The MIBI Agreements and the Law

Second Edition

Cathleen Noctor

B.C.L., Barrister-at-Law

and

Richard Lyons

B.A. (Hons), Senior Counsel

Bloomsbury Professional

Published by
Bloomsbury Professional
Maxwelton House
41–43 Boltro Road
Haywards Heath
West Sussex
RH16 1BJ

Bloomsbury Professional
The Fitzwilliam Business Centre
26 Upper Pembroke Street
Dublin 2

ISBN 978 1 84766 992 6

© Cathleen Noctor and Richard Lyons

British Library Cataloguing-in-Publication Data
A catalogue record for this book is available from the British Library

Typeset by Marie Armah-Kwantreng, Dublin, Ireland
Printed in Great Britain by
CPI Group (UK) Ltd, Croydon, CR0 4YYL

FOREWORD TO THE FIRST EDITION

The MIBI agreements are a relatively recent arrival to the Irish legal scene. Taken in conjunction with EU law and the decisions of our domestic Courts, it is clear that a substantial body of law has emerged that requires specialised treatment.

In dealing with the development and progression of the various agreements over a period of forty years, the authors have provided a valuable and informative insight into their structure and effect. For the practitioner, there is particular assistance in dealing with the difficult issues associated with deciding on the proper form of and parties to proceedings.

In this work Cathleen Noctor and Richard Lyons have displayed great industry in bringing clarity to an aspect of our law which in time I am sure will become the standard text on this complex subject. It is both a pleasure and a privilege to be associated with this very fine book.

Matthew Deery

The Circuit Court

PREFACE TO SECOND EDITION

You might wonder if there is a more tedious read than a road traffic regulation. The answer is probably an EC Directive relating to motor insurance. By comparison the decisions of the European Court of Justice dealing with motor insurance across the EC area are relatively light reading. That was our sorry lot in trying to update the first edition of this book. Those tiresome sources and others had to be ploughed through to recalibrate the first edition of this book which had become increasingly outdated with both the introduction of a new MIBI agreement and several seminal decisions of both the Superior Courts and the European Court of Justice. While one's nature was to recoil from the wearisome task, the embarrassment of seeing practitioners still availing of what was becoming an outdated text led the authors to the masochistic task of its updating and effectively re-writing large tracts of the original text. In addition to updating and re-writing we have included what is hoped are some helpful appendices.

One of the features of this area of law is the extremely high level of out of court settlements given that legal issues invariably arise in the context of personal injury claims defended on the ground by insurance companies. While a huge variety of issues can arise, the nature of the litigation is such that decisions are less common and it is not always possible to predict how particular issues that have been flagged may ultimately be decided.

None of this would have been possible without the unflagging assistance and support of our man in Molesworth Street, namely Aidan Lynch, the claims manager of the Motor Insurers Bureau of Ireland. Over a period of fourteen months or so he put up with numerous queries and unfailingly gave us his time and expertise and indeed made many helpful additions to the text, answering every query however elementary with unfailing good grace. In addition we have had the benefit of the experience of our own colleagues at the Law Library who in different ways made helpful suggestions and comments. In no particular order we would like to thank John Finlay SC, Eoghan Fitzsimons SC and Declan Buckley SC. In addition Lisa Daly BL made a fantastic contribution gathering all recent relevant source material. Thanks also to Frank Turvey BL, Jennifer Good, and Julie O'Brien BL. Finally thanks to Amy Hayes and Jennifer Simpson of Bloomsbury Professional, our publishers.

We have endeavoured to state the law as of 1st August 2012.

Any comments or suggestions on the text are most welcome.

Cathleen Noctor BL

Richard Lyons SC

Law Library,

Four Courts,

Dublin.

Hallowe'en 2012.

Contents

ABBREVIATIONS

First Directive: Council Directive of the European Communities of 24 April 1972, on the approximation of the laws of the Member States relating to insurance against civil liability in respect of the use of motor vehicles and to the enforcement of the obligation to insure against such liability (72/166/EEC).

Second Directive: Second Council Directive on Motor Insurance of 30 December 1983, on the approximation of the laws of Member States relating to insurance against civil liability in respect of the use of motor vehicles (84/5/EEC).

Third Directive: Third Council Directive of 14 May 1990 on the approximation of the laws of the Member States relating to insurance against civil liability in respect of the use of motor vehicles (90/232/EEC).

Fourth Directive: Directive 2000/26/EC of the European Parliament and of the Council of 16 May 2000 on the approximation of the laws of the Member States relating to insurance against civil liability in respect of the use of motor vehicles and amending Council Directives 73/239/EEC and 88/357/EEC.

Fifth Directive: Directive 2005/14/EC of the European Parliament and of the Council of 11 May 2005 amending Council Directives 72/166/EEC, 84/5/EEC, 88/357/EEC and 90/232/EEC and Directive 2000/26/EC of the European Parliament and of the Council relating to insurance against civil liability in respect of the use of motor vehicles.

Sixth Directive: Directive 2009/103/EC of the European Parliament and of the Council of 16 September 2009 relating to insurance against civil liability in respect of the use of motor vehicles, and the enforcement of the obligation to insure against such liability.

2003 Regulations: European Communities (Fourth Motor Insurance Directive) Regulations, 2003 (SI 651/2003).

2008 Regulations: European Communities (Motor Insurance) Regulations, 2008 (SI 248/2008).

TABLE OF CASES

Y

TABLE OF STATUTES

TABLE OF IRISH STATUTORY INSTRUMENTS

TABLE OF EUROPEAN LEGISLATION

TABLE OF MIBI AGREEMENTS

Chapter 1

INTRODUCTION

A. INTRODUCTION

[1.01] In general terms, a person is prohibited from using a mechanically propelled vehicle (vehicle) in a public place in Ireland unless there a vehicle insurer would be liable for injury caused to third parties by the negligent use of that vehicle (compulsory insurance requirements).[1] The compulsory insurance requirements were prescribed by the Road Traffic Act 1933,[2] and are now governed by the Road Traffic Act 1961 (the 1961 Act). The purpose of the compulsory insurance requirements is to ensure that third parties who are caused injury by the negligent use of vehicles are adequately compensated. It is an offence to drive a vehicle without satisfying the compulsory insurance requirements. However, between 5% and 6% of all motorists drive, consciously or unconsciously, without insurance or effective insurance.

B. MOTOR INSURERS' BUREAU OF IRELAND

[1.02] More often than not when an uninsured motorist causes injury to an innocent victim as a result of negligent driving, the uninsured motorist will not be a person of financial means.[3] Given the increase in the use of vehicles, and their use by uninsured motorists, there has been a consequential increase in accidents caused by uninsured motorists. Due to the reality that most uninsured motorists have insufficient assets available to compensate an innocent victim, a gap emerged between the theoretical legal right of an innocent victim to be compensated for his injury and the payment, in practice, of appropriate compensation by uninsured motorists. The MIBI was conceived against this background.

[1.03] The MIBI took the form of a central organisation incorporated and limited by guarantee. In general terms, the MIBI is responsible for compensating innocent victims who are injured by uninsured or untraced motorists. The funds required to pay compensation to innocent victims were made available to the MIBI initially pursuant to an agreement, which became known as the Domestic Agreement, made between it and motor insurers in Ireland. Now, the MIBI is financed by a means of a levy on motor insurers.[4]

[1.04] The MIBI also has responsibilities in relation to Irish vehicles that cause accidents abroad and certain foreign vehicles that cause accidents in Ireland.[5]

---

1. Road Traffic Act 1961, s 56(1).
2. Road Traffic Act 1933, s 56 prohibited the 'driving' of a mechanically propelled vehicle without insurance. Section 56 of the 1961 Act prohibits 'use' without insurance.
3. For further background reading see *Bowes v MIBI* [2000] 2 IR 79 at 85 *et seq*, per Murphy J delivering the majority judgment of the Supreme Court.
4. The Domestic Agreement between the MIBI and the various motor insurers, made on 16 December 1966, is no longer in force. See cl 62 of MIBI's articles of association.

[1.05] In 2011, the MIBI received 3,549 claims and paid out over €54,000,000 in settlements and awards. Of these, 406 claims concerned accidents in Ireland that involved foreign vehicles (a decrease of 11% on the previous year) and 812 claims concerned accidents caused by Irish registered vehicles abroad (an increase of 11% on the previous year).

[1.06] The MIBI is only liable to pay compensation where insurance against such injury was required by law at the time of the accident.[6] The compulsory insurance requirements in Ireland only arise with respect to the 'negligent use' of a mechanically propelled vehicle in a 'public place'.[7] Thus, if an innocent victim is caused injury as a result of a negligent uninsured motorist, otherwise than in a public place, the MIBI is not liable to pay compensation.

C. THE MIBI AND THE 1955 AGREEMENT

[1.07] The Motor Insurers' Bureau of Ireland (the MIBI) is a company limited by guarantee and was established in 1955. Thereafter, the MIBI and the Minister for Local Government entered into an agreement on 30 November 1955 (the 1955 Agreement)[8] which provided a scheme whereby innocent victims caused injury by uninsured motorists would be compensated by the MIBI in certain circumstances. Generally speaking, the 1955 Agreement provided that, if a court made an award of damages in respect of death or personal injury of an innocent victim caused by an uninsured motorist, and the damages were not paid within 28 days, the MIBI would satisfy the award.[9] Thus, the MIBI's liability only arose when an innocent victim, as plaintiff, succeeded in an action and obtained a judgment against the uninsured motorist, as defendant.

[1.08] Under the 1955 Agreement, the MIBI could also handle claims arising out of the use of a vehicle for which there was an insurance policy covering the driving of the vehicle in circumstances where the insurer might have been in a position to repudiate liability for breach of the conditions of the policy.[10]

[1.09] The 1955 Agreement did not apply to damage caused to an innocent victim's property. It also excluded claims for personal injury caused to an innocent victim by the driving of a vehicle where its owner or driver could not be traced. However, the MIBI had a discretion to 'give sympathetic consideration to making some *ex gratia* payment' where a person 'sustained serious and permanent disablement or ... died' as a result of injury caused by an untraced motorist.[11]

---

5. See further below at paras **1.29–1.32**.
6. Road Traffic Act 1961, s 56 prohibits the use of a mechanically propelled vehicle in a public place unless a vehicle insurer or an exempted person would be liable for injury caused by the negligent use of that vehicle. See cl 4 of both the 2004 and 2009 Agreements.
7. As defined by Road Traffic Act 1961, s 3. See **Ch 2**, para **2.04**.
8. The 1955 Agreement operated from 1 January 1956.
9. 1955 Agreement, cl 1. The MIBI was also liable to pay the taxed costs of the action.
10. 1955 Agreement, note 4.
11. 1955 Agreement, note 8.

[1.10] An addendum to the 1955 Agreement was made between the Minister for Local Government and the MIBI on 12 March 1962, the effect of which was to substitute references to the 1933 Act in the 1955 Agreement with references to the 1961 Act.

D. THE MIBI AND THE 1964 AGREEMENT

[1.11] The Minister for Local Government and the MIBI entered into a new agreement on 30 December 1964 (the 1964 Agreement).[12] As with the 1955 Agreement, the 1964 Agreement operated such that, if a person obtained a judgment against the driver (and/or owner) of a vehicle in respect of any liability for injury to a person in circumstances where insurance was compulsory, then, regardless of whether or not there was in fact insurance, the MIBI would, subject to conditions, pay the judgment creditor any amount of the judgment that was not satisfied within 28 days. The insurance industry funded the compensation payments made by the MIBI[13] and, by virtue of s 78 of the 1961 Act,[14] it became mandatory for all vehicle insurers in Ireland to be members of the MIBI.

[1.12] The compulsory insurance requirements were extended by the 1961 Act. The liability of the MIBI to pay compensation was consequentially increased under the 1964 Agreement so that its liability extended to the 'use' rather than just the 'driving' of a vehicle.[15] Furthermore, the 1961 Act made it compulsory to insure against injury to certain passengers and the 1964 Agreement extended the liability of the MIBI to pay compensation to a passenger who obtained a judgment against the owner and/or driver of the relevant vehicle. However, the 1964 Agreement provided that, where a vehicle was used without the consent of its owner, the MIBI was not liable to discharge a judgment obtained against its owner and/or user by a person who was injured while he was in or on the vehicle.[16] In this situation, however, the MIBI could pay compensation, on an *ex gratia* basis, if it was satisfied that the injured person was 'not aware or should

---

12. The 1964 Agreement operated from 1 January 1965. Clause 1 terminated the 1955 Agreement, but without prejudice to its continued operation in respect of accidents that occurred prior to that date.

13. This was the position under an agreement made between the MIBI and various motor insurers on 16 December 1966, whereby the MIBI was funded on a pro rata basis by reference to each insurer's share of the market. This position continues pursuant to cl 62 of the MIBI's articles of association.

14. Road Traffic Act 1961, s 78 Act was substituted by the European Communities (Road Traffic) (Compulsory Insurance) (Amendment) Regulations 1992 (SI 347/1992), art 9. As of 1 August 2012, the motor vehicle insurer members of the MIBI were: ACE European Group Ltd; Aioi Nissay Dowa Insurance Co; Allianz plc.; ARB Insurance Co Ltd; Aviva Insurance Europe SE; AXA Insurance; Brit Insurance; Calpe Insurance Co; Carraig; Catlin Ins Co (UK) Ltd; Chartis Ireland; Chubb; Collingwood Insurance Co Ltd; Ecclesiastical Insurance Office Plc; Electric Ins. (Ire) Ltd; Corinthian; FBD Insurance; Great Lakes U.K.; Greenval; Groupama Insurances; Euro Ins.; International Insurance Company of Hanover Ltd; Irish Public Bodies Mutual; La Parisienne Assurance; Liberty Insurance; Lloyds Underwriters; NFU Mutual; QBE Insurance Ltd; Quinn Direct Insurance; Royal & Sun Alliance; Setanta Ins. Co Ltd; Tradewise Ins. Co Ltd; Travelers Insurance Co Ltd; UPS International; Zenith Insurance Co and Zurich Insurance.

15. Road Traffic Act 1933, s 56 prohibited the 'driving' of a mechanically propelled vehicle without insurance. Section 56 of the 1961 Act prohibits 'use' without insurance.

16. 1964 Agreement, cl 3(1).

not reasonably have known' that there was no consent to user.[17] Furthermore, the MIBI was not liable to satisfy any judgment obtained by a person who was injured in or on a vehicle and who knew, or should reasonably have known, that there was no approved policy of insurance in force in respect of the vehicle.[18]

[1.13] Finally, while the MIBI was not liable to compensate for injury caused by an untraced motorist, it could make an *ex gratia* payment in this situation if it was satisfied that serious injury or death occurred and that this was caused by the negligent use of an untraced motorist.[19]

E. EUROPEAN OBLIGATIONS

[1.14] The various European motor insurance directives are now codified in one directive (the Sixth Directive).[20] The First Directive[21] directed each Member State to ensure that civil liability in respect of the use of vehicles normally based in its territory was covered by insurance and that this insurance covered any loss or injury caused in the territory of another Member State.

[1.15] The Second Directive[22] directed each Member State to introduce minimum compulsory third party liability motor vehicle insurance to be applied in the Member States and extended the obligation of insurance cover to include liability incurred in respect of property damage. Subject to certain limitations, the Second Directive also required that each Member State set up or authorise a body with the task of providing compensation for property damage or personal injury caused by unidentified vehicles or vehicles for which the obligation to insure was not fulfilled.

[1.16] The Third Directive[23] required, inter alia, that the compulsory insurance requirements imposed by the First and Second Directive would cover liability for

---

17. 1964 Agreement, cl 4.
18. 1964 Agreement, cl 3(2).
19. 1964 Agreement, note 8.
20. Directive 2009/103/EC of the European Parliament and of the Council of 16 September 2009 relating to insurance against civil liability in respect of the use of motor vehicles and the enforcement of the obligation to insure against such liability (the Sixth Directive). The Sixth Directive entered into force on 27 October 2009 (Sixth Directive, art 30).
21. Council Directive of the European Communities of 24 April 1972, on the approximation of the laws of the Member States relating to insurance against civil liability in respect of the use of motor vehicles and to the enforcement of the obligation to insure against such liability (72/166/EEC) (the First Directive). The Member States were required to implement the First Directive by 31 December 1973.
22. Second Council Directive on Motor Insurance of 30 December 1983, on the approximation of the laws of Member States relating to insurance against civil liability in respect of the use of motor vehicles (84/5/EEC) (the Second Directive). The Member States were required to implement the First Directive by 31 December 1987. However, Ireland was allowed to exclude property damage claims until 31 December 1992 and was permitted to impose an excess on such claims between that date and 31 December 1995 that exceeded that which was generally permitted by the Second Directive.
23. Third Council Directive of 14 May 1990 on the approximation of the laws of the Member States relating to insurance against civil liability in respect of the use of motor vehicles (90/232/EEC) (the Third Directive).

personal injuries to all passengers, other than the driver, arising out of the use of the vehicle.[24] While the Member States were generally required to comply with the Third Directive by 31 December 1992, Ireland was given until 31 December 1998 to comply with it as regards pillion passengers of motor cycles and until 31 December 1995 as regards other vehicles.[25]

[1.17] The Fourth Directive[26] was concerned with accidents occurring *outside* an injured party's EEA State of residence.[27] In general terms, it sought to simplify and accelerate the means by which compensation could be recovered by a person who resides in a Member State and is caused loss or injury in an accident that, inter alia, occurs in an EEA State (other than his EEA State of residence) and is caused by the use of a vehicle that is insured and normally based in another EEA State (other than his EEA State of residence). Injured parties covered by the Fourth Directive were given a direct right of action against the insurance undertaking that covered the person responsible for the accident.

[1.18] The Fifth Directive[28] required each EEA State to establish a compensation procedure whereby the victim of any accident, caused by a vehicle that is normally based in any EEA State, may claim compensation in his EEA State of residence, regardless of whether or not the vehicle that caused the injury was insured. In addition, where there was insurance, such injured parties were given a direct right of action against the insurance undertaking that covered the responsible person against civil liability.

F. THE MIBI AND THE 1988 AGREEMENT

[1.19] A new agreement was entered into on 21 December 1988 (the 1988 Agreement)[29] between the Minister for the Environment and the MIBI and implemented measures in

---

24. Third Directive, art 1.
25. Third Directive, art 6(2).
26. Directive 2000/26/EC of the European Parliament and of the Council of 16 May 2000 on the approximation of the laws of the Member States relating to insurance against civil liability in respect of the use of motor vehicles and amending Council Directives 73/239/EEC and 88/357/EEC (the Fourth Directive). Member States were required to adopt and publish their domestic implementing provisions before 20 July 2002 and those domestic provisions were required to be operative before 20 January 2003.
27. An 'EEA State' means a State that is a contracting party to the Agreement on the European Economic Area signed at Oporto on 2 May 1992, and the protocol adjusting the Agreement signed at Brussels on 17 March 1993 (reg 2(1)), and as amended by the 2004 and 2007 EEA Enlargement Agreements. In essence, the EEA States are the EU Member States and Iceland, Norway and Liechtenstein.
28. Directive 2005/14/EC of the European Parliament and of the Council of 11 May 2005 amending Council Directives 72/166/EEC, 84/5/EEC, 88/357/EEC and 90/232/EEC and Directive 2000/26/EC of the European Parliament and of the Council relating to insurance against civil liability in respect of the use of motor vehicles (the Fifth Directive). Member States were required to implement the Fifth Directive by 11 June 2007 at the latest.
29. The 1988 Agreement operated from 31 December 1988. Clause 1 determined the 1964 Agreement, but without prejudice to its continued operation in respect of accidents that occurred prior to that date.

compliance with the Second Directive. The changes introduced by the 1988 Agreement extended the liability of the MIBI to pay compensation for property damage caused by uninsured motorists.[30] It further extended its liability to pay compensation for personal injury or death (but not property damage) caused by the negligent driving of a vehicle in a public place where the owner or user thereof remained unidentified or untraced.[31] It also provided a means whereby an innocent victim could make a compensation claim directly to the MIBI without first having to sue the driver (and/or owner) and obtain a judgment against either or both of them. It also permitted a claimant to sue the MIBI as a co-defendant in proceedings against the owner and/or user of a vehicle (except in respect of an untraced motorist) and sue the MIBI as sole defendant for performance of its obligations under the 1988 Agreement.[32]

G. THE MIBI AND THE 2004 AGREEMENT

[1.20] A fourth agreement was entered into between the Minister for Transport and the MIBI on 31 March 2004 (the 2004 Agreement).[33] It repeated most of the provisions of the 1988 Agreement. However, it provided a new protocol for making claims in respect of injury or loss caused by uninsured or stolen vehicles and unidentified or untraced drivers. Many of its provisions were introduced to assist the MIBI in dealing with fraudulent claims and it made the claims procedure more comprehensive than that which was provided for under the 1988 Agreement. For example, it expressly obliged a claimant to co-operate with An Garda Síochána and the MIBI.[34] It also required that a claimant must make himself available for interview by the MIBI in respect of a claim in which the injury or damage is alleged to have been caused by an untraced motorist.[35] Further, the 2004 Agreement expressly stated, for the first time, that the guarantee fund was a fund of last resort.

H. THE MIBI AND THE 2009 AGREEMENT

[1.21] A fifth agreement was entered into between the Minister for Transport and the MIBI on 29 January 2009 (the 2009 Agreement).[36] It was introduced after the European Court of Justice (ECJ) found[37] that cls 5.2 and 5.3 of the 2004 Agreement were incompatible with art 1(4) of the Second Directive.[38] Clause 5.2 of the 2004 Agreement prevented a passenger recovering compensation if he 'ought reasonably to have known'

---

30.   1988 Agreement, cl 4(1).
31.   1988 Agreement, cl 6 and cl 7(2).
32.   1988 Agreement, cl 2.
33.   The 2004 Agreement applies to accidents that occurred on or after 1 May 2004 (see **Appendix 2**). The 2004 Agreement, cl 1 terminated the 1988 Agreement, but without prejudice to its continued operation in respect of accidents that occurred prior to that date.
34.   2004 Agreement, cl 3.4.
35.   2004 Agreement, cl 3.3.
36.   The text of the 2009 Agreement is reproduced in **Appendix 1**.
37.   *Commission v Ireland* (Case C–211/07), Judgment of the Court (Sixth Chamber), 21 February 2008.
38.   Now Sixth Directive, art 10(1). The text of the Sixth Directive is reproduced in **Appendix 3**.

that the vehicle in which he was travelling was uninsured, and cl 5.3 excluded passenger claims arising out of two uninsured vehicles colliding with each other. Now, cl 5.2 of the 2009 Agreement confines the exclusion to a passenger who *knew* that there was no insurance policy in force in respect of the use of the vehicle and the 2009 Agreement contains no equivalent to cl 5.3 of the 2004 Agreement.

[1.22] The 2009 Agreement also introduced compensation for vehicle or property damage against an unidentified vehicle where there are significant personal injuries.[39] For the first time, applications to the Injuries Board were mentioned in the 2009 Agreement. Following the Fourth Directive, the MIBI was designated as the Information Centre and Compensation Body by the European Communities (Fourth Motor Insurance Directive) Regulations 2003,[40] and the MIBI's status as such is referred to in the 2009 Agreement.[41]

I. THE AGREEMENTS – A NOVEL LEGAL MECHANISM

[1.23] The rationale for the 1955 Agreement was to protect victims of uninsured motorists. However, over the course of the various agreements, the role of the MIBI has been developed to take account of the increase in the use of vehicles, and associated claims, and Ireland's obligations under the various European directives in relation to insurance against civil liability in respect of the use of vehicles.

[1.24] Therefore, unlike normal civil liability, the MIBI is not liable on the basis of fault, vicarious liability or statute. Its liability is based on its voluntary submission to the regime established under the agreements.[42] For this reason, the agreements are curious legal animals and have an unusual jurisprudential provenance. Each agreement was concluded between the MIBI and a government minister. Where the MIBI is sued, it could therefore simply assert that there is no privity of contract between it and a claimant/plaintiff. This curious feature has been the subject of much judicial comment in England. Lord Hailsham, commenting on the English agreements noted:

> 'Their foundations in jurisprudence are better not questioned any more than were the demises of John Doe and the behaviour of Richard Roe in the old ejectment actions.'[43]

---

39. 2009 Agreement, cl 7.1.
40. Information Centre and Compensation Body by the European Communities (Fourth Motor Insurance Directive) Regulations 2003 (SI 651/2003) and reproduced in **Appendix 4.1.** The Regulations became operative on 27 November 2003 and were amended by the European Communities (Motor Insurance) Regulations 2008 (SI 248/2008) and are reproduced in **Appendix 4.2.**
41. 2009 Agreement, cl 4.5 and cl 12 respectively. Although not formerly designated by statutory instrument to be the 'central body' that was required by the Fourth Directive, art 6a (as inserted by Fifth Directive, art 5(4) (now Sixth Directive, art 26)), the 2009 Agreement, cl 12 states that the MIBI shall act as the Central Body in accordance with the requirements of the Fourth and Fifth Directives.
42. As noted by Judge McMahon in *Hyland v MIBI and Dun Laoghaire Rathdown County Council* (29 July 2003, unreported) CC, *ex tempore*, Judge McMahon. See **Ch 11**.
43. *Gardner v Moore and MIB* [1984] AC 548 at 556, [1984] 2 WLR 714, [1984] 1 All ER 1100. In *Hardy v MIB* [1964] 2 QB 745, [1964] 3 WLR 433, [1964] 2 All ER 742, [1967] 1 Lloyd's Rep 397, (contd .../)

[1.25] While privity of contract has the potential to create serious legal difficulties for a claimant, it may be said that this potential has been overcome by the fact that the MIBI and, in the United Kingdom, the MIB do not defend claims on this basis. Indeed prior to the conclusion of the 1988 Agreement, the MIBI gave an undertaking that it would not raise this point and the Irish courts proceed on the assumption that the MIBI has, for valuable consideration, contracted with a claimant to perform the agreement or that it is estopped from denying privity of contract.[44]

[1.26] Speaking of the corresponding English agreement, Lord Denning MR said in *Gurtner v Circuit:*[45]

> 'It is true that the injured person was not a party to that agreement between the bureau and the Minister of Transport and he cannot sue in his own name for the benefit of it. But the Minister of Transport can sue for specific performance of it. He can compel the bureau to honour its agreement by paying the injured person, see *Beswick v. Beswick.*[46] If the Minister of Transport obtains an order for specific performance the injured person can enforce it for his own benefit, see by Lord Pearce in *Beswick v. Beswick.*[47] If the Minister of Transport should hesitate to sue, I think it may be open to the plaintiff to make him a defendant: and thus compel performance.'[48]

[1.27] While the issue of privity could theoretically raise its head, it is unlikely that the MIBI would raise this in its defence in circumstances where it is funded by the motor

---

43. (contd) having noted that the MIB agreement was entered into between the Minister of Transport and the MIB, Lord Denning MR observed that: '[n]o point is taken by the [MIB] that [the Agreement] is not enforceable by a third person. I trust that no such point will ever be taken' ([1964] 2 QB 745 at 757). This point was observed in *Fire, Auto and Marine Insurance Co Ltd v Greene* [1964] 2 QB 687, [1964] 2 All ER 761, [1964] 3 WLR 319.

44. See Murphy J in *Bowes v MIBI* [2000] 2 IR 79 at 87.

45. *Gurtner v Circuit* [1968] 2 QB 587, [1968] 2 WLR 668, [1968] 1 All ER 328, [1968] 1 Lloyd's Rep 171.

46. *Beswick v Beswick* [1968] AC 58, [1967] 3 WLR 932, [1967] 2 All ER 1197, HL (E).

47. *Beswick v Beswick* [1968] AC 58 at 91.

48. *Gurtner v Circuit* [1968] 2 QB 587 at 596. The three judges of the Court of Appeal individually held, by reference to ordinary principles of contract law that no person other than the Minister could sue for specific performance of the agreement. Having stated that only the Minister could sue for specific performance of the agreement, Diplock LJ noted that: '[n]evertheless, the courts have on a number of occasions entertained actions by unsatisfied judgment creditors brought against the bureau to enforce on their own behalf undertakings given by the bureau to the Minister under the contract. In these actions, in which the Minister was not joined as a party, the bureau has not taken the point that the plaintiff was not privy to the contract on which he has sued. The court, for its part, has turned a blind eye to this. Unless the point is specifically raised, the court is entitled to proceed on the assumption that the bureau has, before action is brought, contracted for good consideration with the plaintiff to perform the obligations specified in its contract with the Minister or has by its conduct raised an estoppel which would bar it from relying on the absence of privity of contract. But this Nelsonian solution cannot be adopted where a party to the litigation does raise the point that there is no privity of contract ...' ([1968] 2 QB 587 at 599). See also the decision of the House of Lords in *Albert v MIB* [1972] AC 301, [1971] 3 WLR 291, [1971] 2 All ER 1345; wherein Lord Donovan, having referred to *Hardy* and *Gurtner* declined to say anything on the matter because the MIB had not raised any point as to the plaintiff's right to sue under the agreement ([1972] AC 301 at 312).

insurers operating in Ireland[49] who are legally obliged to be members of it.[50] In any event the Supreme Court has held in *Campbell v O'Donnell* that the cause of action against the MIBI is the same as that against an uninsured defendant.[51]

J. A FUND OF LAST RESORT

[1.28] Unlike its predecessors, the 2004 Agreement explicitly stated that the MIBI was the fund of last resort.[52] This clause was omitted from the 2009 Agreement. Where there are other wrongdoers involved in an accident that gives rise to a claim, the MIBI will often try to absolve itself from any liability on the grounds that there is another party with a liability who should meet the claim. Thus, if a claimant is involved in an accident involving two motorists, one of whom is insured and the other not, the MIBI will not pay out if the insured driver has any liability. The so called '1% rule' is invoked by the MIBI. Even if a court finds that the insured motorist is only 40% liable for the accident, a claimant can recover 100% of his award from the insured motorist because the insured and uninsured motorists are concurrent wrongdoers. That being so, the claimant will have no unsatisfied judgment and accordingly the MIBI need not pay out compensation.[53] While the overt reference to a fund of last resort was omitted from the 2009 Agreement, the ECJ has recently stated that the payment of compensation by 'a national body' is considered to be 'a measure of last resort' provided for only when the offending vehicle is uninsured or unidentified.[54]

K. FOREIGN VEHICLES IN IRELAND AND IRISH VEHICLES ABROAD[55]

[1.29] In addition to directing the Member States to take measures to ensure compulsory insurance, the First Directive directed the Member States to ensure that such insurance extended to loss or injury caused in any Member State and accorded with the law of the other Member States in this regard.[56] The Second Directive directed the Member States to introduce minimum compulsory third party liability motor vehicle insurance to be applied in all Member States. Section 56(2A) of the Road Traffic Act 1961[57] implements the compulsory insurance provisions of the First and Second Directives. It provides that an insurance policy covers injury or damage to persons or property incurred by the negligent use of a vehicle in any of the designated territories and to the

---

49. The MIBI is funded on a pro rata basis by reference to each insurer's share of the market.
50. Road Traffic Act 1961, s 78 as substituted by the European Communities (Road Traffic) (Compulsory Insurance) (Amendment) Regulations 1992 (SI 347/1992), art 9.
51. *Campbell v O'Donnell* [2009] 1 IR 133 per Kearns J at p 144–145.
52. 2004 Agreement, cl 13.
53. Civil Liability Act 1961, s 12. See **Ch 8**.
54. *Churchill Insurance Co Ltd v Wilkinson and Evans v Equity Claims Ltd* (Joined cases Case C– 442/10), 1 December 2011.
55. This is considered in detail in **Ch 13**.
56. Article 3.
57. Road Traffic Act 1961, s 56(2A) in its current form was substituted by the EC (Road Traffic) (Compulsory Insurance) (Amendment) Regulations 1992 (SI 347/1992), art 4(1).

extent of the compulsory insurance requirements of the relevant territory or under Irish law, whichever is greater. The designated territories are the European Community and other associated countries.[58]

[1.30] The MIBI has responsibilities regarding Irish vehicles abroad and foreign vehicles from countries that are members of the Council of Bureaux that cause accidents in Ireland. It performs certain functions that were the responsibility of the Irish Visiting Motorists Bureau Ltd until 1992.[59] It operates the green card system in Ireland whereby it issues green cards to Irish motorists travelling to participating countries in which the production of a green card is required. This is equal to and accepted as the national motor insurance certificate relevant to the participating country. If an Irish motorist with a green card causes an accident in a participating country in which the production of a green card is required, the MIBI is deemed to be the vehicle insurer that issued the certificate of insurance. The injured party in the country of accident can claim compensation from the bureau in the country of accident, that bureau can recoup such compensation from the insurer of the Irish vehicle and, in default, from the MIBI. Likewise, if a foreign vehicle with a green card causes an accident in Ireland, the MIBI deals with all third party claims arising out of the driving of that foreign vehicle as though it was the insurer but can recoup this money from the bureau in the country in which the green card issued in the event that it fails to recover from the insurer of that vehicle.[60]

[1.31] Another agreement operates between 33 of the 46 countries participating in the green card system, and Ireland is one such country.[61] Foreign vehicles travelling between 33 of these 46 countries do not require green cards. Instead, liability is determined by reference to the country in which the vehicle is normally based and this is, for the most part, ascertained by reference to the vehicle's registration plate. If an Irish registered vehicle causes an accident in one of the other 33 countries that are parties to this agreement, the MIBI is liable to reimburse the bureau in the country of accident unless the insurer of the Irish registered vehicle does so. If there is no insurer, the MIBI must pay. Likewise, if a foreign vehicle from one of the other 33 countries causes an accident in Ireland, the insurer of that foreign vehicle must reimburse the MIBI in terms of any monies the latter pays out by way of compensation. If it transpires that there was no insurance in place for the foreign vehicle, the bureau of the country in which the foreign vehicle is normally based must repay the MIBI.

[1.32] As referred to above,[62] the Fourth Directive simplified the means by which a resident of an EEA State may recover compensation for injury caused to him by a vehicle in the EEA but outside his EEA State of residence. Certain of the provisions of

---

58. See **Ch 13**, paras **13.17–13.18**.
59. The Irish Visiting Motorists Bureau (IVMB) has been disbanded. The MIBI performs the duties that were previously performed by the IVMB (see the Mechanically Propelled Vehicles (International Circulation) Order 1992 (SI 384/992), art 8, which became operative on 1 January 1993).
60. The Green Card System is now governed by Section II of the Internal Regulations (see **Appendix 6**).
61. See Section III of the Internal Regulations (see **Appendix 6**).
62. At para **1.17**.

the Fourth Directive were implemented in Ireland by the European Communities (Fourth Motor Insurance Directive) Regulations 2003.[63] Under the 2003 Regulations, the MIBI operates as an information centre that is required to provide injured parties with information pertaining to Irish registered vehicles. Having also been designated as the compensation body that was required by the Fourth Directive, the MIBI may also be required to pay compensation to an Irish resident who is injured outside Ireland and in another EEA State or in certain specified territories[64] and on the basis that the MIBI may recover that compensation from another bureau in the EEA State. As also referred to above, the Fifth Directive extended this settlement mechanism.[65]

L. OTHER CONSIDERATIONS

[1.33] In certain circumstances a vehicle will be validly insured but the insurer may have voided the policy on the basis of a material non-disclosure by the insured such as previous drink driving convictions. In those circumstances while the policy may have been voided, the MIBI will not have an involvement as the injured party, subject to certain preconditions, will be entitled to recover from the insurer pursuant to s 76 of the 1961 Act.[66] In addition injured parties may have a remedy against the owner, as well as the driver of a vehicle, if it is being driven with the consent of the owner, pursuant to s 118 of the 1961 Act,[67] although this will not affect the insurance status of the car.

[1.34] Finally, the position of 'insurer concerned' is worthy of mention.[68] In general terms it means that if there was any insurance attaching to a vehicle, even if the driving was not insured, that insurance company will deal with any claims arising out of an accident as 'insurer concerned'. They will defend or settle the claim as appropriate and any monies paid out are paid by that company, as opposed to the MIBI's central funds. While they are MIBI cases, it is the individual insurance company that deals with the claim. While the insurance company is entitled to reimbursement from the negligent uninsured driver, in practical terms recovery is rare. A 'pure' MIBI case is one where the vehicle has no insurance attaching to it and any settlement or award in those circumstances would come out of MIBI central funds.

---

63. See above para **1.22** (see also **Appendix 4.1**).
64. See **Ch 13**, para **13.36**.
65. See para **1.18**.
66. See **Ch 10**, paras **10.57–10.80** and **Ch 13**, paras **13.41–13.55**.
67. See **Ch 9**, para **9.12** and **Ch 10**, para **10.02**.
68. It is defined in the articles of association of the MIBI as meaning 'the member who at the time of the accident which gave rise to a Road Traffic Act liability was providing Motor Insurance in respect of the vehicle from the use and/or ownership of which the liability of the judgment debtor arose' (See **Appendix 5**).

Chapter 2

THE OBLIGATION TO INSURE: LIABILITY OF THE MIBI

A. INTRODUCTION

[2.01] In general terms, s 56 of the Road Traffic Act 1961 (the 1961 Act) provides that a person who uses a mechanically propelled vehicle must be insured against his negligent use of that vehicle.

[2.02] Section 56 requires unlimited insurance cover against personal injury caused by the negligent use of a mechanically propelled vehicle[1] and imposes minimum compulsory insurance requirements in respect of property damage caused to another person.[2]

[2.03] Clause 4.1.1 of the 2009 Agreement benefits a person who is caused damage or injured by the user of a mechanically propelled vehicle that is 'required to be covered by an approved policy of insurance under Section 56 of the [1961] Act'. If such a person obtains a judgment in court, or an order to pay from the Personal Injuries Assessment Board ('PIAB') against the user and that judgment or order to pay is not discharged, the

---

1.   Road Traffic Act 1961, s 56(1)(a). Second Directive, art 1(2) required minimum insurance for personal injuries of €350,000 for one victim and €500,000 per claim if there was more than one victim. In a combined personal injury and property damage claim, Second Directive, art 1(2) required minimum insurance of €600,000 per claim.

 The Fifth Directive raised the minimum insurance requirement for personal injury to €1,000,000 per victim or €5,000,000 whatever the number of victims (see Fifth Directive, art 2 substituting Second Directive, art 1). The foregoing minimum insurance requirement is now contained in Sixth Directive, art 9 which codified the earlier directives. However, as of 1 August 2012, the minimum insurance requirement for personal injury in Sixth Directive, art 9, was increased to €1,120,000 per victim or €5,600,000 per claim whatever the number of victims, pursuant to the European Commissioner's Notice regarding the adaptation in line with inflation of certain amounts laid down in the Sixth Directive (2010/C 332/01).

2.   Road Traffic Act 1961, s 56(2)(a) originally mandated minimum insurance against property damage of £1,000 caused by an act of negligence or a series of acts of negligence collectively constituting one event. This was increased to £40,000 in respect of acts occurring on or after 31 December 1987 and prior to 31 December 1990 (Road Traffic Act 1961, s 56 as substituted by the European Communities (Road Traffic) (Compulsory Insurance) (Amendment) Regulations 1987 (SI 322/1987), art 4(1)). From 31 December 1990 to 31 December 1995, inclusive, the minimum was £80,000 (Road Traffic Act 1961, s 56(2) as substituted by the European Communities (Road Traffic) (Compulsory Insurance) (Amendment) Regulations 1987 (SI 322/ 1987), art 4(1)). As of 1 January 1996, this was increased to £90,000 (Road Traffic Act 1961, s 56(2) as substituted by the European Communities (Road Traffic) (Compulsory Insurance) (Amendment) Regulations 1995 (SI 353/1995), art 3(1)). In practice, however it seems that this property damage limit was generally not relied upon with respect to non-commercial vehicles. Road Traffic Act 2002, s 17, made provision for increasing the limit to €200,000. However, the Road Traffic Act 2002, s 17 was never commenced by statutory instrument pursuant to the Road Traffic Act 2002, s 26. (contd .../)

MIBI may be liable to satisfy the judgment. However, the MIBI is not obliged to discharge any judgment that falls outside the scope of cl 4.1.1 of the 2009 Agreement.[3]

B. COMPULSORY INSURANCE

[2.04] The MIBI is required to meet unsatisfied orders to pay made by the PIAB and unsatisfied court judgments in respect of liability for injury to persons or damage to property caused by the user of a vehicle for which an approved policy of insurance is required by law.[4] It has no liability to meet claims made by persons for whom compulsory insurance is not required by law. The cornerstone provision is s 56 of the 1961 Act[5] which now provides:

'(1) A person (in this subsection referred to as the user) shall not use in a public place,[6]

---

2.   (contd) The Fifth Directive raised the minimum insurance requirements for property damage to €1,000,000 per claim, whatever the number of victims (see Fifth Directive, art 2 substituting Second Directive, art 1). The same requirement is repeated by Sixth Directive, art 9 which codified the earlier directives. In Ireland, the European Communities (Motor Insurance) Regulations 2008 (SI 248/2008), reg 2(b) (the 2008 Regulations) amended Road Traffic Act 1961, s 56(2)(a) to implement the requirements of the Fifth Directive. The 2008 Regulations became operative at the end of 3 July 2008 (see the Interpretation Act 2005, s 16(3)). Sixth Directive, art 9(1) also provided that, if necessary, Member States could establish a transitional period extending until 11 June 2012 at the latest within which to adapt their minimum amounts of cover to the aforementioned amounts. It further provided, however, that until 11 December 2009 at the latest, Member States should increase guarantees to at least half of the minimums specified in art 9(1). In addition, Sixth Directive, art 9(2) provides, *inter alia*, that every five years, after 11 June 2005, or at the end of any transitional period as referred to in art 9(1), the amounts referred to therein shall be reviewed in line with the European Index of Consumer Prices (EICP) established pursuant to Regulation (EC) No 2494/95. It states that the amounts shall be adjusted automatically and increased by the percentage change indicated by the EICP for the relevant period, ie the five years immediately preceding the review provided for in art 9(1) and rounded up to a multiple of €10,000. On 9 December 2010, and following the review required by the Sixth Directive, art 9(1) of the European Commission published a notice regarding the adaptation of monetary amounts in the Sixth Directive. This increased the minimum insurance requirement to €1,120,000 for property damage. Road Traffic Act 1961, s 56(2)(a) was again amended to reflect the foregoing increase by the European Union (Motor Insurance) (Limitation of Insurance in relation to Property) Regulations 2011 (SI 702/11 and made 21 December 2011).

3.   This is subject to any views expressed as to whether or not various provisions of the various directives have been properly implemented.

4.   See cl 4.1.1 of the 2009 Agreement and cl 4.1 of the 2004 Agreement.

5.   As modified by Road Traffic Act 1968, s 53 (the 1968 Act) and the European Communities (Motor Insurance) Regulations 2008 (SI 248/2008), reg 2(a).

6.   A 'public place' is defined as: '(a) any public road, and (b) any street, road or other place to which the public have access with vehicles whether as of right or by permission and whether subject to or free of charge' (Road Traffic Act 1961, s 3(1) as substituted by Road Traffic Act 1994, s 49). *Stanbridge v Healy* [1985] ILRM 290 held that public (in the context of public place) means the public generally and not any particular class of the public. In *Lynch v Lynch* [1995] 3 IR 496, a car park outside a factory, that was used by its employees, customers and suppliers, the public attending nearby football matches and farmers attending local marts, was held to be a public place, whereas in *Hunter v Gray* [1970] NI 1 a car park outside an apartment block (with no gates or barriers) was not a public place even though, (contd .../)

a mechanically propelled vehicle[7] unless either a vehicle insurer[8] ...[9] or an exempted person[10] would be liable for injury caused by the negligent use of the vehicle by him at that time or there is in force at that time ...

    (a)   an approved policy of insurance[11] whereby the user or some other person who would be liable for injury caused by the negligent use of the vehicle at that time by the user, is insured against all sums without limit (save as is hereinafter otherwise provided) which the user or his personal representative or such other person or his personal representative shall

---

6.   (contd) in addition to tenants of the flats using it, it was used by persons attending there on lawful business and wherein the court attached significance to the fact that there was no evidence that it was frequented by the public. In terms of the MIBI's obligations, see *Buchanan v MIB* [1955] 1 QB 607 which held that the MIBI was not obliged to pay compensation for injuries caused by an uninsured motorist on a road on which passes were required to be produced by persons entering the area and *Charlton v Fisher* [2001] 1 All ER (Comm) 769, [2001] RTR 479, in which the Court of Appeal noted that the MIB would not have any obligation in respect of the use of an uninsured vehicle 'off the road' (in a hotel car park) because insurance was only required for the 'use of the vehicle on a road'. For further reading, see Pierse, *Road Traffic Law* (3rd edn, First Law, 2003).

7.   A 'mechanically propelled vehicle' is defined as 'a vehicle intended or adapted for propulsion by mechanical means, including:

(a) a bicycle or tricycle with an attachment for propelling it by mechanical power, whether or not the attachment is being used,

(b) a vehicle the means of propulsion of which is electrical or partly electrical and partly mechanical ...'.

However, a mechanically propelled vehicle is not to be regarded as such if it is substantially disabled (through accident, breakdown or the removal of the engine or other such vital part) as to be no longer capable of being propelled mechanically (Road Traffic Act 1961, s 3(1)–(2)).

For further reading, see Pierse, *Road Traffic Law* (3rd edn, First Law, 2003) at p 1046.

Prior to the European Communities (Motor Insurance) Regulations 2008 (SI 248/2008) a mechanically propelled vehicle was further defined to include a semi-trailer or trailer (whether coupled or uncoupled to a mechanically propelled vehicle) used in a public place (Road Traffic Act 1961, s 56(9) as substituted by the European Communities (Road Traffic) (Compulsory Insurance) Regulations 1975 (SI 178/1975), reg 3 (effective 5 August 1975), and substituted by the European Communities (Road Traffic) (Compulsory Insurance) (Amendment) Regulations 1992 (SI 347/1992), art 5 (effective 1 January 1993)). Road Traffic Act 1961, s 56(9) (as substituted by the European Communities (Motor Insurance) Regulations 2008 (SI 248/2008), reg 2(b)) now defines a 'mechanically propelled vehicle' to include 'a semi-trailer or trailer when used in a public place'. Road Traffic Act 1961, s 56(10), which provided '[n]othing in [Part VI of the 1961 Act] shall be deemed to extend compulsory motor insurance cover to any person in or on a semi-trailer or trailer when used in a public place', was effectively repealed by the European Communities (Motor Insurance) Regulations 2008 (SI 248/2008), reg 2(b). Thus, it appears that the combined effect of the Road Traffic Act 1961, s 56(1) and (9) is that insurance is compulsory for persons in or on a semi-trailer or trailer in a public place.

8.   Road Traffic Act 1961, s 58 defines 'vehicle insurer'.

9.   Road Traffic Act 1961, s 56(1) also provides for a 'vehicle guarantor' having liability for injury caused by the negligent use of a vehicle. Road Traffic Act 1968, s 53, however, provides that the provisions of Road Traffic Act 1961, Pt VI relating to such an approved guarantor shall cease to have effect.

10.   Road Traffic Act 1961, s 60 defines 'exempted person' (see **Section D**, below).

11.   Road Traffic Act 1961, s 62 defines 'approved policy of insurance'.

become liable to pay to any person ...[12] by way of damages or costs on account of injury to person or property caused by the negligent use of the vehicle at the time by the user...'[13]

[2.05] Thus, if a plaintiff obtains a judgment against a user in respect of injury or damage arising out of the use of a vehicle for which insurance was not required by law at the time of the accident, the MIBI will not satisfy the judgment. For example, if the injury was not sustained in a public place, the MIBI may reject a claim against it.[14] Likewise, if the MIBI succeeds in making the case that the plaintiff's injuries were not caused by the 'negligent use'[15] of the vehicle by the uninsured, it may reject a claim for

---

12.   Prior to the amendment made by the European Communities (Motor Insurance) Regulations 2008 (SI 248/2008), reg 2(a), the words '(exclusive of the excepted persons)' appeared immediately after 'liable to pay to any person' in Road Traffic Act 1961, s 56(1)(a). Although Road Traffic Act 1961, s 65(1) defines 'excepted person', the significance of 'excepted person' cannot be considered in isolation from the Regulations that were made under s 65(1), case law interpreting same, Ireland's obligations under the various directives and its transposition of same. See **Sections E–G** below.

13.   In recent times, Road Traffic Act 1961, s 56 was analysed by the Supreme Court in *DPP v Donnelly* [2012] IESC 44 (23 July 2012, unreported) SC, (Fennelly J) (see further **Ch 10** para **10.69**) and *DPP v Leipina and Suhanovs* [2011] IESC 3 (2 February 2011, unreported) SC, (Finnegan J) (see further **Ch 13**, paras **13.14–13.15**).

14.   A person who suffers injury otherwise than in a public place might contend that the direction to the Member States to 'take all appropriate measures to ensure civil liability in respect of the use of vehicles normally based in its territories is covered by insurance' is not confined to users in a public place (First Directive, art 3(1) and now contained in the Sixth Directive, art 3, first paragraph). While Sixth Directive, art 3, second paragraph (and previously First Directive, art 3(1)) further provides that: '[t]he extent of the liability covered and the terms and conditions of the cover shall be determined on the basis of the measures referred to in the first paragraph [of art 3 of the Sixth Directive]', it might be successfully argued that the freedom given to Member States by the foregoing only applies to the type of civil liability (eg fault or risk as analysed in *Ferreira and Ferreira v Companhia de Seguros Mundial Confianca SA* (Case C–348/98) [2000] ECR I–06711 discussed below at paras **2.29–2.33**), rather than giving Member States a discretion to exclude the requirements of compulsory insurance for user of vehicles in certain areas of its territory. Such a contention gains support from the direction to Member States to ensure that compulsory insurance against civil liability covers 'the entire territory of the Community' (Third Directive, art 2 and now Sixth Directive, art 14(a)). The various remedies that might be claimed by a person who is aggrieved by an alleged failure on the part of the State to properly implement the various directives are considered in the context of **Sections F** and **G** below.

15.   Road Traffic Act 1961, s 56, as amended. The Sixth Directive does not make negligence a pre-condition to the MIBI's obligations. However, the fact that Ireland makes 'negligent use' a pre-condition, and thereby enabling the MIBI to resist a compensation claim on the basis that injuries were caused by something other than this, must be considered in the context of the ECJ decision in *Ferreira and Ferreira v Companhia de Seguros Mundial Confianca SA* [2000] ECR I-06711 (see below, para **2.30**). Prior to *Ferreira*, the issue was considered in England in *Hardy v MIB* [1964] 2 QB 745, [1964] 3 WLR 433, [1964] 2 All ER 742, [1967] 1 Lloyd's Rep 397. The uninsured driver drove off in a mechanically propelled vehicle while the plaintiff was holding onto the open door and had his head through its window. The MIB defended the case on the basis that the injury was caused by an assault and therefore not a liability against which the defendant was obliged to be insured. The Court of Appeal held that the driver's deliberate attempt to flee fell within 'the use of the vehicle on a road', and for which compulsory third party liability insurance was required, and that this phrase must be construed widely enough to cover innocent or criminal use. (contd .../)

compensation.[16] Furthermore, as seen below, there are circumstances where insurance is not necessary. For example, insurance is not required for certain vehicles[17] and exempted persons are not required to obtain insurance.[18] Hence, it will be seen that the MIBI is not liable to compensate for injury or damage caused by vehicles for which insurance is not required or for injury or damage caused by an exempted person. It will also be seen below that, until the European Communities (Motor Insurance) Regulations 2008 (the 2008 Regulations),[19] it was not mandatory to insure against injury to excepted persons.[20]

---

15. (contd) It considered that, if a policy was good at its inception, then, notwithstanding a criminal act by the insured, a victim of his criminality could recover under the policy even though the insured could not. The House of Lords unanimously approved *Hardy* in *Gardner v Moore and MIB* [1984] AC 548, [1984] 2 WLR 714, [1984] 1 All ER 1100. Gardner was injured when an uninsured driver drove his motor vehicle at him. The MIB's reliance on the public policy doctrine that a person was not entitled to profit from his own wrongdoing was rejected. The Law Lords held that satisfaction of the uninsured driver's liability to the plaintiff was incidental to the main purpose of the MIB Agreement, namely to protect innocent third parties. Lord Hailsham LC considered that invoking the principle contended for by the MIB would 'stand the principle of public policy on its head' ([1984] AC 548 at 561–562). Subsequently, in *Charlton v Fisher* [2001] RTR 479, [2001] 1 All ER (Comm) 769; an insured driver deliberately rammed the plaintiff's car in a hotel car park and pleaded guilty to criminal damage. His policy covered: 'accident[s] involving [his] car' and the Court of Appeal held that his insurer was not obliged to indemnify him in respect of this 'deliberate criminal act'. Because the driver was obliged to be insured in respect of injury caused by 'use of the vehicle on a road', the Court of Appeal noted, *obiter dictum*, that, but for the fact that the incident occurred 'off the road', the MIB would have been obliged to compensate the plaintiff. See also *Bristol Alliance Limited Partnership v Williams* [2011] EWHC 1657 (QB). In that case, a property owner claimed against his own insurance for damage caused by an insured driver and, by subrogation, the property insurer claimed against the driver. The driver's insurer asserted that cover was excluded because the damage was deliberate. The High Court held that the *obiter dicta* in *Charlton* gave effect to the policy of the legislation that innocent third parties should be protected from harm inflicted by dangerous and criminal drivers. The High Court said that this would 'simply achieve by a direct route that which is already the indirect effect of the MIB scheme, at least in all but a minority of cases (of which this is one)' (at paras 54–55). It held, *obiter dictum*, that, even if the court was wrong in its interpretation of the domestic law, there was nothing to justify a definition of victim under the motor insurance directives that excluded third parties who have suffered personal injury or damage, but who are also insured, and whose insurers exercise their rights of subrogation (see paras 83–84).

16. Furthermore, cl 4.1.1 of the 2009 Agreement (and cl 4.1 of the 2004 Agreement) states that the liability of the MIBI to satisfy judgments is subject to the general provisions of the Agreement. Thus, by way of example, the MIBI might justifiably reject a claim in circumstances where a claimant has failed to comply with the conditions precedent in cl 3 of the 2009 Agreement (and cl 3 of the 2004 Agreement).

17. See **Section C** below.

18. See **Section D** below.

19. SI 248/2008.

20. See **Section E** below.

C. VEHICLES FOR WHICH INSURANCE IS NOT REQUIRED

[2.06] Section 4(2) of the 1961 Act provides that insurance is not compulsory[21] for:

'(a)   a vehicle owned by the State or a person using such vehicle in the course of his employment,

(b)   a vehicle under seizure by a person in the service of the State in the course of his duty or a person using such vehicle in the course of his employment, or

(c)   a member of the Garda Síochána or an officer of any Minister using a vehicle for the purpose of a test, removal or disposition of the vehicle pursuant to this Act or any regulation thereunder.'[22]

[2.07] These include vehicles owned by government departments and state agencies, including An Garda Síochána and the defence forces.

D. EXEMPTED PERSONS

[2.08] Section 56(1) of the 1961 Act prohibits the use of a mechanically propelled vehicle in a public place unless an exempted person (or a vehicle insurer) would be liable for injury caused by the negligent use of the vehicle.

[2.09] 'Exempted person' is defined in section 60(1) of the 1961 Act[23] as:

(a)   a board or other body established by an Act of the Oireachtas;

(b)   a company as defined by section 2(1) of the Companies Act 1963, in which the majority of shares are held by or on behalf of a Minister of State; or

(c)   a company as defined by section 2(1) of the Companies Act 1963, in which a majority of the ordinary shares are held by either (a) or (b) above.

[2.10] A certificate of exemption must be obtained from the Minister for the Environment.[24] A certificate cannot issue unless the Minister is of the opinion that the applicant for exemption is, and will be, capable of meeting any liability arising out of the negligent use of a mechanically propelled vehicle in respect of which the applicant for the certificate would otherwise be required to have an approved policy of insurance.[25] In addition, under s 78(2) of the 1961 Act,[26] exemption status will not apply in the absence of an undertaking by the applicant to deal with third party claims against it in respect of mechanically propelled vehicles on similar terms to those applicable as between the Minister and the MIBI.[27]

---

21.   The provisions concerning the 'compulsory insurance of mechanically propelled vehicles' are contained in Road Traffic Act 1961, Pt VI.

22.   Road Traffic Act 1961, s 4(1) provides that the extent of the exclusion from the obligation to insure is defined by s 4(2).

23.   As substituted by Road Traffic Act 1968, s 54.

24.   Road Traffic Act 1961, s 60(1) as substituted by Road Traffic Act 1968, s 54.

25.   Road Traffic Act 1961, s 60(2) as substituted by Road Traffic Act 1968, s 54.

26.   As substituted by the European Communities (Road Traffic) (Compulsory Insurance) (Amendment) Regulations 1992 (SI 347/1992), art 9.

27.   Road Traffic Act 1961, s 61 (as substituted by Road Traffic Act 1968, s 55(1)) enables the Minister to require an applicant for exemption status to deposit money with the High Court.

Exempted persons include Dublin Bus, Bus Éireann and Iarnród Éireann.

[2.11] The MIBI agreements expressly provide that the liability of the MIBI extends to circumstances where an approved policy of insurance is actually in force in respect of a vehicle that is owned by, or in possession of, the State or an exempted person.[28, 29]

[2.12] Furthermore, if such a vehicle is unlawfully removed from the possession of the State or an exempted person, the MIBI agreements deem the vehicle to continue in the possession of the State or exempted person for the duration of the unlawful removal.[30]

E. EXCEPTED PERSONS

1. Persons for whom insurance is not compulsory

[2.13] Excepted persons are persons for whom compulsory insurance under approved policies of insurance was not required under Irish law until the European Communities (Motor Insurance) Regulations 2008 (the 2008 Regulations).[31] Thus, it was not necessary to insure against injury or damage caused to excepted persons. An excepted person who suffered injury or damage could not recover against the MIBI and was in the same position as a plaintiff in any other area of the law in that he could only sue the

---

28.   See cl 11.1 of the 2009 Agreement (and cl 11.1 of the 2004 Agreement).

29.   In *Lynch v MIBI* [2005] IEHC 184 (10 May 2005, unreported) HC, (Macken J), the plaintiff's van skidded on an oil spillage on a road. He claimed that this was caused by the owner/driver of an untraced vehicle and sued the MIBI for personal injury. The MIBI defended the claim, *inter alia*, on the basis that the plaintiff did not comply with a condition precedent in the 1988 Agreement, namely that the plaintiff failed to establish that the vehicle that caused the accident was not a 'state vehicle' *nor* establish that it was one for which the Road Traffic Act 1961 obliged the driver thereof to have insurance. The MIBI relied on cl 11 of the 1988 Agreement which provided: '[the MIBI's] acceptance of liability in respect of vehicles the use of which is required to be covered by an approved policy of insurance shall extend to vehicles owned by or in possession of the State or of an "exempted person" as defined in ... the Act so long as there is in force an approved policy of insurance purporting to cover the use of the vehicle'. Clause 6 of the 1988 Agreement required the MIBI to pay compensation in respect of injury or death caused by the negligent driving of a vehicle in a public place 'where the owner or user of the vehicle remains unidentified or untraced'. Macken J noted that cl 3 of the 1988 Agreement (in prescribing conditions precedent to the MIBI's liability) did not require a claimant to establish that a vehicle was a 'state vehicle' or was being driven by an 'exempted person'. Macken J concluded that: '[a]n interpretation of the agreement which would have as its effect the removal from the plaintiff of the right to proceed against the [MIBI] unless the plaintiff could first establish, on the balance of probabilities, a negative, that is to say, that the vehicle in question was not a state vehicle, as defined, or was not driven by an exempted person, as defined, would mean that clause 6 of the [1988] agreement would have to be given an interpretation which is at odds with the very wording of [that clause]. It would further have as its effect that, where a vehicle remains untraced, such as in the case of so-called "hit-and-run" accidents ... the agreement could never be invoked, or could only be invoked in circumstances of singular coincidence' (at pp 6–7). Having further commented that the interpretation advanced by the MIBI would 'scarcely comply' with the objectives of the Second Directive, Macken J held that the plaintiff was entitled to invoke the 1988 Agreement (at p 8).

30.   See cl 11.2 of the 2009 and 2004 Agreements.

31.   European Communities (Motor Insurance) Regulations 2008 (SI 248/2008).

wrongdoer personally in the hope that the wrongdoer had assets or was indemnified by some other means.

[2.14] Section 65(1) of the 1961 Act, as amended,[32] defines excepted persons in the following terms:

> '(a) any person claiming in respect of injury to himself sustained while he was in or on[33] a mechanically propelled vehicle (or a vehicle drawn thereby) to which the relevant document relates, other than a mechanically propelled vehicle, or a drawn vehicle, or vehicles forming a combination of vehicles, of a class specified for the purposes of this paragraph by regulations made by the Minister,[34] provided that such regulations shall not extend compulsory insurance in respect of civil liability to passengers to—
>
> (i) any part of a mechanically propelled vehicle, other than a large public service vehicle,[35] unless that part is designed and constructed with seating accommodation[36] for passengers, or
>
> (ii) a passenger seated in a caravan attached to a mechanically propelled vehicle while such a combination of vehicles is moving in a public place.'

---

32. As substituted by the Road Traffic Act 1968, Sch, and subsequently by the European Communities (Road Traffic) (Compulsory Insurance) (Amendment) Regulations 1992 (SI 347/1992), art 7(1).

33. References to injury sustained while in or on a vehicle include 'injury sustained while entering, getting on to, being put into or on, or alighting from, (or being taken out of or off, the vehicle, and injury caused by being thrown out of or off the vehicle' (Road Traffic Act 1961, s 65(2)(b)). See also *Kenny v MIBI and The Minister for the Environment* (3 April 1995, unreported) SC, *per* Blayney J (Hamilton CJ and O'Flaherty J concurring), discussed below at para **2.54**.

34. The upshot of Road Traffic Act 1961, s 65(1)(a) is that insurance for passengers is not compulsory unless the Minister makes regulations compelling such insurance. The only restriction upon the Minister's power (in s 65(1)(a)) to make regulations to compel passenger insurance is that the Minister is expressly precluded from using this power to compel insurance in respect of the two categories of passengers that are specified in the section. For the foregoing reason, it was submitted in the first edition of this book that s 65(1)(a) effected an impermissible delegation of the sole and exclusive power of the Oireachtas to legislate for the State and violated Art 15.2.1 of the Constitution (see *The MIBI Agreements and the Law* (1st edn, First Law, 2005) para 2.5.1. The constitutionality of s 65(1)(a) was raised in *Delargy v Minister for the Environment and Local Government, Ireland, Attorney General and MIBI* [2005] IEHC 94, (18 March 2005, unreported) HC, Murphy J. However, the court disposed of the issues before it on the basis that Road Traffic (Compulsory Insurance) Regulations 1962 (SI 14/1962), art 6(2) made thereunder was unconstitutional.

35. A 'large public service vehicle' is 'a public service vehicle having seating passenger accommodation for more than eight persons exclusive of the driver'; a 'public service vehicle' is 'a mechanically propelled vehicle used for the carriage of persons for reward'; a 'small public service vehicle' is 'a public service vehicle which is not a large public service vehicle'; (Road Traffic Act 1961, s 3(1)).

36. 'Seating accommodation for a passenger' is:
    '(i) in the case of a vehicle other than a cycle, a fixed or folding seat permanently and securely installed in or on the vehicle, and (ii) in the case of a cycle, a seat for one passenger behind the driver or a seat in a sidecar, in each case permanently and securely installed, and "seating accommodation for passengers" shall be similarly construed' (Road Traffic Act 1961, s 65(2)(c) as inserted by the European Communities (Road Traffic) (Compulsory Insurance) (Amendment) Regulations 1992 (SI 347/1992), art 7).

[2.15] The combined effect of ss 65(1) and 56(1) of the 1961 Act (until the 2008 Regulations) was four-fold. Firstly, as a general principle, insurance was not compulsory for passengers. Secondly, the Minister could make regulations compelling insurance for certain passengers. Thirdly, ministerial regulations could not be used to compel insurance for passengers to any part of a vehicle (other than a large public service vehicle) unless that part was designed and built with passenger seating. Fourthly, compulsory insurance for passengers seated in a caravan attached to a moving vehicle could not be introduced by ministerial regulation.

[2.16] Other statutory categories of excepted persons include:

(a) where a person suffers personal injuries which causes his death ('the deceased'), a person who claims for the personal injuries sustained by the deceased cannot recover if the deceased (had he not died) would have been an excepted person in terms of s 65(1)(a);[37]

(b) a person who claims for personal injuries sustained by a second person is an excepted person if that second person (had he personally made the claim) would have been an excepted person;[38]

(c) a person claiming for property damage sustained while the property was 'in or on'[39] the mechanically propelled vehicle;[40] and

(d) a person claiming for damage sustained to property while it was owned by or was in the possession, custody or control of the insured.[41]

2. Compulsory insurance requirements under the 1962 Regulations

[2.17] The Road Traffic (Compulsory Insurance) Regulations 1962[42] (the 1962 Regulations) were made pursuant to, *inter alia*, s 65(1)(a) of the 1961 Act.[43] Article 6(1) of the 1962 Regulations[44] extended the requirements of compulsory insurance. Its

---

37. Road Traffic Act 1961, s 65(1)(b)(i).
38. Road Traffic Act 1961, s 65(1)(b)(ii).
39. References to injury sustained while in or on a vehicle include 'injury sustained while entering, getting on to, being put into or on, or alighting from, or being taken out of or off, the vehicle, and injury caused by being thrown out of or off the vehicle' (Road Traffic Act 1961, s 65(2)(b)).
40. Or property on a vehicle drawn by a mechanically propelled vehicle (Road Traffic Act 1961, s 65(1)(c) as amended by the Road Traffic Act 1968, Sch).
41. Road Traffic Act 1961, s 65(1)(d).
42. Road Traffic (Compulsory Insurance) Regulations 1962 (SI 14/1962).
43. It should be noted that when the Road Traffic (Compulsory Insurance) Regulations 1962 were introduced (including art 6(1)), Road Traffic Act 1961, s 65(1) had not been amended and, pursuant to the original s 65(1), the Minister was authorised to make regulations compelling insurance for passengers to any class of mechanically propelled vehicle. This position continued after s 65(1) was amended by the Road Traffic Act 1968. The power to make regulations was only circumscribed when the Road Traffic Act 1961, s 65(1) was substituted by the European Communities (Road Traffic) (Compulsory Insurance) (Amendment) Regulations 1992 (SI 347/1992), art 7(1) (the Second 1992 Regulations).
44. Road Traffic (Compulsory Insurance) Regulations 1962, art 6(1) was amended by the Road Traffic (Compulsory Insurance) (Amendment) Regulations 1992 (SI 346/1992), (the First 1992 Regulations), see below at para **2.19**.

provisions operated until 30 December 1995. It specified three classes of vehicle for the purpose of s 65(1)(a) of the 1961 Act as follows:

'(a)   public service vehicles;

(b)   vehicles[45] constructed primarily for the carriage of one or more passengers;

(c)   station wagons, estate cars and other similar vehicles which are constructed or adapted for alternative purposes (including the carriage of one or more passengers) and which are fitted with seats, whether rigid, collapsible or detachable in the area to the rear of the driver's seat.'

[2.18] Thus, the effect of the 1962 Regulations was to require compulsory insurance for passengers in these categories of vehicles and remove their status as excepted persons.

3. Compulsory insurance requirements brought about by the First 1992 Regulations

[2.19] The 1962 Regulations were subsequently amended by the Road Traffic (Compulsory Insurance) (Amendment) Regulations 1992 (the First 1992 Regulations).[46] Article 4 of the First 1992 Regulations substituted a new art 6 into the 1962 Regulations. Article 6(1) of the 1962 Regulations now provides:

'The following vehicles are hereby specified for the purpose of [s 65(1)(a) of the 1961 Act]:

(a)   vehicles, other than cycles,[47] designed and constructed with seating accommodation for passengers;[48]

(b)   cycles designed and constructed with seating accommodation for passengers.'

[2.20] This means that compulsory insurance is now required for passengers in these categories of vehicles and their previous status as excepted persons has been removed.

[2.21] The first category took effect as of 31 December 1995,[49] and the second has applied since 31 December 1998.[50]

---

45.   'Vehicle' is defined as a mechanically propelled vehicle (Road Traffic (Compulsory Insurance) Regulations 1962, art 2).

46.   SI 346/1992.

47.   'Cycle' simpliciter is not defined in the legislation. However, mechanically propelled vehicle is defined as 'a vehicle intended ... for propulsion by mechanical means' (see para **2.04**).

48.   'Seating accommodation for a passenger' is '(i) in the case of a vehicle other than a cycle, a fixed or folding seat permanently and securely installed in or on the vehicle, and (ii) in the case of a cycle, a seat for one passenger behind the driver or a seat in a sidecar, in each case permanently and securely installed, and 'seating accommodation for passengers' shall be similarly construed' (Road Traffic Act 1961, s 65(2)(c), as inserted by the European Communities (Road Traffic) (Compulsory Insurance) (Amendment) Regulations 1992 (SI 347/1992), art 7).

49.   Road Traffic (Compulsory Insurance) Regulations 1962 (SI 14/1962), art 6(2) as substituted by the Road Traffic (Compulsory Insurance) (Amendment) Regulations 1992 (SI 346/1992), art 4 (the First 1992 Regulations). The original Road Traffic (Compulsory Insurance) Regulations 1962 (SI 14/1962), art 6 ceased to have effect on this date.

50.   Road Traffic (Compulsory Insurance) Regulations 1962 (SI 14/1962), art 6(3) as substituted by Road Traffic (Compulsory Insurance) (Amendment) Regulations 1992 (SI 346/1992), art 4. The original Road Traffic (Compulsory Insurance) Regulations 1962 (SI 14/1962), art 6 ceased to have effect on this date.

F. PASSENGERS OTHER THAN ON A MOTORCYCLE

1. Vehicles designed and constructed with seating accommodation

[2.22] As seen above at para 2.19, art 4 of the First 1992 Regulations extended the requirements of compulsory insurance for vehicles designed and constructed with seating accommodation for passengers (other than cycles).

2. Vehicles not designed and constructed with seating accommodation

[2.23] The First 1992 Regulations extended the requirements of compulsory insurance to passengers of the categories of vehicles enumerated therein. Aside from motorcycles, the First 1992 Regulations did not compel insurance for passengers in vehicles that were *not* designed and constructed with passenger seating accommodation.

[2.24] The purpose of the First 1992 Regulations was to implement art 1 of the Third Directive,[51] and in respect of which Ireland was given until 31 December 1995, to comply with its provisions as they affected vehicles other than motorcycles.

[2.25] The fifth recital in the preamble to the Third Directive observes: '[w]hereas there are, in particular, gaps in the compulsory insurance cover of motor vehicle passengers in certain Member States; whereas, to protect this particularly vulnerable category of potential victims, such gaps should be filled.' Furthermore, art 1 of the Third Directive,[52] in directing that compulsory insurance 'shall cover liability for personal injuries to all passengers, other than the driver, arising out of the use of the vehicle' does not distinguish between seated and unseated passengers.

[2.26] As a consequence of the foregoing, the position under Irish legislation appeared to be that a passenger in unseated accommodation was an excepted person as defined by s 65(1)(a) of the 1961 Act.[53] For this reason, the MIBI could refuse an application for compensation made by an unseated passenger who suffered injury as a result of the negligent driving of the vehicle in which he was an unseated passenger. The question therefore arose as to whether or not such an unseated passenger had any remedy in circumstances where Ireland appeared to have failed to properly implement the provisions of the Third Directive, insofar as the Third Directive made no distinction between seated and unseated passengers.

3. *Withers v Delaney and MIBI*

[2.27] The issue of the State's transposition of the various directives was raised in *Withers v Delaney and MIBI*.[54] It must be emphasised, however, that this case concerned

---

51. Third Directive, art 1 is now contained in Sixth Directive, art 12(1). Sixth Directive, art 12(1) provides '... the insurance referred to in Article 3 shall cover liability for personal injuries to all passengers, other than the driver, arising out of the use of a vehicle'.
52. Third Directive, art 1 is now contained in Sixth Directive, art 12(1).
53. This was the position prior to the European Communities (Motor Insurance) Regulations 2008 (SI 248/2008) at which time the general exception to the compulsory insurance requirements for excepted persons was removed.
54. *Withers v Delaney and MIBI* (Case C–158/01) [2002] ECR I–08301.

an accident that occurred on 23 July 1995, and therefore prior to the deadline for Ireland's implementation of the Third Directive. For this reason, when the matter was referred to the European Court of Justice (the ECJ), it held that the plaintiff could not rely on the provisions of the Third Directive.

[2.28] In this case, the plaintiff's son was killed when the car in which he was travelling, and being driven by the first defendant, left the road and hit a ditch. The vehicle contained two seats, one for the driver and one for a passenger. The deceased was travelling in the rear of the vehicle in a covered area that contained no seating. On the date of the accident, the deceased was an excepted person, in terms of s 65(1)(a) of the 1961 Act, because he was a passenger in part of a vehicle that was *not* designed and constructed with seating accommodation for passengers.[55] At the hearing before Cork Circuit Court, the plaintiff claimed that the Irish legislation did not properly transpose the First and Second Directives. On 9 March 2001, Judge McMahon stayed the proceedings and referred three questions to the ECJ for a preliminary ruling pursuant to art 234 of the EC Treaty. The first question was:

> '[w]hether on the true interpretation of the [First and Second Directives], Ireland was entitled on 23 July 1995, to maintain legislation (Section 65 of the 1961 Act and the Road Traffic (Compulsory Insurance) Regulations, 1962) which did not make compulsory insurance mandatory for passengers injured in a "part of a vehicle, other than a large public service vehicle, unless that part of the vehicle is designed and constructed with seating accommodation for passengers"?'

[2.29] The ECJ[56] considered that the net issue was whether or not the First and Second Directives left to the Member States the power to determine the extent and the detailed provisions of passenger cover.[57] The ECJ followed the decision in *Ferreira and Ferreira v Companhia de Seguros Mundial Confianca SA*[58] and held that, pursuant to the First and Second Directives, Member States remained competent to determine 'the extent of passenger cover'.[59]

---

55.   The requirements of compulsory insurance were extended by way of ministerial regulations (Road Traffic (Compulsory Insurance) Regulations 1962 (SI 14/1962), as amended by Road Traffic (Compulsory Insurance) (Amendment) Regulations 1992 (SI 346/1992), art 4). However, these Regulations did not affect the plaintiff because Road Traffic Act 1961, s 65(1)(a) expressly precluded the Minister from extending the requirements of compulsory insurance by way of regulations for passengers to any part of a vehicle (other than a large public service vehicle) unless that part was designed and built with passenger seating.

56.   In circumstances where it was considered that the answer to this question could be clearly deduced from existing case law, the ECJ gave its decision by way of reasoned order under art 104(3) of the Rules of Procedure of the ECJ and made on 14 October 2002.

57.   *Withers v Delaney and MIBI* (Case C–158/01) [2002] ECR I–08301, para 16.

58.   *Ferreira and Ferreira v Companhia de Seguros Mundial Confianca SA* (Case C–348/98) [2000] ECR I–06711. In this case, the ECJ held that Second Directive, art 3 (now Sixth Directive, art 12(2)) required compulsory insurance against civil liability in respect of the use of motor vehicles to cover personal injuries to passengers who are members of the family of the insured person or of the driver, where those passengers are carried free of charge, whether or not there is any fault on the part of the driver of the vehicle which caused the accident, only if the domestic law of the Member State concerned requires such cover in respect of personal injuries caused in the same conditions to other third party passengers (para 35).

59.   At para 18 of *Withers v Delaney and MIBI* (Case C–158/01) [2002] ECR I–08301.

[2.30] In *Ferreira,* the ECJ reviewed the provisions of the First, Second and Third Directives (the three directives). It observed that, as was clear from the aim and wording of the three directives, they did not seek to harmonise the rules of the Member States governing civil liability.[60] Having outlined the purpose of the three directives,[61] the ECJ in *Ferreira* concluded that, in the absence of Community rules defining the type of civil liability, it was for the Member States to lay down the system of civil liability applicable to road traffic accidents.[62] This meant that, provided that the Member States ensured that the civil liability arising under their domestic law was covered by insurance that complied with the three directives, they were free to determine the type of civil liability applicable to road traffic accidents.[63]

[2.31] As in *Ferreira,* the Court in *Withers* observed that while art 1 of the Third Directive[64] had extended the compulsory insurance cover imposed by art 3(1) of the First Directive[65] to passengers other than the driver, the accident in *Withers* occurred before the deadline of 31 December 1995 for Ireland's transposition of the Third Directive for vehicles, other than cycles.

[2.32] For this reason, the Third Directive could not be relied upon before the Irish courts.[66] The Court held that the First and Second Directives did not require Member States to ensure that compulsory insurance 'cover[ed] personal injuries to passengers carried in a part of a vehicle that was not adapted for the transport of seated passengers'.[67]

[2.33] The order of the ECJ in *Withers,* however, clearly forecast that, if the accident had occurred on or after the deadline, the plaintiff could have relied upon the Third Directive.[68]

---

60. At para 23 of *Ferreira and Ferreira v Companhia de Seguros Mundial Confianca SA* (Case C–348/98) [2000] ECR I–06711. The ECJ in *Ferreira* further referred to the decision in *Ruiz Bernaldez* (Case C–129/94) [1996] ECR I–01829, [1996] 2 CMLR 889, wherein the ECJ held that the preambles to the directives showed that their aim was, first, to ensure the free movement of vehicles normally based on Community territory and of persons travelling in those vehicles and, second, to guarantee that the victims of accidents caused by those vehicles receive comparable treatment irrespective of where in the Community the accidents occur. In this regard, it expressly referred to the fifth recital in the preamble to the Second Directive and the fourth recital in the preamble to the Third Directive.
61. At paras 25–27 of *Ferreira and Ferreira v Companhia de Seguros Mundial Confianca SA* (Case C–348/98) [2000] ECR I–06711.
62. At para 28 of *Ferreira and Ferreira v Companhia de Seguros Mundial Confianca SA* (Case C–348/98) [2000] ECR I–06711.
63. At para 29 of *Ferreira and Ferreira v Companhia de Seguros Mundial Confianca SA* (Case C–348/98) [2000] ECR I–06711.
64. Third Directive, art 1 is now contained in Sixth Directive, art 12(1).
65. First Directive, art 3(1) is now contained in Sixth Directive, art 3, first and second paragraphs.
66. At para 20 of *Withers v Delaney and MIBI* (Case C–158/01) [2002] ECR I–08301. See also *Ferreira and Ferreira v Companhia de Seguros Mundial Confianca SA* (Case C–348/98) [2000] ECR I–06711 (para 33).
67. At para 21 of *Withers v Delaney and MIBI* (Case C–158/01) [2002] ECR I–08301.
68. It has been noted that it could be argued that an individual travelling in a part of a vehicle that is not fitted with seating is not a 'passenger' within the meaning of the Third Directive, art 1. (contd .../)

4. *Farrell v Whitty, the Minister for the Environment, Ireland, the Attorney General and the MIBI*

[2.34] In *Farrell v Whitty, the Minister for the Environment, Ireland, the Attorney General and the MIBI*,[69] the plaintiff suffered personal injury in an accident in January 1996, while she was sitting on the floor in the rear of a van (which had no seating) that was bring driven by the first defendant. The first defendant was an uninsured driver. The plaintiff sought to recover compensation from the MIBI pursuant to the 1988 Agreement. The MIBI refused to compensate her on the basis that she was travelling in a part of the vehicle that was not fitted with seating and accordingly insurance was not compulsory. The plaintiff obtained a default judgment against the uninsured driver in July 2001 and the assessment of damages was deferred to the trial of the action. In the proceedings issued by the plaintiff in 1997, the plaintiff claimed, *inter alia*:

1.   Damages for personal injuries against the uninsured driver;

2.   A declaration that the plaintiff was entitled to rely upon the provisions of the First Directive as amended by the Third Directive in the proceedings;

3.   A declaration that the European Communities (Road Traffic) (Compulsory Insurance) (Amendment) Regulations, 1992[70] (the Second 1992 Regulations) failed to implement adequately or at all the relevant provisions of the First Directive as amended by the Third Directive.

[2.35] Thereafter, the parties agreed that a number of points could be determined as preliminary issues in the High Court, namely:

1.   Insofar as s 65(1) of the 1961 Act, as amended by article 7 of the Second 1992 Regulations provided that regulations made by the Minister 'shall not extend compulsory insurance in respect of civil liability to passengers to – (i) any part of a mechanically propelled vehicle, other than a large public service vehicle,

---

68.   (contd) See Murphy, 'Unseated Passengers and the MIBI', 8(3) 2003 *Bar Review* 96 at pp 98–99. Murphy, however, submits that it is clear from the judgment of the ECJ in *Withers v Delaney and MIBI* (Case C–158/01) [2002] ECR I–08301 that this cannot be a correct interpretation of the Third Directive. Murphy also considers the decision in *Ruiz Bernaldez* (Case C–129/94) [1996] ECR I–01829, [1996] 2 CMLR 889 in which the ECJ was concerned with Spanish legislation that discharged an insurer from liability for injury caused to a third party by an insured's drunk driving. In an art 177 reference, the ECJ held that the First Directive, art 3(1) (as amended and now Sixth Directive, art 3, first and second paragraphs) had to be interpreted as meaning that compulsory insurance must enable third party victims of accidents caused by vehicles to be compensated for all damage suffered by them up to the amounts specified by Second Directive, art 1(2) (and now contained in the Sixth Directive, art 9). It considered that any other interpretation would have operated to allow Member States to limit the payment of compensation to third party victims of road traffic accidents to certain types of damage and would thereby cause disparities in the treatment of victims depending on where an accident occurred. The ECJ in *Ruiz Bernaldez* noted that this would bring about a situation that the directives sought to avoid and it would deprive the First Directive, art 3(1) (now Sixth Directive, art 3, first and second paragraphs) of its effectiveness (at paras 18–19).

69.   *Farrell v Whitty, the Minister for the Environment, Ireland, the Attorney General and the MIBI*, [2008] IEHC 124, (31 January 2008, unreported) HC, Birmingham J.

70.   European Communities (Road Traffic) (Compulsory Insurance) (Amendment) Regulations, 1992 (SI 347/1992).

unless that part is designed and constructed with seating and accommodation for passengers...', does s 65(1), as amended, implement the First, Second and Third Directives in a proper and permissible manner?

2.   If the answer to 1 was in the negative, were the relevant provisions of the First, Second and Third Directives directly effective such that the plaintiff could rely on same in respect of the matters complained of in the proceedings?

3.   If the answer to 2 was in the affirmative, was the plaintiff entitled to recover from the MIBI pursuant to the 1988 Agreement?

[2.36] On 30 July 2004, the High Court (Ó Caoimh J), in dealing with the preliminary issues, referred the following two questions to the ECJ for a preliminary ruling under art 234 of the EC Treaty, namely:

1.   As of 31 December 1995, the date by which Ireland was obliged to implement the provisions of the Third Directive, in respect of passengers on vehicles other than motorcycles, did art 1 of the Third Directive oblige Ireland to render insurance compulsory in respect of civil liabilities for injury to individuals travelling in that part of a motor vehicle not designed or constructed with seating accommodation for passengers?

2.   If the answer to 1 was in the positive, did art 1 of the Third Directive confer rights on individuals that could be relied upon directly before the national courts?

[2.37] On 19 April 2007, the ECJ answered the reference as follows:[71]

1.   Article 1 of the Third Directive[72] is to be interpreted as precluding national legislation whereby compulsory motor vehicle liability insurance does not cover liability in respect of personal injuries to persons travelling in a part of the motor vehicle which has not been designed and constructed with seating accommodation for passengers;

2.   Article 1 of the Third Directive satisfies all the conditions necessary for it to produce direct effect and accordingly confers rights upon which individuals may rely directly before the national courts. However, it is for the national courts to determine whether that provision may be relied upon against a body such as the MIBI.

[2.38] Thereafter, the matter came before Birmingham J in the High Court, at which time the net issue for determination was '[m]ay a directive (in this case article 1 of [the Third Directive]) which confers rights upon which individuals may rely directly before the national Court be relied upon against the [MIBI]?' Before the High Court, it was agreed that the issue could be determined by deciding whether the MIBI was or was not an 'emanation of the State' as that phrase was understood in European law.[73]

---

71.   *Farrell v Whitty, Minister for the Environment, Ireland, Attorney General and the MIBI* (Case 356/05) [2007] ECR I–03067.

72.   Third Directive, art 1 is now contained in the Sixth Directive, art 12(1).

73.   *Farrell v Whitty, the Minister for the Environment, Ireland, the Attorney General and the MIBI*, [2008] IEHC 124, (31 January 2008, unreported) HC, Birmingham J, at p 10. This judgment is analysed in detail in **Ch 12**.

Birmingham J, in an analytical judgment, concluded that the MIBI, in substance if not in form, operated as a quasi state claims agency giving effect to an important aspect of public social policy and therefore was to be regarded as an emanation of the State.[74] On this basis, the plaintiff was entitled to recover from the MIBI pursuant to the 1988 Agreement.[75] This decision is under appeal to the Supreme Court.[76]

5. *Smith v Meade, Meade, FBD Insurance Plc, Ireland and the Attorney General*

[2.39] In *Smith v Meade, Meade, FBD Insurance Plc, Ireland and the Attorney General*,[77] the plaintiff suffered personal injury in June 1999 when the van in which he was travelling as a passenger, owned by the second defendant (the van owner) and driven by the first defendant (the van driver), collided with another vehicle as a result of the alleged negligent driving of the van driver. At the time of the collision, the plaintiff was travelling in an area that was not designed or constructed with seating accommodation for passengers. The van owner had an insurance policy with the third defendant (the insurer) in respect of any loss or damage suffered by third parties as a consequence of any negligent driving by him or any persons driving with his consent and authority and, at the time of the accident, the van driver was driving with the van owner's consent. The insurer, however, declined to indemnify the van owner in respect of the plaintiff's injuries on the basis that the policy did not cover liability in respect of personal injuries to a person being carried as a passenger in a part of the vehicle that was not designed or constructed with seating accommodation for passengers.

[2.40] The plaintiff submitted that, having regard to the provisions of the First, Second and Third Directives, the exclusion clause in the insurance policy should be held void notwithstanding the fact that the Third Directive had not been transposed into Irish law by either the date by which its transposition was required *or* the subsequent date of the accident. The insurer submitted that it was entitled to rely on the exclusion contained in s 65 of the 1961 Act, as amended, and contended that the plaintiff's remedy was one against the State on the basis of its failure to transpose the Third Directive into Irish law by the required date.

[2.41] Peart J said that there was no doubt that the insurance policy excluded any indemnity in respect of the plaintiff's injuries in circumstances where he was seated in the rear part of the vehicle which was not fitted with a seat. Furthermore, there was no dispute that, on the date of the accident, the Third Directive had not been transposed into

---

74. *Farrell v Whitty, the Minister for the Environment, Ireland, the Attorney General and the MIBI*, [2008] IEHC 124, (31 January 2008, unreported) HC at p 35.

75. *Farrell v Whitty, the Minister for the Environment, Ireland, the Attorney General and the MIBI*, [2008] IEHC 124, (31 January 2008, unreported) HC at p 36.

76. Indeed, cl 3.10.3 of the 2009 Agreement expressly provides that cl 3 of that agreement will be reviewed in light of the Supreme Court judgment in *Farrell v Whitty, the Minister for the Environment, Ireland, the Attorney General and the MIBI*.

77. *Smith v Meade, Meade, FBD Insurance Plc, Ireland and the Attorney General* [2009] 3 IR 335.

Irish law and the time within which this was required to be done by Ireland had passed. He also considered that it was clear from the case law of the ECJ that the Third Directive had direct effect against the State or any emanation of the State, but this did not provide a remedy against any individual such as the insurance company.[78]

[2.42] Peart J concluded:

> '[36] All passengers being carried in vehicles and who are injured as a result are intended to be guaranteed equal treatment throughout the European Community regardless of in which member state the injury is caused. The Second Directive required each member state to take necessary measures to ensure that any statutory provision or any contractual clause contained in an insurance policy which excludes from insurance persons, *inter alia*, such as this plaintiff shall for the purpose of article 3(1) of the First Directive be void. I should perhaps note that this obligation is one imposed upon member states, *i.e.*, to put measures in place to so ensure. The Directive does not itself state that such a clause *is* void. Nevertheless the objective is clear. The amendment to s. 65 of the [1961 Act by article 7 of the Second 1992 Regulations] is clearly in conflict with these objectives, and the failure to transpose the Third Directive by the date required has meant that on the date of the accident in which the plaintiff received his injuries, the law of this State was out of line with what was required by Community law.

> [37] [The ECJ judgment in *Marleasing S.E. v La Comercial Internacional de Alimentación* (Case C–106/89) [1990] ECR I–4135 ...] requires a national court, when applying national law, to do so as far as possible in the light of the wording and purpose of the directive in order to pursue the result sought to be pursued by the directive. It seems inescapable that in the present case this court is required to read s. 65 of the Act, as amended by the two Regulations of 1992,[79] by overlooking or ignoring the exclusion permitted therein in respect of liability for injuries caused to persons such as the plaintiff in this case. It seems to follow inevitably from this that the court must conclude that the clause to that effect contained in the policy of insurance ... must be regarded as void, therefore disentitling the [insurer] from relying upon it in order to refuse to indemnify [the van driver and van owner] in respect of the plaintiff's claim for damages ... in the event that he is found at hearing to have so suffered as a result of the negligence of [the van driver]. I so find.'[80, 81]

---

78.   *Smith v Meade, Meade, FBD Insurance Plc, Ireland and the Attorney General* [2009] 3 IR 335 at p 347.

79.   That is, the Road Traffic (Compulsory Insurance) (Amendment) Regulations 1992 (SI 346/1992) and European Communities (Road Traffic) (Compulsory Insurance) (Amendment) Regulations 1992 (SI 347/1992).

80.   *Smith v Meade, Meade, FBD Insurance Plc, Ireland and the Attorney General* [2009] 3 IR 335 at p 348. See also **Ch 10**, paras **10.57–10.83**.

81.   The defendants subsequently settled this action with the plaintiff and the settlement was ruled by the High Court (Quirke J) on 10 February 2009 (see [2009] 3 IR 335 at p 349). As between the defendants, however, the matter remains under appeal. For an analysis of, *inter alia*, the decision of the ECJ in *Farrell v Whitty* and *Smith v Meade* and others, see Murphy, 'Uninsured Passengers and EU law', 14(6) 2009 *Bar Review* 123.

G. MOTORCYCLE PASSENGERS

1. Motorcycle passengers – development of the law

[2.43] The original art 6(2) of the 1962 Regulations expressly provided that the compulsory insurance requirements of art 6(1) of the 1962 Regulations did not extend to the driver of a cycle or to a person being conveyed by a cycle, whether in a side car or otherwise. Thus, while the original art 6(1) made passenger insurance obligatory in respect of the three categories (a)–(c) specified above at para **2.17**, this obligation did not extend to pillion or rear-seat motorcycle passengers ('motorcycle passengers').

[2.44] The exception of motorcycle passengers from the requirements of compulsory insurance in Ireland until 30 December 1998, has been noted above.[82] Hence, until this date, a motorcycle passenger who was injured as a result of the negligent driving of that motorcycle could not require the MIBI to meet an unsatisfied judgment.

[2.45] Article 4 of the First 1992 Regulations, which substituted a new art 6 into the 1962 Regulations, made insurance compulsory for motorcycle passengers. The purpose of the First 1992 Regulations was to implement certain provisions of the Third Directive.

[2.46] In terms of the chronological development, the position may be summarised as follows:

1. Article 3(1) of the First Directive required each Member State to take all appropriate measures to ensure that civil liability in respect of the use of vehicles in its territory was covered by insurance; [83]

2. Article 1(1) of the Second Directive required that the insurance required by Article 3(1) of the First Directive covered damage to person and property;[84]

3. Article 1 of the Third Directive provided that the insurance required by Article 3(1) of the First Directive 'shall cover liability for personal injuries to all passengers, other than the driver, arising out of the use of the vehicle.'[85]

---

82. See paras **2.19**–**2.21**.
83. The First Directive, art 3(1) provided '[e]ach Member State shall, subject to Article 4, take all appropriate measures to ensure that civil liability in respect of the use of vehicles normally based in its territory is covered by insurance. The extent of the liability covered and the terms and conditions of the cover shall be determined on the basis of these measures'. This obligation is now contained in the Sixth Directive, art 3.
84. Second Directive, art 1(1) provided: '[t]he insurance referred to in Article 3(1) of [the First Directive] shall cover compulsorily both damage to property and personal injuries'. When Second Directive, art 1(1) was substituted by Fifth Directive, art 2, its text was unaltered. This obligation is now contained in Sixth Directive, art 3.
85. Third Directive, art 1(1) as set out above is now contained in Sixth Directive, art 12(1). Fifth Directive, art 4(2) inserted Third Directive, art 1a, and which provided that '[t]he insurance referred to in Article 3(1) of [the First Directive] shall cover personal injuries and damage to property suffered by pedestrians, cyclists and other non-motorised users of the roads who, as a consequence of an accident in which a motor vehicle is involved, are entitled to compensation in accordance with national civil law. This Article shall be without prejudice either to civil liability or to the amount of damages.' (contd .../)

[2.47] While the general implementation date for the Third Directive was 31 December 1992,[86] Ireland was given until 31 December 1998 to comply with art 1 as regards requiring compulsory insurance for pillion passengers on motorcycles.[87] A pillion passenger who suffers injury on or after 31 December 1998, in circumstances where there was no insurance covering his personal injury and subject to the other general provisions of the relevant MIBI Agreement, may make a claim to the MIBI in respect of his injuries.

2. *Delargy v Minister for the Environment and Local Government, Ireland, Attorney General and MIBI*

[2.48] In *Delargy v Minister for the Environment and Local Government, Ireland, Attorney General and MIBI*,[88] the plaintiff was a pillion passenger on a motorcycle and suffered significant injuries in an accident in September, 1987, in which the owner of the motorcycle was driving it. The plaintiff sued the motorcycle owner and in April 1996 obtained judgment against him in an uncontested action. The judgment was unsatisfied. Thereafter, in these proceedings, the plaintiff claimed, *inter alia*:

1. A declaration that s 65(1)(a) of the 1961 Act was unconstitutional;

2. A declaration that s 56 of the 1961 Act was unconstitutional;

3. A declaration that reg 6 of the 1962 Regulations was unconstitutional, that the Minister was acting *ultra vires* the powers conferred on him by the Oireachtas and that the same was null and void;

4. A declaration that the 1964 MIBI Agreement was void insofar as it purported to exclude the plaintiff's claim;

5. A declaration that the First Directive as amended by the Third Directive had direct effect and that the plaintiff was entitled to rely on it;

6. A declaration that the First Directive as amended obliged the State parties to ensure that the liability of the motorcycle owner and driver to the plaintiff on foot of the judgment obtained by her was covered by insurance;

---

85. (contd) The text of Fifth Directive, art 4(2) (as it inserted a new art 1a into the Third Directive) is now contained in Sixth Directive, art 12(3). Fifth Directive, art 4(1) also inserted a new paragraph into Third Directive, art 1 which provided that 'Member States shall take the necessary measures to ensure that any statutory provision or any contractual clause contained in an insurance policy which excludes a passenger from such cover on the basis that he knew or should have known that the driver of the vehicle was under the influence of alcohol or of any other intoxicating agent at the time of the accident, shall be deemed to be void in respect of the claims of such passenger.' The Commission considered that it was important to clarify this issue along the lines established by the ECJ in *Ruiz Bernaldez* (Case C–129/94) [1996] ECR I–01829, [1996] 2 CMLR 889 (see above fn **68**). The text of Fifth Directive, art 4(1) (as it amended Third Directive, art 1) is now contained in Sixth Directive, art 13(3).

86. Third Directive, art 6(1).

87. Third Directive, art 6(2).

88. *Delargy v Minister for the Environment and Local Government, Ireland, Attorney General and MIBI* [2005] IEHC 94, (18 March 2005, unreported) HC, Murphy J.

7.   Damages for failure to implement the First and Third Directives;

8.   A declaration that the plaintiff was entitled to claim against the MIBI in respect of the liability of the motorcycle owner and driver to the plaintiff on foot of the judgment obtained by her against him.

[2.49] Murphy J observed that the relevant legislation permitted the Minister to distinguish between various classes of vehicles but did not provide any guidance as to the principle(s) upon which the Minister was to draw that distinction. He noted that the Minister had been given the power to introduce a provision which made a difference between a case where one person, injured by the negligence of another (without the means to satisfy a judgment), could be compensated *and* a case where another person similarly injured with the same level of fault (on the part of a similarly situated defendant) could not be so compensated.[89] Murphy J considered, however, that it was clear that, in the absence of seats, there was no requirement for passengers to be compulsorily insured. He noted that, as regards vehicles in which there is no provision made for seating for passengers such as tractors, there might be a rational basis for excluding compulsory insurance for passengers.[90]

[2.50] With respect to the plaintiff, and in circumstances where there was accommodation for a passenger on the motorcycle, he stated:

'Motor cycles are usually constructed for the carriage of single passengers. It is difficult to see by what principle of policy the Minister had excluded cover under Regulation 6(2) of the [1962 Regulations].

What the Minister has done is not merely regulatory or administrative only, but is an attempt to arbitrarily restrict cover to a category of otherwise insured passengers.'

[2.51] In the foregoing circumstances, Murphy J declared that reg 6(2) of the 1962 Regulations was unconstitutional and that the Minister had acted *ultra vires* the powers conferred on him by the Oireachtas and that same was null and void.[91] For this reason, it was unnecessary to consider the issue of direct effect of the First and Third Directives.

[2.52] With respect to the liability of the MIBI, Murphy J noted that the Third Directive, which required cover for 'all passengers', gave Ireland until 31 December 1998, to comply as regards motorcycle passengers, that is more than 11 years after the plaintiff's 1987 accident. He concluded that, at the time of the accident, there was no requirement to have cover for pillion passengers and therefore the MIBI had no obligation under the

---

89. *Delargy v Minister for the Environment and Local Government, Ireland, Attorney General and MIBI* [2005] IEHC 94, (18 March 2005, unreported) HC, at p 8.

90. At pp 8–9. In this regard, he noted that a passenger in an unseated area in the back of a van or lorry was not compulsorily insurable (at p 9). However, the foregoing comment must be considered in the context of *Farrell v Whitty* before the ECJ and the decision of Birmingham J. in the High Court (under appeal). See paras **2.34–2.38** above.

91. In the judgment of 18 March 2005, Murphy J said that he would make a declaration that Road Traffic (Compulsory Insurance) Regulations 1962 (SI 14/1962), reg 6 was unconstitutional. However, in a supplemental judgment delivered on 10 August 2005 (and discussed below), Murphy J stated that the declaration of unconstitutionality should refer specifically to reg 6(2) of the Regulations, rather than reg 6.

1964 Agreement to satisfy the plaintiff's judgment against the motorcycle owner and driver.[92]

H. INJURY TO EXCEPTED PERSON AFTER DISEMBARKING VEHICLE

[2.53] Prior to the 2008 Regulations,[93] a person who suffered injury while 'in or on' a part of a vehicle that was not 'designed and constructed with seating accommodation[94] for passengers' (that is an unseated passenger) was an excepted person. Hence, it was

---

92. At p 10. Murphy J said that there was no issue regarding the intervention of European Community law which was not in contemplation at that time and he said that it followed that, prior to 31 December 1998, the Third Directive had no direct effect in Ireland of any kind, either against a public body, a private body or individual. Murphy J said that he had considered the judgment of the ECJ in *Withers v Delaney and MIBI* (Case C–158/01) [2002] ECR I–08301. Finally, Murphy J said that he was not satisfied that there was evidence that the MIBI could be considered an 'emanation of the State'. He referred to *Mighell v Reading* [1999] 1 CMLR 1251 (Court of Appeal) and *White v White* [1999] 1 CMLR 1251 (Court of Appeal), [2001] 1 WLR 481, [2001] 2 All ER 43, [2001] 1 Lloyds Rep 679 and [2001] RTR 379 (House of Lords). He considered that the English conclusion that the MIB was not an emanation of the State was more persuasive than the Irish decision in *Dublin Bus v MIBI* (29 October 1999, unreported) CC, Judge McMahon, (at p 12). Obviously, however, the foregoing comments predated the decision in *Farrell v Whitty, the Minister for the Environment, Ireland, the Attorney General and the MIBI* [2008] IEHC 124, (31 January 2008, unreported) HC, Birmingham J.

A supplemental judgment was delivered in *Delargy v Minister for the Environment and Local Government, Ireland, the Attorney General and the MIBI* [2006] IEHC 267, (10 August 2005, unreported) HC, Murphy J. In advance of this judgment, the court heard submissions with respect to the appropriate form of ancillary relief that might be available to the plaintiff in light of the court's findings in the substantive proceedings. In this regard, Murphy J concluded that the plaintiff was entitled to a remedy against the Minister. In the supplemental judgment, he described the issue as follows: 'the question arises as to the consequences of the Minister acting *ultra vires* the powers conferred on him by the Oireachtas in relation to the exclusion of cover for pillion passengers. There is no direct relationship between the power of the court to null an administrative act and liability to pay damages or monetary compensation. When a court nulls an administrative act on procedural grounds, that decision is deemed to be *ultra vires* and void *ab initio*. However, it does not follow that a declaration of invalidity of an administrative decision in and of itself gives rise to a cause of action and damages' (at p 4). However, Murphy J concluded that in acting as the Minister did, reg 6(2) arbitrarily restricted and excluded cover to a category of otherwise insurable passengers. He said that the court had held that it was difficult to see by what principle or policy such exclusion was made and to have acted in such an arbitrary manner was a breach of duty (at p 5). Murphy J concluded that the effect of Road Traffic (Compulsory Insurance) Regulations 1962 (SI 14/1962), reg 6(2) was to exclude a defined category of persons, which included the plaintiff, from having the benefit of the mandatory requirement to have cover. On the authorities of *O'Neill v Clare County Council* [1983] ILRM 141, *Bakht v Medical Council* [1990] 1 IR 515, *Emerald Meats v Minister for Agriculture and Food* [1997] 2 ILRM 275 and *Moyne v London Port and Harbour Commissioners* [1986] IR 299, the court held that the plaintiff was entitled to a remedy against the Minister (at pp 5–6).

93. European Communities (Motor Insurance) Regulations 2008 (SI 248/2008) and which became operative at the end of 3 July 2008 (see the Interpretation Act 2005, s 16(3)). See **Section E**.

94. 'Seating accommodation for a passenger' is: '(i) in the case of a vehicle other than a cycle, a fixed or folding seat permanently and securely installed in or on the vehicle, and (contd .../)

not obligatory to insure against injury or damage caused to such a person. The foregoing statement must, however, be read and considered in the context of the decision in *Farrell v Whitty, the Minister for the Environment, Ireland, the Attorney General and the MIBI*[95] and *Delargy v Minister for the Environment and Local Government, Ireland, Attorney General and MIBI.*[96]

[2.54] However, if such an excepted person was caused injury by the vehicle after disembarking, he no longer came within the definition of an excepted person and could therefore claim compensation from the MIBI. This was established in *Kenny v MIBI and The Minister for the Environment.*[97] In that case, a child fell off the back of a flat bed truck and onto the ground. He then sustained injuries when the back wheel of the lorry was driven over him.[98] The High Court held that the plaintiff was an excepted person and therefore was not entitled to recover against the MIBI. The Supreme Court allowed the plaintiff's appeal. It considered that the plaintiff would have been an excepted person if he had received his injuries while he was 'in or on' the truck[99] and noted that 'in or on' was defined by the Act to include injuries received 'while ... being thrown out of or off the vehicle.'[100] On the facts as found by the trial judge, the Supreme Court was satisfied that two events occurred: firstly, the plaintiff was thrown off the truck; and, secondly, the plaintiff was then run over by one of its wheels. Thus, the plaintiff's injuries were not sustained while he was 'in or on' the truck and were not sustained 'while' he was being thrown out of or off the truck. The plaintiff suffered injuries *after* he was thrown off the truck and therefore was not an excepted person.

---

94.   (contd) (ii) in the case of a cycle, a seat for one passenger behind the driver or a seat in a sidecar, in each case permanently and securely installed, and 'seating accommodation for passengers' shall be similarly construed' (Road Traffic Act 1961, s 65(2)(c) as inserted by the European Communities (Road Traffic) (Compulsory Insurance) (Amendment) Regulations 1992 (SI 347/ 1992), art 7).

95.   *Farrell v Whitty, the Minister for the Environment, Ireland, the Attorney General and the MIBI*, [2008] IEHC 124, (31 January 2008, unreported) HC, Birmingham J..

96.   *Delargy v Minister for the Environment and Local Government, Ireland, Attorney General and MIBI* [2005] IEHC 94, (18 March 2005, unreported) HC, Murphy J.

97.   *Kenny v MIBI and The Minister for the Environment* (3 April 1995, unreported) SC, *per* Blayney J (Hamilton CJ and O'Flaherty J concurring).

98.   *Kenny v MIBI and The Minister for the Environment* (3 April 1995, unreported) SC, *per* Blayney J (Hamilton CJ and O'Flaherty J concurring), p 10.

99.   Road Traffic Act 1961, s 65(1)(a).

100.   Road Traffic Act 1961, s 65(1)(b). References to injury sustained while 'in or on' a vehicle include 'injury sustained while entering, getting on to, being put into or on, or alighting from, or being taken out of or off, the vehicle, and injury caused by being thrown out of or off the vehicle' (Road Traffic Act 1961, s 65(2)(b)).

Table 2.1 Obligation to insure (potential claim against MIBI if no insurance)

> User of mechanically propelled vehicle in a public place must have insurance that will cover that user's negligent use of that mechanically propelled vehicle which causes injury to another person or another person's property.
>
> Insurance must be without limit for personal injury.[101] For property damage, the minimum insurance is €1,120,000 per claim, whatever the number of victims.[102]
>
> This is subject to those categories summarised at **Table 2.2.** below.

(a) Vehicles, other than cycles, designed and constructed with passenger seating accommodation [31 December 1995][103]

(b) Cycles designed and constructed with seating accommodation for passengers [31 December 1998][104]

(c) All passengers (other than passengers on (b) above) [31 December 1995][105]

Table 2.2 No obligation to insure (no claim against MIBI if no insurance)

No obligation	A State owned vehicle or a State employee using such a vehicle in his employment.
	A vehicle seized by the State or a State employee using such a vehicle in his employment.
	A Garda or officer of any Minister testing, removing or disposing of a vehicle under the Road Traffic Act.
	eg vehicles owned by Government Departments and State agencies, including An Garda Síochána and Defence Forces.
Exempted Person	A board or other body established by an Act of the Oireachtas;
	A State sponsored company;
	A company in which majority shareholder is a statutory board or body or state sponsored company;
	eg Dublin Bus, Bus Éireann and Iarnród Éireann.

---

101. Road Traffic Act 1961, s 56(1)(a) requires insurance 'against all sums without limit' in respect of personal injury.
102. Road Traffic Act 1961, s 56(1)(b), as amended by the European Communities (Motor Insurance) Regulations 2008 (SI 248/2008), reg 2(b) and the European Union (Motor Insurance) (Limitation of Insurance in Relation to Property) Regulations 2011 (SI 702/11), reg 2.
103. This must be read in the context of **Section F** above.
104. This must be read in the context of **Section G** above.
105. In light of *Farrell v Whitty, Minister for the Environment, Ireland, Attorney General and the MIBI* (Case 356/05) [2007] ECR I–03067.

Chapter 3

EXCLUSION OF CLAIMS

A. INTRODUCTION

[3.01] The Sixth Directive provides:

> 'Member states may, however, exclude the payment of compensation by [the body responsible for paying compensation] in respect of persons who voluntarily entered the vehicle which caused the damage or injury when the body can prove that they knew it was uninsured.'[1]

[3.02] The Sixth Directive also provides that insurance policies may exclude claims by persons who:

> '... voluntarily entered the vehicle which caused the damage or injury, when the insurer can prove that they knew the vehicle was stolen.'[2]

[3.03] The exclusions permitted by the Sixth Directive deal with two separate scenarios. Firstly, a body such as the MIBI may exclude the payment of compensation to a person who is injured in an uninsured vehicle where the MIBI can prove that he entered the vehicle voluntarily and knew it was uninsured.[3] Insurers, on the other hand, can expressly exclude a passenger from claiming for injury suffered in a stolen vehicle where it can prove that he knew the vehicle was stolen.[4]

[3.04] Clause 5 of the 2009 Agreement,[5] entitled 'Exclusion of certain user and passenger claims' provides:

> '5.1. Where at the time of the accident the vehicle had been stolen or taken by violence, the liability of the MIBI shall not extend to any judgment or claim in respect of injury, death or damage to property sustained while the person injured or killed or the owner of the property damaged voluntarily entered the vehicle which caused the damage or injury and MIBI can prove that they knew it was stolen or was taken by violence.

---

1. See Sixth Directive, art 10(2) second subparagraph (previously Second Directive, art 1(4) third subparagraph and thereafter substituted in Second Directive, art 1(5) by Fifth Directive, art 2). The Sixth Directive is reproduced in **Appendix 3**.

2. See Sixth Directive, art 13(1) second subparagraph (previously Second Directive, art 2(1) second subparagraph). This article was purportedly transposed into Irish law by the Road Traffic (Compulsory Insurance) Regulations 1962 (SI 14/1962), art 5 and the First Schedule, as amended by: the Road traffic (Compulsory Insurance) Regulations, 1964 (SI No 58 of 1964), art 2; the Road Traffic (Compulsory Insurance) (Amendment) Regulations 1977 (SI No 359 of 1977), art 2; and the Road Traffic (Compulsory Insurance) (Amendment) Regulations 1987 (SI No 321 of 1987), art 4. See **Ch 10**, paras **10.57–10.61**.

3. See the Sixth Directive, art 10(2) (and fn **1** above).

4. See the Sixth Directive, art 13(1) (and fn **2** above).

5. Clause 5.2 of the 2004 Agreement excluded the MIBI's liability where the injured party 'knew, or ought reasonably to have known' that there was no insurance. Clause 5.3 of the 2004 Agreement excluded liability for users of two colliding vehicles, in circumstances where both users were uninsured. The 2009 Agreement is reproduced in **Appendix 1**. The 2004 Agreement is reproduced in **Appendix 2**.

> 5.2. Where at the time of the accident a person injured or killed or who sustained damage to property voluntarily entered the vehicle which caused the damage or injury and MIBI can prove that they knew that there was not in force an approved policy of insurance in respect of the use of the vehicle, the liability of MIBI shall not extend to any judgment or claim either in respect of injury or death of such person while the person injured or killed was by his consent in or on such vehicle or in respect of damage to property while the owner of the property was by his consent in or on the vehicle.'

[3.05] In the first edition of this book it was suggested that the previous MIBI agreements were inconsistent with the Second Directive insofar as they purported to exclude claims from passengers who 'knew, or ought reasonably to have known, that there was not in force an approved policy of insurance in respect of the use of the vehicle'[6] and claims from passengers where two uninsured vehicles collided with each other.[7, 8]

[3.06] Since then, the European Commission obtained a declaration from the European Court of Justice (ECJ) that the maintenance in force of cls 5.2 and 5.3 of the 2004 Agreement constituted a failure on the part of Ireland to fulfil its obligations under the Second Directive. The ECJ held that:

> '[b]y excluding from the right to compensation persons who entered any uninsured vehicle, without restricting that exclusion to persons present in an uninsured vehicle which caused damage or injury and, in relation to collisions between uninsured vehicles, to persons who, at the time of the accident, were aware that the vehicle which they had entered was uninsured, clauses 5.2 and 5.3 of the Agreement infringed the third subparagraph of article 1(4) of the [Second] Directive.'[9, 10]

[3.07] Subsequent to this judgment of the ECJ, the 2009 Agreement was introduced and includes a new cl 5.[11]

[3.08] The exclusions in cl 5 of the 2009 Agreement provide a full defence to claims against the MIBI. The MIBI bears the onus of proof in respect of these defences. The case law to date has only considered the old 'knew or ought reasonably to have known' test under cl 5.3 of the 2004 Agreement.[12] The extent to which knowledge might be inferred has yet to be tested by the Irish courts. Under the old test, however, a plaintiff who did not saddle himself with actual knowledge, due to his own inaction, or made no enquiry despite all the indicators pointing to there being no insurance, was deemed to be one who ought reasonably to have known.[13]

---

6.   Clause 5.2 of the 2004 Agreement.
7.   Clause 5.3 of the 2004 Agreement.
8.   See *The MIBI Agreements and the Law* (1st edn, First Law, 2005) pp 47–49.
9.   See fn **1**.
10. *Commission v Ireland* (Case C–211/07), Judgment of the Court (Sixth Chamber), 21 February 2008, at para 14.
11. See para **3.04**.
12. And cl 5(3) of the 1988 Agreement and equivalent provisions in earlier MIBI Agreements.
13. *Ward v Ward and MIBI* (18 February 2003, unreported) SC, *ex tempore*, and *Devlin v Cassidy and MIBI* [2006] IEHC 287, (31 July 2006, unreported) HC. See further paras **3.22–3.26**.

[3.09] To successfully defend a claim under the 2009 Agreement, the MIBI must prove that the plaintiff 'knew' that there was not in force an approved policy of insurance. It is submitted, however, that there is no reason why a court could not infer knowledge, based on circumstantial evidence given a suitable case. In the UK, 'knew' has been held to mean possessing information leading one to the conclusion that a driver might not be insured but deliberately refraining from asking the question. However, it does not extend to a situation where a passenger did not think about insurance, even though an ordinary prudent passenger in his position, and with his knowledge, would have enquired about it.[14]

[3.10] Thus, while it may seem that the MIBI will be faced with an insurmountable task in terms of proving that a plaintiff knew that there was no insurance, there is no reason, in principle, why a court would be precluded from inferring that a plaintiff knew that there was no insurance on the balance of probabilities. The criminal courts regularly return verdicts of guilty beyond reasonable doubt in trials in which the prosecution's case is based on circumstantial evidence.[15] There is no reason why, in an appropriate case, the MIBI could not successfully argue that actual knowledge encompasses imputed knowledge as discussed in the House of Lords in *White v White*,[16] and in which such a construction was held to be compliant with the Second Directive.[17] Indeed in *Kinsella v MIBI*,[18] although dealing with the wording of the 1964 MIBI Agreements, Finlay CJ specifically upheld a trial judge drawing inferences from the plaintiff's lack of credibility in other aspects of the case.

---

14. *White v White* [2001] 1 WLR 481, [2001] 2 All ER 43, [2001] 1 Lloyd's Rep 679, [2001] RTR 379.
15. For example, *DPP v O'Reilly* [2009] IECCA 1, (6 March 2009, unreported) Court of Criminal Appeal, in which the main plank of the prosecution's case for murder concerned the locations from which the accused made mobile telephone calls after the deceased's death.
16. *White v White* [2001] 1 WLR 481, [2001] 2 All ER 43, [2001] 1 Lloyd's Rep 679, [2001] RTR 379.
17. *Per* Lord Nicholls of Birkenhead at p 486 and see paras **3.30–3.37** for discussion. In explaining how the word 'knew' was to be construed in the context of the permitted exception to Second Directive, art 1(4) (now Sixth Directive, art 10(2), second subparagraph), Lord Nicholls of Birkenhead stated at para 14: 'The context is an exception to a general rule. The Court of Justice has stressed repeatedly that exceptions are to be construed strictly. Here, a strict and narrow interpretation of what constitutes knowledge for the purpose of article 1 is reinforced by the subject matter. The subject matter is compensation for damage to property or personal injuries caused by vehicles. The general rule is that victims of accidents should have the benefit of protection up to specified minimum amounts, whether or not the vehicle which caused the damage was insured. The exception, therefore, permits a member state, contrary to the general rule, to make no provision for compensation for a person who has suffered personal injury or damage to property. Proportionality requires that a high degree of personal fault must exist before it would be right for an injured passenger to be deprived of compensation. A narrow approach is further supported by the other prescribed limitation on the permissible ambit of any exclusion; the person claiming compensation must have entered the vehicle voluntarily. The need for the passenger to have entered the vehicle voluntarily serves to confirm that the exception is aimed at persons consciously colluding in the use of a uninsured vehicle. And it can be noted that the Directive emphasises the exceptional nature of the exclusion of compensation by placing the burden of proving knowledge on the party who seeks to invoke the exception, namely, the institution responsible for paying compensation.'
18. *Kinsella v MIBI* [1997] 3 IR 586.

B. DAMAGE CAUSED TO PERSONS OR PROPERTY IN STOLEN VEHICLES

[3.11] Clause 5.1 is self explanatory. A passenger in a stolen vehicle cannot recover from the MIBI if he voluntarily entered the vehicle which caused his injury and the MIBI can prove that he knew it was stolen. If a passenger, who is initially unaware that the vehicle in which he is travelling is stolen, subsequently becomes so aware and fails to alight if the opportunity presents itself, this may allow the MIBI to avail of what is known in the UK as 'the petrol station' defence. Stopping at a petrol station or such like may enable a passenger, newly appraised of information that the vehicle was stolen, to get out. Failure to do so may prevent recovery.[19]

[3.12] It would be contrary to the spirit of the MIBI agreement if a passenger, colluding with an uninsured driver of a stolen vehicle, could claim compensation for the negligence of that driver when the ultimate paymaster is the pool of insured motorists subsidising the MIBI.[20] This exclusion does not extend to injury caused to joyriding passengers injured as a result of negligence of other uninsured vehicles.[21]

C. THE SUBJECTIVE TEST OF KNOWLEDGE

[3.13] Pursuant to cl 5.2 of the 2009 Agreement, and by way of example, a passenger in a car who is injured when its uninsured driver veers off a road and crashes into a brick wall cannot look to the MIBI for compensation for any injury if he knew that the driver was uninsured at the time of the accident.[22]

[3.14] In *Kinsella v MIBI*,[23] which concerned the 1964 Agreement, the Supreme Court held that a subjective test of knowledge of the absence of insurance must be applied when determining a passenger's entitlement to recover from the MIBI. A plaintiff is

---

19. See *McMinn v McMinn* [2006] EWHC 827 (although note that the High Court disproved of the reasoning of *McMinn* in *Stych v Dibble* [2012] EWHC 1606 – see further below at paras **3.52–3.54**). Whether or not a passenger had voluntarily allowed himself be carried in a vehicle was considered in *Pickett v Roberts and MIB* [2004] AII ER 685, [2004] 1 WLR 2450. In this case, the plaintiff sought to argue that she had done enough to withdraw her consent to the use which involved her boyfriend defendant performing handbrake turns despite her protestations. The Court of Appeal held that the plaintiff, who had voluntarily entered the vehicle, could not withdraw her consent except by an unequivocal repudiation of the common venture to which she consented when she entered the vehicle. An unequivocal request to alight from the vehicle was enough but an objection to the way the vehicle was being driven was not.
20. See the judgment of Finlay CJ In *Kinsella v MIBI* [1997] 3 IR 586, and his comments in respect of blameworthiness at p 588.
21. As noted above, previous MIBI agreements had excluded claims where one uninsured vehicle collided with another uninsured vehicle prior to this being held to be contrary to the Second Directive in *Commission v Ireland* (Case C–211/07), Judgment of the Court (Sixth Chamber), 21 February 2008 (see cl 5.3 of the 2004 Agreement and cl 5(3) of the 1988 Agreement).
22. This statement must, however, be considered in the context of the decision of the ECJ in *Churchill Insurance Company Limited v Wilkinson and Evans v Equity Claims Ltd* (Case C–442/10), 1 December 2011, and discussed below at paras **3.39–3.51** (see also **Ch 10**, paras **10.54–10.56**).
23. *Kinsella v MIBI* [1997] 3 IR 586.

entitled to recover if he had a *bona fide,* though mistaken, belief that the use of the vehicle at the time of the accident was covered by insurance. The MIBI bears the onus of proving that the person knew (or, prior to the 2009 Agreement, ought reasonably to have known) that the use of the vehicle on the occasion was not covered by insurance. The Court held that the test was whether the particular passenger, having regard to all relevant circumstances, should have known that the driving was not covered by an approved policy of insurance. Thus, notwithstanding the fact that all the objective evidence may tend to suggest that the injured person knew about the absence of insurance, it may be extremely difficult for the MIBI to disprove a plaintiff's assertion that he did not know about the absence of insurance.

D. DECISIONS PRIOR TO 2009 – KNEW OR OUGHT REASONABLY TO HAVE KNOWN

1. *Kinsella v MIBI*

[3.15] The facts in *Kinsella v MIBI* were uncontroversial. The uninsured driver was the plaintiff's aunt. The plaintiff was 28 years old at the date of the accident and had limited educational qualifications. Having failed State examinations, the plaintiff left school at 16 years of age to work as a farm labourer and was the owner of a car that was insured on an owner-driver basis. Although he was aware that no one other than himself was insured to drive his car, the plaintiff assumed that his aunt was insured to drive it under the terms of his uncle's policy. The plaintiff was injured while he was travelling as a passenger in his own car while his aunt was driving it.

[3.16] The plaintiff sued his aunt and obtained a judgment against her and this was not satisfied within 28 days. The plaintiff instituted proceedings against the MIBI and claimed that it was obliged to pay the plaintiff the amount of the judgment pursuant to cl 2 of the 1964 Agreement.[24] The MIBI defended the claim by reference to cl 5(2) of the 1964 Agreement[25] on the grounds that the plaintiff ought reasonably to have known that there was no insurance in relation to the use of the vehicle. The trial judge concluded that the plaintiff should have known that there was no insurance in place and dismissed the claim. The Supreme Court allowed the plaintiff's appeal. Delivering the unanimous opinion of the Supreme Court, Finlay CJ[26] stated the following proposition:

> 'I am satisfied that certain principles apply to the interpretation of [the 1964 Agreement], in respect of this particular issue, which are relevant to this action. Firstly, it is clear that the onus is upon the defendant to prove that a person claiming on foot of a judgment in the circumstances in which the plaintiff is claiming in this case either knew, or should reasonably have known, that the use of the vehicle on the occasion was not covered by insurance.

---

24. Clause 2 of the 1964 Agreement is similar in format and wording to cl 4.1.1 of the 2009 Agreement (and cl 4.1 of the 2004 Agreement).

25. Clause 5(2) of the 1964 Agreement is similar in format and wording to cl 5.2 of the 2004 Agreement (and cl 5(2) of the 1988 Agreement).

26. Blayney and Denham JJ concurring.

Secondly, I am satisfied that having regard to the terms of clause 5(2) [of the 1964 Agreement] that the question as to whether or not a claimant 'should reasonably have known' of the absence of insurance is essentially a subjective question. The issue is not: 'would a reasonable person have known?', but rather: 'should the particular individual, having regard to all relevant circumstances have known?'. For example, obviously, obviously, a person with defective reasoning or mental powers, or a young child, could not possibly be defeated by this clause.'[27]

[3.17] Finlay CJ proceeded to state:

'It is also, in my view, relevant that a person who travels in a vehicle which he knows is being used by a person who is not covered by insurance under the Road Traffic Act is, essentially, blameworthy for he is clearly condoning, though probably not technically participating in the commission of a serious offence. Having regard to that principle, I am satisfied that a court in reaching a conclusion as to whether a person claiming under the agreement should reasonably have known of the absence of insurance, is to some extent, at least, concerned to assess as to whether the attitude or conduct of the person concerned at the time of the accident was in this particular sense blameworthy.'[28]

2. Each case turns on its facts

[3.18] Whether or not a plaintiff knew that there was no insurance at the time of the accident will depend on the facts of each individual case. This was illustrated in the High Court in *Cranny v Kelly and MIBI*.[29] In *Cranny*, the deceased (the plaintiff's husband) was killed while travelling as a passenger in an unregistered and uninsured hybrid car.[30] The deceased had painted the registration number on the car. The deceased was a member of An Garda Síochána and the car was owned by his friend, the first defendant. On the facts of the case, Lavan J concluded that the deceased must reasonably have known that the vehicle in which he was travelling was uninsured.[31]

---

27. *Kinsella v MIBI* [1997] 3 IR 586 at p 588.
28. *Kinsella v MIBI* [1997] 3 IR 586 at p 588. *Kinsella* was applied in *Bracken v Commissioner of An Garda Síochána* (31 July 1998, unreported) HC, O'Sullivan J.
29. *Cranny v Kelly and MIBI* (5 April 1996, unreported) HC, Lavan J; [1998] 1 IR 54 (Supreme Court).
30. A car manufactured from two cars and reassembled.
31. The plaintiff's case was that the first defendant was driving the car at the time of the accident but no witness could give this evidence. At the end of the plaintiff's case, the first defendant applied for a non-suit on the basis that the evidence did not establish who was driving. The trial judge put the first defendant on his election in relation to the calling of evidence and the first defendant confirmed that he did not intend to go into evidence. The trial judge refused the application for a non-suit and invited the first defendant to reverse his decision. The first defendant then gave evidence that the deceased was driving the car. Thereafter, the trial judge ruled that he could not decide on the balance of probabilities that the first defendant was driving at the time of the accident but he proceeded to consider whether the passenger knew or ought to have known about the absence of insurance. On appeal, the Supreme Court remitted the matter for a retrial on the basis that, firstly, the trial judge had departed from established practice when he refused the non-suit application and then proceeded to hear evidence from the first defendant and, secondly, the trial judge's decision on the passenger's knowledge at the time was based upon the evidence that was given by the first defendant (*per* Murphy J (Hamilton CJ and Keane J concurring)).

[3.19] In *Curran v Gallagher, Gallagher and MIBI*,[32] the Supreme Court reaffirmed the *Kinsella* decision. The plaintiff in that case was 19 years old when the car in which he was a passenger collided with a wall. The plaintiff sued and obtained judgment in default of defence against the owner and driver of the uninsured vehicle (the first and second defendants). The MIBI relied on cl 5(2) of the 1988 Agreement and claimed that the plaintiff knew or ought to have known that the owner and driver were uninsured. The trial judge held that the plaintiff lied when he gave evidence that the owner had handed the car keys to the driver. The trial judge held that the keys were taken by the driver from under a mat in the car and drew an inference from this that the plaintiff must have known that the driver had no authority to take the car. The trial judge dismissed the plaintiff's action.

[3.20] The Supreme Court allowed the plaintiff's appeal. Delivering the majority judgment of the Court, Lynch J[33] stated that, while the plaintiff might have known by the time of the hearing of the action that the driver had no authority to take the car at the relevant time, the case had to be decided on the plaintiff's state of knowledge at the date of the accdent.[34]

[3.21] The Supreme Court held that there was nothing in the evidence to alert the plaintiff to a want of authority on the part of the driver to take the car at the relevant time. The trial judge was wrong to infer, from the fact that the plaintiff lied in relation to the taking of the keys, that he knew that the driver had no authority on the night in question.[35] Lynch J stated:

> 'Knowing that that was the [MIBI's] case against him, on the facts as found by the learned trial judge, he grossly distorted the facts by inventing the story of the keys being passed through the open window and other details as well. Does that reprehensible conduct establish as a matter of probability that he knew that the [driver] had no authority to take the car? If he had fully agreed with the evidence of the [driver] that the car was unlocked and that [the driver] got the key from under the mat, how would that have established knowledge on [the plaintiff's] part that [the driver] had no authority to take the car? In my view it certainly would not ... It must be remembered that the test of knowledge is a subjective one and the onus of proof is on the [MIBI].'[36]

[3.22] The Supreme Court revisited *Kinsella* in *Ward v Ward and MIBI*.[37] The plaintiff was injured while travelling as a passenger in an uninsured vehicle being driven by the first defendant, the plaintiff's 19-year-old nephew. At the time of the accident, the plaintiff was visiting Ireland and left his own new car in Dublin. The plaintiff and his nephew were travelling in a 25-year-old car that the nephew had purchased the day before the accident. The accident occurred after the plaintiff and his nephew left a bank

---

32. *Curran v Gallagher, Gallagher and MIBI* (7 May 1997, unreported) SC.
33. Keane J concurring. Murphy J dissented and considered that the plaintiff was or should have been aware that the driver was not covered by insurance.
34. *Curran v Gallagher, Gallagher and MIBI* (7 May 1997, unreported) SC, at p 12.
35. *Curran v Gallagher, Gallagher and MIBI* (7 May 1997, unreported) SC, at p 15.
36. *Curran v Gallagher, Gallagher and MIBI* (7 May 1997, unreported) SC, at pp 16–17.
37. *Ward v Ward and MIBI* (18 February 2003, unreported) SC, *ex tempore* (*per* Keane CJ, Geoghegan and McCracken JJ concurring).

at a time when the cashier was getting alarmed and had sent for the porter. At that stage, the plaintiff and his nephew made eye contact with and were observed by gardaí and the plaintiff and his nephew took off at a relatively fast speed in their car. They were pursued by the gardaí and, following a chase, the car overturned and the plaintiff was injured.

[3.23] The MIBI defended the claim against it on the basis that the plaintiff knew or ought to have known that the vehicle was uninsured. The trial judge dismissed the case and this was appealed. Keane CJ delivered the unanimous judgment of the Supreme Court which dismissed the appeal. Having commented upon the trial judge's entitlement to find that the appellant was a person whom he did not consider worthy of belief on many aspects of his story, the Supreme Court considered that the trial judge was perfectly entitled to conclude that there was every indication that there was some illicit activity going on so far as the appellant and his nephew were concerned. In these circumstances, the appellant's failure to enquire from his nephew about the insurance was almost certainly because the appellant either had no interest in the matter or knew the vehicle was probably uninsured and simply did not ask a question to which he did not want to know the answer.[38] Having emphasised that the onus was unquestionably on the MIBI to establish that the appellant knew or ought to have known that the car was uninsured, Keane CJ said:

> 'I am satisfied in this case that the failure of the [appellant] to make any inquiries in the circumstances of this case, bearing in mind everything that the trial judge heard about the circumstances of their visit to Ireland, the circumstances in which they came to be travelling in that particular car and the fact that the driver of the car was 19 years old, all of those circumstances entitled the trial judge to reach a conclusion, that if he did not actually know that the car was uninsured, he ought to have known and the fact that he did not have actual knowledge of it was due to his own actions in making sure that he did not saddle himself with knowledge of that nature.'[39]

[3.24] Having reiterated that the onus was on the MIBI to establish that the appellant knew or ought to have known about the absence of insurance, Keane CJ further stated:

> 'In a case where one has a situation in which this issue is expressly raised, in which the [appellant] is cross-examined about it, in which the [appellant] denies that he knew that it was uninsured, in which there is evidence which would have put a responsible person in a situation like this on inquiry as to whether the car was insured or not, the trial judge was entitled to draw the inference, having regard to the lack of credibility he found in the [appellant] throughout all other aspects of the case, that he was about an illicit enterprise and that he therefore was not interested in the question of whether it was insured or not. In circumstances where if he had been approaching the matter in a responsible manner, he would certainly have inquired whether this recently acquired car by his 19 year old nephew was insured or not, he expressly refrained from asking any such question.'[40]

---

38. *Ward v Ward and MIBI* (18 February 2003, unreported) SC, *ex tempore* (*per* Keane CJ, Geoghegan and McCracken JJ concurring), at pp 7–8.
39. *Ward v Ward and MIBI* (18 February 2003, unreported) SC, *ex tempore* (*per* Keane CJ, Geoghegan and McCracken JJ concurring), at p 8.
40. *Ward v Ward and MIBI* (18 February 2003, unreported) SC, *ex tempore* (*per* Keane CJ, Geoghegan and McCracken JJ concurring), at p 10.

[3.25] This approach was broadly followed by Peart J in *Devlin v Cassidy and the MIBI*.[41] One of the issues was whether the plaintiff 'knew or ought reasonably to have known' of the existence of an insurance policy. Peart J stated that the relevant date of knowledge of the insurance matter is at the time of the accident:

'The question is did he know that the driver had no insurance, or ought to have so known, at the date of the accident. In this regard we note that he made no inquiry at the date of the accident. He did not give it a moment's thought. The fact that [the driver] may have driven his girlfriend's car sometime previously is hardly reason to believe that some time later he was insured to drive yet another car which he did not own... All one's instincts are against finding for the plaintiff in this regard. It seems wrong that a plaintiff who in a drunken state gets into a car which he knows is being driven by another drunken man who he knows does not own the car, and to whom he addresses no inquiry about whether or not that drunken man is insured to drive, can nevertheless recover damages for his injuries under the agreement on the basis that he did not know, and ought not to have known, that the driver was uninsured.'[42]

[3.26] Later in the judgment, Peart J stated:

'The [MIBI] in my view has discharged the onus found to be upon it of proving that this plaintiff ought to have known that the driving [by the driver] was not covered by any policy of insurance. It has done so by the eliciting of evidence in this regard from the plaintiff himself, which is sufficient for the court to reach a conclusion on the balance of probabilities.'[43, 44]

E. THE POSITION IN THE UNITED KINGDOM

[3.27] In the United Kingdom compensation is not recoverable by a person who knew or ought to have known that there was no insurance. Clause 6(1)(e) of the Motor Insurers' Bureau (Compensation of Victims of Uninsured Drivers) Agreement 1999 ('the 1999 MIB Agreement') excludes liability in circumstances where a passenger:

'... at the time of the use[45] giving rise to the relevant liability was voluntarily allowing himself to be carried in the vehicle and, either before the commencement

---

41.   *Devlin v Cassidy and the MIBI* [2006] IEHC 287, (31 July 2006, unreported) HC.

42.   *Devlin v Cassidy and the MIBI* [2006] IEHC 287, (31 July 2006, unreported) HC, at p 9.

43.   *Devlin v Cassidy and the MIBI* [2006] IEHC 287, (31 July 2006, unreported) HC, at p 12.

44.   See also the judgment of De Valera J in *Corrigan v Conway, Drumgoole and MIBI* [2007] IEHC 32, (31 July 2007, unreported) HC. While in a restaurant, the plaintiff, who was five months pregnant, believed that there might be a problem with her pregnancy. For this reason, the plaintiff's husband (the second defendant) drove her car to take her to a hospital. In the course of their journey, the plaintiff suffered injury as a result of her husband's negligent driving. De Valera J considered that the threat of a miscarriage could cause anxiety to such an extent that the plaintiff's mind could not be expected to address the question of insurance and which he considered to be a 'relevant circumstance' as envisaged by Finlay CJ in *Kinsella* above (at p 3). He considered that this anxiety and worry 'was sufficient to drive other matters, such as the insurance situation, from her mind' and held that the MIBI could not rely on the exclusion in cl 5(2) of the 1988 agreement (at p 4).

45.   Notably, cl 5.1–5.2 of the 2009 Agreement (and the same provisions in the 2004 Agreement) is concerned with knowledge 'at the time of the accident'.

of his journey in the vehicle,[46] or after such commencement if he could reasonably be expected to have alighted from it, knew or ought to have known that:

(i)   the vehicle had been stolen or unlawfully taken;

(ii)   the vehicle was being used without there being in force in relation to its use such a contract of insurance as would comply with Part VI of the 1988 Act. ...

(iii)   the vehicle was being used in the course of furtherance of a crime ...'

[3.28] In *Delaney v Pickett*[47] the Court of Appeal dismissed a passenger's appeal against the High Court's decision refusing his claim for compensation from the MIB in circumstances where it held that the passenger and the uninsured driver had been involved in a joint enterprise to acquire cannabis for resale and the driving by the uninsured had caused the injury. The claim was excluded by cl 6(1)(e)(iii) of the 1999 MIB agreement because the vehicle was being used in the course of furtherance of a crime. In that case no point was taken as to the compatibility of that exclusion clause with the motor insurance directives and there must be some doubt as to whether that particular exclusion would survive the scrutiny of the ECJ.[48]

[3.29] However, guilty knowledge of a deceased passenger does not affect a claim made by his or her dependants. The 1999 MIB Agreement in the UK is different to its predecessor and has been held not to exclude a fatal claim by dependants of a fatally injured passenger against a negligent driver.[49]

[3.30] In *White v White*,[50] the plaintiff passenger suffered injury when the car in which he was travelling overturned. The driver was the plaintiff's brother. The plaintiff sued his brother and the MIB. The MIB defended the claim by reference to cl 6(1)(e). The trial judge held that, while it could not be said that the plaintiff knew that his brother was uninsured, he clearly ought to have known. However, the plaintiff was entitled to rely directly on the Second Directive and the MIB was liable to satisfy the plaintiff's claim in circumstances where art 1(4) thereof only permitted the Member States to exclude compensation where the injured party 'knew that [the vehicle] was uninsured'. The MIB appealed and the Court of Appeal considered the appeal in tandem with the appeal in *Mighell v Reading*.[51]

[3.31] In *Mighell v Reading*, the appellant was injured in an accident caused by the negligent driving of the uninsured driver of his car. The trial judge held that the plaintiff knew that the driver was uninsured by reference to the fact that the driver was unemployed and did not have a car of his own. The Court of Appeal upheld the trial

---

46.   As above.

47.   *Delaney v Pickett* [2012] 1 WLR 2149.

48.   However, the Court of Appeal allowed the passenger's appeal against the High Court's dismissal of his claim against the driver of the vehicle in which he was travelling.

49.   See *Phillips v Rafiq* [2007] 1 WLR 1351, [2007] 3 All ER 382.

50.   *White v White* [2001] 1 WLR 481, [2001] 2 All ER 43, [2001] 1 Lloyd's Rep 679, [2001] RTR 379, (House of Lords).

51.   *White v White* [2001] 1 WLR 481, [2001] 2 All ER 43, [2001] 1 Lloyd's Rep 679, [2001] RTR 379, (House of Lords)

judge's finding that *Mighell* knew that his driver was uninsured and dismissed the appeal.[52]

[3.32] In *White v White,* the Court of Appeal was prepared to *assume* that England and Wales had failed to properly transpose the Second Directive. However, it held that the doctrine of direct effect[53] did not apply and allowed the appeal brought by the MIB.

[3.33] *White* appealed to the House of Lords[54] and it held that the 1988 English MIB agreement must be interpreted in line with the Second Directive.

[3.34] The Law Lords[55] held that 'knowledge' means 'primarily possession of information by the passenger from which the passenger drew the conclusion that the driver was uninsured'. The most obvious and simple example of this knowledge arises where a driver tells a passenger that he is not insured. In this regard, the Law Lords considered that 'information from which a passenger drew the conclusion that the driver was uninsured may be obtained in other ways'. A passenger who is aware, from his familial or other connections with the driver, that the driver has not passed a driving test ('if he'd taken the test, I would have known') was used as an example. The Law Lords noted that knowledge of this character was often labelled actual knowledge in order to distinguish it from other cases in which a person, although lacking knowledge, is treated by the law as having knowledge of the relevant information.

[3.35] The Law Lords considered that there was one category of case which was so close to actual knowledge that the law treated the person as having knowledge:

> 'It is the type of case where, as applied to the present context, a passenger had information from which he drew the conclusion that the driver might well not be insured but deliberately refrained from asking questions lest his suspicions should be confirmed. He wanted not to know ('I will not ask, because I would rather not know'). The law generally treats this state of mind as having the like consequences as would follow if the person, in my example, the passenger, had acted honestly rather than disingenuously. He is treated as though he had received the information which he deliberately sought to avoid. In the context of the [Second] Directive that makes good sense. Such a passenger as much colludes in the use of an uninsured vehicle as a passenger who actually knows that the vehicle is uninsured. The principle of equal treatment requires that the two persons shall be treated alike. The [Second] Directive is to be construed accordingly.'[56]

[3.36] The Law Lords considered that it was *acte clair* that these categories of cases were within the scope of the exception permitted by the Second Directive. However, the exception did not include a passenger who did not think about insurance, even though an

---

52. *White v White* [2001] 1 WLR 481 at p 486 (House of Lords).
53. See **Ch 12**, para **12.01–12.10** in relation to direct effect.
54. *White v White* [2001] 1 WLR 481, [2001] 2 All ER 43, [2001] 1 Lloyd's Rep 679, [2001] RTR 379, (House of Lords).
55. *Per* Lord Nicholls of Birkenhead, with whom Lord Mackay of Clashfern, Lord Cooke of Thorndon and Lord Hope agreed (Lord Scott of Foscote dissenting).
56. *White v White* [2001] 1 WLR 481 at p 486 (*per* Lord Nicholls of Birkenhead).

ordinary prudent passenger in his position and with his knowledge would have enquired about it:

> 'Conversely, I am in no doubt that "knew" in the [Second] Directive does not include what can be described broadly as carelessness or "negligence". Typically this would cover the case where a passenger gave no thought to the question of insurance, even though an ordinary prudent passenger, in his position and with his knowledge, would have made inquiries. He "ought" to have made inquiries, judged by the standard of the ordinary prudent passenger. A passenger who was *careless* in this way cannot be treated as though he *knew* of the absence of insurance. As Lord Denning MR said in *Cia Maritima San Basilio SA v Oceanus Mutual Underwriting Association (Bermuda) Ltd*[57] negligence in not knowing the truth is not equivalent to knowledge of it. A passenger who was careless in not knowing did not collude in the use of an uninsured vehicle, and he is not to be treated as though he did. To decide otherwise would be to give a wide, rather than a narrow interpretation to the exception by the [Second] Directive. This also seems to me to be acte clair.'[58]

[3.37] For this reason, *White*'s claim was not excluded and the House of Lords allowed his appeal.

F. EUROPEAN DEVELOPMENTS

[3.38] The ECJ has been very protective of its role as guardian of the motor insurance directives. The exclusions in the various MIBI agreements have consequently narrowed over the years. In *Candolin v Pohjola*,[59] a car accident occurred in Finland in which the driver and all passengers were drunk. One of the passengers was killed and the others were seriously injured. Finnish law expressly excluded the recovery of compensation under insurance for personal injury in a road accident where a passenger knew or should have known that the driver was above the legal limit for driving. The ECJ found that this limitation was contrary to European law as it was a disproportionate interference with the passenger's right to compensation under compulsory motor vehicle insurance, as provided for under the motor insurance directives. The court held that art 2(1) of the Second Directive[60] and art 1 of the Third Directive[61] precluded a national rule that allowed the compensation, that might otherwise be payable under the insurance, to be refused or limited in a disproportionate manner on the basis of the passenger's contribution to the injury or loss suffered by him. The ECJ considered that it was irrelevant that the passenger concerned was also the owner of the vehicle. The Court held that national rules must not deny passengers the right to be compensated or limit

---

57.   *Cia Maritima San Basilio SA v Oceanus Mutual Underwriting Association (Bermuda) Ltd* [1977] QB 49 at 68.
58.   *White v White* [2001] 1 WLR 481 at 486–487.
59.   *Candolin v Pohjola* (Case C–537/03) [2005] ECR 1–5745, [2005] 3CMLR 17.
60.   Now Sixth Directive, art 13(1).
61.   Now Sixth Directive, art 12(1).

compensation in a disproportionate manner. It is for the national courts to determine whether the limit on compensation is disproportionate.[62]

[3.39] More recently, in joined cases *Churchill Insurance Company Limited v Wilkinson* and *Evans v Equity Claims Limited*[63] the ECJ, on a preliminary reference from the English Court of Appeal, held that the motor insurance directives prevented an insurer from refusing to indemnify where the insured person suffers personal injury as a passenger in his own vehicle that is being driven by an uninsured driver. This remains the position even if the insured victim was aware that the person to whom he gave permission to drive the vehicle was not insured.

[3.40] The joined cases considered the specific situation where a person, who is an insured person under a policy of insurance, gives permission to another person (who is not so insured) to drive the vehicle and the uninsured person then causes an accident in which the insured person suffers personal injury ie the insured and the victim are one and the same (the insured victim). In each case the insurer of the insured victim claimed that, while it was liable to compensate the insured victim, it was entitled to an indemnity from the insured victim (as insured) in the same amount as the compensation payable to him under s 151(8) of the English Road Traffic Act 1988.[64]

[3.41] The ECJ was concerned with arts 12(1) and 13(1) of the Sixth Directive. Article 12(1) of the Sixth Directive provides:

> 'Without prejudice to the second subparagraph of Article 13(1), the insurance referred to in Article 3[65] shall cover liability for personal injuries to all passengers, other than the driver, arising out of the use of a vehicle.'

[3.42] Article 13(1) of the Sixth Directive provides:

> 'Each Member State shall take all appropriate measures to ensure that any statutory provision or any contractual clause contained in an insurance policy issued in accordance with Article 3[66] shall be deemed to be void in respect of claims by third parties who have been victims of an accident where that statutory provision or contractual clause excludes from insurance the use or driving of vehicles by:
>
> (a)   persons who do not have express or implied authorisation to do so;

---

62.   *Candolin v Pohjola* (Case C–537/03) [2005] ECR 1–5745, [2005] 3CMLR 17 at paras 29 and 31. In *Hussey v Twomey* [2009] 3IR 293 the Supreme court upheld a finding of contributory negligence in the amount of 40% against the plaintiff who was a passenger in a car driven by the second defendant on the grounds that she knew or should reasonably have known that the driver had consumed alcohol. *Candolin* does not appear to have been cited in argument.

63.   *Churchill Insurance Company Limited v Wilkinson and Evans v Equity Claims Ltd* (Case C–442/10), 1 December 2011.

64.   English Road Traffic Act 1988, s 151(8) provides that, when an insurer has become liable to pay an amount in respect of the liability of a person not insured by a policy, he is entitled to recover that amount from the insured person who caused or permitted the use of the vehicle that gave rise to that liability. The lower courts in England came to different views in relation to the application and interpretation of s 151 and the Court of Appeal referred the matter to the ECJ for a preliminary ruling.

65.   Previously First Directive, art 3.

66.   Previously First Directive, art 3.

    (b)   persons who do not hold a license permitting them to drive the vehicle concerned;

    (c)   persons who are in breach of the statutory technical requirements concerning the condition and safety of the vehicle concerned.

However, the provisions or clause referred to in point (a) of the first subparagraph may be invoked against persons who voluntarily entered the vehicle which caused the damage or injury, when the insurer can prove that they knew the vehicle was stolen.'

[3.43] The ECJ held that the motor insurance directives must be interpreted as precluding national rules, the effect of which is to omit automatically the requirement that the insurer compensate a passenger who is a victim of a road traffic accident caused by a driver who was not insured under the insurance policy in circumstances where the victim, who was a passenger in the vehicle at the time of the accident, was insured to drive the vehicle himself but he had given permission to the driver to drive it.[67]

[3.44] Interestingly, and in what may prove to be a significant ruling, the ECJ went on to find that the answer to the question referred would not be different depending on whether the insured victim was aware that the person to whom he gave permission to drive the vehicle was not insured to do so, ie 'whether he believed that the driver was insured or whether or not he had turned his mind to that question.'[68] The court held that:

'... national rules formulated in terms of general and abstract criteria, may not refuse or restrict to a disproportionate extent the compensation to be made available to a passenger by compulsory insurance against civil liability in respect of the use of motor vehicles solely on the basis of his contribution to the occurrence of the loss which arises. It is only in exceptional circumstances that the amount of compensation may be limited on the basis of an assessment of that particular case. ....'[69]

[3.45] The ECJ held that the only situation in which a third party, who has been a victim of an accident, may be excluded from insurance cover is that provided for in what is now the second subparagraph of art 13(1) of the Sixth Directive, ie persons who voluntarily enter the vehicle when the insurers can prove that the person knew the vehicle was stolen. It does appear difficult to square the ECJ's finding that the fact that an insured victim was aware that the person that he permitted to drive was not insured had no bearing on the question referred, with art 10(2) of the Sixth Directive which permits Member States to exclude the payment of compensation 'in respect of persons who voluntarily entered the vehicle which caused the damage or injury when the [the MIBI]

---

67.   *Churchill Insurance Company Limited v Wilkinson and Evans v Equity Claims Ltd* (Case C–442/10), 1 December 2011, at para 36.

68.   Indeed, it was common case that *Wilkinson* knew that the driver was not insured to drive the vehicle under the insurance policy and, at first instance, the court in *Evans* had found that the plaintiff had given no thought to the question of whether or not the driver was insured to drive her motorcycle.

69.   At para 49 and citing *Candolin v Pohjola* (Case C–537/03) [2005] ECR 1–5745, [2005] 3CMLR 17, paras 29, 30 and 35; *Farrell v Whitty, Minister for the Environment, Ireland, Attorney General and MIBI* (Case 356/05) [2007] ECR I–03067, para 35; *Carvalho Ferreira Santos* (Case C–484/09), 17 March 2011, para 38; and *Ambrósio Lavrador and Olival Ferreira Bonifácio* (Case C–409/09), 9 June 2011.

can prove that they knew it was uninsured'. Article 10(2) is reflected in cl 5.2 of the 2009 Agreement which excludes the payment of compensation by the MIBI where it can prove that a claimant knew there was no insurance in force in respect of the vehicle.[70]

[3.46] *Churchill*,[71] however, was concerned with a situation where the vehicle had a policy of insurance (although it did not cover the driver) as opposed to a situation where a vehicle had no policy of insurance. Article 10(2) of the Sixth Directive allows the 'body responsible for compensation' (i e the MIBI in Ireland) to refuse compensation where there was no insurance cover on the vehicle. Article 13(1) of the Sixth Directive is concerned with exclusion clauses in insurance policies where there was insurance in respect of the vehicle (although it may not have covered the driver) and only permits exclusion where the insurer can prove that the injured party knew that the vehicle was stolen. The ECJ held that the aim of the directives is to protect victims and the legal position of the owner of the vehicle, as a passenger in that vehicle, was the same as any other passenger.[72] The only permitted derogation from the foregoing is that insurers may exclude compensation for a passenger who voluntarily enters a vehicle and the insurer can prove that the passenger knew that it was stolen.[73]

[3.47] The ECJ held:

'40.   In that regard, it is first necessary to point out that the situation in which the vehicle that caused the damage was driven by a person not insured to do so, while a driver was, moreover, insured to drive that vehicle, and the situation specified in the third subparagraph of Article 1(4) of the Second Directive in which the vehicle which caused the accident was not covered by any insurance policy, are situations neither similar nor comparable. The fact that a vehicle is driven by a person not named in the relevant insurance policy cannot, having regard, in particular, to the aim of protecting victims of road traffic accidents, pursued by the First, Second and Third Directives, support the view that that vehicle was not insured for the purpose of that provision.

41.   Second, as noted by the Commission, the payment of compensation by a national body is considered to be a measure of last resort, provided for only in cases in which the vehicle that caused the injury or damage is uninsured or unidentified or has not satisfied the insurance requirements referred to in Article 3(1) of the First Directive.[74]

42.   This explains why, despite the general aim of protecting victims of EU rules relating to civil liability in respect of the use of motor vehicles, the EU legislature allows Member States to exclude the payment of compensation by that national body in certain limited cases, and in

---

70.   A plaintiff in Ireland, in a similar situation to *Wilkinson* or *Evans*, would be likely to join the MIBI to the proceedings on the basis that the insurer is likely to claim that there is no valid policy of insurance. See **Ch 10**, paras **10.06** and **10.50–10.83**.

71.   *Churchill Insurance Company Limited v Wilkinson and Evans v Equity Claims Ltd* (Case C–442/10), 1 December 2011.

72.   *Churchill Insurance Company Limited v Wilkinson and Evans v Equity Claims Ltd* (Case C–442/10), 1 December 2011, at para 30.

73.   *Churchill Insurance Company Limited v Wilkinson and Evans v Equity Claims Ltd* (Case C–442/10), 1 December 2011, at para 35 and referring to Second Directive, art 2(1) second subparagraph (now Sixth Directive, art 13(1) second subparagraph).

74.   Now Sixth Directive, art 3.

particular, in respect of persons who voluntarily entered the vehicle which caused the damage or injury when the body can prove that they knew that neither the driver nor the vehicle was insured.'

[3.48] As to whether an injured passenger would be entitled to compensation, if he was aware that the person that he permitted to drive the vehicle was uninsured, the court held:

> '46.   In that regard ... the insurance against civil liability in respect of the use of motor vehicles referred to in Article 3(1) of the First Directive must cover all of the victims other than the driver of the vehicle which caused the damage or injury, unless one of the exceptions expressly provided for by the First, Second or Third Directive applies.
>
> 47.   The fact that the insured victim was aware that the person to whom he gave permission to drive the vehicle was not insured to do so, or that he believed that the driver was insured or whether or not he had turned his mind to that question therefore has no bearing on the answer to question 1.'[75]

[3.49] Some light can be shed on the reasoning of the court if one looks to the opinion of Advocate General Mengozzi.[76] He states:

> '31.   As regards this alleged difference in treatment, I believe that two observations are called for. In the first place, as noted for example by the Commission too, the situation of an insured vehicle and that of an uninsured vehicle are not comparable. For the uninsured vehicle the Directive provides for obligatory action by bodies designated by the Member States, in order to guarantee in any event a certain level of cover for victims: the rules governing uninsured vehicles may well, therefore, be considered to be exceptional and may consequently differ from the rules applicable to the vehicles that are regularly insured.'

[3.50] He further considered:

> '... when one and the same person is both victim and negligent insured, the first status – that of victim – must prevail over the second ...'.[77]

[3.51] The judgment of the ECJ must be read in light of the fact that, in most Member States, insurance simply covers a vehicle, without indicating authorised drivers and there is "implied" authorisation by the insurer for all potential drivers of that vehicle.[78]

---

75.   The first question referred was: '1. Are Articles 12(1) and 13(1) of [the Sixth Directive] to be interpreted as precluding national provisions the effect of which, as a matter of the relevant national law, is to exclude from the benefit of insurance, a victim of a road traffic accident, in circumstances where:

  that accident was caused by an uninsured driver;

  that uninsured driver had been given permission to drive the vehicle by the victim; and

  that victim was a passenger in the vehicle at the time of the accident; and

  that victim was insured to drive the vehicle in question?...' .

76.   Delivered on 6 September 2011.

77.   At para 37 of the opinion.

78.   As observed at para 46 of the opinion.

[3.52] The recent English High Court decision in *Stych v Dibble and Tradax Insurance Company Ltd*[79] is also worthy of mention. In that case, the plaintiff suffered permanent injuries while travelling as a passenger (the passenger) in a vehicle being driven by the first defendant (the driver) who was not insured to drive it. The vehicle was owned by a customer of the garage in which the driver worked and it was used by the driver without the owner's knowledge or consent. The passenger obtained judgment in default of defence against the driver and the issue was whether or not the second defendant (the owner's insurer) was bound to satisfy that judgment.

[3.53] Section 151(2)(b) of the Road Traffic Act 1988 (the 1988 Act) provides that an insurer is liable to meet a judgment obtained against a person (other than the insured person), except in respect of an 'excluded liability', which is defined by s 151(4) of the 1988 Act as, *inter alia*, a liability in respect of injury to a person 'who, at the time of the use which gave rise to the liability, was allowing himself to be carried in or upon the vehicle and knew or had reason to believe that the vehicle had been stolen or unlawfully taken ...'.

[3.54] The High Court held that s 151(4) must be interpreted consistently with what is now art 13(1) of the Sixth Directive[80] and which refers only to a passenger who 'knew' that the vehicle was stolen ie the words 'or ought to have known' bore no additional meaning. The court did not address the issue of whether the words 'unlawfully taken' were consistent with the Second Directive in circumstances where counsel for the passenger conceded that a taking short of theft would bring the exception into play. On the facts, however, the insurers failed to prove that the passenger knew that the vehicle was taken without permission and therefore he recovered against the insurer.

G. CONCLUSION

[3.55] Most motor policies in Ireland include a provision giving the insurer a right of recovery to the effect that if, by law, it must make a payment that would not be covered under the policy, the insured must refund that amount to the insurer. In the normal course of events if an insured was a passenger in his own vehicle (insured passenger), and it was involved in a collision caused by the negligent driving of a driver whom the insured passenger knew was not insured to drive the vehicle, any claim brought against the driver by the insured passenger would name both the driver and the MIBI as co-defendants. The insured passenger's insurer would be the insurer concerned dealing with the claim on behalf of the MIBI. The MIBI would be entitled to plead that the plaintiff was excluded from recovering on the grounds that he knew that the driver was uninsured.[81] The validity of the MIBI maintaining a defence of this nature in such an insurer concerned situation (where the vehicle had a policy of insurance attaching to it) must now be questionable in light of *Churchill*.[82] However, Member States may take

---

79.   *Stych v Dibble and Tradax Insurance Company Ltd* [2012] EWHC 1606.
80.   Previously Second Directive, art 2(1).
81.   Pursuant to cl 5.2 of the 2009 agreement (see also cl 5.2 of the 2004 Agreement).
82.   This issue is discussed in greater detail in **Ch 10**, para **10.06, 10.54–10.56**, and **10.71–10.83**.

account of their own rules relating to civil liability provided that they are exercised in compliance with EU law. The decision would, however, appear to rule out a blanket exclusion in this scenario but would allow for a contributory negligence defence.[83]

---

83.   See *Churchill Insurance Company Limited v Wilkinson and Evans v Equity Claims Ltd* (Case C–442/10), 1 December 2011, wherein the ECJ stated: 'Accordingly, national rules, formulated in terms of general and abstract criteria, may not refuse or restrict to a disproportionate extent the compensation to be made available to a passenger by compulsory insurance against civil liability in respect of the use of motor vehicles solely on the basis of his contribution to the occurrence of the loss which arises. It is only in exceptional circumstances that the amount of compensation may be limited on the basis of an assessment of that particular case ...' (at para 49).

Chapter 4

CLAIMING COMPENSATION FROM THE MIBI: CONDITIONS PRECEDENT AND DECISIONS ON CLAIMS

A. INTRODUCTION

[4.01] Clause 2 of the 2009 Agreement[1] prescribes the means by which a person who wishes to claim compensation from the MIBI in respect of an accident that occurred on or after 30 January 2009 must proceed against the MIBI. One of the options available is to '[make] a claim directly to [the MIBI] for compensation which may be settled with or without an admission of liability'.[2]

[4.02] A claimant must comply with the conditions precedent prescribed by the MIBI agreement that applies on the date of his accident. For example, pursuant to the 2009 Agreement, it is a condition precedent to the MIBI's liability that prior notice of a claim be given within the time limits prescribed by the Statute of Limitations.

[4.03] The obligations on a claimant were substantially increased by the 2004 Agreement. Since then, a claimant is required, *inter alia*, to:

1. be available for interview by the MIBI if the accident is alleged to have involved an untraced motorist. If the 2009 Agreement applies, the claimant must also make himself available for interview within 30 days of completing an application to the Personal Injuries Assessment Board (the Injuries Board[3]) so as to enable the Injuries Board and the MIBI to reach a decision on the claim within 90 days;

2. notify An Garda Síochána within two days of the accident or as soon as he 'reasonably could' and co-operate with An Garda Síochána; and

3. furnish the MIBI with all medical information reasonably required in relation to the processing of the claim.

[4.04] Under the 2009 Agreement, a claimant must give the MIBI at least 28 days notice before 'issuing a motion for judgment' against any person which may give rise to an obligation on the part of the MIBI, whereas under the 2004 Agreement the same notice period applied to 'obtaining judgment' against the MIBI.[4]

[4.05] Since 2004, the extent of the information that must be provided to the MIBI has greatly increased. Notification of the intention to claim compensation may be achieved

---

1. See cl 2 of the 2004 Agreement in respect of accidents that occurred between 1 May 2004 and 29 January 2009 inclusive.
2. Clause 2.1 of the 2009 Agreement; see also cl 2.1 of the 2004 Agreement which does not include the word 'directly'.
3. injuriesboard.ie has been the trading name of PIAB as a service provider since June 2008.
4. See cl 3.9 of the 2009 and 2004 Agreements.

by electronic mail as an alternative to registered post. Under the 2009 Agreement, however, notification cannot be given to the MIBI in the first two months after the accident unless a claimant can furnish the details of any involved persons for whom an approved policy of insurance existed on the date of the accident. Under the 2004 Agreement, the relevant period is three months.[5]

[4.06] For the first time, the 2009 Agreement expressly refers to the Injuries Board. Clause 2.2 of the 2009 Agreement provides that:

'A person claiming compensation by virtue of this Agreement (hereinafter referred to as 'the claimant') must seek to enforce the provisions of this Agreement by:

2.1 making a claim directly to MIBI for compensation which may be settled with or without admission of liability, or

2.2 making an application to the Injuries Board citing MIBI as a respondent under the terms of the PIAB Act 2003 which, pursuant to s.12(1), provides that unless and until such an application is made, no proceedings in court may be brought in respect of the claim …[6]

B. MAKING A COMPENSATION CLAIM TO THE MIBI

1. Making a compensation claim and simultaneously issuing proceedings

[4.07] It is seen in **Ch 5** that, in addition to making a compensation claim directly to the MIBI, a claimant may make an application for compensation to the Injuries Board. A claimant, who applies to the MIBI for compensation pursuant to cl 2.1 of either the 2009 Agreement or 2004 Agreement, might simultaneously make an application for compensation to the Injuries Board pursuant to s 11 of the Personal Injuries Assessment Board Act 2003 (the PIAB Act 2003), and with a view to protecting himself against the Statute of Limitations 1957–2000.[7] In this way, if the MIBI fails to propose any or any

---

5.   See cl 3.6 of the 2009 and 2004 Agreements.

6.   The word 'or' is omitted between the end of sub-cl 2.2 and the beginning of sub-cl 2.3 of the 2009 Agreement.

7.   The Civil Liability and Courts Act 2004, s 7(1), amended the Statute of Limitations (Amendment) Act 1991, s 3(1), by reducing the limitation period within which a person may bring an action claiming damages for personal injuries from three years to two years. This provision took effect from 31 March 2005 (Civil Liability and Courts Act 2004 (Commencement) Order 2004 (SI 544/2004)). Furthermore, the Civil Liability and Courts Act 2004, s 7(d) inserted a new Statute of Limitations (Amendment) Act 1991, s 5A. This introduced a new concept, 'the relevant date', which is defined as 'the date of the accrual of the cause of action or the date of knowledge of the person concerned as respects that cause of action, whichever occurs later'. Section 5A(1) provides, *inter alia*, that, where the relevant date falls before 31 March 2005, an action claiming damages for personal injuries shall not be brought after either the expiration of two years from 31 March 2005, *or* three years from the relevant date, whichever occurs first. In *Lavery v MIBI* [2009] IEHC 628, (1 May 2009, unreported) HC (Laffoy J), the plaintiff endeavoured to get around the fact that the proceedings issued outside the then three-year limitation period, applicable to actions for damages for personal injuries caused by negligence, (contd …/)

adequate settlement,[8] the claimant has preserved the option of litigation.[9] Clause 2.1–2.2 of the 2009 Agreement, however, appear to envisage a claimant taking one or other course of action, insofar as the word 'or' appears between cls 2.1 and 2.2 of the 2009 Agreement.[10]

2. Reporting to An Garda Síochána

[4.08] The 2004 Agreement introduced a condition whereby any accident giving rise to a claim to the MIBI must be reported by a claimant to An Garda Síochána 'within two days of the event or as soon as the claimant reasonably could'.[11]

3. Prior notice to the MIBI of claim

[4.09] A claimant or his legal advisor must give prior notice by registered post or electronic mail of the intention to seek compensation.[12] Prior notice of a claim, for

---

7.   (contd) by making the case that a six-year limitation applied to an action in respect of the actions of an unidentified motorist and in which the relief sought was a mandatory order or specific performance of the 1988 MIBI Agreement. Following the reasoning of *Campbell v O'Donnell* [2009] 1 IR 133, [2008] 2 ILRM 241, however, Laffoy J held that the plaintiff's cause of action against the MIBI was the same as the cause of action against the unidentified and untraced owner or user of the vehicle would have been if those parties had been identified and therefore the plaintiff was statute barred pursuant to the Statute of Limitations (Amendment) Act 1991, s 3(1) (at p 11).

8.   It should be noted, however, that before a claimant sues the MIBI pursuant to cl 2 of either the 2009 or 2004 Agreement, he must have applied to the MIBI for compensation (and/or applied to the PIAB under the 2009 Agreement) and either been refused or offered inadequate compensation. Under cl 2.4 of the 2009 Agreement, he must also have obtained an authorisation from the Injuries Board to proceed with legal action. In *Lavery v MIBI* [2009] IEHC 628, (1 May 2009, unreported) HC (Laffoy J), the plaintiff tried to get around the then three-year limitation period applicable to her claim by arguing that cl 2(3) of the 1988 Agreement (which provides for suing the MIBI as sole defendant where a plaintiff is a seeking a court order for performance of the agreement) displaced the Statute of Limitations (Amendment) Act 1991, s 3(1), because cl 2(3) provides that the MIBI can only be sued thereunder if he has first applied to the MIBI for compensation under cl 2(1) and has either been refused compensation or offered what the claimant considers to be inadequate compensation. Laffoy J rejected the foregoing argument on the basis that the terms of the MIBI agreement could not, and could not have been intended to, displace the provisions of the Statute of Limitations and therefore a claimant must issue his proceedings within the limitation period irrespective of the manner in which the MIBI has processed his claim (at p 12).

9.   The likelihood of the MIBI settling a claim, in terms of cl 2.1 of either the 2009 or 2004 Agreements, would seem confined to a situation where it is the only potential defendant to an action (that is where responsibility for the injury lies with an unidentified or untraced owner/ user). In practice, settlements prior to the issuing of proceedings are usually confined to material damage claims caused by uninsured motorists. It is almost impossible to image a settlement being proposed by the MIBI in circumstances where it is only one of a number of potential defendants to an action or where the circumstances are such that it is appropriate to sue the MIBI as a sole defendant to one of two actions arising out of the claim.

10.   There is no equivalent to cl 2.2 of the 2009 Agreement in the 2004 Agreement.

11.   Clause 3.13 of the 2009 and 2004 Agreements.

12.   Clause 3.1 of the 2009 and 2004 Agreements.

personal injuries or death or property damage, in respect of an accident that occurred on or after 30 January 2009 must be given within the time limits prescribed by the Statute of Limitations.[13] As regards an accident that occurred between 1 May 2004 and 29 January 2009, inclusive, a claim for personal injuries or death must also be given within the time limits prescribed by the Statute of Limitations, whereas notice of a claim for property damage is required to be given within one year of the accident.[14]

[4.10] Notice may be given by registered post. This is normally achieved by way of a solicitor's letter setting out all relevant particulars of the accident including the name of the alleged wrongdoer or proposed defendant, details in relation to the offending vehicle, and the place and date of the accident. A claimant also has the option of giving notice by electronic mail as specified on the MIBI's website.[15]

[4.11] The details that must accompany a claimant's notice were extended in 2004.[16] Under the 2009 Agreement, a claim is deemed not to be notified to the MIBI unless all of the following information is supplied or good cause is shown as to why it is not available:

- the name, date of birth, PPS number and address of the claimant;

- the registration of the vehicle alleged to be uninsured and, where available, the type and make of such vehicle;

- the name of the Garda Station to which the accident was reported;

- the reason why the claimant considers the vehicle to be uninsured;

- what steps have been taken to establish the insurance position;

- the name and address of the owner and/or driver of the uninsured vehicle;

- the date and time of the accident;

- the place of the accident;

---

12.   (contd) The Sixth Directive, art 10(2) provides that '[t]he victim may in any event apply directly to the body which, on the basis of information provided at its request, by the victim, shall be obliged to give him a reasoned reply regarding the payment of any compensation'.
13.   Clause 3.1 of the 2009 Agreement.
14.   Clause 3.1 of the 2004 Agreement. The corresponding provision of the 1988 Agreement was considered by the High Court in *Galvin v Dennehy, Dennehy and the MIBI* [2005] IEHC 90, (18 March 2005, unreported) HC, McCracken J. Clause 3(1) of the 1988 Agreement made it a condition precedent to the MIBI's liability that '... the claimant or the claimant's legal representative shall have given notice in writing, by registered post, of intention to seek compensation: (a) ... (b) in respect of damage to property not later than one year from the date of the accident giving rise to the damage to property'. The High Court concluded that the only possible interpretation of cl 3(1) of the 1988 Agreement was that, in relation to damage to property, a claimant must give the notice in writing referred to therein to the MIBI and it was not sufficient to give such notice to any other insurer against whom there might possibly be a claim. In the circumstances, the MIBI was not liable to the plaintiff in respect of his property damage claim.
15.   Clause 3.1 of the 2009 and 2004 Agreements.
16.   Clause 3.14 of the 2004 Agreement.

- a brief description of the accident;

- if any other vehicle was involved, its registration number and, where available, the type and make of such vehicle; and

- the name and address of the owner and/or driver of any other such vehicle, and insurance details.[17]

[4.12] Where a claimant attempts to give notice via the MIBI's website,[18] it is not actually possible to complete the notification process without furnishing each and every piece of information required by the MIBI. A claimant who completes and submits a claim in this way may rest assured that he has duly complied with the requirement to provide the information set out above.

[4.13] Where a claimant gives notice by way of registered post, however, he may find that the MIBI subsequently rejects the claim on the grounds that he failed to provide all the details that are required by cl 3.14 of either the 2009 or 2004 Agreements. For this reason, a claimant who notifies the MIBI of a claim by registered post would be well advised to include a cover letter stating that the claimant assumes that the notice complies with cl 3.14 and calling upon the MIBI to revert in the event that it considers the position to be otherwise.

4. Provision of all material information

[4.14] The 2009 and 2004 Agreements state that a claimant must provide the MIBI with 'all material information (including all medical reports) reasonably required' in relation to the processing of the compensation claim. This includes information relating to the relevant accident, personal injury or death, medical treatment, funeral expenses, property damage and other costs incurred on behalf of a claimant.[19]

[4.15] Any ambiguity as to *when* the MIBI may call upon a claimant to hand over any information that it reasonably requires (and which now includes medical reports) was

---

17. Clause 3.14 of the 2009 Agreement. The only difference between the information required by the 2009 Agreement and the 2004 Agreement is that cl 3.14.1 of the 2009 Agreement requires a claimant's date of birth whereas cl 3.14(a) of the 2004 Agreement does not require this information.

18. www.mibi.ie.

19. Clause 3.2 of the 2009 and 2004 Agreements. Even before the 2004 Agreement expressly obliged a claimant to furnish 'all medical reports' to the MIBI, the High Court held that the MIBI was entitled to see copies of the medical reports upon which the plaintiff intended to rely in proceedings against it. In *McCormack v Boileau and MIBI* (7 April 1997, unreported) HC, *ex tempore*, Smyth J, the High Court held that that the plaintiff had failed to comply with cl 3(2) of the 1988 Agreement in refusing to furnish his medical reports to the MIBI without a court order. Clause 3(2) of the 1988 Agreement obliged the claimant to furnish the MIBI 'with all material information reasonably required in relation to the processing of the compensation claim including information relating to the relevant accident, personal injuries or death, medical treatment, funeral expenses, damage to property, and legal, professional or other costs reasonably incurred by or on behalf of the claimant'.

removed by the new requirement in 2004 Agreement that the information be furnished 'on demand'.[20]

[4.16] Thus, it seems that the MIBI can insist on seeing a claimant's medical reports at any time after a claimant has notified it of the intention to claim compensation.[21]

5. Availability for interview

[4.17] Where a claimant claims in respect of an accident that is alleged 'to have been caused or contributed' to by 'an untraced motorist', the claimant must be available for interview by the authorised agents of the MIBI. This obligation in cl 3.3 of the 2009 Agreement[22] appears to be justified on the basis that the MIBI 'is unable to obtain details of the accident from the driver'.[23] However, cl 3.3. is framed in sufficiently broad terms to require a claimant to submit for interview if the circumstances of the accident necessitate the claimant bringing two actions ie the first action against the MIBI as sole defendant (where the owner and user of one or more vehicles are unidentified or untraced) and the second action against other owners and/or drivers of other vehicles involved in the accident and, in which case, the MIBI will only be a defendant if the driving of one or more of the vehicles involved was uninsured.

[4.18] The claimant's solicitor may 'be present' for any such interview. The claimant must answer all reasonable questions relating to the circumstances of the accident. This requirement was introduced by the 2004 Agreement.[24] Furthermore, the 2009 Agreement requires that a claimant make himself available for interview within 30 days of completing an application to the Injuries Board so as to enable the Injuries Board and the MIBI to reach a decision on the claim within 90 days.[25] A claimant's answers can only be used for 'progressing the claimant's claim against the MIBI and for no other purpose' and in any court hearing which may arise to determine the liability of the MIBI

---

20.   Clause 3.2 of the 2004 and 2009 Agreements. Notably the obligation to furnish medical reports is not confined to those upon which the claimant intends to rely in the proceedings.

21.   It is also clear from the Supreme Court decision in *McGrory v ESB* [2003] 3 IR 407, *per* Keane CJ (*nem diss*) that, where the MIBI is a party to any proceedings (or acting on foot of a mandate), it can require a plaintiff to submit to a medical examination, disclose medical records and permit the MIBI to interview the plaintiff's treating doctors. This entitlement arises prior to the closure of pleadings in the case. In the event of a plaintiff's failure to comply with any of the foregoing, the courts have an inherent jurisdiction to stay the proceedings.

22.   And cl 3.3. of the 2004 Agreement.

23.   Apart from the MIBI, the only other possible co-defendant to such an action would be the identified owner of the vehicle. However, in the unlikely event that the driver of the vehicle that allegedly caused the accident is traced (but the owner is not), cl 3.3 of the 2009 Agreement does not appear to provide a basis upon which the claimant might be required to submit to an interview.

24.   Clause 3.3 of the 2004 Agreement.

25.   Clause 3.3 of the 2009 Agreement. This suggests that the MIBI will not call upon a claimant to submit to an interview at any time before this ie would not call upon him to do so in the context of the claimant making an application directly to MIBI for compensation pursuant to cl 2.1 without first making an application to the Injuries Board.

to the claimant.[26] The answers may not be used by any party other than the MIBI or its servants or agents. The Agreement provides that a claimant's answers may not be used in criminal proceedings in any circumstances.[27]

6. Co-operation with An Garda Síochána

[4.19] A claimant must co-operate fully with 'An Garda Síochána or any other authorised person in their investigations of the circumstances giving rise to the claim'. This condition was introduced by the 2004 Agreement.[28]

7. Furnishing all relevant information

[4.20] A claimant must furnish the MIBI with copies of all relevant documentation in relation to the accident and any subsequent legal proceedings relating thereto, including copies of all correspondence, statements and pleadings.[29]

8. Furnishing all insurance information

[4.21] A claimant must endeavour to establish if an approved policy of insurance[30] exists covering the use of any vehicle involved in the accident.[31] A claimant or his legal representative can make a written demand, by registered post, of the user and/or owner of a motor vehicle for their insurance particulars under s 73 of the Road Traffic Act 1961.[32]

---

26.   A literal reading of cl 3.3 of the 2009 and 2004 Agreements suggests that, while the answers given by a claimant in interview may be used by the MIBI to defend a 'court hearing' in which its liability to the claimant is being determined, a claimant's answers in interview cannot be used to reject a claim for compensation under cl 2.1 of either agreement as this would entail using the answers for reasons other than 'progressing' the claim.

27.   If, however, the answers were false and a claimant repeated those answers in a court, in theory there is no reason why the claimant's evidence might not be used in a subsequent prosecution for fraud or perjury.

28.   Clause 3.4 of the 2009 and 2004 Agreements.

29.   Clause 3.5 of the 2009 and 2004 Agreements.

30.   'Approved policy of insurance' is defined by the Road Traffic Act 1961, s 62, as amended by: the European Communities (Road Traffic) (Compulsory Insurance) Regulations 1975 (SI 178/1975), arts 4 and 5, the European Communities (Road Traffic) (Compulsory Insurance) (Amendment) Regulations 1987 (SI 322/1987), art 5, and the European Communities (Road Traffic) (Compulsory Insurance) (Amendment) Regulations 1992 (SI 347/1992), art 4.

31.   Clause 3.6 of the 2009 and 2004 Agreements. Previously, cl 3(4) of the 1988 Agreement required a claimant to endeavour to establish if there was a policy covering the use 'in a public place' of any vehicle involved in the accident. However, it is submitted that nothing turns on the omission of these words from the 2004 and 2009 Agreements in circumstances where insurance is only required in respect of the user of a mechanically propelled vehicle in a public place.

32.   The Road Traffic Act 1961, s 73(1)(a) (as modified by the Road Traffic Act 1968, s 53), provides that, where a claim is made against a person in respect of a liability that should be insured against by an approved policy of insurance, such person, on demand in writing by registered post served by the claimant or his agent, shall, if the liability was so covered, state that fact and furnish particulars of the vehicle insurer and provide particulars of the relevant certificates of insurance. (contd .../)

[4.22] Clause 3.6 of the 2009 Agreement suggests that the MIBI should not be notified of a claim any earlier than two months after the accident unless the claimant has obtained written confirmation of the insurance position from An Garda Síochána or the owner/user of the relevant vehicle(s). If, having made a written demand for particulars, the insurance position is not established in the two-month period following the accident, the claimant can notify the MIBI of the claim. Under the 2004 Agreement, a three-month period is specified.[33]

9. Making a property damage claim

[4.23] A claimant must furnish the MIBI with details of any property damage claim, arising from the accident, made under any policy of insurance or otherwise, and any report made or notification given in respect of the damage or the use of the vehicle giving rise to that damage. The requirement to furnish the MIBI with these particulars is stated in terms of details, reports or notifications of which the claimant is aware and that the MIBI reasonably requires.[34]

[4.24] Under the 1988 Agreement, if a claimant recovered under his own comprehensive motor insurance for a *property* damage claim, the MIBI could refuse a subsequent claim for compensation. This was because, in stating the liability of the MIBI to satisfy judgments, cl 4(2) of the 1988 Agreement provided that, where a person has received benefit or compensation 'from any source in respect of damage to property, [the MIBI] may deduct' the amount of that benefit or compensation.[35] Given this provision, and the possible adverse consequences for a claimant's own premium, a claimant under the 1988 Agreement would have been well advised not to make a material damage claim against his own comprehensive policy and pursue the MIBI for the material damage instead.

[4.25] Pursuant to the 2004 Agreement, the MIBI was given a new discretion to make a deduction where a claimant 'is *entitled* to receive benefit or compensation from *any* source',[36] as opposed to making a deduction where a claimant had in fact obtained compensation elsewhere.[37] The 2009 Agreement, however, provides that the MIBI 'shall' make a deduction in such circumstances.[38] The foregoing implies that the MIBI must now reduce the amount of compensation payable to a claimant who *could* claim on

---

32. (contd) In the event that the liability would have been covered but for an approved policy of insurance having been avoided, cancelled or terminated, s 73(1)(b) requires that the person must state that fact and furnish particulars of the relevant insurer. Section 73(1)(c) provides that, if the liability was not covered by reason of the person against whom the claim is made having been a vehicle insurer or an exempted person, the person must state that fact and furnish particulars of the relevant certificate of exemption. Finally, if none of the foregoing apply, s 73(1)(d) requires the person against whom the claim is made to state that fact.

33. Clause 3.6 of the 2004 Agreement.

34. Clause 3.7 of the 2009 and 2004 Agreements.

35. Pursuant to cl 4(2) of the 1988 Agreement the MIBI could make a deduction where a claimant '[had] received benefit or compensation' from another source.

36. Emphasis added. Clause 4.4 of the 2004 Agreement.

37. Clause 4(2) of the 1988 Agreement.

38. Clause 4.4 of the 2009 Agreement.

his own comprehensive insurance policy, regardless of whether or not a claimant actually makes such a claim. Since late 2003, however, a protocol has operated between the MIBI and all motor insurers in the State and which provides that an innocent motorist, who is caused property damage by an uninsured motorist, can claim against his own comprehensive policy without affecting his no claims bonus/discount even though that claim might be recoverable against the uninsured motorist or the MIBI. Thus, while the protocol respects an insured motorist's right to look to the MIBI for compensation, it appears that cl 4.4 of the 2009 Agreement compels the MIBI to penalise a claimant who takes this course of action.[39]

10. Making a claim for damages for personal injuries or death

[4.26] It is arguable that the obligation on the part of the MIBI to make a deduction under cl 4.4 of the 2009 Agreement is not confined to a property damage claim ie the MIBI may refuse a claim for personal injuries or death on the grounds that compensation may be obtainable elsewhere. This is because of the difference in wording

---

39. In this regard, it should be noted that Second Directive, art 1(4), sixth subparagraph provided that 'each Member State shall apply its laws, regulations and administrative provisions to the payment of compensation by [the body required to be established by Art 1(4)], without prejudice to any other practice which is more favourable to the victim'. An identical provision is now contained in Sixth Directive, art 10(4). This issue is further discussed in **Ch 6**, paras **6.26–6.30**. The appropriate interpretation to be afforded to the corresponding provision in the English Uninsured Drivers Agreement (1999) (the 1999 Agreement) raised its head in *McCall v Poulton, MIB, Helphire (UK) Ltd. and Angel Assistants Ltd.* [2009] 1 CMLR 45, [2008] EWCA Civ 1313, [2009] CP Rep 15, [2009] PIQR P8, [2009] RTR 11. In that case, the plaintiff was the victim of a motor accident caused by the first defendant's negligent driving. The plaintiff's car, a taxi, was damaged. He needed a replacement and so hired one on credit from the third defendant. He was also provided with an insurance policy issued by the fourth defendant. This policy provided the plaintiff with post-accident cover for (a) the legal costs of the plaintiff's resulting claim and (b) the third defendant's charges in the event that they were not recovered from the first named defendant within the credit period. Thereafter, it transpired that the first defendant was uninsured and he did not pay the plaintiff any compensation. The plaintiff made a claim on the policy issued to him by the fourth defendant and it paid the hire charges, thereby discharging the plaintiff's debt to the third defendant. The MIB declined to pay compensation for the hire charges in reliance on either or both of two exclusions in the 1999 Agreement, namely (1) cl 6(1)(c), which excludes the MIB's liability to meet claims made: '[b]y, or for the benefit of a person ('the beneficiary') other than the person suffering death, injury or damage which is made ... pursuant to a right of subrogation or contractual or other right belonging to the beneficiary'; and (2) cl 17(1) providing 'Where a claimant has received compensation from ... (b) an insurer under an insurance agreement or arrangement, or (c) any other source ... MIB may deduct ... an amount equal to that compensation'. In the County Court, the third and fourth defendants contended that, as a matter of Community law, interpreting art 1(4) of the Second Directive, the MIB could not rely on either exclusion. The parties were in dispute as to whether the principle of interpretation identified by the ECJ in *Marleasing SA v La Comercial Internacional de Alimentación SA* (Case C–106/89) [1990] ECR I–4135, [1992] 1 CMLR 305 should be applied to the 1999 Agreement and as to whether the MIB was an emanation of the State such that the plaintiff might claim directly against the MIB under the Second Directive. The County Court (Mitchell J) ordered that a preliminary ruling on those issues should be requested from the ECJ. The Court of Appeal dismissed the MIB's appeal against the decision to refer the matter to the ECJ. The reference has not yet been heard by the ECJ.

and punctuation between cl 4.4 of the 2009 (and 2004) Agreement and cl 4(2) of the 1988 Agreement.[40]

11. Cost of providing information to MIBI

[4.27] Clause 4.2 of the 2009 and 2004 Agreements provides that a claimant cannot recover legal costs or expenses incurred in furnishing the information required by the MIBI under the Agreement. The only exception to this provision arises where the MIBI interviews a claimant pursuant to cl 3.3 of either Agreement in respect of a claim arising from an accident allegedly caused by an untraced motorist. In this situation, the MIBI is liable to pay the 'reasonable costs' of such interview.[41]

12. Pre–2009: Taking all reasonable steps required by the MIBI against any person

[4.28] Clause 3.10 of the 2004 Agreement provides that, if required by the MIBI, and subject to a full indemnity from the MIBI as to reasonable costs, a claimant is obliged to take all reasonable steps against any person against whom the claimant might have a remedy in respect of or arising out of the injury, death or damage to property.[42] Under the 2004 Agreement, a dispute between the MIBI and a claimant, as to the reasonableness of any particular step required to be taken by the claimant, could be referred to the Minister for the Environment whose determination of the dispute was final.[43] In this regard, the MIBI has generally required that all potential tortfeasors are sued and that judgment is obtained as against any or all such persons. This seems

---

40. Clause 4.4 of the 2009 Agreement provides: 'Where a claimant has received or is entitled to receive benefit or compensation from any source, including any insurance policy in respect of damage to property, MIBI shall deduct from the sum payable or remaining payable under clause 4.1 an amount equal to the amount of that benefit or compensation in addition to the deduction of [the excesses in respect of property damage as specified in] clauses 7.2 and 7.3' (cl 4.4 of the 2004 Agreement says 'may' instead of 'shall'). Previously, cl 4(2) of the 1988 Agreement provided: 'Where any person has received benefit or compensation from any source in respect of damage to property, [the MIBI] may deduct from the sum payable or remaining payable under [cl 4(1)] an amount equal to the amount of that benefit or compensation in addition to the deduction of any amounts by virtue of [the excesses in respect of property damage as specified in cls 7(4)– (5)].' The difference may be attributable to the notable absence of a comma after 'policy' in cl 4.4 of the 2004 Agreement and which is also absent in cl 4.4 of the 2009 Agreement. However, it must be noted that the Third Directive, art 3 inserted an additional sentence into the first paragraph of art 1(4) of the Second Directive, and which provided '[h]owever, Member States may not allow the [MIBI] to make the payment of compensation conditional on the victim establishing in any way that the person liable is unable or refuses to pay.' An identical provision is now contained in Sixth Directive, art 10(1) and it is clear from the complete text of art 10(1) that the foregoing statement is applicable to both personal injuries and property damage claims.
41. It is unclear whether this includes the legal costs of having a solicitor present at the interview.
42. See also cl 3(7) of the 1988 Agreement, which referred to a claimant as 'plaintiff'. The change of terminology in cl 3.10 of the 2004 Agreement was probably made in anticipation of the Injuries Board.
43. Clause 3.10 of the 2004 Agreement and cl 3(7) of the 1988 Agreement. It would seem that no such dispute as to 'reasonable steps' was ever referred to the Minister.

prudent in circumstances where the liability of the MIBI only arises when a judgment obtained by a claimant is not satisfied[44] and enables the MIBI to protect its position as the insurer of last resort. In *McCahey v The MIBI*,[45] the Court considered that the description of the MIBI as a fund of last resort was a proposition that was clearly correct having regard to the express terms of the 2004 Agreement.[46]

[4.29] Curiously, the provisions of cl 3.10 of the 2004 Agreement are omitted from the 2009 Agreement. Perhaps this was done because art 10(1) of the Sixth Directive provides that 'Member States may not allow the body to make the payment of compensation conditional on the victim establishing in any way that the person liable is unable or refuses to pay.' It has to be said, however, that an almost identical provision was inserted into the Second Directive by the Third Directive. [47]

[4.30] Clause 13 of the 2004 Agreement introduced a new provision to the effect that 'the Guarantee Fund' (which is not defined) 'is a Fund of Last Resort', but this was omitted from the 2009 Agreement.

[4.31] In *McCahey v The MIBI*[48] an accident occurred to which the 2004 Agreement applied. According to the plaintiff, he was cycling his bicycle in a public place when a car pulled out from a parked position, struck him and caused him to fall and suffer personal injuries. The driver and owner of the vehicle were untraced and the plaintiff brought proceedings against the MIBI as sole defendant. The MIBI defended the proceedings on the basis, *inter alia,* that the plaintiff was obliged to issue proceedings against the owner and/or driver of the vehicle that collided with him.

[4.32] In finding that the plaintiff was entitled to succeed against the MIBI, Birmingham J stated:

> '20. In a situation where the plaintiff and his advisors concluded that the identity of the driver had not been established with sufficient clarity so as to justify the issue of proceedings, even if the situation is, that other plaintiffs and other advices may have concluded differently, what is the position? It seems to me that the plaintiff does not lose his right to look to the MIBI by reason of making a tactical judgment, even if it is not the judgment that would be made by others. In that regard the provisions of [cl] 3.10 of the 2004 agreement are relevant to this issue...
>
> 21. In this case the MIBI did not make any requirement of the plaintiff. All they did do, was to point out that Mr. Doe was insured with Hibernian Insurance and it was their belief that the Hibernian's Insurance Company inquiries were continuing. In fact the plaintiff's solicitor had already been in touch with Hibernian Insurance who had responded that their investigations to date had failed to show that liability was attached to their insured and that their driver had no recollection of the incident.

---

44. Clause 4 of the 2009 and 2004 Agreements. See **Ch 8** and *Lindsay v Finnerty, Kelly and the MIBI* [2011] IEHC 402, (25 October 2011, unreported) HC (*per* Peart J).
45. *McCahey v The MIBI* [2009] IEHC 349, (15 July 2009, unreported) HC.
46. *McCahey v The MIBI* [2009] IEHC 349, (15 July 2009, unreported) HC at p 5.
47. See the Second Directive, art 1(4), as inserted by the Third Directive, art 3.
48. *McCahey v The MIBI* [2009] IEHC 349, (15 July 2009, unreported) HC.

22. In a situation where a plaintiff and his advisors had formed the view that they have insufficient evidence to proceed against a party, who may be the subject of suspicion, they are not to be blamed for deciding not to proceed.

23. Had MIBI wanted the plaintiff to proceed against Mr. and Mrs. Doe, it was open to them to make a requirement under [clause] 3.10 of the 2004 agreement and provide the appropriate indemnity in relation to costs. This was, after all, a case where there was a clear disagreement. The [MIBI] believed that the state of the evidence was such that proceedings should issue against the Does, while the plaintiff and his advisors took the contrary view. When the MIBI failed to do that it became a matter for the plaintiff's judgment as to how to proceed. In choosing to proceed as they did, they ran the risk that it would be established on the balance of probabilities that the accident was the fault of the Does, which would have seen these proceedings fail. However, that has not happened. A cloud of suspicion has undoubtedly been cast over the Does, but it does not go beyond that.

24. In these circumstances I am of the view that the plaintiff is entitled to succeed against the MIBI ...'.[49]

12. Dispute relating to compliance with the 2009 Agreement

[4.33] Clause 3.10.1 of the 2009 Agreement provides that, in the event of a dispute 'relating to compliance with these clauses', the claimant can refer same to be decided by an agreed arbitrator or, in default of agreement, one appointed by the President of the Law Society. Clause 3.10.2 provides that the outcome of any determination of such a dispute may be appealed to the Minister, whose decision shall be final. Clause 3.10.3 provides that 'this clause' will be reviewed following the Supreme Court's decision in *Farrell v Whitty.*

C. NON COMPLIANCE WITH CONDITIONS PRECEDENT

[4.34] The MIBI has successfully defended proceedings against it on the basis of non-compliance with certain conditions precedent to its liability as set out in cl 3 of both the 2009 and 2004 Agreements.

[4.35] By way of example, cl 3.8 of the 2009 Agreement provides:

'Notice of proceedings or application to the Injuries Board shall be given by the claimant by registered post before commencement of such proceedings or application:

3.8.1 to the insurer in any case in which there was in force at the time the accident occurred an approved policy of insurance purporting to cover the use of the vehicle and the existence of which is known to the claimant before the commencement of proceedings or application;

3.8.2 to MIBI in any other case [;]

3.8.3 to the owner and/or user of the vehicle giving rise to the claim except where the owner and user of the vehicle remains unidentified.'

---

49.   *McCahey v The MIBI* [2009] IEHC 349, (15 July 2009, unreported) HC at pp 7–8.

[4.36] In *O'Flynn v Buckley, Walsh, MIBI and Horan*,[50] Kearns J, delivering the unanimous judgment of the Supreme Court, said '... the [MIBI] is entitled to require that litigants respect the strict conditions laid down in the [1988] agreement as a pre-condition to the recovery of compensation.'[51, 52]

[4.37] The Supreme Court decision in *O'Flynn v Buckley* was concerned with cl 2 of the 1988 Agreement.[53] However, the above statement made by Kearns J was subsequently approved in *Patterson v McHugh and MIBI*.[54] In *Patterson*, the plaintiff suffered personal injuries in an accident in June 2004. The proceedings were issued on 21 July 2004, and the MIBI was given notice of the proceedings by registered post on 29 March 2005. On 13 June 2005, the insurer concerned brought the plaintiff's solicitors' attention to a breach of the 2004 Agreement which requires that '[n]otice of proceedings shall be given by the claimant by registered post before commencement of such proceedings' to the insurer concerned (in circumstances where there is an insurance policy in respect of the vehicle and the claimant is aware of it) or to the MIBI in any other case.[55] Despite the fact that the MIBI was not prejudiced by the plaintiff's failure to comply with this condition precedent, the High Court held that the MIBI was entitled to rely on the condition precedent.[56] Furthermore, the High Court held that the MIBI was not obliged to show that it was prejudiced and, in respect of which, the court applied *Application of Butler*.[57]

---

50.   *O'Flynn v Buckley, Walsh, MIBI and Horan* [2009] 3 IR 311.

51.   *O'Flynn v Buckley, Walsh, MIBI and Horan* [2009] 3 IR 311 at p 319.

52.   The UK was held to have failed to have properly implemented the Second Directive in *Byrne v MIB* [2009] QB 66, [2008] 4 All ER 476, [2008] 3 WLR 1421; in circumstances where the MIB (Compensation of Victims of Untraced Drivers) Agreement 1972 (the 1972 Agreement) required that an application for compensation for injury caused by an untraced driver must be made within three years (regardless of whether or not the claimant was a child) whereas, if the plaintiff child's cause of action had been against a traced driver, he could have sued at any time prior to his 21st birthday.

53.   The more recent equivalents being contained in cl 2 of the 2009 and 2004 Agreements.

54.   *Patterson v McHugh and MIBI* (5 March 2010, unreported) HC, *ex tempore*, Smyth J at pp 4–5 of the transcript.

55.   Clause 3.8 of the 2004 Agreement.

56.   *Patterson v McHugh and MIBI* (5 March 2010, unreported) HC, *ex tempore*, at pp 5–7 of the transcript. In so doing, the High Court referred to *Cooper v MIB* [1985] 1 QB 575 at 581 wherein, having dismissed the plaintiff's appeal, Cumming-Bruce LJ said at p 58 (albeit *obiter*): '[i]n the circumstances it becomes unnecessary to say anything about the answer which the plaintiff raises to the [MIB] defence founded on the failure of the plaintiff to give notice of proceedings before or within seven days after commencement thereof. I ventured an argument to describe that defence as meritorious but unattractive. But there is no answer to it. However eager one may be, and there have been great judges in the Queen's Bench Division who have demonstrated that eagerness and enthusiasm over the last 20 years, to extend as far as possible the doctrine of forbearance affirmed in *Hughes v. Metropolitan Railway Co.* (1877) 2 App. Cas 439, I am quite unable to accept the invitation ... to extend it to include the doctrine of forbearance by silence to be collected from the correspondence that has been laid before us' (see p 5 of the transcript in *Patterson*).

57.   *Application of Butler* [1970] 1 IR 45 and wherein the Supreme Court considered a motor insurance policy that required a motorist to give written notice to his insurance company 'as soon as practicable' after the occurrence of any accident in which a motorcar driven by him was involved. (contd .../)

D. DECISIONS ON CLAIMS AND REASONS FOR DECISIONS

[4.38] The MIBI must make a decision on any application that it receives for compensation.[58] Under the 2009 Agreement, the MIBI is required to 'take action' within two months of the date on which a claimant presents a claim to it but the MIBI is required to 'terminate its action if the insurance undertaking, or its claims representative, subsequently makes a reasoned reply to the claim'.[59] Previously, the 2004 Agreement required that the MIBI give its decision on a claim 'as soon as is reasonably practicable' and it was obliged to give reasons.[60] Pursuant to both agreements, where the MIBI and the claimant agree on an amount in respect of compensation, the MIBI is required to pay that sum within 28 days of the agreement being reached.[61]

---

57. (contd) The Supreme Court held that his delay of 13 months before notifying the insurance company of an accident brought about a situation where no sum was due to him on foot of the insurance policy. The applicant's belief in the futility of giving notice shortly after the accident, because he knew that his insurance company was insolvent, was irrelevant to the determination of the issue of whether or not any circumstance had prevented him from giving due notice shortly after the accident.

58. Decisions of the MIBI may be challenged by way of judicial review: see the Supreme Court decision in *Bowes v MIBI* [1989] IR 225 at 228. In *Hurley v MIBI and others* [1993] ILRM 887, Carroll J directed the MIBI, *inter alia,* to give sufficiently clear reasons for its decision to refuse an *ex gratia* payment of compensation under the 1964 Agreement for damage caused by an untraced driver. See also *Shiels v MIBI* (26 June 1998, unreported) HC, O'Higgins J, 26 June 1998, where the applicant succeeded in having the MIBI's refusal of a similar application for an *ex gratia* payment quashed on the grounds that the minutes of the meeting, at which the decision to refuse the claim was made, did not disclose the reasons for the decision.

59. Clause 4.5 of the 2009 Agreement. This obligation in cl 4.5 of the 2009 Agreement is, however, imposed on '[t]he MIBI as Compensation Body'. This is the only place in which the term 'Compensation Body' appears in the 2009 Agreement. It appears that the two-month period referred to this clause was intended (and likely to be judicially interpreted as) only referring to the MIBI's status as 'Compensation Body' afforded by the European Communities (Fourth Motor Insurance Directive) Regulations 2003 (SI 651/2003), reg 6 and the obligations imposed on that body by Sixth Directive, art 24. If this is so, then it appears that the general obligation that appears in the 2004 Agreement (and requiring the MIBI to give reasons for its decision and decide on a claim as soon as is reasonably practicable) has been omitted from the 2009 Agreement. See fn **60**.

60. Clause 4.5 of the 2004 Agreement. The Sixth Directive, art 10(2) mandates that a 'reasoned reply' be given in relation to a compensation claim (previously Second Directive, art 1(5) as replaced by Fifth Directive, art 2).

61. Clause 4.6 of the 2009 and 2004 Agreements.

Chapter 5

SUING THE MIBI: CONDITIONS PRECEDENT AND THE PERSONAL INJURIES ASSESSMENT BOARD ('PIAB')/INJURIES BOARD

A. INTRODUCTION

[5.01] Clause 2 of the 2009 Agreement deals with enforcement and provides:

'A person claiming compensation by virtue of this Agreement (hereinafter referred to as "the claimant") must seek to enforce the provisions of this Agreement by:

2.1.   making a claim directly[1] to MIBI for compensation which may be settled with or without admission of liability, or

2.2.   making an application to the Injuries Board citing MIBI as a respondent under the terms of the PIAB Act 2003 which, pursuant to s. 12(1), provides that unless and until such an application is made, no proceedings in court may be brought in respect of the claim,

2.3.   citing MIBI as co-defendants in any proceedings against the owner and or/ user of the vehicle giving rise to the claim except where the owner and user of the vehicle remain unidentified or untraced, or

2.4.   citing MIBI as sole defendant where the claimant is seeking a court order for the performance of the Agreement by MIBI provided the claimant has first applied for compensation to MIBI under the clause 2.1. and has either been refused compensation by MIBI or has been offered compensation by MIBI which the claimant considers to be inadequate and/or applied to the Injuries Board as at 2.2. and having received a release from the Injuries Board to proceed with legal action.'

[5.02] The first edition of this book questioned whether the Injuries Board[2] had jurisdiction to deal with claims involving the MIBI. This issue was raised in the context of the definition of 'civil action' in the Personal Injuries Assessment Board Act 2003 (the PIAB Act 2003) and to which the PIAB Act 2003 applies. Since then, the Supreme Court, in *Campbell v O'Donnell*[3] has held that a claim against the MIBI is effectively one to recover damages in respect of a wrong and falls within the definition of a 'civil action' as defined by the PIAB Act 2003.

[5.03] In light of the foregoing, the 2009 Agreement expressly provides that an application must be made to the Injuries Board citing MIBI as a respondent pursuant to

---

1.   Curiously, this is the first time the word 'directly' has been used. It did not appear in cl 2 of either the 2004 or 1988 Agreements.

2.   http://www.injuriesboard.ie has been the trading name of PIAB as a service provider since June 2008.

3.   *Campbell v O'Donnell* [2009] 1 IR 133, [2008] 2 ILRM 241.

s 12(1) of the PIAB Act 2003 and unless such an application is made, no court proceedings can be brought.[4]

[5.04] A claim is made by completing an application form (form A) and this, together with a medical assessment form (form B)[5] must be submitted to the Injuries Board at PO Box 8, Clonakilty in County Cork with the appropriate fee. A formal notice of the claim is forwarded by the Injuries Board to the respondent(s) who may or may not consent to an assessment. A respondent has 90 days to confirm whether or not he/it consents to the assessment of the claim.[6] Where there is consent, or a respondent fails to respond, the Injuries Board proceeds to assess the claim. If a respondent does not consent to the assessment, an authorisation will issue permitting the claimant to issue court proceedings.

[5.05] Where deemed necessary, the Injuries Board arranges for an independent medical examination after the respondent has consented to an assessment. Where an assessment is made, the claimant has 28 days after receiving the notice of assessment to confirm in writing whether he is accepting or rejecting it.[7] If the assessment is accepted by the claimant, it must be acknowledged in writing to the Injuries Board. A respondent is given 21 days within which to confirm acceptance of the assessment.[8] If the respondent also accepts the assessment an 'order to pay' will issue and this has the same status as an award of court. If either of the parties rejects the assessment, an authorisation will issue allowing the claim to be pursued through the court system.[9]

[5.06] Where the MIBI is named as a respondent, the Injuries Board will notify it of the claim and send it a copy of the claimant's application in order to ascertain if it will consent to the claim being assessed. The Injuries Board will respond to the claimant after the expiration of the 90-day period within which the MIBI may respond.[10]

[5.07] If the MIBI does not respond, the Injuries Board is obliged to proceed with the assessment of the claim and is required to assess it within nine months from the date of default.[11] It will seek information in relation to any injuries and any special damages incurred by the claimant. If a final prognosis in relation to the injuries sustained is not available within the time frame allowed by the PIAB Act 2003, an authorisation will issue pursuant to s 17 authorising the bringing of court proceedings. The time period within which a claimant may take legal action in connection with the claim is put on

---

4.   Clauses 2.2 and 2.4 of the 2009 Agreement.
5.   Both forms are available at www.injuriesboard.ie.
6.   The Personal Injuries Assessment Board Rules 2004 (SI 219/2004).
7.   PIAB Act 2003, s 30(2)(a). A failure to respond is deemed to be a rejection of the assessment by the claimant (s 31(1)).
8.   PIAB Act 2003, s 30(2)(b). A failure to respond is deemed to be an acceptance of the assessment by a respondent (s 31(2)).
9.   See PIAB Act 2003, Ch 2.
10.   Ninety days is the period specified in the notice to respondents under the PIAB Act 2003, s 13 as specified in the Personal Injuries Assessment Board Rules 2004 (SI 219/2004).
11.   PIAB Act 2003, s 49.

hold from the time that the Injuries Board receives the completed application and remains on hold for a further six months from the date of the authorisation.[12]

B. THE INJURIES BOARD AND CLAIMS AFFECTING THE MIBI

1. Claim to the Injuries Board against uninsured motorist only

[5.08] Having regard to the history of non-participation by uninsured motorists as defendants to legal proceedings, it is more likely than not that an uninsured motorist will not respond and will therefore be deemed to consent to the Injuries Board making an assessment of the claim against him.[13] If the Injuries Board makes an assessment and the uninsured motorist fails to state his attitude to an assessment within 21 days, the uninsured motorist is deemed to have accepted it.[14] In this eventuality, and assuming that the claimant accepts the assessment, the uninsured motorist is bound by the assessment at the end of the 21-day period.[15] Within one month of the assessment becoming binding, the Injuries Board must issue an 'order to pay' to the uninsured motorist stating that he is liable to pay the claimant the amount of damages specified therein.[16] The order to pay operates as if it was a judgment of a court.[17]

[5.09] Subject to compliance with the other provisions of the 2009 Agreement, the MIBI is liable to satisfy the order to pay in the event that the uninsured motorist does not satisfy it within 28 days of the order being served on him. In the event of the MIBI failing to satisfy the order to pay, the claimant can sue the MIBI for satisfaction. As will be seen below, however, a claimant in this situation must name the MIBI as a respondent in his application to the PIAB and the MIBI may or may not consent to the assessment.

2. A number of different respondents

[5.10] If there is more than one respondent, and one consents to an assessment by the Injuries Board (the participating respondent)[18] but at least one other respondent does not consent to the assessment (the non-participating respondent), the non-participating respondent will not be bound by the ensuing assessment made by the Injuries Board.[19] In this situation, and if the claimant and participating respondent have accepted the

---

12. PIAB Act 2003, s 50. If proceedings are issued against a motorist following the issuing of an authorisation from the Injuries Board in respect of that motorist, and it subsequently transpires that the motorist was not insured, the plaintiff cannot simply make a court application to join the MIBI as a co-defendant. Despite the existence of the proceedings, the plaintiff must make a claim to the Injuries Board and obtain an authorisation against the MIBI before it can be joined to the proceedings against the motorist (see *Sherry v Primark Ltd and Grovenor Cleaning Services Limited* [2010] 1 IR 407).
13. PIAB Act 2003, s 14(1).
14. PIAB Act 2003, s 31(2).
15. PIAB Act 2003, s 33(1).
16. PIAB Act 2003, s 38.
17. PIAB Act 2003, s 40.
18. The Injuries Board is funded by fees from the person or entity against whom claims are made.
19. PIAB Act 2003, s 15(1)(b).

assessment made by the Injuries Board, the Injuries Board will issue an authorisation to the claimant that will enable him to commence legal proceedings against the non-participating respondent only.[20] Thereafter the claimant cannot pursue further legal remedies against the participating respondent. An assessment that is accepted and duly paid has the legal effect of a satisfaction under s 16 of the Civil Liability Act 1961.

C. CONDITIONS PRECEDENT UNDER THE MIBI AGREEMENTS

1. Prior notice of proceedings

[5.11] Notice of either an application to the Injuries Board or court proceedings must be given by the claimant by registered post before an application is made to the PIAB or proceedings are commenced. Depending on the circumstances, this advance notification must be given to the MIBI or a specific insurer and must be given by registered post.[21] Notice to either is normally achieved by way of a typical solicitor's initiating letter setting out all relevant details in relation to the claim, such as the place and date of the accident, the identity of the wrongdoer and details of the vehicles involved.[22]

[5.12] If there was an approved policy of insurance covering user of the vehicle (eg the owner of the vehicle is insured to drive it) but the policy did not extend to the particular user at the relevant time (eg the car was stolen and crashed by its thief), the insurer that issued the policy is the one to whom the advance notification must be given.[23] This insurer will handle the claim on behalf of the MIBI. In essence, therefore, if *any* approved policy of insurance was in place in respect of the vehicle that allegedly caused the injury or damage, the insurer that issued that policy will process the claim even though the relevant policy of insurance did not extend to the user at the relevant time. In these circumstances, the insurer processing the claim is referred to as the 'insurer concerned'.[24]

[5.13] If, however, no policy of insurance was in place in respect of the vehicle that allegedly caused the injury or damage, advance notification of the proceedings must be given to the MIBI.[25] The advance notification must also be given to the MIBI where the

---

20. PIAB Act 2003, s 15(1)(c).
21. Clause 3.8 of the 2009 Agreement (see also cl 3.8 of the 2004 Agreement which is only concerned with notice of proceedings. This notification is in addition to the first notice that a claimant must give of the intention to seek compensation (see cl 3.1 of the 2009 and 2004 Agreements) and in respect of which see further **Ch 4**. While cl 3.1 of the 2009 and 2004 Agreements allows prior notice of the intention to seek compensation to be given by electronic mail, cl 3.8 of the 2009 and 2004 Agreements only permits the giving of advance notice of proceedings by means of registered post.
22. The Civil Liability and Courts Act 2004, s 8 requires the service of a letter of claim on the 'wrongdoer' within two months of the date of the cause of action in a personal injuries action.
23. Clause 3.8.1 of the 2009 Agreement and cl 3.8(a) of the 2004 Agreement.
24. The articles of association of the MIBI defines 'insurer concerned' as 'the member who at the time of the accident which gave rise to a Road Traffic Act liability was providing motor insurance' in respect of the vehicle from the use and/or ownership of which the liability of the judgment debtor arose (see art 71). See **Appendix 5**. For a general discussion of the topic of 'insurer concerned' see *Melia v Melia, Lara Ltd and MIBI* [2004] 1 IR 321 (discussed in **Ch 10**, paras **10.62–10.63**).
25. Clause 3.8.2 of the 2009 Agreement and cl 3.8(b) of the 2004 Agreement.

claimant claims compensation for injury alleged to have been caused by an unidentified or untraced owner/user. The MIBI allocates claims against it to its various member insurers to handle on its behalf. Such claims are allocated to the insurers in proportion to their respective shares of the Irish insurance market. The insurer that processes such a claim on behalf of the MIBI is known as the 'handling office'.

[5.14] Thereafter, if a claimant obtains a judgment against an uninsured driver of a vehicle in respect of which *any* approved policy of insurance existed, the insurer concerned will pay out on foot of any judgment that the uninsured motorist fails to satisfy within the requisite 28 days.[26] In this way, the insurer concerned discharges the liability of the MIBI to satisfy the previously unsatisfied judgment.

[5.15] If, however, a claimant obtains a judgment against the owner/driver of a vehicle for which *no* policy of insurance existed, and the defendant fails to satisfy it within 28 days, the MIBI will pay the claimant the amount of the judgment.[27]

2. Advance notice of issuing a motion for judgment against relevant persons

[5.16] Under the 2009 Agreement, a claimant must give no less than 28 days notice to the MIBI before 'issuing a motion for judgment' against any person, which may give rise to an obligation on the part of the MIBI. Previously, the obligation was to give 28 days notice before 'obtaining judgment'.[28]

3. Offers in satisfaction

[5.17] After a claimant gives notification of court proceedings,[29] the MIBI may, no later than 10 days before the hearing of the action, make an offer in satisfaction of its obligation together with the taxed costs up to that date. If a claimant proceeds to hearing, and obtains an award that is less than the offer (exclusive of costs), the MIBI is not required to pay more than the sum of its offer less the costs incurred by the MIBI in defending the proceedings after the date of the offer. This provision is similar to the procedure in place for defendants to personal injury actions making lodgments and tenders. The MIBI, however, reserves the right to vary the amounts offered in satisfaction of the proceedings and an offer can be made up to 10 days before the hearing of the action.[30]

---

26.   Article 74.1 of the articles of association of MIBI. See **Appendix 5**.
27.   The MIBI is funded by a levy charged on each of its member insurers based on the gross written premiums receivable of each member. The levies are apportioned between the members of the MIBI on a *pro rata* basis to the gross written premiums of the members transacted in the State during the preceding calendar year (see art 62 of the MIBI's Articles of Association).
28.   Clause 3.9 of the 2009 and 2004 Agreements. An 'order to pay' made by the Injuries Board operates as if it was a judgment of a court given for the same amount (PIAB Act 2003, s 40).
29.   See paras **5.11–5.13**.
30.   Clause 10 of the 2009 and 2004 Agreements.

4. List of conditions precedent to MIBI's liability:

[5.18] Clause 3 of the 2009 Agreement sets out the full terms of the conditions precedent to the MIBI's liability. Briefly summarised:

1.   A claimant or his legal representative must have given prior notice by registered post or electronic mail of the intention to seek compensation within the time limits prescribed in the Statute of Limitations.

2.   The claimant must upon demand furnish the MIBI with all material information (including all medical reports) reasonably required in relation to the processing of the compensation claim including information relating to the relevant accident, personal injuries or death or medical treatment, funeral expenses, damage to property and legal, professional or other costs reasonably incurred by or on behalf of the claimant.

3.   If the claim concerns an untraced motorist the claimant must make himself available for interview by an authorised agent of the MIBI. The claimant has a right to have a solicitor present at such interview. All reasonable questions relating to the accident must be answered. The answers can only be used for the claim against the MIBI. The answers may be used in subsequent court proceedings which may arise to determine the MIBI's liability but cannot be used in any criminal proceedings. The claimant must make himself available for interview within 30 days of completing the application to the Injuries Board.

4.   The claimant must cooperate fully with An Garda Síochána or any other authorised persons in their investigation of the circumstances giving rise to the claim.

5.   The claimant must furnish the MIBI with copies of all relevant documentation in relation to the accident and any subsequent legal proceedings relating to it including correspondence, statements and pleadings.

6.   The claimant must endeavour to establish if there is an approved policy of insurance covering the use of the vehicle involved in the accident by demanding insurance particulars of the user or owner of the vehicle, pursuant to s 73 of the Road Traffic Act 1961. If the claimant has made demands in writing and has been unsuccessful for two months after the accident, the MIBI may be notified. If, within the two-month period, the claimant can produce a letter from An Garda Síochána or the owner and/or user of the vehicle giving rise to the claim, the notification can take place immediately.

7.   The claimant must furnish the MIBI with details of any claim made under any policy of insurance, in respect of damage to property, arising out of the accident.

8.   Notice of proceedings or an application to the Injuries Board must be given by the claimant by registered post before commencement of such proceedings or application:

     8.1.   to the insurer in any case in which there was in force at the time the accident occurred an approved policy of insurance purporting to cover the use of the vehicle;

8.2.   the MIBI in any other case;

8.3.   to the owner and/or user of the vehicle giving rise to the claim except where the owner and user remains unidentified.

9.   The claimant must give no less than 28 days notice to the MIBI before issuing a motion for judgment against any person which may give rise to an obligation on the part of the MIBI.

10.   Any dispute in relation to compliance with the conditions precedent may be referred to arbitration and the arbitrator's determination may be appealed to the Minister for Transport.

11.   All judgments must be assigned to the MIBI or its nominee.

12.   The claimant must give credit to the MIBI for any amounts paid to him or due to be paid to him from any source in respect of any liability for injury to person or property arising out of the event which occasioned the claim against MIBI.

13.   Any accident giving rise to a claim made to the MIBI must be reported by the claimant to An Garda Síochána within two days of the event or as soon as the 'claimant reasonably could' report it.

14.   A claim shall not be deemed to be notified unless all the following information is supplied or good cause is shown as to why it is not available.

14.1.   Name, date of birth, PPS number and address of claimant.

14.2.   Registration number of vehicle alleged to be uninsured and where available the type and make of such vehicle.

14.3.   The name of the garda station to which the accident has been reported.

14.4.   The reason why the claimant considers the vehicle to be uninsured.

14.5.   What steps have been taken to establish the insurance position.

14.6.   The name and address of the owner and/or driver of the uninsured vehicle.

14.7.   The date and time of the accident.

14.8.   The place of the accident.

14.9.   A brief description of the accident.

14.10.   If any other vehicle was involved, its registration number and, where available, the type and make of such vehicle.

14.11.   The name and address of the owner and/or driver and insurance details.

[5.19] All the above information can be inserted on the standard claim notification form or on the MIBI online claim notification form available on www.mibi.ie. This form is reproduced in **Appendix 7.1**.

5. Compliance with conditions precedent is important

[5.20] MIBI claims are dealt with by various insurance companies and solicitors dealing with them on its behalf. Most if not all of the conditions precedent have a sound basis in logic. They are not designed to be pitfalls for innocent claims, rather they seek to ensure that the MIBI has ample time to properly investigate all the claims, unmeritorious claims are weeded out, and the pool of insured motorists does not have a needless drain on its resources. Because the day to day handling of claims is dealt with by a number of insurers concerned and handling offices, there is sometimes an inconsistency in the application of the conditions precedent and a claimant may fall foul of a condition precedent in circumstances where non-compliance may not have caused the MIBI any actual prejudice. Occasionally no point will be taken but it certainly cannot be taken for granted that this will be the case.[31]

D. SATISFACTION OF JUDGMENTS BY THE MIBI

1. Assigning judgments[32]

[5.21] A claimant is required to assign any judgment it obtains to the MIBI or its nominee.[33] Curiously, however, the 2009 Agreement does not oblige a claimant to assign

---

31. The MIBI has successfully defended proceedings against it on the basis of non-compliance with the conditions precedent to its liability as set out in cl 3 of both the 2009 and 2004 Agreements. In *O'Flynn v Buckley, Walsh, MIBI and Horan* [2009] 3 IR 311, Kearns J, delivering the unanimous judgment of the Supreme Court, said '... the [MIBI] is entitled to require that litigants respect the strict conditions laid down in the [1988] agreement as a pre-condition to the recovery of compensation' (at p 319). The foregoing statement was approved in *Patterson v McHugh and MIBI* (5 March 2010, unreported) HC, *ex tempore*, Smyth J. In that case, the plaintiff did not give notice of the proceedings by registered post until some months after the proceedings issued. Despite the fact that the MIBI was not prejudiced by non-compliance with the condition precedent in cl 3.8 of the 2004 Agreement, the MIBI raised non-compliance in its defence (at pp 5–7 of the transcript). The MIBI was not required to show that it was prejudiced. See further, **Ch 4**, para **4.37**. The approach taken in *Patterson* is consistent with the English case law. In *Stinton v Stinton* [1995] RTR 167, the plaintiff's claim for a declaration against the MIB was dismissed as the plaintiff had failed to give notice of the proceedings to the MIB in accordance with the UK agreement. Likewise in *Silverton v Goodall and MIB* [1997] PIQR P451 the Court of Appeal dismissed an appeal against the High Court's dismissal of a claim where correct notice had not been given under cl 5(1)(a) of the 1988 Uninsured Drivers Agreement. Subsequently, *Richardson v Watson & Another* [2006] EWCA Civ 1662, (6 December 2006, unreported) Supreme Court of Judicature, Court of Appeal, held that, where a claimant is within time to issue a second action against the English MIB (the first action having been discontinued by the claimant by reason of the MIB's assertion that the claimant had failed to comply with the condition precedent in the 1999 MIB Agreement that required that it be given notice of and served with the proceedings within 14 days of the issuing of the proceedings) it was not an abuse of process to bring a second action. Unlike Irish law, however, the English Limitation Act 1980 permits actions that are not brought within the limitation period to be brought in certain circumstances ie the courts have a discretion to extend the limitation period. While the second action in *Richardson v Watson* was technically out of time, the Supreme Court exercised that discretion to permit the second action to proceed.

32. See **Appendix 7.3** for the document that is currently being used by the MIBI to obtain an assignment of judgments.

33. Clause 3.11 of the 2009 and 2004 Agreements. This obligation extends to any judgment that the claimant obtains in any action that the MIBI calls upon the claimant to take under either Agreement. That said, if the MIBI paid a claimant the amount of an unsatisfied judgment and the claimant then failed to assign the relevant judgment to the MIBI, the MIBI could sue the claimant in quasi contract or unjust enrichment.

the judgment(s) prior to or at the time that the MIBI satisfies the judgment.[34] Where such a judgment is assigned to the MIBI, the MIBI can subsequently enforce the judgment against the relevant defendant. Depending on the circumstances, however, it may be appropriate to defer enforcement pending an improvement in the defendant's financial circumstances. In this regard, the MIBI has twelve years from the date of the judgment (as opposed to the date of assignment) within which to enforce it.[35] The alternative remedies available to the MIBI in terms of recovering the monies paid out from the person against whom judgment was entered depend upon whether or not that person signed a mandate. The remedies are considered in **Ch 9**.

2. Giving credit for any amounts paid to claimant from any source

[5.22] A claimant must give credit to the MIBI for any amounts paid or due to be paid to him from any source in respect of any liability for personal injury or property damage arising out of the event that gave rise to the claim against the MIBI.[36] In addition, the 2009 Agreement provides that, where a claimant is entitled to receive compensation from any source, including any insurance policy in respect of damage to property, the MIBI 'shall' deduct the sum payable from the compensation that is being paid to the claimant.[37] Under the 2004 Agreement, the relevant provision said 'may', rather than 'shall', and thereby gave the MIBI a discretion.[38]

3. Costs of claims paid by the MIBI

[5.23] A claimant's entitlement to legal costs or expenses shall not exceed that which would be payable if the owner or user of the vehicle was covered by an approved policy of insurance or what would be payable by virtue of the fact that the MIBI is or may be a defendant or co-defendant to any legal proceedings relating to his claim.[39]

4. European dimension

[5.24] Finally, the position of a claimant who is unaware of the terms of the relevant MIBI Agreement, or who is ignorant of the existence of the MIBI and its role with respect to claims against uninsured motorists, is worthy of comment.

[5.25] The PIAB Act 2003 does not make any provision for advising a claimant about any alternative means by which he might obtain relief, for example by making a claim for compensation to the MIBI. Despite this, the Injuries Board website does advise a claimant to contact to the MIBI if the claim concerns an uninsured driver.

---

34. This is to be contrasted with the position under the English MIB Agreements. Clause 15 of the MIB (Compensation of Victims of Uninsured Drivers) Agreement 1999 provides that the liability of the MIB to discharge an unsatisfied judgment does not arise unless the claimant assigns the unsatisfied judgment to the MIB.
35. Statute of Limitations 1957, s 11(6)(a).
36. Clause 3.12 of the 2009 and 2004 Agreements.
37. Clause 4.4. of the 2009 Agreement.
38. Clause 4.4 of the 2004 Agreement. For a further discussion, see **Ch 4**, paras **4.23–4.26**.
39. Clause 4.3 of the 2009 and 2004 Agreements.

[5.26] A claimant who obtains an order to pay against an uninsured motorist from the Injuries Board may only subsequently discover that the MIBI may have been liable to discharge the order to pay but is declining to so do because of the claimant's failure to comply with the conditions precedent in the Agreement. This would render the Injuries Board's order to pay valueless.

[5.27] In this regard, the decision of the ECJ in *Evans v The Secretary of State for the Environment, Transport and the Regions and the MIB*[40] is noteworthy. It observes that it is essential for national laws to guarantee that the national authorities will effectively apply the Second Directive in full. It also notes that it is essential that the legal position under national law is sufficiently precise and clear and that individuals are made fully aware of their rights.[41]

[5.28] Furthermore, having noted that the Second Directive 'confine[d] itself to laying down minimum procedural requirements'[42] by providing that victims should be able to apply directly to the body responsible, it said:

> '[I]t is settled case law that in the absence of Community rules governing the matter it is for the domestic legal system of each Member State to designate the courts and tribunals having jurisdiction and to lay down the detailed procedural rules governing actions for safeguarding rights which individuals derive from Community law, provided, however, that such rules ... *do not render virtually impossible or excessively difficult the exercise of rights conferred by Community law*[43] (the principle of effectiveness).[44]

> As regards application of the principle of effectiveness, each case which raises the question *whether a national procedural provision renders application of Community law impossible or excessively difficult*[45] must be analysed by reference to the role of that provision in the procedure, its progress and its special features, viewed as a whole, before the various national instances. In the light of that analysis, the basic principles of the domestic judicial system, such as protection of the rights of the defence, the principle of legal certainty and the proper conduct of procedure, must, where appropriate, be taken into consideration.'[46]

[5.29] An argument could be made that the 2009 Agreement is in breach of the Sixth Directive (and its predecessors) in that victims of uninsured driving are less favourably treated than victims of insured driving in consequence of the conditions precedent to the MIBI's liability eg the requirement that all reasonably required medical reports be

---

40. *Evans v The Secretary of State for the Environment, Transport and the Regions and the MIB* (C–63/01) [2005] All ER (EC) 763, [2003] ECR I–14447, [2004] RTR 32; [2004] 1 CMLR 47, [2004] Lloyd's Rep IR 391, ECJ (5th Chamber).
41. At para 35 and citing *Commission v Greece* [1995] ECR I–499 (para 9) and *Commission v Netherlands* [2001] ECR I–3541 (para 17).
42. At para 44.
43. Emphasis added.
44. At para 45, citing *Upjohn v The Licensing Authority & Ors* (Case C–120/97) [1999] ECR I–223, para 32.
45. Emphasis added.
46. At para 46, citing *Van Schijndel* and *Van Veen* (Joined Cases C–430/93 and C–431/93) [1995] ECR I–4075, para 19. See also **Ch 12**, paras **12.11–12.14**.

furnished on demand and, in untraced driver claims, the requirement to submit to interview. However the ECJ in *Evans v The Secretary of State for the Environment, Transport and the Regions and the MIB*[47] would appear to have rejected such an argument.[48]

[5.30] The Court of Appeal in England had previously rejected a claim that cl 5(1)(a) of the 1988 Uninsured Drivers Agreement, requiring notice within prescribed time limits, was inconsistent with art 3(1) of the First Directive[49] (or indeed any of the motor insurance directives). It said that a competent solicitor, or a layman who pays attention to the language of the agreement and the notes attached to it, should have no real difficulty complying with the requirements.[50]

[5.31] Similarly, McCracken J in *Galvin v Dennehy, Dennehy and MIBI*[51] rejected the argument that the condition precedent, previously contained in cl 3(1)(b) of the 1988 Agreement,[52] requiring notification by registered post of the intention to seek compensation for property damage within one year of the accident was contrary to the First Directive. He said:

> 'Accordingly the specifics as to how each member state will ensure that there is insurance, is a matter of each individual member state. Questions such as

---

47. *Evans v The Secretary of State for the Environment, Transport and the Regions and the MIB* (C–63/01) [2005] All ER (EC) 763, [2003] ECR I–14447, [2004] RTR 32, [2004] 1 CMLR 47 [2004] Lloyd's Rep IR 391, ECJ (5th Chamber).

48. Evans claimed that the English Untraced Drivers Agreement 1972 put a claimant in a worse position vis-à-vis costs to a victim of an insured driver. The court stated 'the compensation awarded for damage or injury caused by an unidentified or insufficiently insured vehicle, paid by the body authorised for that purpose, is not required to include reimbursement of the costs incurred by victims in connection with the processing of their application for compensation except to the extent to which such reimbursement is necessary to safeguard the rights derived by victims from [the Second Directive] in conformity with the principles of equivalence and effectiveness. It is for the national court to consider whether that is the case under the procedural arrangements adopted in the member state concerned'. The Untraced Drivers Agreement 2003 now provides for interest and a discretion to award costs.

49. First Directive, art 3(1) is now contained in Sixth Directive, art 3, first and second paragraphs.

50. *Silverton v Goodall and MIB* [1997] PIQR P451.

51. *Galvin v Dennehy, Dennehy and MIBI* [2005] IEHC 90, (18 March 2005), the High Court on Circuit (McCracken J).

52. This requirement was repeated in cl 3.1(a) of the 2004 Agreement. Now, however, cl 3.1 of the 2009 Agreement requires that notification for personal injury and property damage be given within the period prescribed by the Statute of Limitations. In *Lavery v MIBI* [2009] IEHC 628, (1 May 2009, unreported) HC (Laffoy J), the action was defended on the basis that it was statute barred as having been issued outside the then three-year limitation period applicable to actions for damages for personal injuries caused by negligence. The plaintiff contended that her action, in respect of the actions of an unidentified motorist, and in which she sought a mandatory order or specific performance of the 1988 MIBI Agreement, was governed by the six-year limitation period provided for in s 11(2)(a) of the Statute of Limitations 1957, as amended. Following the reasoning of *Campbell v O'Donnell* [2009] 1 IR 133, [2008] 2 ILRM 241, however, Laffoy J held that the plaintiff's cause of action against the MIBI was the same as the cause of action against the unidentified and untraced owner and user of the vehicle would have been if those parties had been identified. Therefore the plaintiff was statute barred pursuant to the Statute of Limitations (Amendment) Act 1991, s 3(1).

notification of claims or time limits are not dealt with at all in the [First Directive].
I am satisfied that it was perfectly lawful under the terms of the [First Directive]
for the agreement to specify time limits within which claims should be made and
time limits within which notification of proceedings should be given.'[53]

---

53.   At p 6.

Chapter 6

PROPERTY DAMAGE

A. INTRODUCTION

[6.01] Prior to the 1988 Agreement, a person who was caused property damage by an uninsured motorist could not recover compensation from the MIBI.

[6.02] The 1988 Agreement, however, extended the liability of the MIBI to property damage claims caused by an uninsured motorist arising out of an accident occurring on or after 31 December 1992.

[6.03] The liability of the MIBI to meet property damage caused by uninsured motorists is, however, confined to the minimum cover for third party property damage that is required on the date of the accident by the Road Traffic Act 1961 (the 1961 Act).[1] Furthermore, the MIBI's liability does not extend to the first €220 of damage caused to property by a vehicle that is stolen or taken without its owner's consent.[2] Under the 2004 Agreement, the MIBI was not liable for the first €440 of property damage caused to its owner by a vehicle, the use of which was not covered by an approved policy of insurance.[3] This €440 excess was omitted from the 2009 Agreement.

[6.04] Before 2009, the MIBI agreements provided that the MIBI would not be liable for property damage caused by an unidentified vehicle.[4] Now the 2009 Agreement provides that property damage cannot be recovered from the MIBI in these circumstances 'unless compensation for substantial personal injuries involving an in-patient hospital stay for five days or more has also been paid in respect of the event causing the damage subject to an excess of €500.00'.[5]

[6.05] Under the 2009 Agreement, a person who wishes to claim compensation for property damage must give the MIBI prior notice, by registered post or electronic mail, of his intention to do so and such notice must be given within the time limit prescribed by the Statute of Limitations.[6] Under the 2004 Agreement, notice was required to be given within one year of the accident.[7]

---

1. Clause 7.2 of the 2009 and 2004 Agreements. See paras **6.13–6.18** for the minimum compulsory insurance requirements for property damage.
2. Clause 7.3 of the 2009 Agreement and cl 7.3(a) of the 2004 Agreement. See further para **6.19** below.
3. Clause 7.3(b) of the 2004 Agreement.
4. See cl 7.1 of the 2004 Agreement. Prior to that, cl 7(2) of the 1988 Agreement excluded recovery for property damage 'caused by a vehicle the owner or user of which remains unidentified or untraced'.
5. Clause 7.1 of the 2009 Agreement.
6. Clause 3.1 of the 2009 Agreement (ie six years).
7. Clause 3.1(b) of the 2004 Agreement. (contd .../)

B. PROPERTY DAMAGE – 2009 AGREEMENT

[6.06] Clause 7 of the 2009 Agreement provides:

'7.1.　The liability of MIBI for damage to property shall not extend to damage caused by an unidentified vehicle unless compensation for substantial personal injuries involving an inpatient hospital stay for five days or more has also been paid in respect of the event causing the damage subject to an excess of €500.00.

7.2.　The liability of MIBI for damage to property shall not exceed the minimum property damage cover required by Section 56(2)(a) of the Road Traffic Act, 1961 applying at the time of the event giving rise to the claim.

7.3.　The liability of MIBI shall not extend to the first €220 of damage to property suffered by any one property owner due to the negligent use of a vehicle stolen or obtained by violence or threats of violence or used or taken possession of without the consent of the owner of the vehicle or other lawful authority.

7.4.　In cases where the claimant and MIBI agree to accept an Injuries Board award, and if that award includes an allowance for property damage, the acceptance of that award by both parties is subject always to the provisions of Clause 4.4 and this Clause of the Agreement.'

C. EUROPEAN BACKGROUND

[6.07] The First Directive directed the Member States to introduce compulsory motor vehicle insurance for civil liability.[8] The Second Directive directed each Member State to introduce *minimum* compulsory third party liability motor vehicle insurance to be applied in all Member States.[9] It also extended the requirements of compulsory insurance on motor vehicles to include liability for property damage.[10]

7.　(contd) The UK was held to have failed to have properly implemented the Second Directive in *Byrne v MIB* [2009] QB 66, [2008] 4 All ER 476, [2008] 3 WLR 1421 in circumstances where the MIB (Compensation of Victims of Untraced Drivers) Agreement 1972 (the 1972 Agreement) required that an application for compensation for injury caused by an untraced driver must be made within three years (regardless of whether or not the claimant was a child) whereas, if the plaintiff child's cause of action had been against a traced driver, he could have sued at any time prior to his 21st birthday. The foregoing decision, or perhaps *Evans v Secretary of State for the Environment, Transport and the Regions and the MIB* (Case C–63/01) [2005] All ER (EC) 763, [2003] ECR I–14447, [2004] RTR 32, [2004] 1 CMLR 47, [2004] Lloyds Rep 391, ECJ (5th Chamber) which was the background to the *Byrne* decision, may have been the reason for amending cl 3.1(b) of the 2004 Agreement (to cl 3.1 of the 2009 Agreement) from one year to six years for property damage claims.

8.　The First Directive, art 3(1) is now contained in Sixth Directive, art 3. The Member States were also directed to ensure that the insurance extended to loss or injury caused in any Member State and accorded with the law of the other Member States in that regard. For a discussion of the freedom afforded by the directives to the Member States to determine the type of civil liability applicable to road traffic accidents, see *Ferreira and Ferreira v Companhia de Seguros Mundial Confianca SA* (Case C–348/98) [2000] ECR I–06711 (at paras 27 to 29). This decision is considered in **Ch 2**, para **2.30**.

9.　The Second Directive, art 1(2). The minimum amounts initially prescribed by the Fifth Directive, art 2 (and amending the Second Directive, art 1) are now contained in Sixth Directive, art 9(1). See below at para **6.14–6.18**.

10.　The Second Directive, art 1(1) amending First Directive, art 3(1) (now contained in Sixth Directive, art 3, last paragraph).

[6.08] In addition, the Second Directive directed the Member States to set up or authorise the establishment of a body with responsibility for providing compensation for damage to property or personal injury caused by an unidentified or uninsured motor vehicle.[11] The Second Directive acknowledged, however, that in view of the danger of fraud, Member States should be permitted to exclude certain compensation claims and exclude or limit the payment of compensation for property damage caused by an unidentified vehicle.[12] Hence, subparagraphs 4 and 5 of art 1(4) of the Second Directive provided:

'Member States may limit or exclude the payment of compensation by that body in the event of damage to property by an unidentified vehicle.[13]

They may also authorize, in the case of damage to property caused by an uninsured vehicle an excess of not more than €500 for which the victim may be responsible.'[14]

[6.09] Subparagraph 4 of art 1(4) of the Second Directive is now contained in art 10(3) of the Sixth Directive. However, the blanket authority given to the Member States in subparagraph 5 of art 1(5) of the Second Directive to limit or exclude compensation for property damage caused by an unidentified vehicle was removed by the Fifth Directive which amended the Second Directive (see below at para **6.25**).

D. IRISH LEGISLATION IMPLEMENTING THE DIRECTIVES

[6.10] Section 56(2A) of the Road Traffic Act 1961 (the 1961 Act) implemented the compulsory insurance provisions of the First and Second Directives.[15] It provides that the cover provided by an approved policy of insurance extends to damage or costs to persons or property incurred by the negligent use of a vehicle by its user in any of the designated territories, and to the extent of the compulsory insurance requirements of the relevant territory or under Irish law, whichever is greater. Section 62(1)(cc) of the 1961

---

11. The Second Directive, art 1(4) as amended by Third Directive, art 3 (now contained in Sixth Directive, art 10(1), first subparagraph).

12. See the Second Directive, Sixth Recital (and now contained in Sixth Directive, Fourteenth Recital).

13. The Fifth Directive, art 2 substituted the Second Directive, art 1 but this subparagraph remained intact in the Second Directive, substituted art 1(6). The same paragraph now appears as the first subparagraph of Sixth Directive, art 10(3).

14. This excess is effectively retained in Sixth Directive, art 10(3).

15. Road Traffic Act 1961, s 56(2A) in its current form was substituted by the European Communities (Road Traffic) (Compulsory Insurance) (Amendment) Regulations 1992 (SI 347/1992), art 4(1) (the Second 1992 Regulations). The Second 1992 Regulations were introduced to implement the provisions of the First Directive, as amended by the Second and Third Directives and by Council Directive 90/618/EC of 8 November 1990 which amended Directives 73/239 and 88/357 concerning the co-ordination of laws, regulations and administrative provisions relating to direct insurance other than life assurance. The original s 56(2A) was inserted by the European Communities (Road Traffic) (Compulsory Insurance) Regulations 1975 (SI 178/1975), art 3(a), which were introduced to implement the provisions of the First Directive dealing with the abolition of insurance checks on vehicles moving between Member States of the EEC and certain other countries which had made arrangements with the EEC.

Act correspondingly increased the liability of an insurer in the designated territories.[16] The designated territories are the EU Member States[17] (other than the State) and Croatia, Iceland, Norway and Switzerland.[18]

E. MIBI AGREEMENTS AND PROPERTY DAMAGE

1. Extension of the liability of the MIBI to compensate for property damage

[6.11] The 1988 Agreement was drafted as part of the implementation of the Second Directive. It provided that the MIBI would be liable to pay compensation for certain property damage and in respect of accidents that occurred on or after 31 December 1992.[19]

2. Limitation on the liability of the MIBI to compensate for property damage generally

[6.12] The liability of the MIBI is not unlimited. Clause 7.2 of the 2009 Agreement provides that the liability of the MIBI for property damage 'shall not exceed the minimum property damage cover required by section 56(2)(a) of the 1961 Act, applying at the time of the event giving rise to the claim'.

[6.13] Section 56(2)(a) of the 1961 Act originally mandated a minimum insurance against property damage of £1,000 caused by an act of negligence or a series of acts of

---

16. Road Traffic Act 1961, s 62(1)(cc) in its current form was substituted by the European Communities (Motor Insurance) Regulations 2008 (SI 248/2008), reg 3(a)(iii). Prior to that, it was substituted by the European Communities (Road Traffic) (Compulsory Insurance) (Amendment) Regulations 1992 (SI 347/1992), art 4(2). The original s 62(1)(cc) was inserted by the European Communities (Road Traffic) (Compulsory Insurance) Regulations 1975 (SI 178/1975), art 4.

17. There are currently 27 EU Member States: Austria, Belgium, Bulgaria, Cyprus, the Czech Republic, Denmark, Estonia, Finland, France, Germany, Greece, Hungary, Ireland, Italy, Latvia, Lithuania, Luxembourg, Malta, Poland, Portugal, Romania, Slovakia, Slovenia, Spain, Sweden, The Netherlands and the United Kingdom.

18. The foregoing is provided by the Road Traffic Act 1961, s 56(9) as substituted by the European Communities (Motor Insurance) Regulations 2008 (SI 248/2008), reg 2. Initially, the designated territories were prescribed by the Road Traffic Act 1961, s 56(7) which was inserted by the European Communities (Road Traffic) (Compulsory Insurance) Regulations 1975 (SI 178/1975), art 3(b), and pursuant to which the associated countries were Austria, Finland, Norway, Sweden, Switzerland, Hungary, Czechoslovakia and the German Democratic Republic. The Road Traffic Act 1961, s 56(7) was then substituted by the European Communities (Road Traffic) (Compulsory Insurance) (Amendment) Regulations 1995 (SI 353/1995), s 3(2), and pursuant to which the associated countries were the Czech Republic, Hungary, Iceland, Norway, the Slovak Republic and Switzerland. The 1995 Regulations became effective on 1 January 1996. The effect of the European Communities (Road Traffic) (Compulsory Insurance) (Amendment) Regulations 2001 (SI 463/2001), which operated from 12 October 2001 until European Communities (Motor Insurance) Regulations 2008 (SI 248/2008), was to extend the associated countries to incorporate Slovenia, Croatia and Cyprus.

19. Clause 7(1) of the 1988 Agreement expressly provided that the provisions of the 1988 Agreement that extended the liability of the MIBI to property damage would only apply to accidents that occurred on or after 31 December 1992.

negligence collectively constituting one event. This was increased to £40,000 in respect of acts occurring on or after 31 December 1987, and prior to 31 December 1990.[20] From 31 December 1990 to 31 December 1995, inclusive, the minimum was £80,000.[21] As of 1 January 1996, this was increased to £90,000.[22] The Road Traffic Act 2002 (the 2002 Act), made provision for increasing the limit to €200,000,[23] but the relevant provision was never commenced by statutory instrument.[24]

[6.14] The Fifth Directive raised the minimum insurance requirements for property damage to €1,000,000 per claim, whatever the number of victims.[25] The same requirement is repeated in art 9(1) of the Sixth Directive.

[6.15] Article 9(1) of the Sixth Directive also provided that, if necessary, Member States could establish a transitional period extending until 11 June 2012 at the latest within which to adapt their minimum amounts of cover to the aforementioned amounts. It further provided, however, that until 11 December 2009 at the latest, Member States must increase guarantees to at least half of the minimums specified in art 9(1).

[6.16] In addition, art 9(2) of the Sixth Directive provides that, *inter alia*, every five years, after 11 June 2005, or at the end of any transitional period as referred to in art 9(1), the amounts referred to therein must be reviewed in line with the European Index of Consumer Prices (EICP) established pursuant to Regulation (EC) No 2494/95. It states that the amounts shall be adjusted automatically and increased by the percentage change indicated by the EICP for the relevant period, ie the five years immediately preceding the review provided for in art 9(1) and rounded up to a multiple of €10,000.

[6.17] In Ireland, reg 2(b) of the European Communities (Motor Insurance) Regulations 2008[26] (the 2008 Regulations) amended s 56(2)(a) of the 1961 Act to implement the minimum requirements set out in the Fifth Directive ie €1,000,000 per claim, whatever the number of victims.[27]

[6.18] Thereafter, on 9 December 2010, and following a review provided for in the Sixth Directive, the European Commission published a notice regarding the adaptation of monetary amounts in the Sixth Directive. This increased the minimum insurance

---

20. Road Traffic Act 1961, s 56(2) as substituted by the European Communities (Road Traffic) (Compulsory Insurance) (Amendment) Regulations 1987 (SI 322/1987), art 4(1).
21. Road Traffic Act 1961, s 56(2) as substituted by European Communities (Road Traffic) (Compulsory Insurance) (Amendment) Regulations 1987 (SI 322/1987), art 4(1).
22. Road Traffic Act 1961, s 56(2) as substituted by the European Communities (Road Traffic) (Compulsory Insurance) (Amendment) Regulations 1995 (SI 353/1995), art 3(1). In practice, however it seems that this property damage limit was not generally relied upon with respect to non-commercial vehicles.
23. Road Traffic Act 2002, s 17.
24. Required by the Road Traffic Act 2002, s 26.
25. See the Fifth Directive, art 2 substituting a new Second Directive, art 1.
26. European Communities (Motor Insurance) Regulations 2008 (SI 248/2008). The 2008 Regulations became operative at the end of 3 July 2008 (see Interpretation Act 2005, s 16(3)).
27. The Fifth Directive, art 2 (substituting a new Second Directive, art 1) and now the Sixth Directive, art 9(1).

requirement to €1,120,000 for property damage. Section 56(2)(a) of the 1961 Act[28] was amended to reflect the foregoing increase by the European Union (Motor Insurance) (Limitation of Insurance in Relation to Property) Regulations 2011.[29]

3. Excess on claims

[6.19] Clause 7.3 of the 2009 Agreement provides that the MIBI's liability shall not extend to the first €220 of property damage suffered by any one property owner due to the negligent use of a vehicle stolen or obtained by violence (or threats thereof) or used or taken possession of without the consent of the owner of the vehicle or other lawful authority.[30]

4. Property damage caused by an unidentified vehicle

The 1988 Agreement

[6.20] Clause 7(2) of the 1988 Agreement provided that the liability of the MIBI for property damage 'shall not extend to damage caused by a vehicle the owner or user of which remains unidentified or untraced'.

[6.21] The object of this clause appears to have been to prevent a person, who caused damage to his own vehicle, from fraudulently claiming that it was caused by a hit-and-run motorist. However, a literal reading of cl 7(2) of the 1988 Agreement suggests that the MIBI is not liable for property damage caused by a vehicle where either its owner *or* user remains either unidentified or untraced. Clause 7(2) of the 1988 Agreement was, however, interpreted by the Circuit Court in *Dublin Bus v MIBI*[31] as meaning that property damage suffered by the victim of a hit-and-run incident cannot be recovered if the offending vehicle is not identified. If the vehicle is identified, however, the property damage caused is recoverable from the MIBI, regardless of whether or not its owner or driver is identified or traced.

The 2004 Agreement

[6.22] Clause 7.1 of the 2004 Agreement provides that the liability of the MIBI for property damage 'shall not extend to damage caused by an unidentified vehicle'.

[6.23] The change in the 2004 Agreement reflected the interpretation that was placed upon cl 7(2) of the 1988 Agreement in *Dublin Bus v MIBI*.[32]

---

28. As amended by the European Communities (Motor Insurance) Regulations 2008 (SI 248/2008) to reflect the minimum insurance requirements for property damage that were prescribed by the Fifth (now Sixth Directive).

29. European Union (Motor Insurance) (Limitation of Insurance in Relation to Property) Regulations 2011 (SI 702/2011), and made 21 December 2011.

30. Clause 7.3(b) of the 2004 Agreement provided that the MIBI was not liable for the first €440 of property damage suffered by any one property owner due to the negligent use of a vehicle that is not covered by an approved insurance policy. This excess was omitted from the 2009 Agreement.

31. *Dublin Bus v MIBI* (29 October 1999, unreported) CC, Judge McMahon.

32. *Dublin Bus v MIBI* (29 October 1999, unreported) CC, Judge McMahon.

The 2009 Agreement

[6.24] Clause 7.1 of the 2009 Agreement provides:

> 'The liability of the MIBI for property damage shall not extend to damage
> caused by an unidentified vehicle *unless compensation for substantial personal*
> *injuries involving an inpatient stay for five days or more has also been paid in*
> *respect of the event causing the damage subject to an excess of €500.'*[33]

[6.25] The addition to cl 7.1 of the 2009 Agreement can be explained by reference to the
provisions of art 2 of the Fifth Directive and now contained in art 10(3) of the Sixth
Directive. This prohibits the exclusion of compensation for property damage caused by
an unidentified vehicle in circumstances where the victim has suffered 'significant
personal injuries' in the accident in which the property damage was also caused. At the
same time, Member States are allowed to provide for a maximum excess of €500 to be
borne by such a victim of property damage. Furthermore, it provides that the conditions
in which personal injuries are to be regarded as 'significant' shall be determined in
accordance with the legislation or administrative provisions of the Member State in
which the accident takes place but also states that Member States may take into account,
inter alia, whether the injury required hospital care.

F. COMPREHENSIVE POLICIES

[6.26] In late 2003, the MIBI applied a new protocol among its member insurance
companies, and it was updated following the transposition of the Fifth Directive in 2008.
This protocol applies to an insured person who, arising out of an accident, is entitled to
make a claim under the damage section of his comprehensive policy, even though that
claim might also be recoverable as a third party claim against an uninsured driver or the
MIBI. The protocol provides that, where an insured person makes a claim against his
comprehensive policy for damage caused by an *uninsured motorist,* the insured person's
no claims bonus or no claims discount (NCD) will not be affected. It therefore improves
the position of an insured person with comprehensive cover because heretofore an
insured who made a claim against his policy might have adversely affected his NCD.

[6.27] An insured person who has suffered property damage has no legal standing to
enforce the terms of the protocol because it does not form part of a contract of insurance
and is not a term of any of the MIBI agreements. However, motor insurance companies
are obliged by law to be members of the MIBI[34] and any breach of the protocol could be
reported to the MIBI and/or the Insurance Ombudsman.

[6.28] In essence, the protocol agrees that the following standards will be implemented
by all member insurance companies of the MIBI:

• Where a customer makes the claim under his own policy, the Insurer will not,
on that account, cancel or reduce the customer's No Claims Discount. In doing
so the Insurer applies the policy excess.

---

33. Emphasis added.
34. The Road Traffic Act 1961, s 78.

- Each Insurer will specifically inform the customer that they, the Insurer, will deal with the claim on behalf of the MIBI.

- An Insurer who pays a claim in these circumstances will not pursue a subrogation claim against the MIBI. This does not affect the Insurer's right to pursue an uninsured driver if they wish.

[6.29] Since the transposition of the Fifth Directive[35] the MIBI no longer applies an excess to property damage claims where the uninsured vehicle was identified except where the damage has been caused by a stolen vehicle in which case the excess is €220. If the offending vehicle is identified, the comprehensive insurer deals with the claim, applies the policy excess, and the claimant can then seek reimbursement of the excess from the MIBI which should be refunded. Where the offending vehicle was stolen, the MIBI will deduct €220 when refunding the policy excess.

[6.30] That said, cl 4.4 of the 2009 Agreement now provides that where a claimant 'has received or is entitled to receive benefit or compensation from any source, including any insurance policy in respect of damage to property', the MIBI *shall* reduce the compensation payable by the amount of that compensation. This provision was in fact introduced by cl 4.4 of the 2004 Agreement, the only difference being that the 2004 Agreement contained the word 'may' rather than 'shall'.[36] It therefore remains to be seen whether or not the MIBI will resist a property damage claim from an innocent insured motorist who declines to recover against his own comprehensive policy.[37]

---

35. The European Communities (Motor Insurance) Regulations 2008 (SI 248/2008) made 4 July 2008 were introduced to give effect to the Fifth Directive.

36. Under the 1988 Agreement, if a claimant recovered under his own comprehensive motor insurance for a *property* damage claim, the MIBI could refuse a subsequent claim for compensation. This was because, in stating the liability of the MIBI to satisfy judgments, cl 4(2) of the 1988 Agreement provided that, where a person has received benefit or compensation 'from any source in respect of damage to property, [the MIBI] may deduct' the amount of that benefit or compensation. Given this provision, and the possible adverse consequences for a claimant's own premium, a claimant under the 1988 Agreement would have been well advised not to make a material damage claim against his own comprehensive policy and pursue the MIBI for the material damage instead.

37. In this regard, cl 4.4 of the 2004 Agreement permitted the MIBI to reduce the compensation payable where a claimant 'has received or is entitled to receive' alternative compensation (see further **Ch 4**, paras **4.23–4.25**) whereas cl 4(2) of the 1988 Agreement only provided for a reduction in circumstances where a claimant had actually received compensation elsewhere.

Chapter 7

UNIDENTIFIED OR UNTRACED OWNER OR USER

A. INTRODUCTION

[7.01] Prior to the 1988 Agreement, the liability of the MIBI was confined to paying compensation for personal injury or death caused by the negligent driving of an uninsured motorist. The 1988 Agreement broadened the liability of the MIBI by requiring it to pay compensation for personal injury or death caused by the negligent driving of a vehicle whose owner or user remained unidentified or untraced. The 2004 Agreement continued to exclude the recovery of compensation for property damage caused by an unidentified vehicle.[1] Under the 2009 Agreement, however, compensation for property damage caused by an unidentified vehicle is excluded unless compensation for substantial personal injuries involving an inpatient hospital stay for five days or more has also been paid in respect of the event causing the damage.[2]

B. EUROPEAN BACKGROUND

[7.02] The 1988 Agreement was drafted as part of the implementation of the Second Directive. The recitals to the Second Directive acknowledge the necessity for a body to guarantee that an accident victim does not remain without compensation 'where the vehicle which caused the accident is uninsured or unidentified.'[3] In pursuit of this objective, art 1(4), subparagraph 4, of the Second Directive provided:

> 'Each Member State shall set up or authorize a body with the task of providing compensation, at least up to the limits of the insurance obligation for damage to property or personal injuries caused by an unidentified vehicle or a vehicle for which the insurance obligation provided for in paragraph 1[4] has not been satisfied.'[5]

C. COMPENSATION UNDER 2009 AGREEMENT FOR DAMAGE BY UNIDENTIFIED VEHICLES

[7.03] Clause 6 of the 2009 Agreement provides:

> 'The liability of MIBI shall, subject to the exclusions of Clause 5[6] above, extend to the payment of compensation for the personal injury or death of any person caused

---

1. Clause 7.1 of the 2004 Agreement.
2. Clause 7.1 of the 2009 Agreement (and subject to an excess of €500).
3. The Second Directive, Sixth Recital (now Sixth Directive, fourteenth Recital).
4. The Second Directive, art 1(1) , refers to the compulsory insurance requirements imposed by the First Directive, art 3(1).
5. The Second Directive, art 1(4) was amended by the Third Directive, art 3 and the Fifth Directive, art 2. This is now contained in Sixth Directive, art 10(1).
6. Clause 5 is entitled 'Exclusion of certain user and passenger claims'. See **Ch 3**.

by the negligent use of a vehicle in a public place, where the owner or user of the vehicle remains unidentified or untraced.'[7]

[7.04] Clause 7.1 of the 2009 Agreement provides:

'The liability for damage to property shall not extend to damage caused by an unidentified vehicle unless compensation for substantial personal injuries involving an inpatient hospital stay for five days or more has also been paid in respect of the event causing the damage subject to an excess of €500.

Prior to the 2009 Agreement, property damage caused by an unidentified vehicle was not recoverable in any circumstances.

D. PROCEDURE FOR BRINGING A CLAIM AGAINST THE MIBI FOR PERSONAL INJURY CAUSED BY A VEHICLE WHOSE OWNER AND OR USER REMAINS UNIDENTIFIED OR UNTRACED

[7.05] A person who suffers personal injury caused by a vehicle, whose owner or user remains unidentified or untraced, may claim compensation from the MIBI.[8] A claimant in respect of an accident caused or contributed to by an 'untraced motorist' must make himself available for interview by the MIBI and must answer all reasonable questions relating to the circumstances of the accident.[9] If the MIBI refuses to compensate the claimant or the claimant is dissatisfied with the offer of compensation made to him, he must give the MIBI advance notification of his intention to institute proceedings.[10]

[7.06] The first stage is to make an application to the Injuries Board citing MIBI as a respondent under the terms of the PIAB Act 2003 which, pursuant to s 12(1), provides that unless such an application is made no court proceedings may be brought in respect of the claim.[11]

[7.07] Where proceedings are necessary, cl 2.3 of the 2009 Agreement provides that the MIBI is to be cited as co-defendant in proceedings against the owner and/or user of the vehicle giving rise to the claim *except* where the owner *and* user of the vehicle remain unidentified or untraced. In other words, where an accident occurs involving only an unidentified or untraced owner and user, a claimant may sue the MIBI as sole defendant. Where, however, an accident occurs involving more than one vehicle and it is alleged that part of the blame lay with a vehicle, the owner and user of which remains unidentified or untraced, separate proceedings must issue against the MIBI in relation to the unidentified or untraced owner and user.[12] This means that two sets of proceedings arising out of the one accident must be issued, ie one against the MIBI and the other

---

7. See also cl 6 of the 2004 Agreement.
8. Clause 6 of the 2009 and 2004 Agreements. For the procedure in respect of making a claim for compensation see **Ch 4**.
9. Clause 3.3 of the 2009 and 2004 Agreements.
10. See **Ch 4** generally.
11. Clause 2.2 of the 2009 Agreement (see **Ch 10** generally). For obvious reasons, no reference was made to the Injuries Board in the 2004 Agreement.
12. See further below at **Section E**.

against the identified motorist(s).[13] The rationale behind this is that if any blame is apportioned against the identified motorist(s) it would be his/their insurer(s) or possibly an insurer concerned who would compensate the plaintiff,[14] rather than the claim being met from MIBI funds.

[7.08] This issue was considered by the Supreme Court in *O'Flynn v Buckley*.[15] This was a fatal claim arising out of an accident involving two motor vehicles which collided with the deceased. The plaintiff claimed that the deceased had been struck by the first defendant (who was uninsured) and then by the second defendant. The first defendant contended that the deceased had been struck by an untraced and unidentified motorist before the first defendant collided with him. In these circumstances, the MIBI was joined in respect of the first defendant's uninsured driving and the driving of the untraced and unidentified motorist that the first defendant claimed had also struck the deceased. In an application to have the plaintiff's claim against it dismissed, the MIBI submitted that cl 2 of the 1988 Agreement did not permit the MIBI to be joined as a co-defendant where there was also a case being made against an untraced driver. The plaintiff submitted that the court was entitled to direct the disjoinder of the issues prior to the trial and that the MIBI had delayed four years in moving for relief and as such was disentitled to it. Both the High Court (Johnson J) and the Supreme Court held against the MIBI and found that the interests of justice and the legitimate concerns of the MIBI could have been met by providing for the disjoinder of issues pursuant to Order 18 of the Rules of the Superior Court 1986 but the delay, in moving for relief, was such as to disentitle the MIBI to disjoinder.

[7.09] While this decision was very much decided on its particular facts, it provides some comfort for litigants who have joined the MIBI as co-defendants when it should have sued it separately on the basis that the owner and user were unidentified or untraced. In *O'Flynn*, Kearns J (as he then was)[16] in the Supreme Court distinguished the unreported cases which had been relied on by the MIBI.[17] Noting the unusual facts of this case where there was a combination of insured and uninsured drivers, and the possible involvement of an untraced driver, he noted that the difficulty arose because the MIBI was effectively wearing two different hats, one as the body responsible to compensate the plaintiff in respect of an untraced motorist and the other in relation to an uninsured but identified driver. He did however state that the MIBI was correct in

---

13. For the purposes of this discussion, 'identified motorist' encompasses the identified owner and/or user. Indeed, if one or more of the identified motorists are uninsured ('uninsured motorist'), then apart from naming the MIBI as sole defendant in any proceedings in relation to the unidentified and untraced owner and user, the MIBI will also be a necessary co-defendant to proceedings against the uninsured motorist.

14. Pursuant to what is colloquially referred to as 'the 1% rule'. See **Ch 8**.

15. *O'Flynn v Buckley* [2009] 3 IR 311.

16. With whom Denham and Hardiman JJ agreed.

17. *Devereux v Minister for Finance and the MIBI* (10 February 1998, unreported) HC, O'Sullivan J, and *Kavanagh v Reilly and the MIBI* (14 October 1997, unreported) HC, Morris J. Both these decisions were *ex tempore* and in respect of which there are no written judgments, but both are referred to by Jones in 'Counsel's note: "Citing the MIBI of Ireland as a co-defendant"' 3(9) 1998 *Bar Review* 450.

requiring a litigant's respect for the strict conditions laid down in the MIBI Agreement as a pre-condition to the recovery of compensation. Notwithstanding this, he stated:

> 'I am satisfied that the interests of justice and all the legitimate concerns of the MIBI would be met by an order prior to trial providing for the disjoinder of issues under O.18 of the Rules of the Superior Court 1986. In my view it would on the facts of this case, be a superfluous requirement verging upon the absurd to require the plaintiffs to institute a second set of proceedings where the MIBI had been validly joined in a particular capacity in the first instance and where the possible involvement of an untraced motorist had been flagged from the time of the originating letter notifying the claims to the MIBI without any suggestion from the MIBI that a second set of proceedings might be necessary. On the face of it, there was, and is, no irregularity in the form and constitution of the proceedings'.[18]

[7.10] A claimant who sues the MIBI for compensation for injury caused by a vehicle 'the owner and user of which remain unidentified or untraced' must name the MIBI as the sole defendant.[19]

E. TWO ACTIONS MAY BE NECESSARY

[7.11] If a claimant considers that responsibility for his injuries lies between a vehicle (the owner and user of which remain unidentified or untraced) and any other identified persons, and the MIBI refuses to adequately compensate the claimant, he will be required to bring two actions[20]. In this regard, cl 2.2 of the 2009 Agreement provides that a person claiming compensation under the Agreement '*must*' seek to enforce the provisions thereof, *inter alia,* by:

> 'citing the MIBI as co-defendants in any proceedings against the owner and/or user of the vehicle giving rise to the claim *except* where the owner and user of the vehicle remain unidentified or untraced.'

F. NEGLIGENCE AS A CONDITION PRECEDENT

[7.12] In *Rothwell v MIBI*,[21] the plaintiff submitted that it was unnecessary to prove negligence on the part of the driver of an unidentified vehicle as a condition precedent to

---

18. At p 320.
19. Clause 2.3 of the 2009 Agreement provides that a claimant may cite the MIBI 'as co-defendants in any proceedings against the owner and/or user of the vehicle giving rise to the claim except where the owner and user of the vehicle remain unidentified and untraced'. This suggests that where *either* the owner or user is actually identified and traced, the claimant may sue that owner or user and the MIBI as co-defendants. This procedure was adopted in *Breslin v Corcoran and MIBI* (17 July 2001, unreported) HC, Butler J, [2003] 2 IR 203 (Supreme Court), (see also Clause 2.2 of the 2004 Agreement).
20. See **Chs 10** and **11**. See also the decisions in *O'Flynn v Buckley* [2009] 3 IR 311, *Kavanagh v Reilly and MIBI* (14 June 1997, unreported) HC, *ex tempore,* Morris P, *Devereux v Minister for Finance and MIBI* (10 February 1998, unreported) HC, *ex tempore,* O'Sullivan J (see Jones, 'Counsel's note: "Citing the MIBI of Ireland as a co-defendant"', 3(9) 1998 *Bar Review* 450), *Feeney v Dwane and O'Connor* and *Feeney v MIBI* (30 July 1999, unreported) HC, *ex tempore,* Johnson J, *Bowes v MIBI* [2000] 2 IR 79 and *Byrne v Bus Átha Cliath and MIBI* [2005] IEHC 20, O'Leary J.
21. *Rothwell v MIBI* [2003] 1 IR 268, *per* Hardiman J (Murray and Geoghegan JJ concurring) and also at [2003] 1 ILRM 521.

succeeding in an action against the MIBI. The plaintiff claimed that it was sufficient to show he was caused personal injury by an unidentified vehicle. This submission was made on the basis that art 1(4) of the Second Directive did not refer to negligence and required each Member State to establish a body that would be responsible for compensating persons who are caused injuries by an uninsured or unidentified vehicle. The plaintiff submitted that this obligation was enforceable against the MIBI because it was an emanation of the State. Having noted that a similar contention failed in the United Kingdom in *White v MIB*,[22] the Supreme Court declined to consider the argument because the point was not argued in the High Court. The Court commented, however, that if this contention was accepted, it would result in a situation whereby a plaintiff injured by an identified and insured defendant would be required to prove negligence whereas one injured by an unidentified or uninsured vehicle would not be so required.[23]

G. NEGLIGENT DRIVING

[7.13] The phrase 'negligent driving'[24] was considered by the Supreme Court in *Rothwell v MIBI*.[25] The plaintiff lost control of his car, left the correct carriageway and struck an oncoming vehicle. He claimed that he was caused to do so as a result of skidding on an oil spillage on the road and that the spillage was caused by the negligent driving of an unidentified or untraced owner and user. The High Court held that, while the origin of the spillage was unknown, its most likely cause was a truck on which the fuel tank cover was missing, defective or improperly fitted and that the spillage was caused by a sudden movement of the truck. Having accepted that there was no evidence as to why the spillage occurred, the High Court noted that it could have occurred with or without negligence on the part of the truck driver.

[7.14] On this basis, the High Court rejected the plaintiff's assertion of *res ipsa loquitur*.[26] It accepted that the plaintiff did not, and could not, know what happened. It was satisfied that the accident was probably caused by a fuel spillage and that there were circumstances in which this could constitute negligent driving by the driver of the spilling truck. The High Court noted that the plaintiff could not prove any matter beyond

---

22. *White v MIB* [2001] 2 CMLR 1, [2001] 2 All ER 43.
23. *Rothwell v MIBI* [2003] 1 IR 268 at 277. The ECJ has held, however, that the Member States have been afforded a freedom by the directives to determine the type of civil liability applicable to road traffic accidents, see *Ferreira and Ferreira v Companhia de Seguros Mundial Confianca SA* (Case C–348/98) [2000] ECR I–06711 (at paras 27–29) and considered in **Ch 2**, at para **2.30** and **Ch 12** at para **12.18**.
24. As noted above, cl 6 of the 2009 Agreement (and the 2004 Agreement) provides for the payment of compensation in circumstances of 'negligent use' as opposed to 'negligent driving' which is the terminology used in the 1988 Agreement. Neither phrase appears in the Second Directive which is concerned with damage or injury 'caused by' unidentified or inadequately insured or uninsured vehicles.
25. *Rothwell v MIBI* [2003] 1 IR 268, [2003] 1 ILRM 521. See also, [2001] IEHC 103 (6 July 2001, unreported) HC, McCracken J.
26. *Rothwell v MIBI* [2003] 1 IR 268 at p 273 of the Supreme Court judgment. The High Court did observe, however, that if the defendant was known and identified, there was sufficient evidence to shift the onus on to him to show that the spillage had occurred under circumstances that did not constitute negligence on his part (at p 273).

this and that the MIBI could not provide an explanation that might excuse liability on the part of the unidentified or untraced driver. The High Court considered, however, that a situation whereby a plaintiff would not receive compensation unless he could prove that the unidentified or untraced driver could not have any defence would be contrary to the 1988 Agreement. It noted that the plaintiff would not bear such a burden if he knew the identity of the driver. The High Court found in favour of the plaintiff.

[7.15] The Supreme Court allowed the appeal. It deemed the net issue to be whether a condition precedent to the MIBI's liability under the 1988 Agreement was established, namely whether or not there was evidence of negligent driving of the unidentified vehicle.[27] Having noted that neither party could go any further than the trial judge's findings that the spillage might have arisen with or without negligence on the truck driver's part and that the plaintiff bore the burden of proof, the Supreme Court held that the plaintiff was bound to lose unless the deficiency in his case was compensated by some presumption or rule of law in his favour.[28]

[7.16] The Supreme Court was satisfied that there was no ambiguity in the 1988 Agreement that might justify the admission of extrinsic evidence to aid its construction. The Agreement did not identify the MIBI with the unidentified person at any stage prior to the time at which the plaintiff fulfilled the conditions precedent to the MIBI's liability. The Supreme Court emphasised the establishment of negligent driving as a condition precedent to the MIBI's liability.[29] In its absence, the plaintiff could not discharge the burden of proof and the MIBI was not liable. Hardiman J. stated:

> 'Negligence in the driving of the unknown vehicle by the untraced driver is a condition precedent to the liability of the [MIBI]. There is no proof of negligence

---

27.   *Rothwell v MIBI* [2003] 1 IR 268 at p 274. Hardiman J noted that the parties made submissions as to the scope of 'driving' and as to whether or not it extended to improperly securing a fuel tank cap and whether it had the same meaning in the Agreement as it had in the road traffic legislation. Hardiman J, however, concluded that none of these issues was central to the principle question of '[was] there evidence of negligence?'.

28.   *Rothwell v MIBI* [2003] 1 IR 268 at p 274. The Supreme Court rejected the plaintiff's argument that the doctrine of *res ipsa loquitur* applied. Having noted that there was no cross appeal against the High Court's finding that proof that the accident was caused by a fuel spillage did not give rise to an inference of negligence on the basis of *res ipsa loquitur* (at p 273), the Supreme Court considered the evolution of the doctrine of *res ipsa loquitur* (at pp 274–276). It noted that, in certain circumstances, pursuant to *Hanrahan v Merck Sharp & Dohme* [1988] ILRM 629, the onus of proof may shift in civil litigation. The Supreme Court in *Rothwell* considered that, in order to shift the onus to a defendant in respect of a certain matter, *Hanrahan* required that the matter must be within the defendant's exclusive knowledge and 'peculiarly within the range of the defendant's capacity of proof'. The Supreme Court noted that this was not the position in *Rothwell* and, as the High Court held, neither party could go further. The matter was not within the knowledge, exclusive or otherwise, of either of them and this situation could exist whether the defendant was the MIBI or an individual owner (at p 276).

29.   *Rothwell v MIBI* [2003] 1 IR 268 at p 276. Contrast this with the decision of Denning LJ in *Elizabeth v MIB* [1981] RTR 405. In that case the plaintiff was riding his motor cycle behind a van which stopped suddenly and the motorcycle collided with its rear. The van driver drove away and was untraced. Overturning the arbitrator's decision, Denning LJ held that the burden of proving why the van driver braked suddenly was on the van driver and he had not stopped, reported the accident or given evidence and accordingly had not discharged the burden of showing that he had stopped for good reason.

and (as I have held) the onus of proof in this regard is not shifted. If it is unjust that the plaintiff should carry an onus of proof which, practically speaking, he cannot discharge, it would be equally unjust that the defendant should do so. The agreement provides for the circumstances in which, alone, liability is to be attributed to the [MIBI] for the negligence of an unknown person. In the absence of proved causative negligence on the part of that person, the defendant has no liability. The agreement does not, in my view, identify the [MIBI] with the unknown person at any stage prior to demonstration that the conditions precedent to its liability have been met.'[30]

H. NO NEED TO ESTABLISH A NEGATIVE

[7.17] In *Lynch v MIBI*[31] the plaintiff claimed that his van skidded as a result of an oil spillage caused by an unknown driver of an untraced vehicle. The High Court rejected the MIBI's contention that it was incumbent upon the plaintiff to prove that the vehicle that deposited the oil was not an 'exempted person'.[32] Macken J considered that the interpretation of the 1988 Agreement contended for by the MIBI was unduly restrictive. She noted that to give the 1988 Agreement this effect would result in plaintiffs never being able to recover in hit and run accidents.[33]

[7.18] On the facts of this particular case, the court was satisfied on the balance of probabilities that the oil spillage which caused the plaintiff to lose control came from a vehicle travelling along the road and losing oil. The first proposition put forward by the plaintiff's engineers as to how the oil escaped was that the oil cap had not been replaced correctly. The second possible route of escape was a leaking valve of some type. Macken J stated:

'While there is no clear factual evidence available upon which to conclude that either alternative was the definite cause of oil on the roadway, I am of the view that the plaintiff has established, on the balance of probabilities, sufficient facts which, at least on the second proposition put forward on his behalf, would constitute negligence, the first being also reasonably possible, but perhaps less likely. Unlike the case of Rothwell ..., the circumstances are not those in which the oil spillage is a single spill, nor a small spill of about a few pints, as in that case, nor of circumstances in which the spillage could reasonably have occurred with or without negligence on the part of the unidentified driver of the untraced vehicle. The preponderance of the evidence is such as to suggest a spillage of the type in question, over the distance involved, would have been or ought to have been noticed by the driver of the vehicle.

---

30.   *Rothwell v MIBI* [2003] 1 IR 268 at p 276. See also *Rogers v MIBI* [2009] IESC 30 (31 March 2009) SC and see also [2003] IEHC 142 (5 December 2003, unreported) HC, Herbert J.

31.   *Lynch v MIBI* [2005] IEHC 184 (10 May 2005, unreported) HC, Macken J.

32.   Compulsory insurance under the Road Traffic Act 1961 is not required for exempted persons (s 56(1) and defined in the Road Traffic Act 1961, s 60(1)) and currently include Dublin Bus, Bus Éireann and Iarnród Éireann (see **Ch 2**).

33.   Macken J noted that such an interpretation would hardly comply with the objectives of the Second Directive which was introduced for the purpose of ensuring a body existed to guarantee that the victims of injury would not remain without compensation where the vehicle which caused the accident was unidentified (p 7).

Having regard to the foregoing matters established, I am satisfied that the Plaintiff has established negligence on the part of the untraced driver.'[34]

[7.19] While at first blush this finding appears to be at odds with *Rothwell,* it was decided very much on its own particular facts. Thus, a plaintiff may still succeed in a case where he claims that he crashed as a result of an oil spill caused by an untraced motorist, provided he can prove that an untraced motorist probably negligently caused the spill.

I. CAUSATION – STOLEN MOTOR CAR

[7.20] In *Breslin v Corcoran and MIBI,*[35] the first defendant left his car unlocked and with the keys in the ignition. An untraced driver stole the car and negligently collided with the plaintiff. The plaintiff sued the MIBI, pursuant to cls 2(2) and 6 of the 1988 Agreement,[36] and the car owner. The defendants agreed that the plaintiff was entitled to recover against one or other of them. The net issue was which of them was liable to the plaintiff.

[7.21] The High Court accepted the owner's assertion that, although he was negligent and in breach of statutory duty in leaving the car as he did, the acts of the untraced driver broke the chain of causation between the owner's negligence and the plaintiff's injuries. The High Court considered that liability could not be imposed on the car owner in the absence of evidence that he had left it in an area where it should have been known to him that people routinely stole cars for the purpose of driving them around in a reckless and dangerous fashion. The High Court awarded damages against the MIBI and the MIBI appealed.

[7.22] The MIBI asserted that the owner was negligent in circumstances where it was probable that the car would be stolen and asserted that it was reasonably foreseeable that the thief would injure someone. The Supreme Court dismissed the appeal. While it was reasonably foreseeable that the unattended car would be stolen, it was not reasonably foreseeable that it would be driven negligently.[37]

[7.23] Having recited the principles relevant to determining whether or not a duty of care arises in a particular case,[38] the Court noted that, in addition to foreseeability and

---

34. *Lynch v MIBI* [2005] IEHC 184 (10 May 2005, unreported) HC, Macken J at p 33.

35. *Breslin v Corcoran and MIBI* [2001] IEHC 238, (17 July 2001, unreported) HC, Butler J, [2003] 2 IR 203 (Supreme Court).

36. Clause 6 of the 1988 Agreement renders the MIBI liable for injury caused by the negligent driving of a vehicle in a public place, 'where the owner or user of the vehicle remain unidentified or untraced.' Clause 6 of the 2009 Agreement contains the same provision, save that it refers to 'negligent use' as opposed to 'negligent driving'.

37. *Breslin v Corcoran and MIBI* [2003] 2 IR 203. The Court delivered a unanimous judgment *per* Fennelly J (Denham and Murray JJ concurring).

38. The Court approved of a passage from *Glencar Explorations Ltd v Mayo County Council (No 2)* [2002] 1 IR 84 where Keane CJ considered that there was no reason why the courts should feel compelled to hold, in the absence of powerful public policy considerations, that a duty arose in every case in which reasonable foreseeability and proximity were established (at 139).

proximity, it was natural to have regard to considerations of fairness, justice and reasonableness in ruling on the existence of a duty of care.[39] It was necessary to have regard to all the relevant circumstances and consider whether it was probable that the unattended car, if taken, would be driven so carelessly as to cause damage to others. It could not be seriously disputed that it was reasonably foreseeable, as well as likely, that the unattended car, with its keys in the ignition, would be stolen. The Court considered that this act in a busy city street was, in the absence of mitigating circumstances, an act of gross carelessness. However, the plaintiff's injury was not caused by the fact that the car was taken. It was caused by the 'negligent driving' of its thief.

[7.24] The Supreme Court held that, in order to impose liability on the car owner, it would have to be shown that, in addition to foreseeing the theft, he should have foreseen the negligent driving.[40] Fennelly J. stated:

> 'A person is not normally liable, if he has committed an act of carelessness, where the damage has been directly caused by the intervening independent act of another person, for whom he is not otherwise vicariously responsible. Such liability may exist, where the damage caused by that other person was the very kind of thing which he was bound to expect and guard against and the resulting damage was likely to happen, if he did not.'[41]

[7.25] There would have to be some basis in the evidence for finding that the car, if stolen, was likely to be driven in such a way as to endanger others. The Supreme Court observed that cars may be stolen for reasons which do not carry such implications (eg theft for resale) and dismissed the appeal on the basis that there was no evidence to suggest that the car owner should have anticipated as a reasonable probability that the car, if stolen, would be driven so carelessly as to cause injury to another road user.[42] Thus, the plaintiff was entitled to recover from the MIBI.

J. ONUS AND STANDARD OF PROOF WHERE UNIDENTIFIED OR UNTRACED OWNER OR USER

[7.26] In *Bennett v MIBI*[43] the High Court recognised the ease with which a plaintiff might sue the MIBI for personal injury caused by an unidentified vehicle and driver and present a story that could not be contradicted. The Court commented upon the very high onus on such a plaintiff to satisfy a court that everything he says is true.[44] Morris J considered that one must view the plaintiff 'in a critical light to be sure and to be certain on a high balance of probabilities that what he is telling the Court is true'.[45] The Court

---

39. *Breslin v Corcoran and MIBI* [2003] 2 IR 203, at p 208.
40. *Breslin v Corcoran and MIBI* [2003] 2 IR 203, pp 214–215.
41. *Breslin v Corcoran and MIBI* [2003] 2 IR 203, p 214.
42. *Breslin v Corcoran and MIBI* [2003] 2 IR 203, p 215.
43. *Bennett v MIBI* (22 April 1994, unreported) HC, *ex tempore,* Morris J.
44. *Bennett v MIBI* (22 April 1994, unreported) HC, *ex tempore,* Morris J at p 1 of the transcript of the judgment.
45. *Bennett v MIBI* (22 April 1994, unreported) HC, *ex tempore,* Morris J at p 2 of the transcript of the judgment. While Morris J (as he then was) referred to a 'high balance of probabilities', it is submitted that the standard of proof on a plaintiff suing in respect of the actions of an untraced or unidentified motorist is the same as that which is borne in civil litigation generally, namely the balance of probabilities. (contd .../)

dismissed the plaintiff's action for damages for injuries caused by an untraced driver by reference, *inter alia,* to the fact that the plaintiff's evidence of the date of the accident and what he had been doing prior to the accident did not correspond with his hospital records. In addition, the court attached some significance to the plaintiff's failure to report the incident of dangerous driving that was alleged to have caused the relevant collision.[46]

[7.27] In *Walsh v MIBI,*[47] the plaintiff claimed that he suffered injury when, while driving on a narrow road at night, he was approached by an oncoming vehicle driving on the incorrect side of the road. He claimed that this compelled him to take evasive action by pulling to the left and, thereafter, his right outside mirror was hit and dislodged by the oncoming untraced vehicle.[48] The MIBI denied that there was another car. Alternatively, it claimed that the driver of the other car was not negligent. The court considered that the onus of proof was the 'normal civil onus' but noted that:

> 'It is important that a court should be extra careful in assessing the truth, accuracy or otherwise of the evidence of a plaintiff. Because no opposing story will be heard. It follows therefore that independent evidence assumes a particular importance.'[49]

[7.28] Having heard evidence from a garda sergeant who inspected the locus, the Court was satisfied that there was another car and that the plaintiff's outside mirror was struck. The Court also accepted the sergeant's evidence, however, that he found tyre marks from the plaintiff's vehicle over the centre of the road and on the wrong side of the road. On this basis, the Court held that the accident was not caused by the negligent driving of the mystery car.[50]

[7.29] In *Buckley v MIBI,*[51] the plaintiff appealed against the High Court's dismissal of his claim arising out of an oncoming vehicle travelling on the incorrect side of the road and forcing him to swerve off the road. The plaintiff claimed that the car did not stop and was untraced. The Supreme Court accepted the reality that the defendant could have no witnesses and noted that:

> '[i]t was for the Plaintiff to prove that his case is true and to satisfy the learned trial judge on the balance of probabilities that his case is a true case and that on those facts which he alleges he is entitled to succeed.'[52]

---

45.   (contd) A court would obviously, however, have to be vigilant in considering a plaintiff's evidence in circumstances where the defendant (the MIBI) would usually not be in a position to call rebutting evidence.

46.   *Bennett v MIBI* (22 April 1994, unreported) HC, *ex tempore,* Morris J at p 4 of the transcript of the judgment.

47.   *Walsh v MIBI* (15 May 1996, unreported) HC, *ex tempore,* Geoghegan J.

48.   *Walsh v MIBI* (15 May 1996, unreported) HC, *ex tempore,* Geoghegan J, p 3.

49.   *Walsh v MIBI* (15 May 1996, unreported) HC, *ex tempore,* Geoghegan J, p 3.

50.   *Walsh v MIBI* (15 May 1996, unreported) HC, *ex tempore,* Geoghegan J, pp 4–5.

51.   *Buckley v MIBI* (12 November 1997, unreported) SC, *ex tempore, per* Lynch J (Hamilton CJ and Murphy J concurring).

52.   *Buckley v MIBI* (12 November 1997, unreported) SC, p 2.

[7.30] In the transcript of the High Court judgment, however, the trial judge noted that he could only speculate as to what might have happened on the night in question and he was satisfied that the position was not as the plaintiff had made out. In those circumstances, the Supreme Court held that the plaintiff's claim had to fail.[53]

[7.31] In *Kavanagh v MIBI*,[54] submissions were made in the opening of the case regarding the correct standard of proof to be reached by a plaintiff who sued the MIBI in place of an untraced and unidentified motorist. In his judgment, McKechnie J noted that the Supreme Court in *Duffy v MIBI*[55] indicated that the onus was on the plaintiff but *Duffy* did not address the issue of the standard of proof.[56] McKechnie J acknowledged that the decision in *Bennett v MIBI*[57] expressed a view that the plaintiff had to prove his case on 'the higher balance of probability' in such circumstances.[58] While expressly stating that he was not derogating from *Bennett*, McKechnie J found it unnecessary to express a view on that decision because he was satisfied that the plaintiff before him did not meet the normal civil standard and he dismissed his action.

[7.32] In *Rogers v MIBI*,[59] the High Court made an award to the plaintiff in circumstances where the court was satisfied on the balance of probabilities that he was struck by an untraced motorist while he was walking on a public footpath.[60] In allowing the MIBI's appeal, however, the Supreme Court reiterated that the onus is on a claimant against the MIBI to prove negligence. It reaffirmed the *Rothwell*[61] principles and rejected the contention that it was not necessary to prove negligence at all in a claim against the MIBI. Finnegan J stated:

> '... the onus is on the respondent here to satisfy the court of the following:
>
> 1.   That he sustained his injuries as a result of being struck by a motor vehicle, the owner or user of which is unidentified or untraced.
> 2.   That the owner or user was negligent.
>
> The legal burden of proof in all civil cases lies upon the person who asserts the affirmative on each issue in the case. If at the completion of the evidence the burden has not been discharged the decision must go against the party on whom the burden lay. To find for the plaintiff in an action such as the present the judge must be satisfied on the evidence that a particular fact or state of affairs is more likely to have occurred than not. If he is not so satisfied then he must find that the burden has not been discharged.' [62]

---

53.   *Buckley v MIBI* (12 November 1997, unreported) SC, p 4.
54.   *Kavanagh v MIBI* (22 February 2001, unreported) HC, *ex tempore,* McKechnie J.
55.   *Duffy v MIBI* (12 November 1997, unreported) SC.
56.   At pp 4–5 of the transcript of the judgment in *Kavanagh v MIBI* (22 February 2001, unreported) HC, *ex tempore,* McKechnie J.
57.   *Bennett v MIBI* (22 April 1994, unreported) HC, *ex tempore,* Morris J, .
58.   At p 5 of the transcript of the judgment in *Kavanagh v MIBI* (22 February 2001, unreported) HC, *ex tempore,* McKechnie J.
59.   *Rogers v MIBI* [2009] IESC 30 (31 March 2009, unreported) SC and see also [2003] IEHC 142 (5 December 2003, unreported) HC, Herbert J.
60.   At pp 23–24 and 31.
61.   *Rogers v MIBI* [2009] IESC 30 (31 March 2009, unreported) SC at p 30.
62.   *Rogers v MIBI* [2009] IESC 30 (31 March 2009, unreported) SC at p 23.

[7.33] On the facts of the case, the respondent had not discharged the onus of proof. There were a number of factual matters that were all unanswered by the evidence adduced at the trial. Finnegan J held that it was not permissible to resort to conjecture to answer unanswered questions and *res ipsa loquitur* did not apply on the facts. The respondent had failed to establish causation as a matter of probability and his claim had to fail.

Chapter 8

THE '1% RULE'

A. CONCURRENT WRONGDOERS

[8.01] Section 11(1) of the Civil Liability Act 1961 (the 1961 Act), provides that, for the purpose of Pt III of the 1961 Act:[1]

> 'two or more persons are concurrent wrongdoers when both or all are wrongdoers and are responsible to a [plaintiff] for the same damage, whether or not judgment has been recovered against some or all of them.'[2]

[8.02] Section 11(2) of the 1961 Act provides:

> 'Without prejudice to the generality of [s. 11(1)] –
>
> (a)　persons may become concurrent wrongdoers as a result of vicarious liability of one for another, breach of joint duty, conspiracy, concerted action to a common end or independent acts causing the same damage;
>
> (b)　the wrong on the part of one or both may be a tort, breach of contract or breach of trust, or any combination of them;
>
> (c)　it is immaterial whether the acts constituting concurrent wrongs are contemporaneous or successive.'

[8.03] Section 12(1) of the 1961 Act provides, *inter alia,* that, subject to other provisions of the 1961 Act, 'concurrent wrongdoers are each liable for the whole of the damage in respect of which they are concurrent wrongdoers'.

[8.04] Section 13 of the 1961 Act provides that 'an action may be brought against all concurrent wrongdoers or against any of them without joining the other or others'. Section 14 deems concurrent wrongdoers jointly and severally liable.

[8.05] The effect of the foregoing provisions has given rise to the term 'the 1% rule'.[3] This means that if a plaintiff sues two defendants who are concurrent wrongdoers, in respect of the same damage caused by both of them, and they are both found responsible to some degree for the damage suffered by the plaintiff, the plaintiff may execute the entire judgment against one or other of them. This is notwithstanding the fact that one may be found to have more responsibility for the damage than the other. Where a plaintiff is caused damage by an insured and an uninsured defendant, the practical implication of 'the 1% rule' , insofar as the MIBI is concerned, is that, because it has traditionally been 'the payer of last resort',[4] the insured defendant must pay the plaintiff.

1.　Civil Liability Act 1961, Pt III is entitled 'Concurrent Wrongdoers'.

2.　See *Moloney v Liddy & Ors (t/a Hughes & Liddy Solicitors)* [2010] 4 IR 653 (*per* Clarke J) for an analysis of 'same damage', in which the court concluded that there was a real, substantial and significant difference between the damages claimed by the plaintiff against (a) his former solicitors for professional negligence for failing to issue proceedings against his former architects prior to the expiration of the relevant limitation period and (b) his former architects for alleged negligence in the construction of a house.

3.　Sometimes referred to in England as 'the rule of meaningful degree'.

4.　*Bowes v MIBI* [2000] 2 IR 79 and see paras **8.16–8.17** below.

[8.06] A co-defendant can, however, obtain some protection by serving a notice of indemnity and contribution on the other co-defendant(s) to the proceedings if the co-defendant(s) is/are a concurrent wrongdoer(s).[5] If a judgment entered against two or more defendants is enforced against one of the defendants, then, provided that the defendant against whom the judgment has been enforced has served a notice(s) of indemnity and contribution on the other(s), the defendant against whom the judgment is enforced can recover a contribution from the other co-defendant(s) in proportion to the degree to which the other co-defendant(s) was or were deemed liable for the damage. Obviously, it is worthwhile for a co-defendant to pursue such a concurrent wrongdoer where the latter is a mark for damages.

B. CONSTITUTIONALITY OF SECTIONS 12 AND 14 OF THE CIVIL LIABILITY ACT 1961

[8.07] The constitutionality of ss 12 and 14 of the 1961 Act was tested in *Iarnród Éireann v Ireland*.[6] This was a case in which Iarnród Éireann and a cattle owner/farmer were held 30% and 70% liable respectively in proceedings brought by passengers in a train that derailed following its collision with a herd of cattle. As the cattle owner/farmer was a person without significant means, the effect of ss 12 and 14 of the 1961 Act was that Iarnród Éireann was obliged to compensate the injured passengers for all the damage they had sustained, even though it was only responsible for 30% of the damage. This case reiterated the common law position that concurrent wrongdoers are liable for the whole of the damage in respect of which they are concurrent wrongdoers. Thus a plaintiff who obtains a judgment jointly and severally against more than one defendant may enforce the whole judgment against any one of them. Pursuant to the notice of indemnity and contribution served by Iarnród Éireann on the cattle owner/farmer, Iarnród Éireann could, however, pursue the latter for 70% of the money that it paid to the plaintiff.

C. THE MIBI: NEVER A CONCURRENT WRONGDOER

[8.08] It is submitted that the MIBI does not fall within the statutory definition of a concurrent wrongdoer. Its liability to satisfy an award of damages derives only from the various agreements that it has entered into over the years with various government ministers.[7, 8]

[8.09] Where a plaintiff suffers injury in a single accident that is caused by an insured motorist and an uninsured motorist (ie they are concurrent wrongdoers), then the

---

5.   Civil Liability Act 1961, s 21.

6.   *Iarnród Éireann v Ireland* [1996] 3 IR 321.

7.   The MIBI concluded the 1955 Agreement (and the 1962 addendum thereto) and the 1964 Agreement with the Minister for Local Government, the 1988 Agreement with the Minister for the Environment and the 2004 and 2009 Agreements with the Minister for Transport.

8.   Curiously, in *Yang v MIBI and Xiang* [2009] IEHC 318, (17 July 2009, unreported) HC, Quirke J, which concerned a claim brought by a passenger in a car being driven without insurance by the second defendant, it appears from the judgment that the defendants admitted that the plaintiff was entitled to recover damages from both of them on a joint and several basis (at p 2).

plaintiff will normally proceed against three persons: firstly, the insured motorist; secondly, the uninsured motorist; and thirdly, the MIBI.[9] However, assuming that a court is likely to hold that the uninsured motorist was 70% liable and the insured motorist 30% liable, the MIBI is likely to resist the compensation claim or defend proceedings against it, even if it is clear that a finding of some negligence will be made against the uninsured motorist. This is because, as long as some finding of negligence is made against the insured motorist, he and the uninsured motorist are concurrent wrongdoers and the insured motorist will be bound to satisfy the total judgment obtained by the plaintiff.[10] A judgment of this kind will be discharged by the insured motorist's insurer. This insurer is legally obliged to be a member of the MIBI[11] and will be only too familiar with its obligation as a concurrent wrongdoer to discharge the full amount of the judgment. Thus the judgment will be satisfied by the insurer and the issue of the MIBI's liability to discharge an unsatisfied award will not arise.[12]

[8.10] *Lindsay v Finnerty, Kelly and the MIBI*[13] is a very useful recent example of how the rules in relation to concurrent wrongdoers (and how the MIBI is not categorised as one) operate in practice. In this case, the plaintiff had spent the evening in the company of the first and second defendants and, at the conclusion of which, the plaintiff suggested that all three of them return to his home nearby. The plaintiff travelled as a passenger in a car driven by the first defendant, who, it transpired, was uninsured ('the uninsured'). The second defendant ('the insured') drove his own car behind the uninsured and for a distance had the uninsured in his sight until another car got between them. While en route, the uninsured's car drove too close to the left hand edge of the road and, while endeavouring to correct this, it went out of control, hit a wall and ultimately ended up stationery and facing the direction in which the insured's car was

---

9. This example assumes that each motorist also owned the vehicle that he was driving. In the event that any motorist does not own the vehicle being driven by him, it may also be appropriate to name its owner as a co-defendant (Road Traffic Act 1961, s 118).
10. Civil Liability Act 1961, s 12.
11. See the Road Traffic Act 1961, s 78.
12. In practice, the circumstances are rare in which the damage caused by a number of persons involved in an accident might be discrete to the extent that they are not concurrent wrongdoers.

    In *Hayes v Minister for Finance* [2007] 3 IR 190, the Supreme Court commented upon the fact that McMahon and Binchy, *Irish Law of Torts* (3rd edn, Bloomsbury Professional, 2000) opined that the courts, in recent times, were more likely to settle for a 'multiple cause' finding and apportion losses between concurrent wrongdoers and that it was only in very extreme cases that the nature of a third party's act would break the chain completely between a defendant's original conduct and the plaintiff's damage. In *Hayes*, a motorcyclist (carrying the plaintiff as a pillion passenger) was travelling at high speed and being chased by a garda vehicle when he collided with a third party (who did not cause or contribute to the accident) after the motorcyclist had driven around a bend on the wrong side of the road and where the road bore a continuous white line. The Supreme Court considered that this case was an extreme one of the nature identified by McMahon and Binchy such that the motorcyclist's driving amounted to a *novus actus interveniens* and it was this which caused the plaintiff's injuries.
13. *Lindsay v Finnerty, Kelly and the MIBI* [2011] IEHC 402, (25 October 2011, unreported) HC (*per* Peart J).

travelling. Thereafter, the uninsured's car was hit head-on by the insured's vehicle. The impacts happened in very quick succession.

[8.11] Judgment in default was obtained against the uninsured and the assessment of damages was adjourned to the hearing of the action.

[8.12] One of the issues for the court's determination was whether the collisions were separate accidents or whether the uninsured and the insured were, or were deemed to be, concurrent wrongdoers in terms of s 11 of the 1961 Act. The MIBI argued that, if the insured had any liability, the MIBI would not have been required to provide any indemnity in respect of the uninsured driver on the basis of the so-called '1% rule'.

[8.13] In terms of the evidence, Peart J noted that liability had been determined against the uninsured, insofar as judgment in default had been obtained against him. On the facts, Peart J held that the uninsured was liable to the extent of 80%, the insured was liable for 20% (arising out of the second impact), they were concurrent wrongdoers and they were liable on a joint and several basis.[14]

[8.14] In considering the 1961 Act, Peart J emphasised the fact that s 11(1) defined persons as being concurrent wrongdoers where both or all 'are responsible to ... the plaintiff ... for the same damage'. He considered s 11(2)(a) and (c) to be 'particularly illuminating', insofar as the former provides that 'persons may become concurrent wrongdoers as a result of ... independent acts causing the same damage' and the latter providing that 'it is immaterial whether the acts constituting concurrent wrongs are contemporaneous or successive'.[15] Having considered the foregoing, Peart J stated:

> '21 ... It is clear from [s 11(2)(a) and (c)] that if two persons are responsible for the same damage, it matters not firstly that the act of one person is independent of the act of the other, and secondly that the acts take (sic) in succession to each other and not simultaneously. In the present case the available evidence is to the effect that the injuries suffered by the plaintiff may have been caused by either defendant's act or both in combination. In my view that is sufficient to meet [s 11(2)(a)] as it is perfectly possible that each act caused the same damage even if to different degrees. It is clear also that the two acts occurred in close succession, and that is sufficient to meet the provisions of [s 11(2)(c)].'[16]

[8.15] This case is of interest in that there is judicial reference, albeit fleeting, to the so-called '1% rule'. While the term is in common use, there is no legal authority for it. However, as a matter of practicality, if a plaintiff obtains judgment against both an insured and an uninsured defendant, the insured defendant is obliged to satisfy the judgment in full, thereby leaving no unsatisfied judgment in being that the MIBI would

---

14. At p 7. Peart J explained the practical consequences in simple terms 'whereby [the uninsured and the insured] can be pursued for the recovery of damages. Each is liable for the plaintiff's damages and loss, but as concurrent wrongdoers each would be entitled to pursue the other in respect of any portion of those damages and loss which he has had to discharge in respect of the other's share of liability. Put simply, in the present case, the [insured] will be obliged to discharge whatever judgment is awarded to the plaintiff, but would be entitled to seek to pursue the [uninsured] in respect of 80% thereof, should he wish to do so'.

15. At pp 6–7.

16. At p 7.

be required to meet. A failure on the part of the insured defendant's insurers to meet the judgment could result in sanction.[17]

D. THE MIBI: PAYER OF LAST RESORT

[8.16] The MIBI exists for the purpose of, *inter alia,* meeting a judgment that is made against an uninsured motorist and which is not satisfied within 28 days of its making.[18] The 2004 Agreement is the only MIBI agreement that ever expressly referred to the principle that recourse to the MIBI should be taken as a matter of last resort.[19] The principle was, however, previously acknowledged by the judiciary. In *Bowes v MIBI,*[20] Murphy J, with reference to the substance of the MIBI agreements prior to 1988, stated:

> 'Moreover, the procedure ensured that the [MIBI] would be the payer of last resort. Any persons whose negligence contributed to the injuries could be made a defendant by the victim, either at his election or at the direction of the [MIBI], and no matter how small a part the negligence of that defendant played in causing the accident, the fact that the judgment could be recovered against him for the entire amount relieved the [MIBI] of any liability whatever.'[21]

[8.17] The Supreme Court, by a majority of four to one, endorsed the view that the MIBI was the payer of last resort. In delivering the majority judgment, Murphy J held that the liability of the MIBI in respect of the actions of an uninsured motorist was conditional upon the plaintiff proceeding to judgment against the uninsured motorist, unless the MIBI negotiated an acceptable compromise of the plaintiff's claim.[22]

[8.18] While the 2009 Agreement does not explicitly state that the MIBI is the fund of last resort, it remains the case. Indeed in *Churchill Insurance Co Ltd v Wilkinson* and *Evans v Equity Claims Ltd*[23] the ECJ specifically stated:

> 'The payment of compensation by a national body is considered to be a measure of last resort, provided for only in cases in which the vehicle that caused the injury or damage is uninsured or unidentified or has not satisfied the insurance requirements referred to in Article 3(1) of the First Directive.'[24]

---

17.   Pursuant to Road Traffic Act 1961, s 78, the insurer is bound to be a member of the MIBI.
18.   Clause 4.1.1 of the 2009 Agreement and cl 4.1 of the 2004 Agreement.
19.   Clause 13 of the 2004 Agreement, entitled 'Fund of Last Resort', provided '[s]ubject to the generality of the foregoing, the Guarantee Fund is a Fund of Last Resort'.
20.   *Bowes v MIBI* [2000] 2 IR 79.
21.   *Bowes v MIBI* [2000] 2 IR 79 at pp 87–88. However, see the dissenting judgment of Barron J where, in particular at p 99, he appears to state that the MIBI can in certain circumstances be the insurer of first resort.
22.   *Bowes v MIBI* [2000] 2 IR 79 at p 89. Notably, Murphy J considered (albeit *obiter dictum*) that the 1988 Agreement, 'for all its faults and interpreted in the manner which I have indicated' gave full effect to the Second Directive.
23.   *Churchill Insurance Co Ltd v Wilkinson* and *Evans v Equity Claims Ltd* (Joined Cases C–442/10) 1 December 2011 at para 41.
24.   First Directive, art 3(1) is now contained in Sixth Directive, art 3.

[8.19] The 1% rule is more a colloquial term as opposed to a rule of law. It has entered the legal lexicon as it has obvious importance when a plaintiff is suing a number of defendants, one of whom is the MIBI. Where the MIBI is dealing with a claim on behalf of an uninsured driver, or in lieu of a negligent untraced driver, then, in circumstances where there are other defendants,[25] the MIBI will often fight tooth and nail in anticipation of some finding of negligence being made against one of the other defendants. If that happens, and the plaintiff can proceed to enforce the judgment against one of the other defendants, the MIBI is relieved of any obligation to satisfy the plaintiff's judgment, notwithstanding a finding of liability having been made against the uninsured motorist or, in separate proceedings, against the untraced driver.

E. THE MIBI, AN UNINSURED DEFENDANT, AND A NON-MOTORIST AS CO-DEFENDANTS

[8.20] The position of the MIBI as a co-defendant to proceedings brought against it, an uninsured motorist and an insured motorist is considered above. It is noted that the MIBI is likely to defend the proceedings in anticipation that the insured motorist will be found responsible for the accident to some degree and that the plaintiff will recover the judgment from that insured defendant's insurer. However, the position becomes somewhat more complex in circumstances where the MIBI is made a co-defendant to proceedings against it, an uninsured motorist and a *non-motorist* defendant who, by definition, has no relationship with the MIBI, for example a local authority. The issues that arise in the enforcement of judgments obtained in an action of this nature are considered below in **Ch 10**.[26]

F. VISITING VEHICLES FROM OUTSIDE THE STATE: FOREIGN VEHICLES

[8.21] The fact that an accident in Ireland may involve a foreign vehicle does not change Irish domestic law. Accordingly, the provisions of the 1961 Act still apply. The Internal Regulations governing relations between international bureaux recognise this position[27] and allow claims to be handled by a national insurers' bureau in conformity with legal and regulatory provisions applicable in the country of accident.

[8.22] Uncertainty can arise where an accident occurs in which two vehicles are at fault, and one of which is foreign and uninsured. The MIBI takes the view that it is 'deemed insurer' of certain foreign vehicles and will deal with such claims on behalf of the bureau of the country in which the foreign vehicle is 'normally based' and on the basis

---

25. Whether co-defendants in an action that is also brought against the MIBI where there is an uninsured defendant *or* whether there is one action against various insured defendants and a second action against the MIBI in lieu of an untraced motorist.

26. See paras **10.36–10.41**.

27. The Internal Regulations of the Council of Bureau, art 3(4) ('Internal Regulations'), see **Appendix 6** (The Internal Regulations are contained in Appendix I to 2003/564/EC: Commission Decision of 28 July 2003 on the application of Council Directive 72/166/EEC relating to checks on insurance against civil liability in respect of the use of motor vehicles).

that it will ultimately be reimbursed by that national insurers' bureau.[28] However, the 'normally based' concept referred to in Section III of the Internal Regulations 'only [applies] when the relations between bureaux are based on deemed insurance cover ...'. 'Deemed insurance cover' is not defined in the Internal Regulations. The significance is that, if the MIBI is deemed insurer, the MIBI agreements do not apply because a claimant can recover from the MIBI as the insurer of the foreign vehicle,[29] with the MIBI ultimately being reimbursed by the foreign bureau. Indeed, the MIBI itself takes the view that the MIBI agreements have no part to play in foreign vehicle claims although, as a matter of practice, claimants invariably cite the relevant MIBI agreement when dealing with a foreign uninsured vehicle and this would appear to accord with good sense. If it wished, there appears to be no legal reason why the MIBI could not seek to rely on the so-called '1% rule' when dealing with an accident in Ireland caused by an insured Irish vehicle and such a foreign vehicle.[30]

[8.23] 'Deemed' insurer is also referred to in art 8(2) of the Mechanically Propelled Vehicles (International Circulation) Order 1992[31] (the 1992 Order). It provides:

> 'For the purpose of Part VI of the Road Traffic Act, 1961[32]... the following provisions shall apply regarding an international motor insurance card in respect of the use of the vehicle referred to in the said card:
>
> (a)   the said card shall be deemed to be evidence that a certificate issued to the insured named thereon for the period shown thereon as the period of validity in Ireland;
>
> (b)   the [MIBI] shall be deemed to be the vehicle insurer which issued the evidence that a certificate was issued, and to be competent to act as a vehicle insurer;'[33]

[8.24] For the purposes of the 1992 Order, 'international motor insurance card' is defined as meaning 'a duly completed international motor insurance card issued by a bureau or by the [MIBI] in, or substantially in, the form set out in the Schedule to [the 1992] Order'.[34] A 'bureau' is, in effect, defined to refer to a central organisation

---

28.   For a definition, see the Internal Regulations, art 11 Appendix I to 2003/564/EC, (**Appendix 6**). In practice, however, it is common for victims of accidents in Ireland, caused by foreign vehicles, to cite the relevant MIBI agreement, regardless of whether or not the foreign vehicle is in fact insured. Many such victims do not actually know the insurance position in respect of the foreign vehicle when they notify the MIBI.

29.   Pursuant to the Road Traffic Act 1961, s 76, subject to prior notification. See further, **Ch 10**, paras **10.57–10.83**.

30.   Where the foreign vehicle was insured at the time of the accident, the MIBI could be faced with a notice of indemnity from the Irish insurer as the MIBI would be dealing with the claim as deemed insurer (as opposed to under the relevant MIBI agreement, in which case it would not be a concurrent wrongdoer).

31.   Mechanically Propelled Vehicles (International Circulation) Order 1992 (SI 384/1992).

32.   The Road Traffic Act 1961, Pt VI is entitled 'Compulsory Insurance of Mechanically Propelled Vehicles' and comprises ss 56 to 81, inclusive.

33.   Mechanically Propelled Vehicles (International Circulation) Order 1992 (SI 384/1992), art 8(2)(b) is identical to that which was previously contained in the Mechanically Propelled Vehicles (International Circulation) (Amendment) Order (SI 269/1961), art 13(2)(b).

34.   Mechanically Propelled Vehicles (International Circulation) Order 1992 (SI 384/1992), art 4.

established by motor insurers in any country outside the State that is established to perform the same functions as are performed by the MIBI in the State.[35]

[8.25] By way of example, if there was a car pileup caused by two motor vehicles, namely an insured Irish vehicle and a foreign vehicle in respect of which an international motor insurance card of the prescribed nature exists, it seems that the MIBI is deemed insurer in respect of the foreign vehicle. In such circumstances, a plaintiff may recover against the MIBI as the foreign vehicle's insurer.[36] In this way, the MIBI might not avail itself of the 1% rule whereby it could (if it was sued pursuant to one of the MIBI agreements in respect of the actions of an uninsured) avoid having to pay out anything on foot of any judgment that might be entered jointly and severally against the Irish insured and the foreign driver/owner.

[8.26] The position of the MIBI as 'deemed insurer' appears, from the 1992 Order, to be predicated on the basis that a certificate of insurance exists in respect of the foreign vehicle *and* that an international motor insurance card issued in respect of it. Thus, it appears that, if the foreign vehicle was uninsured, there would be no certificate that would render the MIBI deemed insurer. In this situation, it appears that the MIBI's

---

35. Mechanically Propelled Vehicles (International Circulation) Order 1992 (SI 384/1992), art 4. 'Bureau' means 'a central organisation established by motor insurers in any country outside the State for the purpose of giving effect to international agreements for facilitating compliance by visitors with the laws of countries requiring motorists to insure against third party risks, between whom and the [MIBI] there is in force for the time being an agreement whereby, in particular, [the MIBI] agrees to accept in the State on behalf of the said central organisation the same legal liability in respect of an international insurance card as is placed on a vehicle insurer under the Road Traffic Act 1961 in respect of a certificate of insurance issued by an insurer in accordance with section 66 of the Road Traffic Act 1961 certifying that an approved policy of insurance has been issued'. 'Visitor' is defined to mean 'a person resident outside the State making a temporary stay in the State'.

36. Pursuant to Road Traffic Act 1961, s 76, and subject to the MIBI being given prior notification. Section 76(1) provides, *inter alia*: 'Where a [claimant] claims to be entitled to recover from the owner of a mechanically propelled vehicle or from a person (other than the owner) using a mechanically propelled vehicle (in this section referred to as the user), or has in any court of justice (in proceedings of which the vehicle insurer hereinafter mentioned had prior notification) recovered judgment against the owner or user for, a sum (whether liquidated or unliquidated) against the liability for which the owner or user is insured by an approved policy of insurance, the claimant may serve by registered post, on the vehicle insurer by whom the policy was issued or on the vehicle insurer, a notice in writing of the claim or judgment for the sum and upon the service of such notice such of the following provisions as are applicable shall, subject to [s 76(2)], have effect – (a) ... (b) where the claimant has so recovered judgment for the sum, or after service of the notice so recovers judgment for the sum or any part thereof, the insurer shall pay to the claimant so much of the moneys (whether damages or costs) for which judgment was or is so recovered as the insurer has insured and is not otherwise paid to the claimant, and the payment shall, as against the insured or principal debtor, be a valid payment under the policy (c) where the claimant has so recovered judgment for the sum or after service of the notice so recovers judgment for the sum or any part thereof, and has not recovered from the owner or user or such insurer the whole amount of the judgment, the claimant may apply to the court in which he recovered the judgment for leave to execute the judgment against the insurer, and thereupon the court may, if it thinks proper, grant the application either in respect of the whole amount of the judgment or in respect of any specified part of that amount. (d)... (e) ...'.

position would be the same as it adopts in respect of an uninsured vehicle in the State and hence avail itself of the 1% rule.

[8.27] It is submitted that there is no valid legal reason why an uninsured foreign vehicle should be treated any differently to an uninsured Irish vehicle by the MIBI notwithstanding that the MIBI might be entitled to reimbursement in a foreign vehicle scenario.[37] The issue is considered further in **Ch 13**.

---

37.   See the Internal Regulations, art 10, fn **36** and **Appendix 6**.

Chapter 9

MANDATES AND RECOVERY RIGHTS OF THE MIBI

A. INTRODUCTION

[9.01] Once a claimant notifies the MIBI of his intention to claim compensation, the claim is dealt with by one of the MIBI's member insurers, either as 'insurer concerned' or 'handling office'.[1] The member insurer, through its accident investigators, will try to obtain an authority from the uninsured motorist (the uninsured) that will allow the MIBI to act on behalf of the uninsured.[2] To this end, it will call upon the uninsured to sign a 'mandate form'.[3]

B. WHAT IS A MANDATE?

[9.02] In ordinary legal parlance, a mandate is a direction, request and/or of an authoritative command.[4] It is therefore similar to a power of attorney, which is a formal instrument by which one person empowers another to represent him or act in his stead for certain purposes. Once a mandate form is signed, the MIBI (as mandatory) owes a duty of care to the uninsured (as mandator) in relation to the conduct of the proceedings.

C. PROVISIONS OF MANDATE FORM

[9.03] Once signed by the uninsured, the mandate form authorises the MIBI to:

(a) take over and conduct the defence of any claim against the uninsured arising out of the accident[5] and instruct solicitors on behalf of the uninsured;

(b) make admissions on behalf of the uninsured;

(c) pursue any person against whom the uninsured might have a claim for contribution; and

(d) take legal proceedings against the uninsured to recover any monies that the MIBI pays out on behalf of the uninsured by way of settlement or award.

---

1.   See **Ch 5**, paras **5.12–5.15**. The term 'insurer concerned' is defined by the MIBI's articles of association, art 1.2 and the provisions concerning an insurer concerned are contained in arts 71–76 thereof. The text of the foregoing is reproduced in **Appendix 5**.

2.   For obvious reasons, a signed mandate form cannot be obtained from an unidentified or untraced owner or user.

3.   The MIBI Agreements do not use the term 'mandate'. The mandate form that is currently used by the MIBI is reproduced at **Appendix 7.2**.

4.   *Mandare*: 'to give' in Latin.

5.   Clause (a) of the mandate form that is currently being used by the MIBI amounts to an admission of the occurrence of the accident. One would have thought that it would be appropriate to frame this clause in terms of an 'alleged' accident having occurred on a particular date.

[9.04] Furthermore, an uninsured who signs a mandate form undertakes to:

(a) give the MIBI all possible assistance and information in the handling of the claim and the conduct of the proceedings; and

(b) reimburse the MIBI for all monies paid out by it by way of settlement or satisfaction of an award made against the uninsured arising out of the accident and the uninsured acknowledges that he may be sued by the MIBI for recovery of this money.

D. EFFECT OF SIGNED MANDATE FORM

[9.05] Unless or until the MIBI is made a co-defendant to proceedings, it has no standing to participate in the proceedings against an uninsured. The effect of a signed mandate form, however, is that the MIBI takes over and deals with the claim on behalf of the uninsured. This authority extends to the MIBI settling the claim against the uninsured (either before or after the commencement of proceedings) and satisfying any award made against the uninsured by a court. Thereafter, the uninsured is liable to repay to the MIBI the monies paid out by it on his behalf by way of settlement or satisfaction of an award against the uninsured.

E. A CONTRACT OR AN AUTHORITY?

[9.06] The term 'mandate' clearly suggests that the MIBI has authority to act on behalf of an uninsured. The current mandate form provides that an uninsured must reimburse the MIBI for all sums paid out by it in respect of any judgment or settlement. It also states that the sums paid out may be recovered from the uninsured by the MIBI and it acknowledges that the uninsured is aware that the MIBI may take proceedings to recover this money. A further clause specifies that the uninsured understands and consents to the MIBI instructing solicitors on his behalf. It is notable that the foregoing provisions of the current mandate form provide a good basis upon which the MIBI may, as an alternative, recover from an uninsured the monies paid out and the legal costs incurred by it on a *quantum meruit* basis. Given that previously used mandate forms expressly stated that the MIBI would instruct legal advisors to act for the uninsured at the MIBI's expense, the amendment to the current mandate form appears to allow the MIBI recoup every cent paid out by it on behalf of an uninsured as well as the MIBI's own costs.

[9.07] In *Motor Insurers' Bureau of Ireland v Hanley*,[6] Peart J held that a mandate is a contract. In that case the MIBI pursued the defendant by way of summary summons seeking to recover an amount of €127,170.01 paid by the MIBI to an injured party by way of settlement of a claim for compensation. The uninsured defendant had deleted cl (d) of the mandate where it stated that he accepted liability for any sums paid by the plaintiff to the injured party. The uninsured defendant submitted that, as cl (d) had been removed from the mandate, the MIBI's claim was not made under 'a contract, express or

---

6. *Motor Insurers' Bureau of Ireland v Hanley* [2007] 2 IR 591.

implied' and therefore the summary summons procedure was not available to the MIBI. Peart J stated:

> 'If one looks at the mandate, it is certainly a contract by which legal obligations and consequences are contemplated. The defendant clearly is authorising the plaintiff to take over and conduct in his name the defence of the third party claim and is authorising the plaintiff to make admissions on his behalf, and he undertakes to assist them "in the handling of the claim and conduct of the proceedings". That must in my view be taken as including the settlement of those proceedings. He also agrees that if he has any claim for contribution against any other person, the [MIBI] may prosecute that claim in his name but for the benefit of the [MIBI]. Whatever way one looks at this document it is a contract of some kind. Legal consequences flow in either direction from it. For example, the defendant could sue the [MIBI] in the event that it failed or refused to discharge the defendant's liability to the third party. Equally, the [MIBI] could sue the defendant for breach thereof if he failed to give them necessary information and assistance. It is a contract. There is consideration passing. There is offer and acceptance. It is a document intended to give rise to legal obligations and consequences.'[7]

[9.08] Assuming that a signed mandate form would otherwise withstand legal scrutiny,[8] this case would seem to indicate that a mandate is a valid contract for consideration.[9] If the MIBI defends an action or settles an action on behalf of an uninsured who has signed a mandate it can claim that, in consideration for the uninsured signing the mandate, the MIBI agreed to and did provide a service to the uninsured.[10]

F. WHY SIGN A MANDATE FORM?

[9.09] Unless there is a very good defence on the merits of a case, it is hard to give a reason why an uninsured should agree to sign a mandate form. In simple terms, there is little if anything in it for the uninsured. While the MIBI may be more receptive to input from an uninsured as to how a case should be run if he has signed a mandate form, the

---

7. *Motor Insurers' Bureau of Ireland v Hanley* [2007] 2 IR 591 at pp 610–611.
8. For example, it might be challenged on grounds of duress or undue influence.
9. Valuable consideration in the legal sense may consist either in some right, interest, profit or benefit accruing to one party or some forbearance, detriment, loss or responsibility given, suffered or undertaken by the other. Even if a court finds that there is consideration for signing a mandate form, the enforceability of one signed by a minor (even if accompanied by a consent form obtained by the minor's parents) must be questionable in terms of classifying any benefit accruing to the minor being "necessary goods" pursuant to s 2 of the Sale of Goods Act 1893. Legal services may be necessaries (*Helps v Clayton* (1864) 17 CB (NS) 553; *De Stacpoole v De Stacpoole* (1887) 37 Ch D 139).
10. If, instead of signing a mandate, the uninsured retained his own legal team, he would do so on foot of a contract for services. Where a mandate is signed, the lawyers appointed by the MIBI may succeed in effecting a reduction on the liability issue and/or quantum, a benefit which would not otherwise have inured to the uninsured's benefit if the proceedings had not been defended and judgment had been obtained against the uninsured in default of entering an appearance or delivering a defence. Furthermore, the lawyers appointed by the MIBI may obtain evidence from private investigators or medical experts to expose a fraudulent and/or exaggerated claim against an uninsured.

MIBI is not obliged to take cognisance of the mandator's view. While an uninsured may be exposed to reimbursing the MIBI for monies paid out even if he does not sign a mandate form,[11] an uninsured who signs a mandate form eases the reimbursement process for the MIBI.

[9.10] Where an uninsured has clearly been negligent and responsible for damage or injury, there seems to be little incentive for him to sign a mandate form and give the MIBI a carte blanche in relation to the case. If, however, an uninsured believes that he has a good defence on the merits of the case, the availability of legal representation nominated by the MIBI may be attractive.[12] Of course, the uninsured could always instruct his own legal representatives and retain control of his defence. If successful, he could recover his legal costs.

[9.11] An uninsured could, prior to signing the mandate form, delete the paragraph that expresses his agreement to repaying the MIBI any monies that it pays out, although this may have little practical significance in light of the decision in *Hanley*.[13] Depending on the circumstances, the MIBI may have no option but to accept the varied mandate form if it is anxious to secure the uninsured's co-operation. As discussed later,[14] the MIBI may, however, be able to recoup its outlay from the uninsured on the basis of an unjust enrichment.

G. UNINSURED SIGNS MANDATE FORM

[9.12] If the MIBI unsuccessfully defends proceedings against an uninsured who has signed a mandate form, and the MIBI discharges the award made in favour of the plaintiff, the MIBI may recover these monies by suing the uninsured on foot of the judgment against the uninsured[15] rather than pursuant to the signed mandate form. The disadvantage to the former course, however, is that the legal costs incurred by the MIBI

---

11.   See below at paras **9.17–9.27**.

12.   Where the MIBI obtains one signed mandate form from the uninsured driver of a motor vehicle and another from the owner of that vehicle, there is potential for a conflict of interest to arise (eg the issue of whether or not the driver had the owner's consent to use the vehicle in terms of s 118 of the Road Traffic Act 1961). For this reason, it would appear prudent to appoint different firms of solicitors to act for the driver and owner. There is also a potential for a conflict in a case in which the MIBI intends to defend proceedings against it and an uninsured driver (from whom the MIBI has obtained a signed mandate form) on the basis that the plaintiff knew that the vehicle in which he was travelling was uninsured and where the MIBI proposes to adduce evidence from the uninsured driver defendant ie that the plaintiff knew he was uninsured. If a court accepted this defence, it would result in a situation whereby the plaintiff could only recover his award against the (most probably impecunious) uninsured and could not look to the MIBI for satisfaction of that award.

13.   *Motor Insurers' Bureau of Ireland v Hanley* [2007] 2 IR 591. See above at para **9.07**.

14.   See below at paras **9.19–9.27**.

15.   The plaintiff is required to assign any judgment obtained to the MIBI (cl 3.11 of the 2009 and 2004 Agreements). See **Appendix 7.3** for the document that is currently being used by the MIBI to obtain an assignment of a judgment.

in unsuccessfully defending the proceedings against the uninsured are not included within the plaintiff's judgment. For this reason, the MIBI may prefer to rely on the terms of the signed mandate form, in the alternative or in addition to the judgment.

H. CAN THE MIBI DEFEND A CLAIM WITHOUT A SIGNED MANDATE FORM?

[9.13] Where a claim is brought against an uninsured and he does not sign a mandate form, the claimant is likely to find that the uninsured fails to participate in the proceedings. While the MIBI can participate in proceedings in which it is a co-defendant, it cannot represent an uninsured defendant in the absence of it being authorised to do so by way of a mandate. A plaintiff/claimant may obtain a judgment in default of appearance or defence against the uninsured who has not signed a mandate form, in which event the case is adjourned for an assessment of damages.[16] If the MIBI is a defendant to the proceedings, the damages are assessed at the same time as the hearing of the action against the MIBI.[17] However, the MIBI is not automatically liable to discharge the damages that are assessed against the uninsured. It is clear from *Curran v Gallagher, Gallagher and MIBI*[18] that a judgment in default against an uninsured defendant is a finding of liability in default of denial by that uninsured defendant and is binding only as between the plaintiff and that uninsured defendant. It does not bind the MIBI and the MIBI may therefore defend the claim against it.[19] Thus, the MIBI is still entitled to put liability in issue at the hearing of the action. It is only liable to satisfy judgments in respect of any liability for injury for which insurance is required under s 56 of the Road Traffic Act 1961 (injury caused by 'negligent use' and in a 'public place').[20] At the hearing, the MIBI might prove that the uninsured was not guilty of negligent driving or was not driving in a public place and, if it does so, it will not be obliged to indemnify the uninsured in respect of the award of damages assessed against him.[21]

---

16. See the Rules of the Superior Courts 1986, O 13, r 9, and the Circuit Court Rules 2001, O 27, r 2.

17. See the Rules of the Superior Courts, O 13, r 9 (in default of appearance) and the Rules of the Superior Courts 1986, O 27, r 10 (in default of defence). Alternatively, the MIBI might seek an order directing an issue to be tried as to whether or not it is obliged to satisfy a judgment obtained against the uninsured in circumstances where the MIBI claims that the plaintiff knew that there was no insurance policy in existence. This procedure was adopted in *Curran v Gallagher, Gallagher and MIBI* (7 May 1997, unreported) SC (Lynch J,).

    Where the MIBI is not made a party to the proceedings, it may refuse to discharge any judgment that the plaintiff obtains against the uninsured on the basis that it was not sued in the manner dictated by cl 2.3 of the 2009 Agreement and which provides for naming of the MIBI as a co-defendant to the proceedings (see also cl 2.2 of the 2004 Agreement).

18. *Curran v Gallagher, Gallagher and MIBI* (7 May 1997, unreported) SC, *per* Keane and Lynch JJ (Murphy J dissenting).

19. See also *Gurtner v Circuit* [1968] 2 QB 587, [1968] 2 WLR 668, [1968] 1 All ER 328 [1968] 1 Lloyd's Rep 171.

20. Clause 4.1.1 of the 2009 Agreement and cl 4.1 of the 2004 Agreement.

21. Such a defence might be difficult in the absence of the uninsured. It may, however, be demonstrable by the evidence of independent witnesses.

I. UNINSURED DOES NOT CO-OPERATE WITH THE MIBI

[9.14] An uninsured who signs a mandate form may subsequently fail to co-operate with the MIBI and/or, for whatever reason, fail or refuse to give evidence or otherwise assist the MIBI. The absence of the uninsured will hinder the MIBI in its defence of the action. Even if it has been made a party to the proceedings, the MIBI may find that it cannot maintain its defence in the absence of the evidence of the uninsured. If, however, a judgment is entered against the uninsured, and the MIBI satisfies the judgment, it can require the plaintiff to assign the judgment to it.[22] Thereafter, it can take steps to enforce the judgment against the uninsured.[23]

[9.15] If judgment is entered against an uninsured, in default of appearance or defence, and the assessment of damages is adjourned to the hearing of the action, it is submitted that, regardless of whether or not the uninsured has signed a mandate form, the uninsured should be put on notice of the trial date and an affidavit proving service of the notice should be available and produced to the trial judge to illustrate that the uninsured was given the option of participating. At the trial, the trial judge either assesses the amount of damages or, if quantum has been settled, makes an order entering judgment against the uninsured for the amount of the settlement and strikes out the proceedings against the MIBI.

[9.16] It is submitted that, in the same way, an uninsured should be put on notice of any settlement meetings between the MIBI and a plaintiff, particularly if the MIBI wishes to preserve its right to pursue the uninsured for recovery of the monies paid out. This course of action gives the uninsured an opportunity to have an input into the settlement and would assist the MIBI in dealing with any subsequent attempt to challenge the propriety of any settlement it makes.[24]

J. RECOVERY RIGHTS OF THE MIBI WHERE NO SIGNED MANDATE FORM

[9.17] The position of the MIBI in terms of recovering the monies paid out by it on behalf of an uninsured is more problematic where the uninsured does not sign a mandate form, and the MIBI settles a claim against that uninsured without judgment being entered against him and/or without damages being assessed in the normal manner.

[9.18] Where an uninsured does not sign a mandate form, he can defend the proceedings in the normal course and obtain his own legal representation. If the uninsured successfully defends the case on its merits, that will be the end of the matter. However, if the MIBI, in the absence of a signed mandate form, pays out money in settlement of a claim in which no defence is or could reasonably have been maintained by the uninsured, and the

---

22. Clause 3.11 of the 2009 and 2004 Agreements. See **Appendix 7.3** for the document that is currently being used by the MIBI to obtain an assignment of a judgment.
23. Although whether or not it is worthwhile for the MIBI to attempt to enforce the judgment against the uninsured will depend on the circumstances.
24. See merely by way of analogy, the Civil Liability Act 1961, s 22, which provides that a settling tortfeasor can claim contribution from another concurrent wrongdoer once a court is satisfied of the reasonableness of a settlement.

amount of the settlement cannot reasonably be queried, a clear benefit accrues to the uninsured as a result of the settlement. The MIBI in the normal course would have settled the case on reasonable terms and would have avoided a situation where the legal costs (and possibly the award) would have been greater if the matter had proceeded to trial. In these circumstances, it may be said that, if the case had proceeded to trial, it would have been inevitable that a judgment would have been obtained and entered against the uninsured that would have been enforceable by the claimant against the uninsured.[25] In this situation, it may be said that the uninsured has clearly been enriched as a result of the MIBI having discharged the liability to the claimant.[26] The question, however, is whether or not this amounts to an unjust enrichment that would permit the MIBI to rely on the law of restitution to make good its outlay.

K. UNJUST ENRICHMENT

[9.19] The law of restitution is based upon the principle that unjust enrichments must be reversed. All that is required in such proceedings is to state the nature of the claim and the facts upon which the claimant relies, usually an assertion that the defendant has been unjustly enriched at the claimant's expense. The claimant must specify the remedy he seeks. This will usually be an order for the payment of a sum of money by the defendant to the claimant that will operate to reverse the unjust enrichment. The claim may be made where a defendant/uninsured has been unjustly enriched at the expense of the claimant/the MIBI. An enrichment may be positive or negative. A defendant, such as an uninsured, may be incontrovertibly and negatively benefited when he is saved a necessary expense. Where a claimant/the MIBI has paid money to a third party/victim and, in so doing, has discharged a liability of a defendant/uninsured to the third party/victim, the defendant/uninsured may be unjustly enriched at the expense of the claimant/the MIBI because the loss to the claimant/the MIBI, as a result of the payment, is matched by the gain which the defendant/uninsured has made.

[9.20] The remedy of subrogation may also aid the MIBI to prevent the unjust enrichment of an uninsured as a result of the payment of monies by the MIBI in satisfaction of a claim against an uninsured. Where one person has a claim against another, a third person is, in certain circumstances, allowed to have the benefit of the claim and the remedy for its enforcement, even though the benefit of the claim has not been assigned to him. The third person is then said to be subrogated to the rights of the first person.

[9.21] Subrogation was described by Millett LJ in *Boscawen v Bajwa*[27] as follows:

> 'Subrogation ... is a remedy, not a cause of action ... [i]t is available in a wide variety of different factual situations in which it is required in order to reverse the defendant's unjust enrichment. Equity lawyers speak of a right of subrogation, or of an equity of subrogation, but this merely reflects the fact that it is not a remedy which the court has a general discretion to impose whenever it thinks it just to do so. The equity arises from the conduct of the parties on well settled principles and in defined circumstances, which make it unconscionable for the defendant to deny the

---

25. Or the MIBI in the event of the claimant assigning a judgment to the MIBI.
26. Less than 1% of monies paid out are subsequently recovered by the MIBI.
27. *Boscawen v Bajwa* [1996] 1 WLR 328, [1995] 4 All ER 769.

proprietary interest claimed by the plaintiff. A constructive trust arises in the same way. Once the equity is established the court satisfies it by declaring that the property in question is subject to a charge by way of subrogation in the one case or a constructive trust in the other.'[28]

[9.22] In order to satisfy the equity, the MIBI would have to satisfy a court that the uninsured was unjustly enriched at its expense ie firstly, that the uninsured had no chance of successfully defending the case on its merits and, secondly, that the settlement was reasonable in all the circumstances. It would be difficult for an uninsured to take issue with the fact that the MIBI was not pursuing him on foot of an assigned judgment in circumstances where the legal costs would undoubtedly have been greater, as might the award, if the case had actually proceeded to trial.[29] It would be advisable to put the uninsured on notice of any settlement talks between the MIBI and a plaintiff and of the fact that the uninsured may subsequently be pursued by the MIBI for recoupment. The uninsured will then have been given an opportunity to reject the benefit accruing to him and cannot later argue that he did not want the benefit.

[9.23] In *MIBI v Stanbridge and others*[30] Laffoy J rejected the MIBI's claim for a 'remedial constructive trust' when seeking a declaration that a trust arose in respect of the monies inherited by two siblings from their deceased mother on foot of a disclaimer from their father and sister (the uninsured driver and owner respectively of the vehicle giving rise to the claim). The MIBI had the benefit of an assignment of a judgment against the father and sister. A trust did not arise because Laffoy J held that the disclaimers were executed to avoid the MIBI recovering. Laffoy J stated:

'The question for the court, therefore, is whether an intention on the part of [the father and sister] to delay, hinder or defraud the Bureau as a creditor has been proved as an inference of law from the evidence before the court. In this case, I am satisfied that the necessary or probable result of [the father and sister] disclaiming their respective shares of the estate of the deceased on intestacy was to delay, hinder and defeat the payment of the debt due by them to the Bureau as the assignee of the deceased's judgment against them. Therefore, fraud has been proved.'[31]

[9.24] And dealing with the constructive trust argument, Laffoy J held:

'The [MIBI's] reliance on the new model constructive trust is premised on the disclaimers not being void. What it seeks, on the basis of that premise, is a declaration that the respective share of the estate of the deceased to which [the father and sister] would have become entitled, if they had not disclaimed, and to which the [two siblings] would become equally beneficially entitled on disclaimer by virtue of the operation of section 72A of the [Succession] Act of 1965, would be held by the [two siblings] upon trust for the Bureau. In that scenario, in my view, there could be no question of unjust enrichment or unconscionable conduct

---

28. *Boscawen v Bajwa* [1996] 1 WLR 328 at 335.
29. In *Bowes v MIBI* [2000] 2 IR 79, Murphy J, delivering the judgment of the Supreme Court, noted *obiter dictum* that a judgment debtor would be liable to the MIBI either by way of subrogation or assignment for all monies paid by it to a judgment creditor (at p 87).
30. *MIBI v Stanbridge and others* [2011] 2 IR 78.
31. *MIBI v Stanbridge and others* [2011] 2 IR 78 at pp 95–96.

on the part of the [the two siblings], in accepting that to which they would be entitled as a matter of law.

Accordingly, I consider that the argument based on the concept of remedial constructive trust is wholly misconceived.'[32]

[9.25] The minutiae of the law of restitution are beyond the ambit of this work[33] and there is little Irish authority on point.[34] However it is not uncommon for the MIBI to seek to recoup payments made by it in this manner before the courts. More often than not, the proceedings brought by the MIBI are not defended and hence the paucity of authority.

[9.26] In England, it appears to be clear that subrogation is a remedy which is fashioned to the facts of a particular case and which is granted in order to prevent a defendant's unjust enrichment.[35] The law was lucidly expressed by Scarman LJ in *Owen v Tate*[36] as follows:

'If without an antecedent request a person assumes an obligation or makes a payment for the benefit of another, the law will, as a general rule, refuse him a right of indemnity. But if he can show that in the particular circumstances of the case there was some necessity for the obligation to be assumed, then the law will grant him a right of reimbursement if in all the circumstances it is just and reasonable to do so.'[37]

[9.27] The MIBI is clearly obliged to satisfy a judgment obtained against an uninsured.[38] If an uninsured does not defend a case against him and the MIBI can settle the case on terms that are at least as beneficial to an uninsured as if the matter had proceeded to

---

32.   *MIBI v Stanbridge and others* [2011] 2 IR 78 at pp 96–97.

33.   See Goff and Jones, *The Law of Unjust Enrichment (2011)* for a detailed analysis.

34.   However, the Supreme Court has recognised that 'unjust enrichment exists as a distinctive legal concept separate from both contract and tort ...' (*per* Keane J in *Corporation of Dublin v Building and Allied Trade Union* [1996] 1 IR 468 at 483).

35.   See *Banque Financière de la Cité v Parc (Battersea) Ltd.* [1999] 1 AC 221, [1998] 2 WLR 475, [1998] 1 All ER 737. Lord Hoffmann stated '... it is customary for the assured, on payment of the loss, to provide the insurer with a letter of subrogation, being no more nor less than an express assignment of his rights of recovery against any third party. Subrogation in this sense is a contractual arrangement for the transfer of rights against third parties and is founded upon the common intention of the parties. But the term is also used to describe an equitable remedy to reverse or prevent unjust enrichment, which is not based upon any agreement or common intention of the parties enriched and the party deprived. The fact that contractual subrogation and subrogation to prevent unjust enrichment both involve transfers of rights or something resembling transfers of rights should not be allowed to obscure the fact that one is dealing with radically different institutions. One is part of the law of contract and one is part of the law of restitution. Unless this distinction is borne clearly in mind, there is a danger that the contractual requirement of mutual consent will be imported into the conditions for the grant of the restitutionary remedy or that the absence of such a requirement will be disguised by references to a presumed intention, which is wholly fictitious. There is an obvious parallel with the confusion caused by classifying certain restitutionary remedies as *quasi*-contractual and importing into them features of the law of contract' ([1999] 1 AC 221 at 231–232).

36.   *Owen v Tate* [1976] 1 QB 402, [1975] 2 All ER 129, [1975] 3 WLR 369.

37.   *Owen v Tate* [1976] 1 QB 402 at 411–412.

38.   This is subject to the claimant's compliance with the conditions precedent to the relevant MIBI agreement.

judgment, then the remedy of subrogation should be available to the MIBI to avoid the unjust enrichment of the uninsured. While the MIBI has succeeded in claims of this nature before the lower courts, there is no written decision on the issue from the Superior Courts.

Chapter 10

PARTIES TO ACTIONS AFFECTING THE MIBI AND SATISFACTION OF JUDGMENTS

A. INTRODUCTION

[10.01] Clause 2.3–2.4 and cl 3 of the 2009 Agreement[1] prescribe the procedure that must be followed by a person who issues proceedings for the purpose of enforcing the 2009 Agreement. A person who ultimately aspires to recover from the MIBI must comply with the overall provisions of the 2009 Agreement and be aware of the consequences of nonjoinder or misjoinder of the MIBI as a party to such proceedings and the circumstances in which he may be required to institute two actions. In this regard, the 2009 Agreement makes provision for the necessity for a claimant to make an application to the Personal Injuries Assessment Board (Injuries Board[2]) pursuant to the Personal Injuries Assessment Board Act 2003 (the PIAB Act 2003) before issuing proceedings against the MIBI.[3]

B. CLAUSE 2 OF THE 2009 AGREEMENT

[10.02] Clause 2 of the 2009 Agreement provides that a claimant for compensation 'must'[4] seek to enforce the provisions of the Agreement by:

> '2.1 making a claim directly to MIBI for compensation which may be settled with or without admission of liability,[5] or
>
> 2.2 making an application to the Injuries Board citing MIBI as a respondent under the terms of the PIAB Act 2003 which pursuant to s 12(1), provides that unless and until such an application is made, no proceedings in court may be brought in respect of the claim,[6]

---

1. Previously, cl 2.2–2.3 and cl 3 of the 2004 Agreement. The 2009 Agreement is reproduced in **Appendix 1**. The 2004 Agreement is reproduced in **Appendix 2**.
2. injuriesboard.ie has been the trading name of PIAB as a service provider since June 2008.
3. PIAB Act 2003, s 50. If proceedings are issued against a motorist following the issuing of an authorisation from the Injuries Board, and it subsequently transpires that the motorist was not insured, the plaintiff cannot simply make a court application to join the MIBI as a co-defendant. The plaintiff must first make a claim to the Injuries Board and obtain an authorisation against the MIBI before a court can join it as a co-defendant to the proceedings (see *Sherry v Primark Ltd. and Grosvenor Cleaning Services Ltd* [2010] 1 IR 407).
4. The same wording is used in cl 2 of the 2004 Agreement. Clause 2 of the 1988 Agreement stated 'may' rather than 'must'.
5. Clause 2.1 of the 2004 Agreement was in identical terms to cl 2.1 of the 2009 Agreement, save for the addition of 'directly' in cl 2.1 of the 2009 Agreement.
6. The content of cl 2.2 is entirely new to the 2009 Agreement and reflects the provisions of the PIAB Act 2003 and *Campbell v O'Donnell* [2009] 1 IR 133, [2008] 2 ILRM 241, wherein the Supreme Court held that a claim against the MIBI is effectively one to recover damages in respect of a wrong and falls within the definition of a 'civil action' as defined by the PIAB Act 2003. See further **Ch 5**.

2.3 citing MIBI as co-defendants in any proceedings against the owner[7] and/or[8] user of the vehicle giving rise to the claim except where the owner and user of the vehicle remain unidentified or untraced, or

2.4 citing MIBI as sole defendant where the claimant is seeking a court order for the performance of the Agreement by MIBI provided the claimant has first applied for compensation to MIBI under the cl 2.1 and has either been refused compensation by MIBI or has been offered compensation by MIBI which the claimant considers to be inadequate and/or applied to the Injuries Board as at cl 2.2 and having received a release from the Injuries Board to proceed with legal action.'[9]

C. APPROPRIATE DEFENDANTS TO ACTIONS AFFECTING THE MIBI

1. The Personal Injuries Assessment Board

[10.03] The first edition of this book questioned whether the Injuries Board had jurisdiction to deal with claims involving the MIBI. This issue was raised in the context of the definition of 'civil action' in the PIAB Act 2003 and to which the PIAB Act 2003 applies. Since then, the Supreme Court in *Campbell v O'Donnell*[10] has held that a claim

---

7. The Road Traffic Act 1961, s 118 provides the basis upon which a vehicle owner may be sued for the negligence of another person driving his vehicle. It provides that, where a person uses a motor vehicle with the consent of its owner, the user shall, for the purposes of determining the liability of the owner for injury caused by the negligent use of the vehicle by the user, be deemed to have used the vehicle as the servant of the owner but only in so far as the user has acted in accordance with the terms of the consent given by the owner. Section 3(5) of the 1961 Act provides that the owner's consent to user by another includes the implied consent of the owner. The scope of s 118 was considered by the Supreme Court in *Homan v Kiernan and Lombard & Ulster Banking Ltd* [1997] 1 IR 55. The first defendant (the lessee) entered into a lease agreement with the second defendant (the lessor) for the purchase of a truck from a third party. The lease agreement contained a declaration to the effect that the lessee had insured the vehicle in accordance with the lease agreement. The lessee failed to insure the vehicle and he caused a collision with the plaintiff. The lessee signed a mandate to enable the MIBI deal with the proceedings. The lessor accepted ownership of the truck but defended the proceedings on the basis that its consent to the lessee driving the truck was vitiated by the lessee's failure to insure it and that it was therefore not liable to the plaintiff. The High Court held that, in the absence of compliance with the lease agreement, the lessee's liability did not transfer vicariously to the lessor. The Supreme Court allowed the appeal. It held that it would be contrary to the policy of s 118 to allow leasing companies, as owners, allow vehicles out on the road and yet be in a position to say that driving was not with their consent because insurance was not taken out. In the circumstances, the lessee's failure to insure the truck did not vitiate the consent to drive it.
8. Clause 2.3 of the 2009 Agreement is identical in content to cl 2.2 of the 2004 Agreement. Previously cl 2(2) of the 1988 Agreement stated 'owner or user' as opposed to 'owner and/or user'.
9. Clause 2.4 of the 2009 Agreement is the same as cl 2.3 of the 2004 Agreement, save that the 2004 Agreement did not include the words 'and / or applied to the Injuries Board ... and having received a release from the Injuries Board to proceed with legal action', which were clearly added in light of the PIAB Act 2003 and *Campbell v O'Donnell* [2009] 1 IR 133; [2008] 2 ILRM 241. See fn **6** above and para **10.03** below.
10. *Campbell v O'Donnell* [2009] 1 IR 133, [2008] 2 ILRM 241.

against the MIBI is effectively one to recover damages in respect of a wrong and falls within the definition of a 'civil action' as defined by the PIAB Act 2003. It appears to be in light of the foregoing that the 2009 Agreement expressly provides that an application must be made to the Injuries Board citing the MIBI as a respondent pursuant to s 12(1) of the PIAB Act 2003 and unless such an application is made, no court proceedings may be brought.[11] The PIAB Act 2003 provides that the applicable limitation period stops when an application is made to the Injuries Board. It only recommences six months after the date on which the Injuries Board issues an authorisation.[12]

2. Summary of appropriate defendants to actions affecting the MIBI

[10.04] Pursuant to cl 2.3 of the 2009 Agreement, the MIBI is always a co-defendant in proceedings except where the owner and user remains unidentified and untraced.

[10.05] The matters enumerated below are submitted as a summary of the appropriate persons that a claimant should sue in various actions affecting the MIBI. This summary must, however, be considered in light of the contents of paras **10.06** and **Section L** of this chapter. The case law from which these principles are extracted, and the procedure that should be adopted in circumstances where it appears that a claimant must bring two actions, are discussed in **Ch 11**.

1. Where the accident was allegedly caused by the negligent driving of any number of identified and traced owners and/or users of a motor vehicle(s) (and one or more of whom is uninsured), the appropriate defendants to the action are the identified and traced owner(s) and/or user(s) and the MIBI;[13,14]

2. Where the accident was allegedly caused by the negligent driving of any number of unidentified and untraced owners and users of a motor vehicle(s), the appropriate defendant to the action is the MIBI;[15,16,17]

3. Where the accident was allegedly caused by the negligent driving of any number of identified and traced owners and/or users of a motor vehicle(s) (who

---

11. Clauses 2.2 and 2.4 of the 2009 Agreement.
12. PIAB Act 2003, s 50.
13. Clause 2.3 of the 2009 Agreement (cl 2.2 of the 2004 Agreement). See also: *Kavanagh v Reilly and MIBI* (14 June 1996, unreported) HC, *ex tempore*, Morris P; *Devereux v Minister for Finance and MIBI* (10 February 1998, unreported) HC, *ex tempore*, O'Sullivan J, (see Jones, 'Counsel's note: "Citing the MIBI of Ireland as a co-defendant"', 3(9) 1998 *Bar Review* 450); *Feeney v Dwane and O'Connor and Feeney v MIBI* (30 July 1999, unreported) HC, *ex tempore*, Johnson J; *Bowes v MIBI* [2000] 2 IR 79; and *Riordan v MIBI* (24 January 2001 and 1 February 2001, unreported) Circuit Court, the President of the Circuit Court, Judge Smyth. These cases are discussed in **Ch 11**.
14. See Precedent 8.1 in **Appendix 8**.
15. See fn **13** above.
16. See Precedent 8.2 in **Appendix 8**.
17. Clause 2.3 of the 2009 Agreement (cl 2.2 of the 2004 Agreement), in providing that a claimant must cite the MIBI: 'as co-defendants in any proceedings against the owner *and/or* user of the vehicle giving rise to the claim except where the owner and user of the vehicle remain unidentified and untraced' (emphasis added), suggests that where *either* the owner or user is actually identified and traced, the claimant may sue the owner or user and the MIBI as co-defendants. This procedure was adopted in *Breslin v Corcoran and MIBI* (17 July 2001, unreported) HC, Butler J, [2003] 2 IR 203 (Supreme Court).

are insured) *and* any number of unidentified and untraced owners and users, two sets of proceedings must be instituted. One action must be brought against the insured identified and traced owner(s) and/or user(s) as co-defendants.[18] A second action must be brought against the MIBI as sole defendant in respect of the unidentified and untraced owner(s) and user(s);[19]

4. Where the accident was allegedly caused by the negligent driving of any number of identified and traced owners and/or users of a motor vehicle(s) (and one or more of whom is uninsured) *and* any number of unidentified and untraced owners and users, the claimant must bring two actions. The first action must be brought against the identified and traced owner(s) and/or user(s) and the MIBI as co-defendants. In this regard, the MIBI is sued in respect of the uninsured identified and traced owner(s) and/or user(s). A second action must be brought against the MIBI as sole defendant in respect of the unidentified and untraced owner(s) and user(s).[20] Thus, strictly speaking, two sets of proceedings must issue as against the MIBI;

5. Where the accident was allegedly caused by the negligence of any *non*-motorist *and* the negligent driving of any number of unidentified and untraced owners and users of a motor vehicle(s), the claimant must bring two actions. The first action must be brought against the *non*-motorist as sole defendant. A second action must be brought against the MIBI as sole defendant in respect of the unidentified and untraced owner(s) and user(s);[21]

6. Where the accident was allegedly caused by the negligence of any *non*-motorist *and* the negligent driving of any number of identified and traced owners and/or users (who are insured) *and* the negligent driving of any number of unidentified and untraced owners and users, two actions are required. The first action must be brought against the *non*-motorist and the insured owner(s) and/or user(s) as co-defendants. A second action must be brought against the MIBI as sole defendant in respect of the unidentified and untraced owner(s) and user(s);

7. Where the accident was allegedly caused by the negligence of any *non*-motorist *and* the negligent driving of any number of identified and traced owners and/or

---

18. Or as sole defendant if only one insured vehicle is alleged to have caused the accident and its owner/user are the same person.
19. Clause 2.3 of the 2009 Agreement (cl 2.2 of the 2004 Agreement). In *Byrne v Bus Átha Cliath* [2005] IEHC 20, (2 February 2005, unreported) HC, O'Leary J, the plaintiff claimed that she was injured as a result of the negligent driving of the bus in which she had been travelling as a passenger and by an untraced motorist. Having sued both the bus operator and the MIBI in one Circuit Court action, the MIBI succeeded in an application be removed as a co-defendant. While the plaintiff issued a second action against the MIBI, the bus operator appealed against the order and submitted in the High Court that the requirement in Irish law that a claimant must bring two actions was contrary to the motor insurance directives. The High Court, however, held that one defendant could not resist an application by a co-defendant to be dismissed from the proceedings when the application is supported or at least accepted by the plaintiff.
20. Clause 2.3 of the 2009 Agreement (cl 2.2 of the 2004 Agreement).
21. *Hyland v MIBI and Dun Laoghaire Rathdown County Council* (29 July 2003, unreported) CC, *ex tempore,* Judge McMahon. For a discussion of this case, see Abrahamson, 'The MIBI and Co-Defendants Recent Case Law', 8(5) 2003 *Bar Review* 195.

users (and one or more of whom are uninsured) *and* the negligent driving of any number of unidentified and untraced owners and users, the claimant must bring two actions. The first action must be brought against the *non*-motorist, the identified and traced owner(s) and/or user(s) and the MIBI as co-defendants. In this regard, the MIBI is sued in respect of the uninsured identified and traced owner(s) and/or user(s). A second action must be brought against the MIBI as sole defendant in respect of the unidentified and untraced owners and users.

3. MIBI or insurer's liability?

[10.06] Having regard to art 13 of the Sixth Directive[22] and the judgment of the ECJ in *Churchill Insurance Co Ltd v Wilkinson* and *Evans v Equity Claims Ltd,*[23] it is arguable that, in certain circumstances, the MIBI need not be named as a defendant when *someone* was insured to drive a vehicle that negligently caused an accident, even though the driver at the time of the accident may not have been insured. That is, it is arguable that the insurer may not be permitted to rely on certain exclusion clauses in an insurance policy. This raises complex issues and is considered in **Section L** of this chapter,[24] although, in the absence of any definitive judicial determination, there is no conclusive answer to the ultimate question that is raised therein. The contents of **Section L**, including certain decisions of the Irish superior courts, also require to be taken into account before a decision is taken as to the appropriate defendants to an action for damages arising out of an accident in which injuries are caused by a vehicle, and where either (a) the driver thereof was an insured person but a question mark arises over whether the insurer can properly rely on an exclusion clause to avoid liability or (b) the driver thereof was not an insured person but there was an insurance policy in place whereby someone other than the driver was insured to drive the vehicle at the time. Pending a decision from the Superior Courts, caution would dictate that the MIBI should be joined as a co-defendant.

4. Circumstances in which two actions are required

[10.07] Circumstances may arise that necessitate a claimant bringing two actions. In essence, if a claimant claims that his injuries were caused by more than one vehicle, and the owner and user remain unidentified and untraced in respect of one of the vehicles, he must sue the MIBI as a sole defendant in one action. This procedure must be applied even if the claimant has already joined the MIBI as a co-defendant to an action on the basis that responsibility for the accident also lies with an uninsured motorist. Thus a claimant may be compelled to institute two actions in which the MIBI is a defendant to both actions.[25]

---

22. As previously contained in Second Directive, art 2 and see Third Directive, art 1 (now Sixth Directive, art 12(1)). A portion of Sixth Directive, art 13 is reproduced below at para **10.51**. The Sixth Directive is reproduced in **Appendix 3**.
23. *Churchill Insurance Co. Ltd v Wilkinson and Evans v Equity Claims Ltd* (Joined Cases C–442/10) 1 December 2011.
24. See paras **10.50**–**10.83**.
25. On the other hand, see the Supreme Court decision in *O'Flynn v Buckley* [2009] 3 IR 311. In that case, the MIBI was joined in one action as a defendant in respect of *both* the uninsured driving of one defendant *and* the driving of an untraced and unidentified motorist. (contd .../)

5. Hearing of two actions

[10.08] In *Hyland v MIBI and Dun Laoghaire Rathdown County Council*,[26] Judge McMahon in the Circuit Court considered that, where two actions are appropriate, the plaintiff should not prosecute the action to which the MIBI is the sole defendant (in the case of an unidentified and untraced owner and user of a motor vehicle) unless and until the alternative action has been concluded and the plaintiff has failed to recover in that action.[27] On the other hand, in *Feeney v Dwane and O'Connor* and *Feeney v MIBI*,[28] Johnson J ruled that, where a claimant is required to bring two actions, they should be heard together.

[10.09] In *Feeney*, the plaintiff brought one action against an insured motorist and a second action against the MIBI in respect of a vehicle the owner and user of which was unidentified and untraced. Some months prior to the hearing of the actions, Johnson J refused an application by the MIBI to stay the action against it pending the hearing of the plaintiff's action against the insured motorist. Johnson J considered that, if the first action was successfully defended, the matter would have to be re-litigated against the MIBI. For this reason, he directed that both actions be heard together by the same judge, that all the evidence be taken together at the same time and that all parties participate. This principle was endorsed by the High Court in *Kavanagh v MIBI*.[29]

[10.10] It certainly makes practical sense that, where a claimant is obliged to bring two actions (eg, one against an insured motorist and one against the MIBI in respect of a vehicle whose owner and user are unidentified and untraced), the actions should be heard at the same time.

[10.11] Different handling offices acting for MIBI may take different approaches. Sometimes the MIBI will require the proceedings against the identified party to be brought to a conclusion prior to proceeding against the MIBI in respect of the actions of the vehicle whose owner and user are unidentified and untraced. It is submitted that this would be inappropriate for the reasons given in *Feeney* and outlined above.

---

25. (contd) When the MIBI sought to have the claim against it dismissed on the basis that the 1988 Agreement did not permit it to be joined as a co-defendant where there was a case being made against an untraced driver, the court held that the interests of justice and the legitimate concerns of the MIBI could have been met by providing for the disjoinder of issues (under RSC 1986, O 18). The delay in moving for relief, however, was such as to disentitle the MIBI to disjoinder.

26. *Hyland v MIBI and Dun Laoghaire Rathdown County Council* (29 July 2003, unreported) CC, *ex tempore*, Judge McMahon. For a discussion of this case see Abrahamson, 'The MIBI and Co-Defendants Recent Case Law', 8(5) 2003 *Bar Review* 195.

27. In that case, the other alleged wrongdoer, a local authority, was alleged to have negligently maintained the locus.

28. *Feeney v Dwane and O'Connor and Feeney v MIBI* (30 July 1999, unreported) HC, *ex tempore*, Johnson J. See **Ch 11**, para **11.13**.

29. *Kavanagh v MIBI* (22 February 2001, unreported) HC, *ex tempore*, McKechnie J. In *Kavanagh*, however, McKechnie J only heard the second action against the MIBI after the plaintiff's first action against an insured motorist had been heard and dismissed. McKechnie J noted, however, that the first *Kavanagh* case was heard prior to the holding in *Feeney* that both actions should be heard together.

[10.12] If the MIBI was to pursue this course of action, and a claimant was to comply with the MIBI's request in this regard and bring two actions that would be heard separately, the claimant would run the risk of failing in the first action and being made the subject of an order for costs in that action. For this reason, the first edition of this book suggested that it would be prudent for a claimant in such a position to call upon the MIBI to confirm that it was dictating this course of action pursuant to cl 3.10 of the 2004 Agreement which obliges a claimant to 'take all reasonable steps against any person against whom [he] may have a remedy' as he is required to do by the MIBI. If the MIBI duly confirmed this position, the MIBI would, in the event of the claimant's failure in the first action, be liable to fully indemnify the claimant in respect of the reasonable costs thereof.[30] However, the provisions of cl 3.10 of the 2004 Agreement have been entirely omitted from the 2009 Agreement. This may have been done by the MIBI to appear compliant with the Sixth Directive. Article 10(1) of the Sixth Directive provides that 'Member States may not allow the body to make the payment of compensation conditional on the victim establishing in any way that the person liable is unable or refuses to pay'. It has to be said, however, that an almost identical provision was previously inserted into the Second Directive by the Third Directive.[31,32] In the circumstances, therefore, if a claimant under the 2009 Agreement is called upon by the MIBI to bring two actions, he should endeavour to protect himself in relation to the costs of the non-MIBI action by calling upon the MIBI to indemnify him in respect of the costs of that other action.

D. JOINING ALL APPROPRIATE DEFENDANTS (OTHER THAN THE MIBI)

1. Introduction

[10.13] Clause 2.3 of the 2009 Agreement anticipates a claimant suing the MIBI as a co-defendant to proceedings against one or more identified and traced owners and/or users in circumstances where there is no insurance in respect of at least one such owner/user. Clause 2.4 of the 2009 Agreement envisages a claimant suing the MIBI for performance of the Agreement in circumstances where the MIBI has either refused a claim for compensation under cl 2.1 or has offered inadequate compensation.

---

30.   Furthermore, given that the first action might only be determined after the relevant time periods stated in cl 3.1 of the 2009 Agreement (cl 3.1 of the 2004 Agreement) and the Statute of Limitations 1957–2000 had expired, it would be appropriate for the claimant to issue the second action against the MIBI prior to the expiration of the relevant statutory period, notwithstanding the fact that he had agreed not to prosecute it prior to the conclusion of the first action and, only then, if he fails in the first action. As an alternative to issuing a protective writ against the MIBI, the MIBI might be willing to give an undertaking to the claimant that, if he fails in the first action, it will not raise the Statute of Limitations in its defence to any proceedings that the plaintiff may subsequently issue against it. However, if the second action against the MIBI involved another defendant (eg an uninsured motorist), the claimant could not rely on any such undertaking against the uninsured motorist in the absence of the MIBI having obtained a mandate.

31.   See Second Directive, art 1(4), as amended by Third Directive, art 3.

32.   Likewise, the new provision in cl 13 of the 2004 Agreement to the effect that 'the Guarantee Fund' (which is not defined) is 'a Fund of Last Resort' was omitted from the 2009 Agreement.

2. The MIBI calls on a claimant to join defendants

[10.14] Where an accident involves insured and uninsured owners and/or users,[33] a claimant usually joins all relevant motorists (and the MIBI) as defendants to the proceedings in which he seeks to recover compensation for damage or injury caused by all or any of them. If, however, the MIBI takes a view that a claimant has failed to join a party that the MIBI considers that he should sue, the MIBI may call upon the claimant to do so. If the claim is one under the 2004 Agreement, the MIBI may in theory rely upon the provisions of cl 3.10 of the 2004 Agreement, which obliges a claimant to 'take all reasonable steps against any person against whom [he] may have a remedy'.[34] However, it is submitted that, given the omission of the content of cl 3.10 from the 2009 Agreement and art 10(1) of the Sixth Directive, referred to above at para **10.12**, the MIBI is unlikely to expressly rely upon cl 3.10 of the 2004 Agreement. Notwithstanding the fact that the 2004 Agreement was the only one that ever expressly asserted that the guarantee fund was one of last resort,[35] it seems that the MIBI may rely on such a principle as a basis for compelling a plaintiff to sue another party.[36]

E. FAILING TO JOIN THE MIBI AS CO-DEFENDANT WITH UNINSURED MOTORIST

1. Introduction

[10.15] The scenario at point 1 at para **10.05** above outlined a claim arising out of an accident allegedly caused by the negligent driving of any number of identified and traced owners and/or users, and one or more of whom are uninsured. It was noted that the appropriate means by which to proceed is to name all such motorists and the MIBI as defendants to one action. That said, cl 2.3 and cl 2.4 of the 2009 Agreement[37] appear, on one reading, to be inconsistent and this issue is discussed below.

---

33. This issue will not arise in circumstances where the plaintiff's injuries are alleged to have been caused by a vehicle the owner and user of which remain unidentified or untraced, in which case the sole defendant to any action brought by the plaintiff should be the MIBI.

34. See also **Ch 4**, paras **4.28–4.32**.

35. Clause 13 of the 2004 Agreement.

36. See *Bowes v MIBI* [2000] 2 IR 79, wherein Murphy J (delivering the majority judgment of the Court), and with reference to the substance of the MIBI agreements prior to 1988, stated: 'Moreover, the procedure ensured that the [MIBI] would be the payer of last resort. Any persons whose negligence contributed to the injuries could be made a defendant by the victim, either at his election or at the direction of the [MIBI], and no matter how small a part the negligence of that defendant played in causing the accident, the fact that the judgment could be recovered against him for the entire amount relieved the [MIBI] of any liability whatever' (at pp 87–88) (but see also the dissenting judgment of Barron J who appeared to state that the MIBI can in certain circumstances be the insurer of first resort (at p 99)). In *Churchill Insurance Co Ltd v Wilkinson and Evans v Equity Claims Ltd* (Joined Cases C–442/10), 1 December 2011, the ECJ stated that: 'the payment of compensation by a national body is considered to be a measure of last resort, provided for only in cases in which the vehicle that caused the injury or damage is uninsured or unidentified or has not satisfied the insurance requirements referred to in art 3(1) of the First Directive' (at para 41); (First Directive, art 3(1) comprises Sixth Directive, art 3(1)).

37. Previously cls 2.2 and 2.3 of the 2004 Agreement.

2. Nonjoinder of the MIBI as a co-defendant

[10.16] Clause 2.3 of the 2009 Agreement envisages the MIBI being sued as a co-defendant in proceedings against one or more identified and traced owners and/or users of motor vehicles (and one or more of whom is uninsured) and this is the approach that is usually adopted by a claimant.

[10.17] A literal reading of cl 2.4 of the 2009 Agreement, however, suggests that a claimant may sue all identified and traced owners and/or users (*including* an uninsured motorist) in one action and, in the event of the uninsured motorist being found liable for the accident, looking to the MIBI to satisfy any judgment obtained[38] and suing it in the event of its failure to do so.[39] In practice, this is rarely done.

[10.18] This procedure was adopted in *Kinsella v MIBI*.[40] The plaintiff suffered injury while he was a passenger in a vehicle being driven by an uninsured driver. The plaintiff successfully sued and obtained judgment against the uninsured driver. Thereafter, the uninsured driver failed to satisfy the judgment and the plaintiff instituted proceedings against the MIBI as sole defendant and claimed that it was obliged to pay the amount of the judgment under cl 2 of the 1964 Agreement.[41] Neither the 1964 Agreement nor its predecessor[42] made any express provision for joining the MIBI as a party to proceedings.[43] While the route taken by *Kinsella* appears to be envisaged by cl 2.4 of the 2009 Agreement,[44] cl 2.3 of the 2009 Agreement, however, suggests that the MIBI

---

38.   Clause 4.1.1–4.1.2 of the 2009 Agreement (cl 4.1 of the 2004 Agreement).

39.   Clause 2.4 of the 2009 Agreement (cl 2.3 of the 2004 Agreement). In this situation, it should be noted that, if a plaintiff opted to sue all potential defendants other than the MIBI and any one or more of the insured motorist defendants was found liable to some degree, the plaintiff could recover the entire judgment against all or any of the insured motorist defendants found partially liable (pursuant to the concurrent wrongdoer provisions of the Civil Liability Act 1961, ss 11–13). In such circumstances, pursuit of the MIBI would be moot. Further, and in the same way, even if the MIBI was sued as a co-defendant to this action and the uninsured motorist defendant was found liable to some degree, then, provided that an insured motorist defendant was also found liable to some degree, the latter's insurer could be pursued for the total award.

40.   *Kinsella v MIBI* [1997] 3 IR 586. See also *Kelly v MIBI* (24 February 1975, unreported) SC.

41.   This was similar in format and wording to cl 4.1.1–4.1.2 of the 2009 Agreement (cl 4.1 of the 2004 Agreement).

42.   The 1955 Agreement.

43.   The concept of the MIBI as a party to proceedings was first expressly provided for by cl 2 of the 1988 Agreement.

44.   If cl 2 of the 2009 Agreement was interpreted as allowing a *Kinsella* type claimant to proceed without having to join the MIBI as a co-defendant, then such a claimant who complies with the other provisions of the Agreement could, under the existing legislation, make an application to the Injuries Board by naming the uninsured motorist as the sole respondent to his application. Assuming that an order to pay was made by the PIAB, the claimant could then look to the MIBI for satisfaction of the award and, in the event of the MIBI declining to do so, suing the MIBI pursuant to cl 2.3 for satisfaction of the order to pay. Having regard to *Campbell v O'Donnell* [2009] 1 IR 133, [2008] 2 ILRM 241, however, it would be incumbent upon the claimant taking such a course of action to make a further application to the Injuries Board against the MIBI. However, the authors respectfully submit that proceeding by means of two actions would be incorrect. See further fn **45**.

should be joined as a co-defendant to an action brought against an uninsured motorist.[45] This apparent inconsistency is augmented by the fact that cl 2 of the 2009 Agreement[46] states that a person claiming compensation by virtue of the Agreement 'must'[47] seek to enforce its provisions by the means stated in cl 2.

F. MIBI REQUESTS CLAIMANT TO JOIN IT AS CO-DEFENDANT WITH UNINSURED MOTORIST

1. Can the MIBI request a claimant to join it as a co-defendant?

[10.19] Before suing the MIBI for performance of the 2009 Agreement under cl 2.4, it seems that a claimant must have made a claim for compensation to the MIBI under cl 2.2.[48] In addition, cl 3 of the 2009 Agreement prescribes conditions precedent to the MIBI's liability.[49] These oblige a claimant, *inter alia,* to give the MIBI advance notice of an intention to seek compensation.[50] Advance notice of the institution of proceedings must also be given.[51]

[10.20] Subsequent to receiving a claim for compensation or notice of intended proceedings, the MIBI might obtain a mandate[52] from an uninsured motorist. Thereafter,

---

45. In *Bowes v MIBI* [2000] 2 IR 79, Murphy J, delivering the majority judgment of the Supreme Court, observed that the equivalent to cl 2 of the 2009 Agreement (cl 2 of the 1988 Agreement) was:

   'unhappily expressed. On the face of it, it would appear to imply that any person seeking compensation from the [MIBI], having made a claim against it, could then institute proceedings naming the [MIBI] as the sole-defendant. That interpretation would make [cl 2(2) of the 1988 Agreement which is the equivalent to cl 2.3 of 2009 Agreement and cl 2.2 of the 2004 Agreement] irrelevant and unnecessary. Furthermore, such construction would ignore the fact that the liability of the [MIBI] (or the provisions of the agreement enforceable against it by a claimant) arises in two distinct ways. First, the [MIBI] may be liable on foot of a judgment obtained against an uninsured or inadequately insured driver, or alternatively to pay compensation for the negligence of the driver or user of a vehicle (whether insured or not) who is unidentified or untraced. Whatever procedures are adopted, those are the only circumstances in which provisions can be enforced by a claimant against the [MIBI]. Either the claimant seeks to be repaid a judgment debt – in which case he must issue proceedings against a driver – or else he seeks to be compensated for the negligent driving of an untraced and unidentified driver. In that case he may, subject to compliance with the various conditions precedent, institute proceedings against the [MIBI] as the sole-defendant; but his essential proof to obtain compensation would be the negligence of an unidentified and untraced driver.' (at pp 88–89).
46. And cl 2 of the 2004 Agreement.
47. As opposed to 'may' in cl 2 of the 1988 Agreement.
48. As noted above, however, it is arguable that cl 2 of the 2009 Agreement (which effectively states that a claimant 'must' proceed by one of the means stated in that clause) allows a claimant to sue without first claiming compensation. Clause 2 of the 2009 Agreement, however, cannot be read in isolation from cl 3 of the 2009 Agreement, which provides, *inter alia,* that a claimant must give the MIBI prior notice of the intention to seek compensation.
49. And cl 3 of the 2004 Agreement. See **Ch 4**.
50. Clause 3.1 of the 2009 and 2004 Agreements. See **Ch 4**, para **4.09–4.11**.
51. Clause 3.8 of the 2009 and 2004 Agreements. See **Ch 5**, para **5.11**.
52. See **Ch 9**.

the MIBI may defend any proceedings that the claimant issues against the uninsured motorist and do so on behalf of that uninsured motorist. In practice, however, the MIBI may not secure a mandate until after the proceedings have issued or indeed may not secure a mandate at all. In the latter situation, the MIBI might wish to be joined as a co-defendant in order that it can protect its interests. For example, the MIBI might have evidence establishing that the uninsured motorist defendant was not guilty of negligent driving and/or that responsibility lies with another insured motorist or indeed the claimant.

[10.21] Thus, while it may be tempting not to join the MIBI to proceedings against an uninsured motorist defendant, the reality is that cl 2 of the 2009 and 2004 Agreements state that a person 'must seek to enforce the provisions of [the] Agreement by' the means identified therein. It seems therefore that cl 2.3 of the 2009 Agreement requires that, where a claimant sues an uninsured motorist, he must name the MIBI as a co-defendant to the proceedings. Where it is not named as a co-defendant, the MIBI would be well advised to call upon the claimant to so join it in accordance with cl 2.3 of the 2009 Agreement, particularly where there is no mandate and it is unlikely to obtain one. This request might be issued in response to the claimant's compliance with the obligation to make an advance claim for compensation to the MIBI[53] or the obligation to give advance notice of the commencement of proceedings.[54]

2. Can the MIBI refuse to satisfy judgment against uninsured if a claimant refuses to join it as co-defendant?

[10.22] If, notwithstanding the MIBI's request, a claimant refuses to join it as a co-defendant, and the claimant succeeds in his action and obtains an award of damages against an uninsured motorist defendant, the MIBI might decline to satisfy the award on the grounds that it was not proceeded against in the manner dictated by cl 2.3 of the 2009 Agreement (ie as a co-defendant). The same defence would be available if the claimant sued the MIBI under cl 2.4 of the 2009 Agreement for satisfaction of the award.

[10.23] Furthermore, the MIBI could defend an enforcement action by reference to the provisions of the relevant agreement that exclude its liability (eg assert that the claimant voluntarily entered the vehicle and knew that it was stolen).[55]

---

53.   Clauses 2.1 and 3.1 of both the 2009 and 2004 Agreements.
54.   Clause 3.8 of both the 2009 and 2004 Agreements. Alternatively, where the 2004 Agreement applies, the MIBI might rely on cl 3.10 thereof to require a plaintiff to join it as a co-defendant. This permits the MIBI to require a plaintiff to take 'all reasonable steps against any person against whom the plaintiff might have a remedy in respect of or arising out of the [injury or damage]'. Given the difficulties with cl 3.10 of the 2004 Agreement (and its absence from the 2009 Agreement), it is submitted that, where the MIBI wishes to be joined as a co-defendant, it should rely on cl 2.2 of the 2004 Agreement (or cl 2.3 of the 2009 Agreement). See also fn **34** above.
55.   Clause 5.1 of both the 2009 and 2004 Agreements.

3. Can the MIBI refuse to satisfy judgment obtained in default against uninsured if claimant refused its request to join it as co-defendant?

[10.24] A claimant who sues an uninsured motorist defendant (and not the MIBI) may obtain judgment in default of appearance[56] or defence[57] against that defendant. Assuming that the uninsured motorist defendant fails to discharge the judgment within twenty-eight days, the claimant might then look to the MIBI for satisfaction of that judgment.[58]

[10.25] It is submitted, however, that the defences of the nature referred to in paras **10.22–10.23** are also open to the MIBI in this example. Further, it is clear from *Curran v Gallagher, Gallagher and MIBI*[59] that a judgment in default against an uninsured motorist defendant is a finding in default of denial by that uninsured motorist defendant and is binding only as between the plaintiff and that uninsured motorist defendant. It does not bind the MIBI.[60]

[10.26] For this reason, it is also open to the MIBI to defend enforcement proceedings on the merits of the case. For example, it could defend an action brought against it under cl 2.4 of the 2009 Agreement on the grounds that the uninsured motorist against whom the judgment was obtained was not in fact guilty of negligent driving.[61]

---

56. See Rules of the Superior Courts 1986, O 13, r 6.
57. Rules of the Superior Courts 1986, O 27, r 8 (as substituted by the Rules of the Superior Courts (Order 27 (Amendment) Rules) 2004 (SI 63/2004).
58. Pursuant to cl 2.4 of the 2009 Agreement (cl 2.3 of the 2004 Agreement) and in which case the plaintiff would seek a court order 'for the performance of the agreement' and pursuant to cl 4.1.1 of the 2009 Agreement (cl 4.1 of the 2004 Agreement) for payment of the amount of the unsatisfied judgment.
59. *Curran v Gallagher, Gallagher and MIBI* (7 May 1997, unreported) SC (*per* Keane and Lynch JJ, Murphy J dissenting).
60. In *Curran*, the plaintiff obtained judgment in default of defence against the owner and user of a car. By order of the High Court, it was directed that an issue be tried as to whether or not the MIBI was obliged to satisfy any judgment obtained on the grounds that the plaintiff knew (or ought to have known) that there was no insurance policy. This defence to satisfaction was allowed in the High Court and the plaintiff's claim against the MIBI was dismissed. The Supreme Court allowed the appeal on the basis that the MIBI failed to discharge the onus of proving the plaintiff's knowledge of the absence of insurance. In so doing, however, the court acknowledged that a judgment in default of defence against the owner of the vehicle was 'a finding, in default of denial' by that owner that it was used with his consent and was 'a finding as between the plaintiff and the [owner] and [did] not therefore bind the [MIBI] even though the [MIBI] must have been aware of that judgment' (*per* Lynch J, p 3). Later the court repeated the fact that 'the judgment in default of defence against the [owner] does not bind the [MIBI]' (*per* Lynch J, p 17). However, the decision in *Kelly v MIBI* (24 February 1975, unreported) SC, should be noted. In *Kelly*, the Supreme Court refused to allow the MIBI re-open the basis upon which the plaintiff obtained judgment in default against an uninsured motorist and upon which damages were assessed. The MIBI subsequently sought to defend the plaintiff's claim for satisfaction of the award on the basis that the plaintiff was an excepted person. However, the MIBI had full knowledge and prior notice of fact that the judgment was given on the basis that the plaintiff was not an excepted person and it had acknowledged in writing that the plaintiff had complied with the 1964 Agreement. However, this decision was made by reference to the 1964 Agreement, which did not provide for the joinder of the MIBI as a co-defendant to proceedings against an uninsured motorist.
61. Clause 4.1.1 of the 2009 Agreement (cl 4.1 of the 2004 Agreement) as appropriate. (contd .../)

[10.27] In addition, it is notable that cl 3.9 of the 2009 Agreement contains a provision that compels a claimant to give the MIBI no less than twenty-eight days notice before 'issuing a motion' against 'any person' which may give rise to an obligation on the part of the MIBI.[62] This obligation is clearly not confined to proceedings to which the MIBI is a party. Notwithstanding this requirement, it seems that the MIBI cannot do anything to prevent a claimant from proceeding to obtain judgment.[63] Enforcement of such a judgment is, however, an entirely different issue.

G. THE MIBI APPLIES TO COURT TO BE JOINED AS CO-DEFENDANT WITH UNINSURED

[10.28] Order 15, r 13 of the Rules of the Superior Courts 1986, provides, *inter alia:*

> '... The Court may at any stage of the proceedings, either upon or without the application of either party, and on such terms as may appear to the Court to be just, order ... that the names of any parties, whether plaintiffs or defendants, who ought to have been joined, or whose presence before the Court may be necessary in order to enable the Court effectually and completely to adjudicate upon and settle all the questions involved in the cause of matter, be added.'

[10.29] A similar provision existed under the English Rules of the Superior Courts. Order 15, r 6(2)(b) of the Rules of the Superior Courts 1967, as amended, allowed the courts to order any person to be added as a party 'whose presence before the Court is necessary to ensure that all matters in dispute in the cause or matter may be effectually and completely determined and adjudicated upon'.

[10.30] The extent of the English provision was considered in *Gurtner v Circuit,*[64] wherein the MIB applied to be added as a defendant to the proceedings. The plaintiff suffered injury when he was run down by the defendant motorist in June 1961. The plaintiff issued proceedings against the defendant motorist in June 1964. No steps were

---

61.   (contd) In this regard, one must be mindful of the fact that the MIBI is not generally liable to satisfy unpaid judgments. It is only liable to satisfy a judgment in respect of any liability for death or injury to a person or property damage 'which is required to be covered by an approved policy under Section 56 of the [Road Traffic] Act' ie the liability of the MIBI is confined to judgments in respect of liability caused by the negligent use of a motor vehicle in a public place.

62.   A clause of this nature appeared for the first time in cl 3.9 of the 2004 Agreement which obliges a claimant to give no less than 28 days before 'obtaining' judgment against 'any person' which may give rise to an obligation on the part of the MIBI.

63.   In these circumstances, and in respect of a claim governed by the 2004 Agreement, perhaps the MIBI might rely on cl 3.10 of the 2004 Agreement to call upon the plaintiff to abstain from obtaining a judgment in default. However, it is difficult to see how the MIBI could rely on this clause in this way because it provides that '... the Claimant shall take all reasonable steps against any person against whom the Claimant may have a remedy ...'. If the MIBI was to utilise cl 3.10 in these circumstances, it would effectively be calling upon a claimant to abstain from taking action to obtain a judgment against the person whom the claimant asserts is responsible for his injury or damage. In any event, the difficulties with cl 3.10 of the 2004 Agreement are noted above at para **10.12**.

64.   *Gurtner v Circuit* [1968] 2 QB 587, [1968] 2 WLR 668, [1968] 1 All ER 328, [1968] 1 Lloyd's Rep 171.

taken in the proceedings until June 1965, at which time it was discovered that the defendant had gone to Canada in or about 1962. The writ was renewed and, when the plaintiff was still unable to locate the defendant by November 1965, his solicitors wrote to the MIB who asked an insurance company to investigate the matter. Neither the defendant's insurer nor the defendant motorist was located. In June 1967, the plaintiff obtained an order for substituted service on the defendant motorist, care of the insurance company which the MIB had asked to investigate the matter. Thereafter, the MIB sought to be joined as a defendant to the proceedings. The Master of the High Court made an order joining the MIB as a party but this order was overturned by the High Court. On a further appeal, the Court of Appeal considered that it had a discretion to add a party to an action if that party would be affected in his legal rights or in his pocket by the determination of the dispute. Lord Denning MR disagreed with earlier decisions[65] that held that the rule should be interpreted narrowly. He said:

> 'It seems to me that when two parties are in dispute in an action at law, and the determination of that dispute will directly affect a third person in his legal rights or in his pocket, in that he will be bound to foot the bill, then the court in its discretion may allow him to be added as a party on such terms as it thinks fit. By so doing, the court achieves the object of the rule. It enables all matters in dispute to "be effectually and completely determined upon" between all those directly concerned in the outcome.'[66]

[10.31] Having considered the absence of privity of contract between a plaintiff and the MIB, Diplock LJ stated:

> 'Clearly, the rules of natural justice require that a person who is to be bound by a judgment in an action brought against another party and directly liable to the plaintiff upon the judgment should be entitled to be heard in the proceedings in which the judgment is sought to be obtained. A matter in dispute is not, in my view, effectually and completely "adjudicated upon" unless the rules of natural justice are observed and all those who will be liable to satisfy the judgment are given an opportunity to be heard.'[67]

[10.32] The Court of Appeal ordered the joinder of the MIB as a co-defendant on its undertaking to pay any damages that might be awarded to the plaintiff.

H. DEFAULT JUDGMENT AGAINST UNINSURED MOTORIST AS CO-DEFENDANT WITH THE MIBI

1. Can the MIBI prevent a claimant getting judgment in default against uninsured motorist?

[10.33] A claimant who sues an uninsured and the MIBI in one action might find that the uninsured does not sign a mandate and yet fails to participate in the proceedings. Thus, the claimant might be in a position to obtain judgment in default of appearance or

---

65. Including *Fire, Auto and Marine Insurance Co Ltd v Greene* [1964] 2 QB 687, [1964] 2 All ER 761, [1964] 3 WLR 319; wherein the High Court refused the MIB's application to be joined as a co-defendant.
66. *Gurtner v Circuit* [1968] 2 QB 587 at 595.
67. *Gurtner v Circuit* [1968] 2 QB 587 at 602–603.

defence against that uninsured motorist defendant. As noted above,[68] while cl 3.9 of the 2009 Agreement obliges a claimant to give the MIBI advance notice of twenty eight days before issuing a motion for judgment,[69] the MIBI does not appear to have authority to prevent a claimant from obtaining such a judgment.

2. Can the MIBI refuse to satisfy a judgment in default against uninsured motorist where the MIBI is a co-defendant?

[10.34] Where judgment is obtained in default of appearance or defence against an uninsured motorist, the MIBI is not automatically liable to satisfy the judgment. As noted above, judgment in default against an uninsured motorist defendant does not bind the MIBI[70]. Generally, if a claimant sues an uninsured motorist defendant and the MIBI in one action and obtains judgment in default of appearance[71] or defence[72] against the uninsured, the damages to which the claimant may be entitled against the uninsured motorist defendant are ascertained at the same time as the hearing of the action against the MIBI.[73] At that hearing, the MIBI is entitled to defend the proceedings by reference to the provisions of the Agreement that exclude its liability (eg assert that the claimant voluntarily entered the vehicle and knew that it was stolen).[74]

[10.35] Alternatively, the MIBI may defend the proceedings on the merits of the case and, for example, assert that there was no negligent driving on the part of the uninsured motorist defendant.[75] With respect to the latter defence, it is important not to lose sight of the fact that the MIBI is not generally liable to discharge an unpaid judgment. Its liability is to satisfy a judgment in respect of any liability for injury or damage 'which is required to be covered by an approved policy under section 56 of the [Road Traffic] Act' obtained against any person (and whether or not such person is covered by an approved policy of insurance). Section 56 compels insurance against 'negligent use' of a motor vehicle. Hence, the liability of MIBI is confined to discharging judgments obtained

---

68.   See para **10.27**.

69.   To be compared with cl 3.9 of the 2004 Agreement, which obliges a claimant to give the same period of notice before 'obtaining' such a judgment.

70.   See para **10.25**.

71.   See Rules of the Superior Courts 1986, O 13, r 6.

72.   Rules of the Superior Courts, O 27, r 8 (as substituted by the Rules of the Superior Courts (Order 27 (Amendment) Rules) 2004 (SI 63/2004)).

73.   Rules of the Superior Courts, O 13, r 9 (in default of appearance) and O 27, r 10 (in default of defence). Alternatively, the MIBI might seek an order directing an issue to be tried as to whether or not the MIBI is obliged to satisfy a judgment obtained against the owner and/or driver in the circumstances.

74.   Clause 5.2 of the 2009 and 2004 Agreements. Thus, in *Curran v Gallagher, Gallagher and MIBI* (7 May 1997, unreported) SC, the MIBI expressly pleaded in its defence that it was not bound to satisfy any judgment that might be obtained by the plaintiff on the grounds that he knew (or ought to have known) that there was no approved policy of insurance in respect of the vehicle in which he was travelling (under cl 5(2) of the 1988 MIBI Agreement). When the plaintiff obtained judgment in default of defence, the MIBI obtained a High Court order directing that an issue be tried as to whether or not it was obliged to satisfy any judgment on the grounds that the plaintiff knew or ought to have known of the absence of insurance.

75.   Clause 4.1.1 of the 2009 Agreement (Clause 4.1 of the 2004 Agreement).

against persons in respect of their liability for such negligent use. Thus, it is not automatically bound to satisfy any judgment obtained in default.

I. UNINSURED MOTORIST AND NON-MOTORIST AS CONCURRENT WRONGDOERS[76]

[10.36] A further scenario requires consideration, namely where a claimant suffers injury in an accident for which responsibility lies between an uninsured motorist and a *non*-motorist, eg a local authority. It seems that a claimant in this example may properly claim against the local authority, the uninsured motorist and the MIBI in the same action.[77] Assuming that discrete damage cannot be attributed as between the local authority and the uninsured motorist, they are both concurrent wrongdoers and it is appropriate for notices of contribution and indemnity to be exchanged between the two of them.[78]

[10.37] Taking the above example a step further, if a court determined that the local authority was 20% responsible and the uninsured motorist was 80% responsible for the accident, they would be jointly and severally liable for the award.[79] The MIBI would anticipate that the local authority would discharge the total award and that the local authority might then avail of its right to pursue the uninsured motorist for contribution in the amount of 80%.[80]

[10.38] However, what if the local authority failed to discharge the judgment within twenty-eight days? Could the claimant turn to the MIBI for satisfaction of the full judgment under cl 4.1.1 of the 2009 Agreement? From a practical point of view, the MIBI might decide to satisfy the total judgment. Thereafter, it could obtain an assignment of the judgment from the claimant[81] and take steps to enforce the entire judgment against the local authority and recoup all the monies that it paid out to the claimant. If the MIBI succeeded in so doing, the local authority could, in theory, subsequently pursue the uninsured motorist defendant for contribution in the amount of 80%.

[10.39] The foregoing practical approach may well be adopted by the MIBI in circumstances where the *non*-motorist defendant (in our example the local authority) is a mark for damages. However, the MIBI might not be so keen to adopt such an approach if the *non*-motorist defendant in our example was not a mark for damages. For this reason,

---

76. See **Ch 8** for a detailed discussion of concurrent wrongdoers.
77. However, the comments made at para **10.07–10.12** should be noted.
78. In actions such as this, it is not, however, appropriate for the MIBI to serve a notice of indemnity and contribution because it is not a concurrent wrongdoer.
79. In a situation such as this, the MIBI must be alert to ensure that the award is only made jointly and severally as against the concurrent wrongdoers (ie the local authority and the uninsured motorist). See further, *Rogan v Walsh and MIBI* [2004] IEHC 68, (22 April 2004, unreported) HC, Peart J, where, in an action against an uninsured and the MIBI, judgment appears to have been entered against both defendants on a joint and several basis.
80. Assuming of course that a notice of indemnity and contribution has been duly served.
81. Clause 3.11 of the 2009 and 2004 Agreements. See **Appendix 7.3** for the document that is currently being used by the MIBI to obtain assignments of judgments.

it is necessary to consider the precise legal position of the MIBI in the above example ie is it liable to discharge a judgment entered against two concurrent wrongdoers (one of whom is an uninsured motorist and one of whom is a *non*-motorist) in circumstances where the *non*-motorist fails to discharge the judgment entered jointly and severally against both of them? The answer to this question requires a consideration of cl 4.1.1 of the 2009 Agreement, which provides:

> 'Subject to the provisions of Clause 4.4, if Judgment / Injuries Board Order to Pay in respect of any liability for injury to person or death or damage to property which is required to be covered by an approved policy of insurance under Section 56 of the [Road Traffic] Act [1961] is obtained against any person or persons in any court ... or the Injuries Board established by the PIAB Act, 2003 whether or not such person or persons be in fact covered by an approved policy of insurance and any such judgment is not satisfied in full within 28 days from the date upon which the person or persons in whose favour such judgment is given become entitled to enforce it then MIBI will so far as such judgment relates to injury to person or damage to property *and subject to the provisions of this Agreement* pay ... to the person or persons in whose favour such judgment was given any sum payable or remaining payable thereunder in respect of *the aforesaid liability including taxed costs (or such proportion thereof as is attributable to the relevant liability)*[82] or satisfy or cause to be satisfied such judgment whatever may be the cause of the failure of the judgment debtor.'[83]

[10.40] A first reading of cl 4.1.1 suggests that, if the *non*-motorist defendant failed to satisfy the judgment within twenty-eight days, the MIBI would be liable to satisfy the judgment in total. It is arguable, however, that cl 4.1.1 only obliges the MIBI to discharge that portion of the judgment that is attributable to liability for injury which is required to be covered by insurance ie the uninsured motorist in our example. On this interpretation, and using the example above, the MIBI would be liable to discharge only 80% of the award.[84]

[10.41] However, if the MIBI was to succeed in interpreting cl 4.1.1 in this way, and therefore discharged only 80% of the award, an interesting question would arise as to whether or not the MIBI would be entitled to require the claimant to assign a portion of the judgment (ie 80%). In order to pursue the *non*-motorist defendant for recovery of the 80% that it pays out to the claimant, the MIBI would require an assignment of the relevant portion of the judgment. Clause 3.11 of the 2009 Agreement, however, does not appear to contemplate anything less than a judgment being assigned in its entirety.[85]

---

82.   All italics indicate emphasis added.

83.   See also cl 4.1 of the 2004 Agreement.

84.   Clause 4.1.1 of the 2009 Agreement (and cl 4.1 of the 2004 Agreement) lacks clarity. This difficulty may well be referable to the possibility that it was drafted only in contemplation of judgments being obtained in proceedings in which all the defendants (other than the MIBI) are motorists.

85.   Clause 3.11 of the 2009 Agreement provides '[a]ll judgments shall be assigned to MIBI or its nominee' (see also cl 3.11 of the 2004 Agreement).

J. LIABILITY OF AN UNINSURED MOTORIST AS A THIRD PARTY TO PROCEEDINGS

1. Introduction

[10.42] As sole defendant to proceedings, an insured motorist defendant might consider that responsibility for the accident lies totally or partially elsewhere, eg with an uninsured motorist. The claimant might be aware of this but he might decide against suing the uninsured motorist defendant on the basis that he is not a mark for damages. In such a case, the insured motorist defendant is likely to expressly plead in his defence that responsibility for the accident lies with the uninsured motorist. In these circumstances, the claimant might apply to join the uninsured (and the MIBI) as a co-defendant(s). However, what happens if the claimant decides not to join the uninsured motorist (and the MIBI) as a co-defendant(s) and it transpires at the hearing that some responsibility for the accident lies with the uninsured motorist? The answer to this question depends upon whether or not the insured motorist defendant has joined the uninsured motorist as a third party.

2. Insured motorist defendant joins uninsured motorist as a third party

[10.43] If the insured motorist defendant applies to join the uninsured motorist as a third party to the proceedings,[86] the claimant might apply to join the uninsured motorist (and perhaps the MIBI) as co-defendants to the action. If, however, the claimant does *not* so apply (so that the uninsured motorist remains a third party in the proceedings), and a court considers that the uninsured third party has some responsibility for the accident, it will generally enter judgment for the full amount against the insured motorist defendant. This result flows from s 11(1) of the Civil Liability Act 1961 (the 1961 Act).[87] Thereafter, the appropriate contribution that is recoverable by the insured motorist defendant against the uninsured third party is determined in the third party proceedings.[88] Assuming, for example, that the contribution is determined at 40%, the claimant can recover the total damages from the insured motorist defendant who may then proceed against the uninsured third party to recover the 40% contribution.[89] However, this outcome is subject to the provisions of s 35 of the 1961 Act which provides:

'(1) For the purpose of determining contributory negligence—

(i) where the plaintiff's damage was caused by concurrent wrongdoers and the plaintiff's claim against one wrongdoer has become barred by the Statute of Limitations or any other limitation enactment, the plaintiff shall be deemed to be responsible for the acts of such wrongdoer.'

---

86. To this end, Civil Liability Act 1961, s 27(1)(b) requires that the defendant serve a third party notice on the uninsured motorist 'as soon as is reasonably possible'.

87. Civil Liability Act 1961, s 11(1) provides that: '... two or more persons are concurrent wrongdoers when both or all are wrongdoers and are responsible to a [plaintiff] for the same damage, whether or not judgment has been recovered against some or all of them.'

88. Civil Liability Act 1961, s 21(2).

89. Civil Liability Act 1961, ss 21 and 27.

[10.44] Having regard to s 35, it is submitted that, if, at the time that the case is heard, the claimant is statute barred as against the uninsured third party, it is open to the insured motorist defendant to claim that the claimant is guilty of contributory negligence and 'deemed' responsible for the acts of the third party, such that damages should be reduced by 40% and judgment should only be entered against the insured motorist defendant in the amount of 60% of the damages. This avenue is significant when, as in our example, the third party is not a mark for the insured motorist defendant to recover by way of contribution.

3. Insured motorist defendant fails to join uninsured motorist as a third party

[10.45] If the insured motorist defendant does *not* join the uninsured motorist as a third party, then, provided that the court is satisfied that the insured motorist defendant has some responsibility for the accident, it will generally enter judgment for the full amount of damages against the insured motorist defendant. This result flows from s 11(1) of the 1961 Act.[90] Thereafter, the insured motorist defendant might seek to rely on the provisions of s 31 of the 1961 Act which provides:

> '[a]n action may be brought for contribution within the same period as the injured person is allowed by law for bringing an action against the contributor, or within the period of two years after the liability of the claimant is ascertained or the injured person's damages are paid, whichever is the greater.'

[10.46] Thus, the insured motorist defendant has two years, from the date on which the claimant secures judgment against him, within which to institute proceedings against the uninsured motorist for contribution.[91] In our example, the insured motorist

---

90. Civil Liability Act 1961, s 11(1) is reproduced above at fn **87**.

91. However, s 31 cannot be read in isolation from s 27. In circumstances where a concurrent wrongdoer wishes to claim contribution from a person who is not already a party to the action, s 27(1)(b) of the 1961 Act requires that the concurrent wrongdoer 'shall serve a third party notice upon such person as soon as is reasonably possible'. Thereafter, the claim for contribution can only be claimed by way of this third party procedure. Section 27(1)(b) further provides that, if a third party notice is not served in this way, 'the court may in its discretion refuse to make an order for contribution against the person from whom contribution is claimed'. Thus, there is an inconsistency between s 27(1)(b), which anticipates all claims being heard in one action, and s 31, which envisages a further claim being instituted on conclusion of the main action. This inconsistency was considered in *The Board of Governors of St. Laurence's Hospital v Staunton* [1990] 2 IR 31. Judgment was entered in the High Court in an action against the plaintiff hospital. The hospital appealed to the Supreme Court, and prior to the hearing of the appeal, obtained an order from the High Court giving it liberty to serve a third party notice on Staunton who appealed to the Supreme Court against the order joining him as a third party. On appeal against the order joining Staunton, the Supreme Court held that the hospital was barred from proceeding against Staunton for a contribution in the main action because it had not served a third party notice upon him 'as soon as [was] reasonably possible' in terms of s 27(1)(b) of the 1961 Act. However, it further held that to interpret s 27(1)(b) as barring the hospital from instituting original proceedings against Staunton for a claim of contribution would render superfluous the second sentence of s 27(1)(b) which provides that, '[i]f such third party notice is not served as aforesaid, the court may in its discretion refuse to make an order for contribution against the person from whom contribution is claimed'. (contd .../)

defendant might recover contribution in the amount of 40% in a second action brought by him.[92]

K. THE MIBI AS A THIRD PARTY TO PROCEEDINGS?

[10.47] The issue of an insured motorist defendant who wishes to join an uninsured motorist as a third party to the proceedings has been addressed above.[93] Assuming that the claimant does not join the uninsured motorist as a defendant (and the MIBI), the insured motorist defendant may question the merit of joining the uninsured motorist as a third party in circumstances where he is not a mark for damages. In this situation, the insured motorist defendant might also consider joining the MIBI as a third party for the purposes of indemnifying the uninsured motorist. However, the insured motorist defendant cannot join the MIBI as a third party for the simple reason that the MIBI is not a concurrent wrongdoer as defined by s 11(1) of the 1961 Act which provides that 'two or more persons are concurrent wrongdoers when both or all are wrongdoers and are responsible to a [plaintiff] for the same damage, whether or not judgment has been recovered against some or all of them'.[94] The third party procedure provided by s 27 of the 1961 Act is only aimed at the resolution of all issues between concurrent wrongdoers in the same action and, in our example, the concurrent wrongdoers are the insured motorist defendant and the uninsured motorist.[95]

---

91.   (contd) For this reason, s 27(1)(b) had to be interpreted as leaving it open to a defendant to bring a fresh action for contribution, albeit subject to the court's 'new and separate discretion' to refuse an order for contribution in that action. The Supreme Court considered that this interpretation was consistent with s 31, which created 'a very extensive time limit' for making a claim for contribution.

92.   As noted above at paras **10.43–10.44**, however, if, at the time that the case is heard, the claimant is statute barred as against the uninsured concurrent wrongdoer (who is not a party), it is open to the insured motorist defendant to assert that the claimant is guilty of contributory negligence and responsible for the acts of the concurrent wrongdoer who has not been sued. While it may seem peculiar and difficult for a court to embark upon determining the responsibility of an individual who is not a party to the proceedings before it, it is submitted that the court must engage in such an exercise in order to give effect to Civil Liability Act 1961, s 35(1)(i). Thus, the court might find that responsibility for the accident lies between the insured motorist defendant and the non-party uninsured motorist on a 60/40% basis. If this is done, the court may enter judgment against the insured motorist defendant in the amount of 60% of the damage sustained by the plaintiff.

93.   At paras **10.43–10.44**.

94.   In *Byrne v Bus Átha Cliath* [2005] IEHC 20, (2 February 2005, unreported) HC, O'Leary J, in which the plaintiff had incorrectly named the MIBI as a co-defendant to an action (against a bus operator) in lieu of an unidentified and untraced owner and user of a motor vehicle, O'Leary J observed (*obiter dictum*) that '[t]his is not a case in which a notice of indemnity/contribution applies. No such notice has been served as the nature of the MIBI agreement makes such a notice worthless' (at p 3).

95.   Furthermore, cl 2 of the 2009 and 2004 Agreements only envisages the MIBI being joined as a defendant (rather than as a third party) to proceedings. In *Hyland v MIBI and Dun Laoghaire Rathdown County Council* (29 July 2003, unreported) CC, *ex tempore,* Judge McMahon, the court noted that the liability of the MIBI was based upon its voluntary submission to the regime established under the agreement(s) concluded between it and the various government minister(s) and that liability did not attach to it in consequence of its fault, vicarious liability or pursuant to statute.

[**10.48**] Furthermore, in terms of the 2009 and 2004 Agreements, cl 4 only accords rights to a person who has suffered personal injury or damage to property and the insured motorist defendant in the above scenario is not such a person.[96]

[**10.49**] Given that the MIBI exists, *inter alia,* to satisfy unsatisfied judgments, it should not be joined as a third party to proceedings in which a defendant claims that the accident was caused or contributed to by an unidentified or untraced motorist. A defendant in this position can plead this fact in his defence. On receipt of the defence, the appropriate course of action is for the claimant to institute a second action against the MIBI on the basis of the negligence of an untraced and unidentified motorist pursuant to cl 2.4 of the 2009 Agreement.[97]

L. MIBI OR INSURER'S LIABILITY?

1. Introduction

[**10.50**] As mentioned at para **10.06**, it is arguable that, in certain circumstances, the MIBI need not be named as a defendant at all when *someone* was insured to drive the vehicle that caused the accident, even though the driver at the time of the accident may not have been. In order to understand the foregoing statement, it is necessary to consider art 13 of the Sixth Directive.

2. Article 13 of the Sixth Directive

[**10.51**] Article 13 of the Sixth Directive[98] provides that:

'1. Each Member State shall take all appropriate measures to ensure that any statutory provision or any contractual clause contained in an insurance policy issued in accordance with Article 3[99] shall be deemed to be void in respect of claims by third parties who have been victims of an accident where that statutory provision or contractual clause excludes from insurance the use or driving of vehicles by:

(a)   persons who do not have express or implied authorisation to do so;

(b)   persons who do not hold a licence permitting them to drive the vehicle concerned;

(c)   persons who are in breach of the statutory technical requirements concerning the condition and safety of the vehicle concerned.

However, the provision or clause referred to in point (a) of the first subparagraph may be invoked against persons who voluntarily entered the vehicle which caused the damage or injury, when the insurer can prove that they knew the vehicle was stolen.

---

96.   For all the same reasons, it is submitted that, where judgment is entered against an insured motorist defendant in circumstances where the insured motorist wishes to claim a contribution against an uninsured motorist, he could bring an action against the uninsured motorist under s 31 of the 1961 Act but could not proceed in this way against the MIBI.

97.   Previously, cl 2.3 of the 2004 Agreement.

98.   Formerly Second Directive, art 2(1).

99.   Formerly First Directive, art 3(1).

Member States shall have the option – in the case of accidents occurring on their territory – of not applying the provision in the first subparagraph if and in so far as the victim may obtain compensation for the damage suffered from a social security body.

2. In the case of vehicles stolen or obtained by violence, Member States may provide that the body specified at Article 10(1) is to pay compensation instead of the insurer under the conditions set out in paragraph 1 of this Article ....

3. ...'

[10.52] The Sixth Directive appears to direct the EEA States to take measures at national level to prohibit (or void) any condition in an insurance policy that excludes liability for injury caused to a third party by a vehicle (in respect of which an insurance policy exists) solely on the basis that the driver did not have permission to drive or use it.[100] It seems that the only basis upon which Ireland may permit an exclusion clause of this nature is where the injured party actually entered the vehicle (that caused him the damage) in circumstances where he knew that the vehicle was stolen and the insurer can prove this to be the case.[101] Otherwise, it appears that the general requirement that Ireland take steps to prohibit (or void) any condition in an insurance policy that purports to exclude liability for third party injury caused by a vehicle on the basis that the driver did not have express or implied authorisation to do so is if Ireland:

(a) takes "the option" of providing that such a victim will be compensated by a social security body;[102] and

(b) in relation *only* to vehicles that are stolen or obtained by violence (including anyone injured by the driving of it, other than a passenger who voluntarily enters it and knew that it was stolen), Ireland provides that the MIBI will pay compensation 'instead of the insurer'.[103]

---

100. Sixth Directive, art 13(1)(a).
101. Sixth Directive, art 13(1) second subparagraph. See also *Stych v Dibble and Tradax Insurance Company Ltd* [2012] EWHC 1606. The plaintiff in that case suffered permanent injuries while travelling as a passenger (the passenger) in a vehicle being driven by the first defendant (the driver) who was not insured to drive it. The vehicle was owned by a customer of the garage in which the driver worked and it was used by the driver without the owner's consent. The passenger obtained judgment in default of defence against the driver and the issue was whether or not the second defendant (the owner's insurer) was bound to satisfy that judgment. The Road Traffic Act 1988, s 151(2)(b) (the 1988 Act) provides that an insurer is liable to meet a judgment obtained against a person (other than the insured person), except in respect of an 'excluded liability', which is defined by s 151(4) of the 1988 Act as, *inter alia*, a liability in respect of injury to a person 'who, at the time of the use which gave rise to the liability, was allowing himself to be carried in or upon the vehicle and knew or had reason to believe that the vehicle had been stolen or unlawfully taken ...'. The High Court held that s 151(4) must be interpreted consistently with Second Directive, art 2(1) (now Sixth Directive, art 13(1)) which referred only to a passenger who 'knew' that the vehicle was stolen ie the words 'or ought to have known' bore no additional meaning. The court did not address the issue of whether the words 'unlawfully taken' were consistent with the Second Directive in circumstances where counsel for the passenger conceded that a taking short of theft would bring the exception into play.
102. Sixth Directive, art 13(1), third subparagraph.
103. Sixth Directive, art 13(2), first subparagraph.

[10.53] Furthermore, the Sixth Directive directs the EEA States to ensure that any party injured as a result of an accident covered by insurance as referred to in art 3 enjoys a direct right of action against the insurance undertaking covering the person responsible against civil liability.[104]

3. *Churchill Insurance Co Ltd v Wilkinson* and *Evans v Equity Claims Ltd*[105]

[10.54] The European Court of Justice (ECJ) has consistently held that the aim of the various directives is to ensure that compulsory motor vehicle insurance against civil liability in respect of the use of motor vehicles allows *all passengers* who are victims of an accident caused by a motor vehicle to be compensated for the injury or loss they have suffered.[106]

[10.55] In *Churchill Insurance Co Ltd v Wilkinson* and *Evans v Equity Claims Ltd*,[107] however, the ECJ was faced with a situation where the person who suffered injury in a vehicle being driven by an uninsured driver was in fact insured to drive the vehicle that caused the accident (the insured victim). The insured victim had permitted the uninsured driver to drive the vehicle and the insured victim was travelling in that vehicle as a passenger, being driven by the uninsured, at the time of the accident. In that case, the ECJ went as far as to say that the directives:[108]

> 'must be interpreted as precluding national rules the effect of which is to omit automatically the requirement that the insurer should compensate a passenger, the victim of a road traffic accident, on the ground that the passenger was insured to drive the vehicle which caused the accident but that the driver was not'.[109]

[10.56] The ECJ in *Churchill* considered this to be the position even if the insured victim was aware that the person to whom he gave permission to drive the vehicle was not insured to do so.[110]

4. The Road Traffic (Compulsory Insurance) Regulations 1962

[10.57] The Road Traffic (Compulsory Insurance) Regulations 1962, as amended (the 1962 Regulations),[111] which purport to transpose art 13 of the Sixth Directive (as

---

104. Sixth Directive, art 18.
105. *Churchill Insurance Co Ltd v Wilkinson and Evans v Equity Claims Ltd* (Joined Cases C–442/10), 1 December 2011.
106. See *Candolin v Pohjola* (Case C–537/03) [2005] ECR I–5745, at paras 27 and 32; *Farrell v Whitty, Minister for the Environment, Ireland, Attorney General and the MIBI* (Case 356/05) [2007] ECR I–03067 at para 23; and *Churchill Insurance Co Ltd v Wilkinson and Evans v Equity Claims Ltd* (Joined Cases C–442/10), 1 December 2011, at para 29.
107. *Churchill Insurance Co Ltd v Wilkinson and Evans v Equity Claims Ltd* (Joined Cases C–442/10), 1 December 2011.
108. Referring to the Third Directive, art 1, first subparagraph (now Sixth Directive, art 12(1)) and Second Directive, art 2(1) (now Sixth Directive, art 13(1)).
109. *Churchill Insurance Co Ltd v Wilkinson and Evans v Equity Claims Ltd* (Joined Cases C–442/10), 1 December 2011 at para 36.
110. *Churchill Insurance Co Ltd v Wilkinson and Evans v Equity Claims Ltd* (Joined Cases C–442/10), 1 December 2011 at para 47.
111. The Road Traffic (Compulsory Insurance) Regulations 1962 (SI 14/1962), art 5 and First Schedule thereto, (contd .../)

previously contained in the Second Directive[112]), are tortuous and totally lacking in clarity. An analysis of the 1962 Regulations is therefore required. Section 76 of the Road Traffic Act 1961 (s 76) is also relevant to such an analysis.[113]

[10.58] Article 5(1) of the 1962 Regulations defines a prohibited condition and states that any condition, restriction or limitation on the liability of an insurer under an approved policy of insurance 'which comes within any of the classes specified in the First Schedule' thereto, or any condition which has substantially the same effect, is a prohibited condition.[114]

[10.59] Thereafter, para (2) of the First Schedule to the 1962 Regulations (the First Schedule) prohibits:

'[a]ny limitation or restriction on the persons ... whose driving of a vehicle is covered by the approved policy ... except conditions which limit the persons so covered[115] in any one or more of the following ways:

(a)   by specifying by name the persons to be so covered,

---

111.   (contd) as amended by the Road Traffic (Compulsory Insurance) Regulations, 1964 (SI 58/ 1964), art 2; the Road Traffic (Compulsory Insurance) (Amendment) Regulations 1977 (SI 359/ 1977), art 2; and the Road Traffic (Compulsory Insurance) (Amendment) Regulations 1987 (SI 321/1987), art 4.

112.   Second Directive, art 2.

113.   The Road Traffic Act 1961, s 76(1) provides: 'Where a person (in this section referred to as the claimant) claims to be entitled to recover from the owner of a mechanically propelled vehicle or from a person (other than the owner) using a mechanically propelled vehicle (in this section referred to as the user), or has in any court of justice (in proceedings of which the vehicle insurer or vehicle guarantor hereinafter mentioned had prior notification) recovered judgment against the owner or user for, a sum (whether liquidated or unliquidated) against *the liability for which the owner or user is insured by an approved policy of insurance* or the payment of which by the owner or user is guaranteed by an approved guarantee, the claimant may serve by registered post, on the vehicle insurer by whom the policy was issued, or on the vehicle insurer or the vehicle guarantor by whom the guarantee was issued, a notice in writing of the claim or judgment for the sum, and upon the service of the notice such of the following provisions as are applicable shall, subject to subsection 2 (of this section) have effect: ...

    (d) Where the claimant has not so recovered judgment for the sum, the claimant may apply to any court of competent jurisdiction in which he might institute proceedings for the recovery of the sum from the owner or user for leave to institute and prosecute those proceedings against the insurer or guarantor (as the case may be) in lieu of the owner or user, and the court, if satisfied that the owner or user is not in the State, or cannot be found or cannot be served with the process of the court, or that it is for any other reason just and equitable that the application should be granted, may grant the application, and thereupon the claimant shall be entitled to institute and prosecute those proceedings against the insurer or guarantor and to recover therein from the insurer or guarantor any sum which he would be entitled to recover from the owner or user and the payment of which the insurer or guarantor has insured or guaranteed...' (emphasis added).

114.   Without any reference to art 5(1), art 5(2) of the 1962 Regulations provides that an approved policy of insurance shall not contain any condition, restriction or limitation on the liability of the insurer that 'affects the right of any person, except the person to whom the policy ... was issued' to recover, by virtue of the policy, an amount under s 76 of the 1961 Act or which could have the effect of reducing the amount which such a person could so recover, if such condition, restriction or limitation is a prohibited condition.

115.   Emphasis added.

(b)   by specifying by name the persons not to be so covered,

(c)   ...

(d)   ...

(e)   by requiring persons so covered to have the consent of a named person to such driving;

(f)   ...

(g)   ...

(h)   ...

(i)   by specifying that the vehicle must not have been stolen or obtained by violence or taken without the consent of the owner or other lawful authority.'

The conditions referred to at (e), (f) and (g) ... shall provide that the limitations or restrictions shall not apply as respects a claim by a person to recover moneys from the insurer under section 76 of the Act".

[10.60] Paragraph (i) and the last sentence of para (2) of the First Schedule were inserted by Regulations in 1987 (the 1987 Regulations).[116] The explanatory note to the 1987 Regulations states that they give effect to certain provisions of the Second Directive and prevent insurers from 'refusing or reducing a claim by a third party victim of an accident' in specific circumstances and '[t]he effect of this will be to transfer liability for relevant compensation claims from the [MIBI] to motor insurers'.

[10.61] The explanatory note further states that the 1987 Regulations:

'also explicitly provide that insurers can refuse claims arising out of the negligent use, in a public place, of a vehicle which has been stolen or obtained by violence or (contrary to section 112 of the [1961 Act]) taken or used without lawful authority e.g. for "joyriding". The innocent victim of a road traffic accident involving such a vehicle can claim compensation, subject to certain conditions, from the MIBI.'[117]

---

116.   The Road Traffic (Compulsory Insurance) (Amendment) Regulations 1987 (SI 321/1987), art 4.

117.   Curiously, the explanatory note to the European Communities (Road Traffic) (Compulsory Insurance) (Amendment) Regulations 1987 (SI 322/1987) states that the 1987 Regulations (in their original form).
       'implement other provisions of [the Second Directive] and which, in effect, preclude a motor insurer from refusing or reducing compensation by a victim of a road accident *where the driver would otherwise be insured but where*:
       −   the vehicle has been used without the consent of a named person; or
       −   the driver does not hold a valid driving license or, where appropriate, a public service license.' (emphasis added).
       This suggests that the intended purpose of the 1987 Regulations was only to ensure that an insurer could not exclude liability for a technical breach by a person who was otherwise named in the insurance policy, as opposed to generally protecting an innocent victim who is injured by the driving of a vehicle by a person who is not named in the insurance policy (and which appears to have been the intended purpose of the Second Directive).

5. Irish judgments

[10.62] Before analysing the 1962 Regulations, it is appropriate to refer to three particular High Court decisions. The first is *Melia v Melia, Lara Ltd and the MIBI.*[118] In this case, the plaintiff claimed that, while travelling as a passenger in a car, he was injured as a result of the negligent driving of a truck by a servant or agent of the truck owner. The use of the truck was covered by an insurance policy with Quinn Direct. However, a condition of the policy provided that only cardboard could be transported in the truck, as opposed to rubble that was being conveyed at the time of the accident. The insurer purported to repudiate the policy on the basis that the activity engaged in was not an insured risk and that this was not a prohibited condition under the 1962 Regulations.[119] The plaintiff applied under s 76 for leave to proceed against the insurer directly as a new defendant and in lieu of the truck owner.[120]

[10.63] Peart J was satisfied that the condition was not a prohibited condition and concluded that its breach gave rise to a situation where:

> 'for the purposes of s. 76, there was no insurance covering the liability of the user or owner in respect of this accident and [s. 76] cannot therefore be availed of for the purpose of joining Quinn Direct as a fourth defendant... '.[121]

[10.64] The second relevant case (although not concerned with s 76) is *Smith v Meade, Meade, FBD Insurance Plc, Ireland and the Attorney General.*[122] The plaintiff was injured when the van in which he was a passenger was in a collision caused by the van driver. The plaintiff had been travelling in an area that was not designed or constructed with seating accommodation for passengers. The van owner had an insurance policy. The insurer declined to indemnify the van owner in respect of the plaintiff's injuries on the basis that the policy did not cover liability for injury caused to a passenger being carried in a part of the vehicle that was not designed or constructed with seating accommodation. In essence, the insurer asserted that the plaintiff was 'an excepted person' (ie one for whom insurance was not required under Irish law) in circumstances where s 65 of the 1961 Act expressly provided that compulsory insurance was not required for such a passenger.

[10.65] The plaintiff submitted that the exclusion clause in the insurance policy should be deemed void notwithstanding the fact that the Third Directive, which required that insurance cover liability for injuries 'to all passengers' (ie regardless of seating), had not been transposed into Irish law by the date required for its transposition *or* the date of the accident. The insurer submitted that it was entitled to rely on the exclusion from the

---

118. *Melia v Melia, Lara Ltd and the MIBI* [2004] 1 IR 321.
119. Hence, the presence of the MIBI as a defendant in the proceedings.
120. It also transpired that the second defendant did not exist in any legal form (ie there was no registered company by that name) and, on this basis, Quinn Direct also maintained that it could not be an insurer for the purposes of s 76. Peart J considered it unnecessary to decide on this point.
121. At p 332.
122. *Smith v Meade, Meade, FBD Insurance Plc, Ireland and the Attorney General* [2009] 3 IR 335. This decision is under appeal as between the defendants.

obligation to insure (in s 65 of the 1961 Act), and contended that the plaintiff's remedy was one against the State on the basis of its failure to transpose the Third Directive.

[10.66] Peart J said that the insurance policy clearly excluded any indemnity in respect of the plaintiff's injuries in circumstances where he was seated in the rear part of the van which was not fitted with a seat. In circumstances where the date for implementation of the Third Directive had passed, Peart J noted that while its provisions had direct effect against the State, this did not provide a remedy against the insurer.[123]

[10.67] Peart J concluded:

> '[36] All passengers being carried in vehicles and who are injured as a result are intended to be guaranteed equal treatment throughout the European Community regardless of in which member state the injury is caused. The Second Directive required each member state to take necessary measures to ensure that any statutory provision or any contractual clause contained in an insurance policy which excludes from insurance persons, *inter alia*, such as this plaintiff shall for the purpose of article 3(1) of the First Directive be void. I should perhaps note that this application is one imposed upon member states, i.e., to put measures in place to so insure. The Directive does not itself state that such a clause *is* void. Nevertheless the objective is clear. The amendment to s. 65 of the [1961 Act in 1992 that provided that regulations would not be made extending compulsory insurance to passengers in unseated accommodation[124]] is clearly in conflict with these objectives, and the failure to transpose the Third Directive by the date required has meant that on the date of the accident in which the plaintiff received his injuries, the law of this State was out of line with what was required by Community law.'

[10.68] Having made this statement, however, Peart J proceeded to say:

> '[37] [The ECJ] judgment in *Marleasing S.E. v. La Comercial Internacional de Alimentación* (Case C–106/89) [1990] E.C.R. I–4135 ... requires a national court, when applying national law, to do so as far as possible in the light of the wording and purpose of the directive in order to pursue the result sought to be pursued by the directive. It seems inescapable that in the present case this court is required to read s. 65 of the Act, as amended by the two Regulations of 1992,[125] by overlooking or ignoring the exclusion permitted therein in respect of liability for injuries caused to persons such as the plaintiff in this case. It seems to follow inevitably from this that the court must conclude that the clause to that effect contained in the policy of insurance ... must be regarded as void, therefore disentitling the [insurer] from relying upon it in order to refuse to indemnify the [van driver and van owner] in respect of the plaintiff's claim for damages ... in the event that [the plaintiff] is found at hearing to have so suffered as a result of the negligence of the [van driver]. I so find'.[126,127]

---

123. At p 347.
124. By the Road Traffic (Compulsory Insurance) (Amendment) Regulations 1992 (SI 346/1992), art 7.
125. Road Traffic (Compulsory Insurance) (Amendment) Regulations 1992 (SI 346/1992) and EC (Road Traffic) (Compulsory Insurance) (Amendment) Regulations 1992 (SI 347/1992).
126. At p 348.
127. The defendants subsequently settled this action with the plaintiff and the settlement was ruled by the High Court (Quirke J) on 10 February 2009 (see [2009] 3 IR 335 at p 349). (contd .../)

[10.69] The third case that is worthy of mention is *DPP v Donnelly*,[128] in which the Supreme Court recently dealt with the concept of 'vehicle insurer' in the context of a criminal case stated. The question posed by the Circuit Court was:

> '[i]n section 56(1) of the Road Traffic Act 1961,[129] does reference to a Vehicle Insurer being liable for injury caused by the negligent use of a vehicle include liability to pay damages to, or to satisfy judgment obtained by a third party claimant pursuant to section 76 of the said Act?'[130]

[10.70] The Supreme Court answered the question in the negative.[131] It must be noted, however, that it was conceded on behalf of the appellant in the Supreme Court that s 76 would not assist him because it 'proceeds on the assumption that there has been in force

---

127. (contd) As between the defendants, however, the matter remains under appeal. See also **Ch 12**, paras **12.25–12.28**.

For an analysis of, *inter alia*, the decision *Smith v Meade*, see Murphy, 'Uninsured Passengers and EU Law', 14(6) 2009 *Bar Review* 123.

128. *DPP v Donnelly* [2012] IESC 44, (23 July 2012, unreported) SC (Fennelly J).

129. The Road Traffic Act 1961, s 56(1) prohibits a person from using a vehicle in a public place unless either a vehicle insurer (or an exempted person) 'would be liable for injury caused by the negligent use of the vehicle' by him *or* 'there is in force ... an approved policy of insurance whereby the user or some other person who would be liable for injury caused by the negligent use of the vehicle ... by the user, is insured ...'. In this regard, s 68 of the 1961 Act allows a vehicle insurer to issue a certificate of exemption in respect of a vehicle owned by it. This certifies ownership and states the particulars in respect of the vehicle insurer's liability for injury caused by the negligent use of the vehicle.

130. *DPP v Donnelly* [2012] IESC 44, (23 July 2012, unreported) SC (Fennelly J) at para 7.

131. The matter came before the Supreme Court by way of a consultative case stated from the Circuit Court and arising out of a prosecution for the offence of driving without insurance under s 56(3) of the 1961 Act. In this case, the appellant drove his father's vehicle, with the father's consent, but the appellant was not insured on the father's policy. In defending the charge, the appellant contended that, *if* he had caused injury to a third party, the father's insurer (as vehicle insurer) would have been 'liable' to the third party. The DPP, on the other hand, contended that s 56(1) had to be construed in light of s 68 and, on this basis, s 56(1) was only concerned with a situation where the vehicle insurer would be liable directly in tort for the injury caused by the negligent driving of a vehicle owned by it. The essential issue was reduced to whether the reference to 'vehicle insurer' in s 56(1) included the situation that had arisen, namely where an approved policy of insurance existed at the relevant time but did not cover the appellant's driving (at para 11). Delivering the judgment of the Supreme Court, Fennelly J was satisfied that the reference to 'liable for injury' in s 56(1) was concerned with injury suffered by a third party as a result of the negligent driving of a vehicle owned by the vehicle insurer (at para 22). The Court stated that the plain meaning of 'liable' is that the vehicle insurer: 'is liable as a matter of law to pay damages to an injured party for the consequences of its own acts, including acts of the drivers of vehicles which it owns for which it is vicariously liable. The insurer is legally liable in that way only when it owns the vehicle' (at para 27). On the other hand, where an insured person causes injury to a third party, the insured is liable to the third party. The Supreme Court stated that the liability of the insurer in this situation is to indemnify the insured and that '[i]t is not a liability owed directly to the injured party. That liability remains the liability of the insured' (at para 23).

The second question asked of the Supreme Court in the case stated was whether or not, having regard to Second Directive, art 2(1) (now Sixth Directive, art 13(1)), liability could be avoided by an insurer on the basis that the insurance policy limited cover to the persons named therein. In light the Court's conclusion on the appropriate interpretation of s 56(1), however, it was not necessary for the court to answer this question.

an approved policy of insurance covering the driving which has given rise to a claim from an injured person'.[132]

6. Issues concerning insurance policies and the Sixth Directive – by way of examples

[10.71] The apparent effect of the aforementioned provisions of the 1962 Regulations, in light of the Sixth Directive, is probably best considered by way of examples.

Example 1

[10.72] John lives in Ireland, owns a car and takes out an insurance policy that names only John as covered by the policy. The policy provides that the insurance policy applies if the car is being driven by someone who is a named insured. The foregoing does not appear to be a prohibited condition. John permits Mary to use the car. Mary drives it negligently and causes injury to a pedestrian, Anne, in Dublin.

[10.73] Mary's driving is not covered by insurance because she is not a named insured on the policy. This is not a prohibited condition under the 1962 Regulations. Section 76 appears to be of no assistance to Anne in circumstances where Mary's user of the car is not insured by an approved policy of insurance (in terms of *Melia*[133]).

[10.74] However, it is arguable that the position set out above is in conflict with the intended position under art 13(1)(a) of the Sixth Directive (set out above at paras **10.51–10.53**) which required Ireland to ensure that any statutory provision or contractual clause in an insurance policy shall be deemed void (in respect of a third party claim by an injured person) where it excludes from insurance the driving of the vehicle by 'persons who do not have express or implied authorisation to do so'.[134] Thus, while it may be that Anne cannot claim direct effect of the Sixth Directive against the insurer, she may wish to consider whether or not to pursue the State for failing to properly implement the Sixth Directive.[135] Similar issues arise in relation to the apparent intended direct right of action against the insurer under art 18 of the Sixth Directive. In this regard, the direct right of action implemented by the European Communities (Fourth Motor Insurance Directive) Regulations 2003 (the 2003 Regulations)[136] provides that the insurer shall be directly liable to the injured party to the extent that it is liable to the

---

132.   *DPP v Donnelly* [2012] IESC 44, (23 July 2012, unreported) SC (Fennelly J), at para 10.

133.   *Melia v Melia, Lara Ltd and the MIBI* [2004] 1 IR 321 and paras **10.62–10.63**.

134.   The point being made here is that, in circumstances where Sixth Directive, art 13(1)(a) requires that Member States void clauses that exclude cover for persons who drive without authorisation, how can an insurer be permitted to avoid liability in respect of a person who drives with such authorisation.

135.   See **Ch 12**, para **12.07** *et seq* for a consideration of horizontal direct effect. It is also arguable that the provisions of art 13 are not in any event unconditional (which is a prerequisite to a finding that a directive may have direct effect), insofar as the State is given an option as set out in the third subparagraph of art 13(1) to allow an injured party in this situation to recover compensation from a social security body in the State rather than the insurer.

136.   European Communities (Fourth Motor Insurance Directive) Regulations 2003 (SI 651/2003). The 2003 Regulations are reproduced in **Appendix 4**.

insured person.[137] The 2003 Regulations await judicial scrutiny and there is no judicial determination as to the validity or otherwise of a clause of the nature referred to in this example,[138] including whether it is in fact an exclusion clause or a mere term of the contract pursuant to which John has obtained insurance. Perhaps the issue is unlikely to raise its head because, in practical terms, Anne may claim compensation from the MIBI,[139] unless the accident did not occur in a public place, in which case the MIBI is not obliged to discharge any unsatisfied judgment.[140] In this event, the issue of whether or not the insurer would be obliged to indemnify would become significant.

Example 2

[10.75] John lives in Ireland, owns a car and takes out an insurance policy in which Mary is named as a person insured to drive it. The policy provides that the insurance policy applies if the car is being driven by someone who is covered by the certificate of insurance. The foregoing does not appear to be a prohibited condition. Mary takes John's car with his consent. She collects her friend Pamela to go to Wicklow for the day and Pamela is not named as a person insured to drive the car. On their return journey, Mary starts to feel unwell, is unable to drive and asks Pamela to take over. Pamela complies and negligently drives the car and causes injury to herself, Mary and a pedestrian on the road, Rebecca.

[10.76] It appears that Pamela's driving is not covered by insurance because she is not a named insured on the policy. This is not a prohibited condition under the 1962 Regulations. Section 76 appears to be of no assistance to Rebecca in circumstances where Pamela's user of the car is not insured by an approved policy of insurance (in terms of *Melia*[141]).

[10.77] The intention of the Sixth Directive with respect to a situation such as this, however, is unclear. Article 13(1)(a) required Ireland to ensure that any statutory provision or contractual clause in an insurance policy shall be deemed void (in respect of a third party claim by an injured person) where it excludes from insurance the driving of vehicles by 'persons who do not have express or implied authorisation to do so'. It would therefore appear that Ireland is vulnerable to a person in Rebecca's position claiming that it has not properly implemented the Sixth Directive. In the event that such a conflict is found to exist between Irish law and the Sixth Directive, it appears that Rebecca cannot claim direct effect of the Sixth Directive against the insurer.[142] On the

---

137. European Communities (Fourth Motor Insurance Directive) Regulations 2003 (SI 651/2003), reg 3(5).
138. Obviously, however, consideration must be given to *Smith v Meade, Meade, FBD Insurance Plc, Ireland and the Attorney General* [2009] 3 IR 335. This decision is under appeal as between the defendants.) and discussed above at paras **10.64–10.68**.
139. John's insurance company would be 'insurer concerned'.
140. Clause 4.1.1–4.1.2 of the 2009 Agreement (cl 4.1 of the 2004 Agreement).
141. *Melia v Melia, Lara Ltd and the MIBI* [2004] 1 IR 321 and paras **10.62–10.63**.
142. See fn **134** above. In addition, if John's car is treated as having been stolen by Pamela, it is further arguable that the provisions of art 13 are not in unconditional for the reason that the State is given an additional option in this situation to provide that, in the case of stolen vehicles, injured parties are to look to the MIBI for compensation.

other hand, the High Court in *Smith v Meade, Meade, FBD Insurance Plc, Ireland and the Attorney General*[143] prevented an insurer from relying on an exclusion clause that conflicted with the provisions of the Third Directive. Similarly, while the intended position under art 18 of the Sixth Directive appears to have been that Rebecca would have a direct right of action against the insurer, the direct right of action afforded by the 2003 Regulations provides that the insurer shall be directly liable to the injured party to the extent that it is liable to the insured person, which may be of no avail to Rebecca if the position is that there is no insurance in place (in terms of *Melia*[144]). As stated above, the 2003 Regulations await judicial scrutiny and it remains to be seen whether a clause of the nature used in this example would be deemed to be an exclusion clause of the nature that the Sixth Directive intended to outlaw or a mere term of the contract between the parties and pursuant to which John has obtained insurance.

[10.78] In circumstances where Rebecca may apply to the MIBI for compensation,[145] a conflict of the aforementioned nature is unlikely to arise. However, as with example 1, if the accident did not occur in a public place, the MIBI would not be required to discharge any unsatisfied judgment[146] and, in this event, the issue of whether or not the insurer would be obliged to indemnify would become significant.

[10.79] This brings us to Mary who was not driving. On the basis of the insurance contract, the insurer may well claim that there is no insurance in place (in terms of *Melia*[147]) and that there is therefore no basis upon which Mary might recover under s 76. While Mary may well have been aware that Pamela was not insured, the second subparagraph of art 13(1) of the Sixth Directive suggests that such a state of knowledge would only be relevant if John's car is treated as having been stolen. While the insurer might assert that Pamela stole the car in terms of taking the car with the intention of temporarily depriving the owner thereof in terms of the Criminal Justice (Theft and Fraud Offences) Act 2001, s 4, such an approach would appear to be unrealistic in circumstances where John's car was legitimately in Mary's custody and Pamela was merely obliging her by taking over at the wheel when Mary was unwell. Thus, again, it remains to be seen whether an insurer might successfully avoid having to indemnify in respect of injuries caused to Mary in this situation. In the event that the insurer succeeded in asserting that there was no insurance for this reason, and that Mary could not recover in respect of her injuries, the issues in terms of claiming that the State has failed to properly implement the Sixth Directive are similar to those concerning Rebecca. If Mary turns to the MIBI for compensation under 2009 Agreement on the basis that she was caused injury by Pamela as an uninsured driver, the MIBI might well resist the claim on the basis that she voluntarily entered the vehicle and knew that there was no insurance.[148]

---

143. *Melia v Melia, Lara Ltd and the MIBI* [2004] 1 IR 321 and paras **10.62–10.63**. This is decision is under appeal.
144. *Melia v Melia, Lara Ltd and the MIBI* [2004] 1 IR 321 and paras **10.62–10.63**.
145. John's insurance company would be 'insurer concerned'.
146. Clause 4.1.1–4.1.2 of the 2009 Agreement (cl 4.1 of the 2004 Agreement).
147. *Melia v Melia, Lara Ltd and the MIBI* [2004] 1 IR 321 and paras **10.62–10.63**.
148. See cl 5.2 of the 2009 Agreement.

[10.80] With respect to Pamela, she has no recourse in circumstances where she was the cause of the accident.

7. Conclusion

[10.81] It should be apparent from the above that, if the owner's insurance policy does not cover the driver to drive the vehicle, the existence of a valid policy of insurance in relation to the use of the vehicle at the time of the relevant accident is potentially significant. The European case law only appears to envisage a body such as the MIBI having a role when the negligently driven vehicle was either uninsured or unidentified. This may well be because, in mainland Europe as opposed to the UK and Ireland, it is the vehicle that is insured as opposed to the driver.[149] Car insurance premia in Ireland are calculated, *inter alia*, on the basis of risks associated with particular identifiable drivers as opposed to a particular vehicle being insured on the basis that it might be driven by anyone.

[10.82] The effect, if any, of these transposed directives and indeed *Churchill Insurance Co Ltd v Wilkinson* and *Evans v Equity Claims Ltd*[150] has yet to be tested by the Irish courts in a civil context. On one reading, *Churchill* appears to allow a plaintiff to sue an insurer where the use of the vehicle was uninsured, as opposed to the MIBI which has traditionally dealt with such claims as 'insurer concerned'.[151] The significance is that, if the insurance company was defending such a claim as opposed to the MIBI, the MIBI's conditions precedent could not be relied upon by the insurance company, nor could it exclude a claim on the basis that a plaintiff knew that the vehicle was uninsured.

[10.83] In *Churchill* the ECJ held that the derogations from the obligation to insure in art 13[152] are only permitted when the insurer can prove that the claimant knew that the vehicle was stolen. While a claimant may risk not involving the MIBI if he feels that the MIBI could prove that he knew a vehicle he was injured in was uninsured, the safer course, pending a judicial determination on the issue, would appear to be to join the MIBI as a defendant.[153]

---

149. As noted by Advocate General Mengozzi in his opinion in *Churchill Insurance Co Ltd v Wilkinson and Evans v Equity Claims Ltd*, (Joined Cases C–442/10), 6 September 2011, at para 28 (see also para 31 of the ECJ judgment in *Churchill*).
150. *Churchill Insurance Co Ltd v Wilkinson and Evans v Equity Claims Ltd* (Joined Cases C–442/10), 1 December 2011.
151. But see *Melia v Melia, Lara Ltd and the MIBI* [2004] 1 IR 321.
152. Formerly Second Directive, art 2.
153. If the MIBI were not to be involved, the insurers should be given advance notice of the proceedings in accordance with the Road Traffic Act 1961, s 76 and potentially joined as a party to the proceedings.

Chapter 11

COSTS WHERE CLAIMANT MUST BRING TWO ACTIONS

A. INTRODUCTION

[11.01] Clause 2.3 of the 2009[1] Agreement provides that a person claiming compensation by virtue of the agreement must seek to enforce the provisions of the agreement by: 'citing MIBI as co-defendants in any proceedings against the owner and/ or user of the vehicle giving rise to the claim *except* where the owner *and* user of the vehicle remain unidentified or untraced ...' (emphasis added).

[11.02] As indicated in **Ch 10**, the import of the foregoing is that, where there the owner of a vehicle is not identified and its driver is not traced (untraced vehicle[2]), an action in which the MIBI is named as sole defendant must be brought. The rationale behind this is that if an identified defendant, usually a motorist, is involved and is partly to blame for a claimant's injury, that defendant can compensate the claimant for his injury in full, thereby rendering it unnecessary for the MIBI to do so. However, this assumes that the identified defendant is insured and/or a mark for damages.

[11.03] However, there may also be cases in which an accident involves both an identified, but uninsured, defendant and an untraced vehicle. As a matter of practicality, the factual matrix in the claim involving the uninsured defendant and the untraced vehicle are very often similar and there is a needless duplicity in running two actions either consecutively or separately. Again, as a matter of practicality, practitioners often overlook this exception and join the MIBI as a co-defendant in one action and in which the plaintiff sues the MIBI both on the basis of an uninsured defendant and an untraced vehicle, and 'the MIBI is thus involved wearing two different hats'.[3]

[11.04] If the MIBI is named as a defendant to proceedings involving both an uninsured defendant and an untraced vehicle, a defence is often delivered to the effect that the plaintiff is precluded from recovering from the MIBI on the basis that the claimant is in breach of cl 2.3 of the 2009 Agreement. Practitioners met with such a defence might take some solace from the Supreme Court decision in *O'Flynn v Buckley*.[4] In that case the MIBI sought to dismiss the plaintiff's claim against it on the basis that the equivalent cl 2(2) of the 1988 Agreement did not permit the MIBI to be joined a co-defendant (with other identified defendants) to proceedings in which the plaintiff was claiming against the MIBI both on the basis that one of the identified defendants was in fact uninsured *and* on the basis that an untraced vehicle was also responsible for the accident.

---

1.   And cl 2.2. of the 2004 Agreement. The 2009 Agreement is reproduced in **Appendix 1**. The 2004 Agreement is reproduced in **Appendix 2**.

2.   The phrase 'untraced vehicle' is used throughout this chapter to refer to a situation in which the driver of a vehicle is untraced and the owner of the same vehicle is unidentified.

3.   See Kearns J in *O'Flynn v Buckley* [2009] 3 IR 311 at p 319.

4.   *O'Flynn v Buckley* [2009] 3 IR 311.

[11.05] The Supreme Court[5] upheld the High Court decision that dismissed the MIBI's application on the basis that the interests of justice and any legitimate concerns of the MIBI could be met by an order providing for the disjoinder of issues pursuant to O 18 of the Rules of the Superior Court 1986. However, the Supreme Court held that the MIBI's delay in moving for relief was such as to disentitle it to the relief sought. Not only was there a delay in that case but it was a fatal injuries claim in which the possible involvement of an untraced vehicle had been flagged in the originating letter in which the MIBI was notified of the claims and the MIBI never suggested that a second set of proceedings might be necessary in respect of the untraced vehicle. In addition, the MIBI was not willing to give an undertaking not to plead the Statute of Limitations in any further proceedings. The case was decided on:

> '... the unusual facts of [the] case where there is a combination of insured and uninsured drivers and the possible involvement of an untraced driver'.[6]

[11.06] Kearns J did state that:

> '[Counsel for the MIBI] also submitted, I think correctly, that the [MIBI] is entitled to require that litigants respect the strict conditions laid down in the agreement as a pre-condition to the recovery of compensation.'[7]

[11.07] As it transpired, the MIBI never sought amended proceedings subsequent to this decision. Had an actual disjoinder occurred, one wonders which set of proceedings would have been left without the MIBI as a defendant, presumably the case against the identified but uninsured defendant.

[11.08] So while the door is not closed to a plaintiff who incorrectly sues the MIBI as a co-defendant in relation to proceedings involving both an identified, but uninsured, defendant and an untraced vehicle, the correct procedure is to issue two sets of proceedings.

[11.09] What then in relation to the costs of the set of proceedings that ultimately transpires to have been unnecessary, whether the MIBI is a defendant to only one such action or to both actions?

B. PRELIMINARY PROTECTIVE MEASURES BEFORE INSTITUTING TWO SEPARATE ACTIONS

1. Plaintiff considers responsibility lies between an insured motorist and untraced vehicle.

[11.10] Where a claim for compensation is rejected or an inadequate offer of compensation is made by the MIBI, the operation of cl 2.3 of the 2009 Agreement[8] renders it necessary for a claimant to institute two actions where the plaintiff considers that responsibility lies between an insured motorist and an untraced vehicle. In this

---

5.   *O'Flynn v Buckley* [2009] 3 IR 311 *per* Kearns J (Denham and Hardiman JJ concurring).

6.   *O'Flynn v Buckley* [2009] 3 IR 311 *per* Kearns J at p 319.

7.   *O'Flynn v Buckley* [2009] 3 IR 311 at p 319.

8.   And cl 2.2 of the 2004 Agreement.

situation, the plaintiff's exposure to costs must be minimised from the outset. It is therefore advisable that, in addition to the other conditions precedent and the issue of standard O'Byrne type letters,[9] the advance notice of the proceedings to the MIBI should:

(1) refer to the established principle that requires the claimant to bring two separate actions;[10] and

(2) advise that, in default of an admission of liability within a stated period:

    (a) the claimant will be compelled to institute two actions in which case the claimant will apply to have the actions listed for hearing together;

    (b) in the event that the claimant fails in the first action that he will bring against the other defendant(s), and a consequential order for costs is made against the claimant in that first action, the claimant will use the correspondence for the purpose of seeking an order against the MIBI in respect of the costs of the first action; and

    (c) the claimant will also pursue the MIBI for the costs of the claimant's second action against the MIBI and will use the correspondence for the purposes of applying for such an order.[11]

2. Plaintiff considers responsibility lies only with untraced motorist

[11.11] The letter referred to at para 11.10 above requires modification in circumstances where a claimant considers that responsibility for his injuries lies *solely* with an untraced vehicle. If the claimant has no evidence to justify his instituting proceedings against anyone other than the MIBI, the advance notice of the proceedings to the MIBI should:

(1) advise the MIBI that it is the claimant's opinion that responsibility for the accident lies solely with an untraced vehicle and that the claimant has no evidence to suggest that responsibility for the accident lies elsewhere;

(2) advise the MIBI that, in default of an admission of liability within a stated period, the claimant intends to issue proceedings against the MIBI only; and

(3) call upon the MIBI to advise the claimant if it requires the claimant to take a claim against any other person against whom the MIBI considers the claimant might have a remedy.

---

9. Civil Liability and Courts Act 2004, s 8 also requires the service of a letter of claim on the 'wrongdoer' within two months of the date of the cause of action in a personal injuries action.

10. *Feeney v Dwane and O'Connor and Feeney v MIBI* (30 July 1999, unreported) HC, *ex tempore*, Johnson J, and *Devereux v Minister for Finance and MIBI* (10 February 1998, unreported) HC, *ex tempore*, O'Sullivan J. See also Jones, 'Counsel's note: "Citing the MIBI of Ireland as a co-defendant"', 3(9) 1998 *Bar Review* 450.

11. A letter in similar terms should issue to the defendant(s) to the first action. The same letter may be modified for use in a situation where it is necessary for the claimant to institute two actions and in which the MIBI is a defendant to both ie one in respect of the actions of an uninsured motorist and the other in respect of an untraced vehicle.

[11.12] In the event that the MIBI calls upon the claimant to sue another party or parties, the replying correspondence to such a demand should deal with the following matters:

(1) repeat the claimant's assertion that he has no evidence to suggest that responsibility for the accident lies anywhere other than with the untraced vehicle and express the view that the second action that the MIBI calls on him to bring should not in fact be brought;

(2) advise the MIBI that the claimant requires a full indemnity in respect of the costs of the additional action and request confirmation that the MIBI will duly indemnify the claimant;

(3) advise the MIBI that if the claimant is compelled to institute two actions, the claimant will apply to have the actions listed for hearing together; and

    (a) in the event that the claimant fails in the first action that the MIBI has directed the claimant to bring, and a consequential order for costs is made against the claimant in that first action, the claimant will use the correspondence for the purpose of seeking an order over against the MIBI in respect of the costs of the first action;

    (b) the claimant will also pursue the MIBI for the costs of the claimant's second action against the MIBI and will use the correspondence for the purposes of applying for such an order.

C. JURISDICTION TO ORDER COSTS IN FAVOUR OF AND AGAINST NON-PARTIES

1. *Feeney v Dwane* and *O'Connor and Feeney v MIBI*

[11.13] In *Feeney v Dwane and O'Connor* and *Feeney v MIBI*,[12] the plaintiff brought two actions in circumstances where the driving of an untraced vehicle was alleged to have some responsiblility for the accident. The plaintiff succeeded in the first action against the identified motorists and was awarded the costs of the first action against them. The issue of the costs of the second action against the MIBI remained. Johnson J was concerned about the appropriateness of making an order for costs against the defendants to the first action in favour of the MIBI who was not a party to that first action. Ultimately, however, Johnson J made an order for costs in favour of the MIBI against the plaintiff in the second action. He then made an order over against the defendants to the first action in respect of those costs. Finally, he awarded the plaintiff's costs of the second action against the defendants to the first action.[13] Johnson J noted the following matters:

1. the nature of the defence delivered by *Dwane and O'Connor* required that the plaintiff sue the MIBI;

---

12. *Feeney v Dwane and O'Connor and Feeney v MIBI* (30 July 1999, unreported) HC, *ex tempore*, Johnson J.

13. In *Feeney*, Johnson J indicated that, where the MIBI was sued in the case of an untraced vehicle and, arising out of the same circumstances, proceedings were also issued against an identified motorist, the actions should be heard together. In this regard, some months prior to the hearing of the actions, Johnson J refused an application by the MIBI to stay the action against it pending the hearing of *Feeney v Dwane and O'Connor.* (contd .../)

2. the plaintiff was compelled by cl 2(2) of the 1988 Agreement[14] and the decision in *Kavanagh v Reilly and MIBI*[15] to issue a separate action against the MIBI;

3. in terms of procedure, the only means by which to expeditiously deal with the cases was to have both heard together in order to minimise costs;

4. the facts of the case, having regard to the provisions of O 99 of the Rules of the Superior Courts 1986[16] and the definition of 'party' in O 125;[17]

5. notwithstanding the fact that there were two separate actions, *Dwane and O'Connor* were on notice of the case by virtue of the manner in which it was being run and attended and participated in the manner in which it was run;

6. even though the cases were not consolidated, it would be taking a completely artificial view of the cases and the rules to treat them otherwise; and

7. in the exceptional circumstances arising in the MIBI situation, it was unacceptable that the innocent plaintiff might be penalised where all the parties were part of the same *res gestae* and where the proceedings against the MIBI were mandatory in light of the defence delivered by *Dwane and O'Connor*.[18]

---

13. (contd) Johnson J considered that if the first action were successfully defended, the matter would have to be re-litigated against the MIBI. He directed that both actions be heard together by the same judge, all evidence be taken together at the same time and that all parties participate.
For further reading on this topic see Kelly, 'Costs implications of proceeding against the MIBI', 6(6) 2001 *Bar Review* 337.

14. The equivalent to cl 2.3 of the 2009 Agreement (cl 2.2 of the 2004 Agreement).

15. *Kavanagh v Reilly and MIBI* (14 June 1996, unreported) HC, *ex tempore*, Morris P.

16. Order 99, r 1, as amended, provides 'Subject to the provisions of the Acts and any other statutes relating to costs and except as otherwise provided by these Rules: (1) The costs of and incidental to every proceeding in the Superior Courts shall be in the discretion of those Courts respectively. (2) No party shall be entitled to recover any costs of or incidental to any proceeding from any other party to such proceeding except under an order as provided by these Rules. (3) ... the costs of every action, question, or issue tried by a jury shall follow the event unless the Court, for special cause, to be mentioned in the order, shall otherwise direct ... (4) ... the costs of every issue of fact or law raised upon a claim or counterclaim shall, unless otherwise ordered, follow the event ...'. It should also be noted that the Judicature (Ireland) Act 1877, s 53, as amended, provides that: 'Subject to the provisions of this Act and of Rules of Court, the costs of and incidental to every proceeding in the High Court of Justice and Court of Appeal respectively shall be in the discretion of the Court ... . Provided that (subject to all existing enactments limiting, regulating, or affecting the costs payable in any action by reference to the amount recovered therein), the costs of every action, question, and issue tried by a jury shall follow the event, unless, upon application made, the judge at the trial or the Court shall for special cause shown and mentioned in the order otherwise direct ...'.

17. Order 125, r 1, provides that party 'includes every person served with notice of or attending any proceedings, although not named on the record'. Notably, an almost identical definition of party is contained within the Judicature (Ireland) Act 1877, s 3.

18. See also *Walsh v Bus Éireann and McGrory and Walsh v MIBI* (13 November 2002 and 20 November 2002, unreported) HC, *ex tempore*, Kearns J. In this case, the plaintiff sued Bus Éireann and the driver of the bus in which she was travelling as a passenger. Bus Éireann defended the proceedings on the basis that responsibility for the accident lay with an untraced vehicle. The plaintiff was compelled to bring proceedings against the MIBI. The plaintiff failed in her action against Bus Éireann and succeeded against the MIBI. Kearns J awarded Bus Éireann its costs against the plaintiff and gave the plaintiff an order over against the MIBI. (contd .../)

[11.14] It is clear that the courts have jurisdiction to join parties to proceedings for the purpose of making a costs order against them.[19] It would also appear that the courts have a jurisdiction to order the costs of previous associated proceedings to be included as costs in a subsequent claim eg an unsuccessful plaintiff suing an identified defendant who had a costs order made against him in that action may subsequently recover those costs in any successful proceedings taken against the MIBI, on the basis of the negligent driving of an untraced vehicle, on the assumption that the costs application can be supported by appropriate correspondence. The jurisdiction to make an order for costs against a non-party and the criteria by which it should be exercised were considered in detail by Clarke J in *Moorview Developments Ltd v First Active Plc*.[20] That case concerned a 'funder' of litigation as opposed to the MIBI but it is clear authority for the jurisdiction to make a costs order against a non-party.

2. *Riordan v MIBI*

[11.15] In *Riordan v MIBI*,[21] the plaintiff was injured when the bus in which she was travelling collided with an untraced vehicle. The plaintiff sued Dublin Bus. It denied liability and expressly pleaded in its defence that, if the plaintiff suffered any injury, it was caused or contributed to by the negligent driving of the untraced vehicle. In these circumstances, cl 2(2) of the 1988 Agreement[22] required that the plaintiff sue the MIBI in a separate action. Thereafter, the plaintiff's solicitor wrote to the MIBI and, citing *Devereux v Minister for Finance and MIBI*[23] as the basis for separate proceedings, called upon the MIBI to agree to either being joined as a co-defendant to the first action against Dublin Bus or to a consolidation of the actions. The plaintiff received no reply to this letter. Dublin Bus successfully defended the first action.

[11.16] At the hearing of the second action against the MIBI, the accident was found to have been entirely caused by the driving of the untraced vehicle. The plaintiff was awarded the costs of the second action against the MIBI. The issue of the costs of the first action against Dublin Bus remained outstanding. In this regard, the President of the Circuit Court, Judge Smyth, made an order against the MIBI in favour of Dublin Bus in respect of its costs of successfully defending the first action. In addition, the President made an order for costs against the MIBI in respect of the plaintiff's costs in her unsuccessful action against Dublin Bus. In this regard, the plaintiff relied on the decision of Johnson J in *Feeney v Dwane and O'Connor* and *Feeney v MIBI*.[24]

---

18. (contd) In the circumstances, Kearns J equated the position of the MIBI in appearing and participating in the proceedings against Bus Éireann as that of a notice party.
19. See *Byrne v John S. O'Connor & Co* [2006] 3 IR 379.
20. *Moorview Developments Ltd v First Active Plc* [2011] IEHC 117, (16 March 2011, unreported) HC.
21. *Riordan v MIBI* (24 January 2001, and 1 February 2001, unreported) CC, the President of the Circuit Court, Judge Smyth. For a discussion of this case, see Kelly, 'Costs implications of proceeding against the MIBI', 6(6) *Bar Review* 337.
22. Clause 2.3 of the 2009 Agreement (cl 2.2 of the 2004 Agreement).
23. See fn **10**.
24. See para **11.13**. But see also *Hyland v MIBI and Dun Laoghaire Rathdown County Council* (29 July 2003, unreported) CC, *ex tempore*, Judge McMahon. (contd .../)

24. (contd) In that case, the MIBI succeeded in its application to have the proceedings dismissed against it where it was sued in respect of the actions of an untraced vehicle and where a local authority was sued as a co-defendant in the same action for allegedly negligently maintaining the locus. Aside from the fact that, consistent with *Feeney v Dwane and O'Connor and Feeney v MIBI*, the Court was satisfied that the MIBI should be sued as a sole defendant in respect of the actions of the untraced vehicle, the Court did not appear to envisage both actions being heard at the same time. For a discussion of this case see Abrahamson, 'The MIBI and Co-Defendants Recent Case law', 8(5) 2003 *Bar Review* 195.

Chapter 12

THE MIBI: AN EMANATION OF THE STATE?

A. INTRODUCTION

[12.01] The significance of whether or not the MIBI can be categorised as an emanation of the State arises when an individual considers that he has been given a right under a European motor insurance directive (a directive) and it has either not been implemented or not properly implemented into Irish law. A number of matters arise for consideration by an individual who wishes to assert a right that appears to have been given to him pursuant to a directive. Firstly, consideration must be given to the issue of whether or not the directive has direct effect. If it has direct effect, the individual may be in a position to enforce the directive against the State before the Irish courts. Alternatively, the individual may be able to enforce the right against the MIBI if it falls within the definition of an emanation of the State. Secondly, if the directive does not have direct effect, an individual may be able to rely on the concept of indirect effect and call upon the Irish courts to interpret Irish legislation in a manner that is consistent with the directive. Thirdly, if an individual can establish that the State has failed to properly implement the directive, he may recover damages from the State before the Irish courts for its failure to implement or properly implement the directive. This third scenario arises regardless of whether or not the directive has direct effect. While a comprehensive discourse of European law is beyond the scope of this work, each of these issues is considered in general terms.

B. DIRECT EFFECT AGAINST A MEMBER STATE

[12.02] In general terms, it may be said that a directive states certain legal principles and directs Member States to implement those legal principles into their respective legal systems by means of domestic legislation by a prescribed date. The difficulties that arise when a Member State fails to implement or properly implement a directive by the prescribed date (an unimplemented directive) are well established. It is against this background that the concept of direct effect was developed by the European Court of Justice (the ECJ).

[12.03] In essence, direct effect means that, where a State has failed to implement a directive by the prescribed date (the guilty Member State), an individual who has been afforded rights under the unimplemented directive can seek to enforce that unimplemented directive against the guilty Member State on the basis that it has effect notwithstanding the failure to implement it. Thus, the guilty Member State is effectively precluded from defending the claim on the basis that the directive was not implemented and it is liable to the individual as though it had in fact implemented the directive.

[12.04] A claim that a directive has direct effect may be made before an Irish court, which may, by way of a preliminary reference, refer a question to the ECJ as to whether or not the directive has direct effect.

[12.05] Where an individual relies directly upon the terms of an unimplemented directive against a guilty Member State (as opposed to a private individual), the term vertical direct effect is used. By way of a simple example, in *Pubblico Ministero v Ratti*,[1] a manufacturer of solvents was prosecuted for failing to comply with Italian law regulating the manufacturing process of solvents. In his defence, he relied on the direct effect of two directives that Italy had failed to implement. The ECJ held that he was entitled to rely on the direct effect of the unimplemented directives.

[12.06] An individual can also claim vertical direct effect against a body that is sufficiently closely identified with the guilty Member State (ie an emanation of the State) to the extent that it is appropriate for the courts to prevent the body from defending itself by reference to the guilty Member State's failure to implement the directive. This is discussed in general terms below at paras **12.33–12.50**.

C. DIRECT EFFECT AGAINST A PRIVATE INDIVIDUAL

[12.07] An individual cannot, however, rely upon the terms of an unimplemented directive directly against another private individual. Thus, if an employment contract between two private persons contains a term that violates an unimplemented directive, neither person can rely upon the terms of the unimplemented directive against the other. Thus a directive does not have horizontal direct effect, that is, it does not apply as between two private persons.[2]

D. CONDITIONS PRECEDENT TO DIRECT EFFECT

[12.08] *Van Duyn v Home Office*[3] was the first case in which the ECJ declared that a directive could have direct effect. However, certain conditions must be satisfied before a directive can be considered to have direct effect. In *Francovich and Others v Italy*,[4] the ECJ stated the conditions as follows:

> 'wherever the provisions of a directive appear, as far as their subject matter is concerned, to be unconditional and sufficiently precise, those provisions may, in the absence of implementing measures adopted within the prescribed period, be relied upon as against any national provision which is incompatible with the Directive or insofar as the provisions [of the Directive] define rights which individuals are able to assert against the State.'[5]

[12.09] In *Francovich*, the directive at issue required Member States to establish a system under which employees would be protected in the event of the insolvency of their employer. To this end, the directive provided that Member States were to lay down

---

1. *Pubblico Ministero v Ratti* (Case 148/78) [1979] ECR 1629, [1980] 1 CMLR 96.
2. See *Marshall v Southampton and South-West Hampshire Area Health Authority* (Marshall I) (Case 152/84) [1986] ECR 723, [1986] 1 CMLR 688; and *Fratelli Costanzo SpA v Comune di Milano* (Case 103/88) [1989] ECR 1839, [1990] 3 CMRL 239.
3. *Van Duyn v Home Office* (Case 41/74) [1974] ECR 1337, [1975] 1 CMLR 1.
4. *Francovich and Others v Italy* (Joined Cases C–6/90 and C–9/90) [1991] ECR I–5357, [1993] 2 CMLR 66.
5. At para 11.

detailed rules for the organisation, financing and operation of guarantee institutions. The assets of the institutions were required to be independent of employers' operating capital, employers were required to contribute to their financing (unless it was fully covered by public authorities) and the institutions' liabilities could not depend on whether or not obligations to contribute to its financing had been fulfilled.

[12.10] The ECJ found that the provisions at issue were not 'unconditional' as regards the determination of the persons entitled to the guarantee and as regards the content of that guarantee. For this reason, its elements were not sufficient to enable individuals to rely on its provisions before the national courts. This was because the directive did not identify the person liable to provide the guarantee. The State could not be considered liable on the sole ground that it had failed to take transposition measures within the prescribed period.[6] In essence, the directive could not have direct effect because it allowed Italy to identify the one or more guarantee institutions against which the remedy was to be available.[7]

E. DIRECT EFFECT OF MOTOR INSURANCE DIRECTIVES

[12.11] The first edition of this book predated any decision of the ECJ concerning the direct effect of any of the motor insurance directives. At that time, the decision of the ECJ in *Evans v Secretary of State for the Environment, Transport and the Regions and the MIB*,[8] was, however, considered worthy of mention in terms of anticipating the view that the ECJ might adopt to a claim that a motor insurance directive has direct effect.[9]

Evans brought High Court proceedings against the Secretary of State for the Environment, as the person responsible for the implementation of the First and Second Directives in the United Kingdom, and the MIB. He submitted, *inter alia,* that the United Kingdom had failed to implement the Second Directive because its agreement with the MIB failed to provide for the payment of interest on an award of damages.

[12.12] The High Court stayed the proceedings and referred various questions to the ECJ for a preliminary ruling. Although the questions referred to the ECJ did not concern the direct effect of the motor insurance directives against the United Kingdom or the MIB as an emanation of the State, the ECJ observed that the questions referred to it 'raise[d] a number of problems concerning the nature of the body which the Member States are required to establish in order to implement the Second Directive ... and the possible liability of the Member State concerned for failure to transpose [it]'.[10] Having

---

6.   *Francovich and Others v Italy* (Joined Cases C–6/90 and C–9/90) [1991] ECR I–5357, [1993] 2 CMLR 66 at para 26.

7.   The claimant was, however, entitled to damages from Italy for its failure to implement the directive. See below at para **12.53** *et seq.*

8.   *Evans v Secretary of State for the Environment, Transport and the Regions and the MIB* (Case C–63/01), [2005] All ER (EC) 763, [2003] ECR I–14447, [2004] RTR 32, [2004] 1 CMLR 47, [2004] Lloyd's Rep IR 391, ECJ (5th Chamber).

9.   Or indeed as against the MIBI as an emanation of the State.

10.   *Evans v Secretary of State for the Environment, Transport and the Regions and the MIB* (Case C–63/01, [2005] All ER (EC) 763, [2003] ECR I–14447, [2004] RTR 32, [2004] 1 CMLR 47, [2004] Lloyd's Rep IR 391, ECJ (5th Chamber), at para 20.

noted that art 1(4) of the Second Directive[11] was implemented by means of a number of agreements between the Secretary of State and the MIB, the ECJ described the MIB as 'a private-law entity of which all insurance companies which offer motor vehicle insurance in the United Kingdom are members'.[12]

[12.13] Having stated that art 1(4) of the Second Directive required each Member State to 'set up or authorise a body with the task of providing compensation', the ECJ noted that art 1(4) contained no provision concerning the legal status of the body or the detailed arrangements for its authorisation. It expressly allowed the Member States to regard compensation by that body as subsidiary and enabled Member States to provide for the settlement of claims between that body and those responsible for the accident and for relations with other insurers or social security bodies required to compensate the victim in respect of the same accident.[13] It considered that 'a body may be authorised by a Member State' within the terms of art 1(4) where, *inter alia,* 'its obligation to provide compensation ... derives from an agreement concluded between that body and a public authority of the Member State'.[14]

[12.14] Finally, the ECJ noted that the Second Directive 'confine[d] itself to laying down minimum procedural requirements' by providing that victims should be able to apply directly to the body responsible and that:

'it [was] settled case law that in the absence of Community rules governing the matter it [was] for the domestic legal system of each Member State to designate the courts and tribunals having jurisdiction and to lay down the detailed procedural rules governing actions for safeguarding rights which individuals derive from Community law, provided, however, that such rules ... [did] not render virtually impossible or excessively difficult the exercise of rights conferred by Community law'.[15]

[12.15] In England, the Court of Appeal considered the issue of direct effect in *White v White*.[16] In this case, the respondent was awarded compensation against the MIB in respect of injuries that he suffered while travelling in a car being driven by his uninsured brother. The trial judge considered that, while the respondent could not be said to have known that there was no insurance, he ought to have known that this was position. The

---

11. Second Directive, art 1(4) is now contained in Sixth Directive, art 10(4).

12. *Evans v Secretary of State for the Environment, Transport and the Regions and the MIB* (Case C–63/01, [2005] All ER (EC) 763, [2003] ECR I–14447, [2004] RTR 32, [2004] 1 CMLR 47, [2004] Lloyd's Rep IR 391, ECJ (5th Chamber), at paras 5-6.

13. *Evans v Secretary of State for the Environment, Transport and the Regions and the MIB* (Case C–63/01, [2005] All ER (EC) 763, [2003] ECR I–14447, [2004] RTR 32, [2004] 1 CMLR 47, [2004] Lloyd's Rep IR 391, ECJ (5th Chamber), at para 32.

14. *Evans v Secretary of State for the Environment, Transport and the Regions and the MIB* (Case C–63/01, [2005] All ER (EC) 763, [2003] ECR I–14447, [2004] RTR 32, [2004] 1 CMLR 47, [2004] Lloyd's Rep IR 391, ECJ (5th Chamber), at para 1.

15. *Evans v Secretary of State for the Environment, Transport and the Regions and the MIB* (Case C–63/01, [2005] All ER (EC) 763, [2003] ECR I–14447, [2004] RTR 32, [2004] 1 CMLR 47, [2004] Lloyd's Rep IR 391, ECJ (5th Chamber) at para 45. This is the principle of effectiveness and the court cited *Upjohn Ltd v The Licensing Authority and Others* (Case C–120/97) [1999] ECR I–223, para 32.

16. *White v White* [1999] 1 CMLR 1251 (Court of Appeal).

English MIB agreement excluded the payment of compensation in circumstances where a plaintiff 'knew or ought to have known' that there was no insurance. However, the trial judge considered that the Second Directive only permitted Member States to exclude a claim for compensation where a claimant 'knew' that there was no insurance. On appeal, the English Court of Appeal was prepared to *assume* that the State had failed to properly transpose the Second Directive. However, it concluded that the doctrine of direct effect did not apply because the Second Directive left the English government free to fulfil the obligations created by it in any way, whether by using the MIB or any other mechanism. Thus, the conditions precedent to the application of direct effect were not satisfied. The Court of Appeal allowed the MIB's appeal,[17] but White ultimately succeeded in his appeal to the House of Lords.[18]

[12.16] The issue of the State's transposition of the various directives was raised in Ireland in *Withers v Delaney and MIBI*.[19] It must be emphasised, however, that this case concerned an accident that predated the deadline for Ireland's implementation of the Third Directive and, because of this, the ECJ held that the plaintiff could not rely on its provisions. In this case, the plaintiff's son was killed when the car in which he was travelling, and which was being driven by the first defendant, left the road and hit a ditch. The vehicle contained two seats, one for the driver and one for a passenger. The deceased was travelling in the rear of the vehicle in a covered area that contained no seating. On the date of the accident, the deceased was an excepted person, in terms of s 65(1)(a) of the 1961 Act, because he was a passenger in a part of a vehicle that was *not* designed and constructed with seating accommodation for passengers.[20] In the Circuit Court, the plaintiff claimed that the Irish legislation did not properly transpose the First and Second Directives. Judge McMahon stayed the proceedings and referred three questions to the ECJ for a preliminary ruling pursuant to art 234 of the EC Treaty.[21] The first question was:

'[w]hether on the true interpretation of the [First and Second Directives], Ireland was entitled on the [date of the accident], to maintain legislation (Section 65 of the

---

17. *White v White* [1999] 1 CMLR 1251 (Court of Appeal) at p 1266.
18. *White v White* [2001] 1 WLR 481, [2001] 2 All ER 43, [2001] 1 Lloyd's Rep 679, [2001] RTR 379. The Law Lords held that the 1988 English MIB agreement had to be interpreted in line with the Second Directive. In this regard, it held that 'knew' meant that the passenger primarily possessed information from which he drew the conclusion that the driver was uninsured. This included a situation where a passenger possessed information leading him to conclude that the driver might well not be insured but the passenger deliberately refrained from asking, lest his suspicions be confirmed. However, it did not extend to the situation where the passenger did not think about insurance although an ordinary prudent passenger in his position and with his knowledge would have enquired about it ([2001] 1 WLR 481 at pp 486–487).
19. *Withers v Delaney and MIBI* (Case C–158/01) [2002] ECR I–08301.
20. The requirements of compulsory insurance were extended by way of ministerial regulations (Road Traffic (Compulsory Insurance) Regulations 1962 (SI 14/1962), as amended by the Road Traffic (Compulsory Insurance) (Amendment) Regulations 1992 (SI 346/1992), art 4). However, these regulations did not affect the plaintiff because Road Traffic Act 1961, s 65(1)(a) expressly precluded the Minister from extending the requirements of compulsory insurance by way of regulations for passengers to any part of a vehicle (other than a large public service vehicle) unless that part was designed and built with passenger seating.
21. The decision to refer the matter to the ECJ was made on 9 March 2001.

1961 Act and the Road Traffic (Compulsory Insurance) Regulations, 1962) which did not make compulsory insurance mandatory for passengers injured in a "part of a vehicle, other than a large public service vehicle, unless that part of the vehicle is designed and constructed with seating accommodation for passengers"?'

[12.17] The ECJ[22] considered that the net issue was whether or not the First and Second Directives left to the Member States the power to determine the extent and detailed provisions of passenger cover.[23] The ECJ followed the decision in *Ferreira and Ferreira v Companhia de Seguros Mundial Confianca SA*[24] and held that, pursuant to the First and Second Directives, Member States remained competent to determine 'the extent of passenger cover'.[25]

[12.18] In *Ferreira,* the ECJ reviewed the provisions of the First, Second and Third Directives ('the three directives'). It observed that, as was clear from the aim and wording of the three directives, they did not seek to harmonise the rules of the Member States governing civil liability.[26] Having outlined the purpose of the three directives,[27] the ECJ in *Ferreira* concluded that, in the absence of Community rules defining the type of civil liability, it was for the Member States to lay down the system of civil liability applicable to road-traffic accidents.[28] This meant that, provided that the Member States ensured that the civil liability arising under their domestic law was covered by insurance that complied with the three directives, they were free to determine the type of civil liability applicable to road traffic accidents.[29]

---

22. In circumstances where it was considered that the answer to this question could be clearly deduced from existing case law, the ECJ gave its decision by way of reasoned order under the Rules of Procedure of the ECJ, art 104(3) and made on 14 October 2002.
23. *Withers v Delaney and MIBI* (Case C–158/01) [2002] ECR I–08301 at para 16.
24. *Ferreira and Ferreira v Companhia de Seguros Mundial Confianca SA* (Case C–348/98) [2000] ECR I–06711. In *Ferreira,* the ECJ held that the Second Directive, art 3 (now Sixth Directive, art 12(2)) required compulsory insurance against civil liability in respect of the use of motor vehicles to cover personal injuries to passengers who are members of the family of the insured person or of the driver, where those passengers are carried free of charge, whether or not there is any fault on the part of the driver of the vehicle which caused the accident, only if the domestic law of the Member State concerned requires such cover in respect of personal injuries caused in the same conditions to other third party passengers (para 35).
25. At para 18 of *Withers v Delaney and MIBI* (Case C–158/01) [2002] ECR I–08301.
26. At para 23 of *Ferreira and Ferreira v Companhia de Seguros Mundial Confianca SA* (Case C–348/98) [2000] ECR I–06711. The ECJ in *Ferreira* further referred to the decision in *Ruiz Bernaldez* (Case C–129/94) [1996] ECR I–01829, [1996] 2 CMLR 889, wherein the ECJ held that the preambles to the directives showed that their aim was, firstly, to ensure the free movement of vehicles normally based on Community territory and of persons travelling in those vehicles and, secondly, to guarantee that the victims of accidents caused by those vehicles receive comparable treatment irrespective of where in the Community the accidents occur. In this regard, it expressly referred to the fifth recital in the preamble to the Second Directive and the fourth recital in the preamble to the Third Directive.
27. At paras 25–27 of *Ferreira and Ferreira v Companhia de Seguros Mundial Confianca SA* (Case C–348/98) [2000] ECR I–06711.
28. At para 28 of *Ferreira and Ferreira v Companhia de Seguros Mundial Confianca SA* (Case C–348/98) [2000] ECR I–06711.
29. At para 29 of *Ferreira and Ferreira v Companhia de Seguros Mundial Confianca SA* (Case C–348/98) [2000] ECR I–06711.

[12.19] As in *Ferreira,* the Court in *Withers* observed that, while art 1 of the Third Directive[30] had extended the compulsory insurance cover imposed by art 3(1) of the First Directive[31] to passengers other than the driver, the accident in *Withers* occurred before the deadline of 31 December 1995 for Ireland's transposition of the Third Directive for vehicles, other than cycles. For this reason, the Third Directive could not be relied upon before the Irish courts.[32] The Court held that the First and Second Directives did not require Member States to ensure that compulsory insurance 'cover[ed] personal injuries to passengers carried in a part of a vehicle that was not adapted for the transport of seated passengers'.[33]

[12.20] The order of the ECJ in *Withers,* however, clearly forecast that, if the accident had occurred on or after the deadline for implementation of the Third Directive, the plaintiff could have relied on it.[34]

[12.21] In *Farrell v Whitty, the Minister for the Environment, Ireland, the Attorney General and the MIBI,*[35] the plaintiff suffered personal injury in an accident in January 1996, while she was travelling as a passenger in the rear of a van that had no seating. The van was driven by the first defendant and he was an uninsured driver. The plaintiff sought to recover compensation from the MIBI pursuant to the 1988 Agreement. The MIBI refused to compensate her on the basis that she was travelling in a part of the vehicle that was not fitted with seating and accordingly insurance was not compulsory.

---

30.   The Third Directive, art 1 is now contained in Sixth Directive, art 12(1).

31.   The First Directive, art 3(1) is now contained in Sixth Directive, art 3, first and second paragraphs.

32.   At para 20 of *Withers v Delaney and MIBI* (Case C–158/01) [2002] ECR I–08301. See also *Ferreira and Ferreira v Ferreira and Ferreira v Companhia de Seguros Mundial Confianca SA* (Case C–348/98) [2000] ECR I–06711 (para 33).

33.   At para 21 of *Withers v Delaney and MIBI* (Case C–158/01) [2002] ECR I–08301.

34.   It has been noted that it could be argued that an individual travelling in a part of a vehicle that is not fitted with seating is not a 'passenger' within the meaning of the Third Directive, art 1. See Murphy, 'Unseated Passengers and the MIBI', 8(3) 2003 *Bar Review* 96, at pp 98–99. Murphy, however, submits that it is clear from the judgment of the ECJ in *Withers v Delaney and MIBI* (Case C–158/01) [2002] ECR I–08301 that this cannot be a correct interpretation of the Third Directive. Murphy also considers the decision in *Ruiz Bernaldez* (Case C–129/94) [1996] ECR I–01829, [1996] 2 CMLR 889 in which the ECJ was concerned with Spanish legislation that discharged an insurer from liability for injury caused to a third party by an insured's drunk driving. In an art 177 reference, the ECJ held that the First Directive, art 3(1) (as amended and now contained in Sixth Directive, art 3, first and second paragraphs) had to be interpreted as meaning that compulsory insurance must enable third party victims of accidents caused by vehicles to be compensated for all damage suffered by them up to the amounts specified by art 1(2) of the Second Directive (and now contained in Sixth Directive, art 9). It considered that any other interpretation would have operated to allow Member States limit the payment of compensation to third party victims of road traffic accidents to certain types of damage and would thereby cause disparities in the treatment of victims depending on where an accident occurred. The ECJ in *Ruiz Bernaldez* noted that this would bring about a situation that the directives sought to avoid and it would deprive the First Directive, art 3(1) (now contained in Sixth Directive, art 3, first and second paragraphs) of its effectiveness (at paras 18–19).

35.   *Farrell v Whitty, the Minister for the Environment, Ireland, the Attorney General and the MIBI,* [2008] IEHC 124, (31 January 2008, unreported) HC, Birmingham J. This decision is under appeal.

The plaintiff obtained a default judgment against the uninsured driver in July 2001 and the assessment of damages was deferred to the trial of the action. In the proceedings issued by the plaintiff in 1997, the plaintiff claimed, *inter alia*:

1. Damages for personal injuries against the uninsured driver;

2. A declaration that the plaintiff was entitled to rely upon the provisions of the First Directive as amended by the Third Directive in the proceedings;

3. A declaration that the European Communities (Road Traffic) (Compulsory Insurance) (Amendment) Regulations, 1992[36] ('the Second 1992 Regulations') failed to implement adequately or at all the relevant provisions of the First Directive as amended by the Third Directive.

[12.22] Thereafter, the parties agreed that a number of points could be determined as preliminary issues in the High Court, namely:

1. Insofar as s 65(1) of the 1961 Act, as amended by art 7 of the Second 1992 Regulations provided that regulations made by the Minister 'shall not extend compulsory insurance in respect of civil liability to passengers to – (i) any part of a mechanically propelled vehicle, other than a large public service vehicle, unless that part is designed and constructed with seating and accommodation for passengers ...', does s 65(1), as amended, implement the First, Second and Third Directives in a proper and permissible manner?

2. If the answer to 1 was in the negative, were the relevant provisions of the First, Second and Third Directives directly effective such that the plaintiff could rely on same in respect of the matters complained of in the proceedings?

3. If the answer to 2 was in the affirmative, was the plaintiff entitled to recover from the MIBI pursuant to the 1988 Agreement?

[12.23] On 30 July 2004, the High Court (Ó Caoimh J), in dealing with the preliminary issues, referred the following two questions to the ECJ for a preliminary ruling under art 234 of the EC Treaty, namely:

1. As of 31 December 1995, the date by which Ireland was obliged to implement the provisions of the Third Directive in respect of passengers on vehicles other than motorcycles, did art 1 of the Third Directive oblige Ireland to render insurance compulsory in respect of civil liabilities for injury to individuals travelling in that part of a motor vehicle not designed or constructed with seating accommodation for passengers?

2. If the answer to 1 was in the positive, did art 1 of the Third Directive confer rights on individuals that could be relied upon directly before the national courts?

---

36. European Communities (Road Traffic) (Compulsory Insurance) (Amendment) Regulations, 1992 (SI 347/1992).

[12.24] On 19 April 2007, the ECJ answered the reference as follows:[37]

1. Article 1 of the Third Directive[38] is to be interpreted as precluding national legislation whereby compulsory motor vehicle liability insurance does not cover liability in respect of personal injuries to persons travelling in a part of the motor vehicle which has not been designed and constructed with seating accommodation for passengers;

2. Article 1 of the Third Directive satisfies all the conditions necessary for it to produce direct effect and accordingly confers rights upon which individuals may rely directly before the national courts. However, it is for the national courts to determine whether that provision may be relied upon against a body such as the MIBI.

[12.25] In *Smith v Meade, Meade, FBD Insurance Plc, Ireland and the Attorney General*,[39] the plaintiff suffered personal injury in June 1999 when the van in which he was travelling as a passenger, and being driven by the first defendant (the van driver), collided with another vehicle as a result of the alleged negligent driving of the van driver. The plaintiff had been travelling in an area that was not designed or constructed with seating accommodation for passengers. The second defendant (the van owner) had an insurance policy with the third defendant (the insurer) in respect of any loss or damage suffered by third parties as a consequence of any negligent driving by him or any persons driving with his consent and authority and, at the time of the accident, the van driver was driving with the van owner's consent. The insurer, however, declined to indemnify the van owner in respect of the plaintiff's injuries on the basis that the policy did not cover liability in respect of personal injuries to a person being carried as a passenger in a part of the vehicle that was not designed or constructed with seating accommodation for passengers.

[12.26] The plaintiff submitted that, having regard to the provisions of the First, Second and Third Directives, the exclusion clause in the insurance policy should be deemed void notwithstanding the fact that the Third Directive had not been transposed into Irish law by the date required for its transposition *or* the subsequent date of the accident. The insurer submitted that it was entitled to rely on the exclusion contained in s 65 of the 1961 Act, as amended, and contended that the plaintiff's remedy was one against the State on the basis of its failure to transpose the Third Directive into Irish law by the required date.

[12.27] Peart J said that the insurance policy clearly excluded any indemnity in respect of the plaintiff's injuries in circumstances where he was seated in the rear part of the vehicle which was not fitted with a seat. Furthermore, there was no dispute that, on the date of the accident, the Third Directive had not been transposed into Irish law and the

---

37. *Farrell v Whitty, Minister for the Environment, Ireland, Attorney General and the MIBI* (Case 356 / 05) [2007] ECR I–03067.

38. Third Directive, art 1 is now contained in Sixth Directive, art 12(1).

39. *Smith v Meade, Meade, FBD Insurance Plc, Ireland and the Attorney General* [2009] 3 IR 335. This decision is under appeal as between the defendants. Of note, the MIBI was never joined as a co-defendant in the proceedings. If it had been joined, FBD Insurance plc would have been the 'insurer concerned'.

time period within which this was required to be done by Ireland had passed. He also considered that it was clear from the case law of the ECJ that the Third Directive had direct effect against the State or any emanation of the State, but did not provide a remedy as against any individual such as the insurance company.[40]

[12.28] Peart J concluded:

'[36] All passengers being carried in vehicles and who are injured as a result are intended to be guaranteed equal treatment throughout the European Community regardless of in which member state the injury is caused. The Second Directive required each member state to take necessary measures to ensure that any statutory provision or any contractual clause contained in an insurance policy which excludes from insurance persons, *inter alia*, such as this plaintiff shall for the purpose of article 3(1) of the First Directive be void. I should perhaps note that this application is one imposed upon member states, *i.e.*, to put measures in place to so insure. The Directive does not itself state that such a clause *is* void. Nevertheless the objective is clear. The amendment to s. 65 of the [1961 Act by article 7 of the Second 1992 Regulations] is clearly in conflict with these objectives, and the failure to transpose the Third Directive by the date required has meant that on the date of the accident in which the plaintiff received his injuries, the law of this State was out of line with what was required by Community law.

[37] [The ECJ] judgment in *Marleasing S.E. v. La Comercial Internacional de Alimentación* (Case C–106/89) [1990] E.C.R. I–4135] ... requires a national court, when applying national law, to do so as far as possible in the light of the wording and purpose of the directive in order to pursue the result sought to be pursued by the directive. It seems inescapable that in the present case this court is required to read s. 65 of the Act, as amended by the two Regulations of 1992,[41] by overlooking or ignoring the exclusion permitted therein in respect of liability for injuries caused to persons such as the plaintiff in this case. It seems to follow inevitably from this that the court must conclude that the clause to that effect contained in the policy of insurance ... must be regarded as void, therefore disentitling the [insurer] from relying upon it in order to refuse to indemnify the [van driver and van owner] in respect of the plaintiff's claim for damages... in the event that [the plaintiff] is found at hearing to have so suffered as a result of the negligence of the [van driver]. I so find'.[42, 43]

---

40. *Smith v Meade, Meade, FBD Insurance Plc, Ireland and the Attorney General* [2009] 3 IR 335 at p 347.
41. Road Traffic (Compulsory Insurance) (Amendment) Regulations 1992 (SI 346/1992) (the First 1992 Regulations), and the European Communities (Road Traffic) (Compulsory Insurance) (Amendment) Regulations 1992 (SI 347/1992) (the Second 1992 Regulations).
42. *Smith v Meade, Meade, FBD Insurance Plc, Ireland and the Attorney General* [2009] 3 IR 335 at p 348.
43. The defendants subsequently settled this action with the plaintiff and the settlement was ruled by the High Court (Quirke J) on 10 February 2009 (see p 349 of *Smith v Meade, Meade, FBD Insurance Plc, Ireland and the Attorney General* [2009] 3 IR 335). As between the defendants, however, the matter remains under appeal. For an analysis of, *inter alia*, the decision of the ECJ in *Farrell v Whitty, the Minister for the Environment, Ireland, the Attorney General and the MIBI*, [2008] IEHC 124, (31 January 2008, unreported) HC and *Smith v Meade, Meade, FBD Insurance Plc, Ireland and the Attorney General* [2009] 3 IR 335, see Murphy, 'Uninsured Passengers and EU Law', 14(6) 2009 *Bar Review* 123.

F. A BODY AS AN EMANATION OF THE STATE

[12.29] Aside from claiming direct effect against a Member State, an individual may also claim direct effect against a body that is sufficiently closely identified with the guilty Member State (ie an emanation of the State) to the extent that it is proper to prevent that body from claiming that it is not obliged to comply with a directive just because the State has failed to implement it. That said, if a directive does not satisfy the conditions precedent to direct effect, such that the doctrine of direct effect does not apply against the Member State, then it is equally without direct effect as against an emanation of the State.[44]

[12.30] The concept of an 'emanation of the State' was first identified in *Marshall v Southampton and South West Hampshire Area Health Authority*.[45] Marshall was dismissed by her employer on the grounds that she had reached retirement age, which was 60 years for females and 65 years for males. The implementation date for the 1976 Equal Treatment Directive had passed and the United Kingdom had failed to implement it. The ECJ held that a person employed by the State could rely directly upon the directive as against his State employer (vertical direct effect). The ECJ considered that the fact that the State was acting as an employer, as opposed to exercising its governmental powers, was irrelevant. The Court used the terms 'State' and 'local authority' interchangeably. As an employee of a local authority, Marshall could rely on the unimplemented directive directly against her State employer.

[12.31] The concept of the State was further developed in *Foster and Others v British Gas plc*,[46] and in which the ECJ held as follows:

> '... a body, whatever its legal form, which has been made responsible, pursuant to a measure adopted by the State, for providing a public service under the control of the State and has for that purpose special powers beyond those which result from the normal rules applicable in relations between individuals is included in any event among the bodies against which the provisions of a directive capable of having direct effect may be relied upon.'[47]

[12.32] The principle was applied in Ireland in *Coppinger v Waterford County Council*.[48] The plaintiff suffered personal injury when, following a collision between the plaintiff's car and the defendant's truck, the plaintiff's car under-ran the rear of the defendant's truck. One of the issues in the case concerned Ireland's compliance with certain directives that obliged trucks to have anti-run protection devices.[49] At the time of the

---

44.   In this regard, the comments made below at paras **12.53–12.62** about the decision of the ECJ in *Evans v The Secretary of State for the Environment, Transport and the Regions and the MIB* (Case C–63/01), [2005] All ER (EC) 763, [2003] ECR I–14447, [2004] RTR 32, [2004] 1 CMLR 47, [2004] Lloyd's Rep IR 391, ECJ (5th Chamber) are repeated.

45.   *Marshall v Southampton and South West Hampshire Area Health Authority* (Case 152/84) [1986] ECR 723, [1986] 1 CMLR 688.

46.   *Foster and Others v British Gas plc* (Case C–188/89) [1990] ECR I–3313, [1990] 2 CMLR 833.

47.   At para 20.

48.   *Coppinger v Waterford County Council* [1998] 4 IR 220.

49.   Council Directive of 20 March 1970, on the approximation of the laws of the Member States relating to liquid fuel and rear protective devices for motor vehicles and their trailers (70/221/EEC) as expanded and refined by Commission Directive of 18 April 1979 (79/490/EEC).

plaintiff's accident, the relevant directives had not been transposed into Irish law and the dates for their implementation by Ireland had passed. The plaintiff claimed that the directives had direct effect. Geoghegan J was satisfied that the defendant was an emanation of the State.[50] He also found that the obligations created by the directives were 'definite and certain' and '[did] not confer any discretion on the member state'.[51] Geoghegan J held that the directives had direct effect.[52] The defendant was in breach by its failure to have the requisite device fitted to its truck and this breach caused the serious aspect of the plaintiff's injuries.[53]

G. THE MIBI: AN EMANATION OF THE STATE?

[12.33] In *Delargy v Minister for the Environment and Local Government, Ireland, Attorney General and MIBI*,[54] the plaintiff was a pillion passenger on a motorcycle and suffered significant injuries in an accident in September 1987, when the owner of the motorcycle was driving it. The plaintiff sued the motorcycle owner and in April 1996 obtained judgment against him in an uncontested action. The judgment was unsatisfied. Thereafter, in these proceedings, the plaintiff claimed, *inter alia*:

1. A declaration that s 65(1)(a) of the 1961 Act was unconstitutional;

2. A declaration that s 56 of the 1961 Act was unconstitutional;

3. A declaration that art 6 of the 1962 Regulations was unconstitutional, that the Minister was acting *ultra vires* the powers conferred on him by the Oireachtas and that the same was null and void;

4. A declaration that the 1964 MIBI Agreement was void insofar as it purported to exclude the plaintiff's claim;

5. A declaration that the First Directive, as amended by the Third Directive, had direct effect and that the plaintiff was entitled to rely on it;

6. A declaration that the First Directive as amended obliged the State parties to ensure that the liability of the motorcycle owner and driver to the plaintiff on foot of the judgment obtained by her was covered by insurance;

7. Damages for failure to implement the First and Third Directives;

8. A declaration that the plaintiff was entitled to claim against the MIBI in respect of the liability of the motorcycle owner and driver to the plaintiff on foot of the judgment obtained by her against him.

[12.34] Murphy J observed that the relevant legislation permitted the Minister to distinguish between various classes of vehicles but did not provide any guidance as to

---

50. *Coppinger v Waterford County Council* [1998] 4 IR 220 at p 226. Geoghegan J quoted from that portion of the judgment of the ECJ in *Foster and Others v British Gas plc* (Case C–188/89) [1990] ECR I–3313, [1990] 2 CMLR 833, which is reproduced above.

51. *Coppinger v Waterford County Council* [1998] 4 IR 220 at p 227.

52. *Coppinger v Waterford County Council* [1998] 4 IR 220 at p 227.

53. *Coppinger v Waterford County Council* [1998] 4 IR 220 at p 236.

54. *Delargy v Minister for the Environment and Local Government, Ireland, Attorney General and MIBI* [2005] IEHC 94, (18 March 2005, unreported) HC, Murphy J.

the principle(s) upon which the Minister was to draw that distinction. He noted that the Minister had been given the power to introduce a provision which made a difference between a case where one person, injured by the negligence of another (without the means to satisfy a judgment), could be compensated *and* a case where another person similarly injured with the same level of fault (on the part of a similarly situated defendant) could not be so compensated.[55] Murphy J considered, however, that it was clear that, in the absence of seats, there was no requirement for passengers to be compulsorily insured. He noted that, as regards vehicles in which there is no provision made for seating for passengers eg tractors, there might be a rational basis for excluding compulsory insurance for passengers.[56]

[12.35] With respect to the plaintiff, and in circumstances where there was accommodation for a passenger on the motorcycle, he stated:

> 'Motor cycles are usually constructed for the carriage of single passengers. It is difficult to see by what principle of policy the Minister had excluded cover under Regulation 6(2) of the [1962 Regulations].
>
> What the Minister has done is not merely regulatory or administrative only, but is an attempt to arbitrarily restrict cover to a category of otherwise insured passengers.'

[12.36] In the foregoing circumstances, Murphy J declared that art 6(2) of the 1962 Regulations[57] was unconstitutional and that the Minister had acted *ultra vires* the powers conferred on him by the Oireachtas and that the clause was null and void.[58] For this reason, it was unnecessary to consider the issue of direct effect of the First and Third Directives.

[12.37] With respect to the liability of the MIBI, Murphy J noted that the Third Directive, which required cover for 'all passengers', gave Ireland until 31 December 1998 to comply as regards motorcycle passengers, ie more than 11 years after the plaintiff's 1987 accident. He concluded that, at the time of the accident, there was no requirement to have cover for pillion passengers and therefore the MIBI had no

---

55.   *Delargy v Minister for the Environment and Local Government, Ireland, Attorney General and MIBI* [2005] IEHC 94, (18 March 2005, unreported) HC at p 8.

56.   *Delargy v Minister for the Environment and Local Government, Ireland, Attorney General and MIBI* [2005] IEHC 94, (18 March 2005, unreported) HC at pp 8–9. In this regard, he noted that a passenger in an unseated area in the back of a van or lorry was not compulsorily insurable (at p 9)). However, the foregoing comment must be considered in the context of *Farrell v Whitty, the Minister for the Environment, Ireland, the Attorney General and the MIBI* before the ECJ (Case 365/05) [2007] ECR I–03067 and the decision of Birmingham J in the High Court [2008] IEHC 124, (31 January 2008, unreported) HC, and which is currently under appeal. See paras **12.21** *et seq* above.

57.   Road Traffic Road Traffic (Compulsory Insurance) Regulations 1962 (SI 14/1962).

58.   In the judgment of 18 March 2005, Murphy J said that he would make a declaration that the Road Traffic (Compulsory Insurance) Regulations 1962 (SI 14/1962), art 6 was unconstitutional. However, in a supplemental judgment delivered on 10 August 2005 (and discussed below at fn **60**), Murphy J stated that the declaration of unconstitutionality should refer specifically to art 6(2) of the Regulations, rather than art 6.

obligation under the 1964 Agreement to satisfy the plaintiff's judgment against the motorcycle owner and driver.[59, 60]

[12.38] Following the decision of the ECJ in *Farrell v Whitty, Minister for the Environment, Ireland, Attorney General and the MIBI*,[61] the matter came before Birmingham J in the High Court, at which time the net issue for determination was '[m]ay a directive (in this case article 1 of [the Third Directive]), which confers rights upon which individuals may rely directly before the national Court, be relied upon against the [MIBI]?'. Before the High Court, it was agreed that the issue could be determined by deciding whether the MIBI was or was not an 'emanation of the State' as that phrase was understood in European law.[62] This was the first time that the issue of whether the MIBI was an emanation of the State was given express consideration.

59. At p 10. Murphy J said that there was no issue regarding the intervention of European Community law which was not in contemplation at that time and he said that it followed that, prior to 31 December 1998, the Third Directive had no direct effect in Ireland of any kind, either against a public body, a private body or an individual. Murphy J said that he had considered the judgment of the ECJ in *Withers v Delaney and MIBI* (Case C–158/01) [2002] ECR I–08301. Finally, Murphy J said that he was not satisfied that there was evidence that the MIBI could be considered an 'emanation of the State'. He referred to *Mighell v Reading* [1999] 1 CMLR 1251 (Court of Appeal) and *White v White* [1999] 1 CMLR 1251 (Court of Appeal), [2001] 1 WLR 481, [2001] 2 All ER 43, [2001] 1 Lloyds Rep 679, and [2001] RTR 379 (House of Lords). He considered that the English conclusion that the MIB was not an emanation of the State was more persuasive than the Irish decision in *Dublin Bus v MIBI* (29 October 1999, unreported) CC, Judge McMahon (at p 12).

60. A supplemental judgment was delivered in *Delargy v Minister for the Environment and Local Government, Ireland, the Attorney General and the MIBI* [2006] IEHC 267, (10 August 2005, unreported) HC, Murphy J. In advance of this judgment, the court heard submissions with respect to the appropriate form of ancillary relief that might be available to the plaintiff in light of the court's findings in the substantive proceedings. In this regard, Murphy J concluded that the plaintiff was entitled to a remedy against the Minister. In the supplemental judgment, he described the issue as follows: 'the question arises as to the consequences of the Minister acting *ultra vires* the powers conferred on him by the Oireachtas in relation to the exclusion of cover for pillion passengers. There is no direct relationship between the power of the court to null an administrative act and liability to pay damages or monetary compensation. When a court nulls an administrative act on procedural grounds, that decision is deemed to be *ultra vires* and void *ab initio*. However, it does not follow that a declaration of invalidity of an administrative decision in and of itself gives rise to a cause of action and damages' (at p 4). However, Murphy J concluded that in acting as he did, art 6(2) arbitrarily restricted and excluded cover to a category of otherwise insurable passengers and said that the court had held that it was difficult to see by what principle or policy such exclusion was made and to have acted in such an arbitrary manner was a breach of duty (at p 5). Murphy J concluded that the effect of art 6(2) of the 1962 Regulations was to exclude a defined category of persons, which included the plaintiff, from having the benefit of the mandatory requirement to have cover. On the authorities of *O'Neill v Clare County Council* [1983] ILRM 141, *Bakht v Medical Council* [1990] 1 IR 515, *Emerald Meats v Minister for Agriculture and Food* [1997] 2 ILRM 275 and *Moyne v London Port and Harbour Commissioners* [1986] IR 299, the court held that the plaintiff was entitled to a remedy against the Minister (at pp 5–6).

61. *Farrell v Whitty, Minister for the Environment, Ireland, Attorney General and the MIBI* (Case 356/05) [2007] ECR I–03067.

62. *Farrell v Whitty, the Minister for the Environment, Ireland, the Attorney General and the MIBI* [2008] IEHC 124, (31 January 2008, unreported) HC, Birmingham J, at p 10.

Birmingham J, in an analytical judgment, concluded that the MIBI, in substance if not in form, operated as a quasi State claims agency giving effect to an important aspect of public social policy and therefore was to be regarded as an emanation of the State.[63] On this basis, the plaintiff was entitled to recover from the MIBI pursuant to the 1988 Agreement. [64] This decision is under appeal to the Supreme Court.[65]

[12.39] In considering this issue, Birmingham J attached significance, *inter alia*, to the following paragraph of the judgment of the ECJ in *Farrell v Whitty*[66] wherein the court stated:

'40. A Directive cannot be relied on as against individuals, whereas it may be relied on as against a State, regardless of the capacity in which the latter is acting, that is to say, whether as employer or as public authority. The entities against which the provisions of a directive that are capable of having direct effect may be relied upon include a body, whatever its legal form, which has been responsible, pursuant to a measure adopted by the State, for providing a public service under the control of the State and have for that purpose special powers beyond those which result from the normal rules applicable in relations between individuals (Case C–188/89 *Foster and Others* [1990] E.C.R. I–3313, para. 20; Case C–343/98 *Collino and Chiappero* [2000] E.C.R. I–6659, para. 23; and Case C–157/02 *Rieser Internationale Transporte* [2004] E.C.R. I–1477, para. 24)'.[67]

[12.40] The parties in *Farrell v Whitty* were agreed that the starting point for consideration of the issue was *Foster v British Gas Plc*[68] which arose from the actions of the pre-privatised British Gas Plc that required their female employees to retire earlier than their male counterparts, and in apparent breach of the provisions of the 1976 Equal Treatment Directive.[69] Birmingham J noted that the kernel of the judgment was to be found in the following paragraphs:[70]

'16. As the Court has consistently held (see the judgment in case 8/81 *Becker v. Hauptzollamt Wuenster-Innenstadt* [1982] E.C.R. 53, paragraphs 23 to 25), where the Community authorities have, by means of a directive, placed Member States under a duty to adopt a certain course of action, the effectiveness of such a measure would be diminished if persons were prevented from relying upon it in proceedings before a court and national courts were prevented from taking it into consideration as an element of Community law. Consequently, a Member State which has not adopted the implementing measures required by the directive within

---

63. At p 35.
64. At p 36.
65. Indeed, cl 3.10.3 of the 2009 Agreement expressly provides that cl 3 of that agreement will be reviewed in light of the Supreme Court judgment in *Farrell v Whitty, the Minister for the Environment, Ireland, the Attorney General and the MIBI.*
66. *Farrell v Whitty* (Case 356/05) [2007] ECR I–03067.
67. *Farrell v Whitty* (Case 356/05) [2007] ECR I–03067 at p 14.
68. *Foster v British Gas Plc* (Case 188/89) [1990] ECR I–3313.
69. Council Directive 76/207/EEC of 9 February 1976 on the implementation of the principle of equal treatment for men and women as regards access to employment, vocational training and promotion, and working conditions.
70. *Farrell v Whitty, the Minister for the Environment, Ireland, the Attorney General and the MIBI,* [2008] IEHC 124, (31 January 2008, unreported) HC, Birmingham J, at p 17 .

the prescribed period may not plead, as against individuals, its own failure to perform the obligations which the directive entails. Thus, wherever the provisions of a directive appear, as far as their subject-matter is concerned, to be unconditional and sufficiently precise, those provisions may, in the absence of implementing measures adopted within the prescribed period, be relied upon as against any national provision which is incompatible with the directive or insofar as the provisions define rights which individuals are able to assert against the State

...

18. On the basis of those considerations, the Court has held in a series of cases that unconditional and sufficiently precise provisions of a directive could be relied on against organisations or bodies which were subject to the authority or control of the State or had special powers beyond those which result from the normal rules applicable to relations between individuals ...

20. It follows from the foregoing that a body, whatever its legal form, which has been made responsible, pursuant to a measure adopted by the State, for providing a public service under the control of the State and has for that purpose special powers beyond those which result from the normal rules applicable in relations between individuals is included in any event among the bodies against which the provisions of a Directive capable of having direct effect may be relied upon.'

[12.41] Birmingham J reviewed the Irish and English authorities, including the decision of Murphy J in *Delargy v The Minister for the Environment and Local Government, Ireland, the Attorney General and the MIBI*.[71] Birmingham J considered that, notwithstanding the fact that that decision was under appeal, he would be slow not to follow the judgment of Murphy J if the conclusions in it, concerning the status of the MIBI, formed part of the *ratio decidendi*.

[12.42] Birmingham J concluded that the tripartite test in *Foster* was not to be read as if it was a statutory requirement. Thereafter, he concluded:

'The *Foster* formula is a guide or illustration and no doubt a useful guide or illustration but no more than that. I take that view primarily as a result of the consideration of the language of the relevant paragraph of the *Foster* judgment itself. Paragraph 20, it will be recalled, is in the following terms:

"It follows from the foregoing that a body, whatever its legal form, which has been made responsible, pursuant to a measure adopted by the State, for providing a public service under the control of the State and has for that purpose special powers beyond those which result from the normal rules applicable in relation between individuals *is included in any event* among the bodies against which the provisions of a directive capable of having direct effect may be relied upon" [Emphasis added].

12.3 I am of the view that reference to "*is included in any event*" is quite inconsistent with any suggestion that what is being offered is a comprehensive, all embracing test. On the contrary it seems to me that the phrase "*is included in any event*" signals that the category of bodies is wider than those that meet the three tests and that bodies that do meet the three tests constitute only a subset of the entire category.

---

71.   *Delargy v The Minister for the Environment and Local Government, Ireland, the Attorney General and the MIBI* [2005] IEHC 94, (18 March 2005, unreported) HC, Murphy J.

12.4 The opening words of this paragraph "it follows from the foregoing" point in the same direction. What has preceded paragraph 20 are a number of paragraphs setting out general principles. This phrase roots what is to come later in paragraph 20 in what is gone before. The view that I have arrived at that it is not appropriate to apply the tripartite test as though it were a statutory definition accords with the views of the Court of Appeal in England as expressed in *N.U.T. and Others v. St. Mary's Church of England Junior School and Others* [1997] 3 C.L.M.R. 630, a judgment of Scheimann L.J.

12.5 ...

12.6 The closer the subject matter under consideration to those that were at issue in *Foster*, the more helpful will be the application of the tripartite test. Conversely, if the facts to be considered and the nature of the body to be considered diverge significantly from *Foster*, the value of the test will be undermined. *Foster* concerned a commercial undertaking operating in the marketplace. A similar situation existed in *Rolls-Royce v. Doughty* [1992] I.C.R. 538. The present situation is quite different in that we are concerned not with a commercial undertaking, but with the vehicle by which a long-term social policy is delivered.'[72]

[12.43] Thereafter, in his analysis of the MIBI, Birmingham J said that, while there was no doubt that in form it was a private body, he was of the view that, in practice, there was 'a considerable degree of State control or influence'.[73] He also considered the obligation in cl 4(1) of the 1988 Agreement that required the MIBI to satisfy judgments in respect of liability for injury to persons or damage to property for which insurance was mandatory under s 56 of the 1961 Act but which was not in fact covered by such insurance. In circumstances where it was accepted that the MIBI's obligations under the 1961 Act encompassed amendments enacted thereto during the currency of that agreement, Birmingham J considered that '[b]y any standard, this [had] to be regarded as a significant element of control' of the MIBI by the State.[74]

[12.44] On the other hand, Birmingham J considered that, subject to one 'significant exception', the executive arm of the State could not dictate how the MIBI might deal with individual claims. That said, Birmingham J considered it an unusual feature of a contract between two parties (ie the Minister and the MIBI) that it should provide that, in the event of a disagreement between the MIBI and a claimant, one party to the contract (ie the Minister) should determine how the dispute might be resolved.[75] He noted the difference between cl 3(7) of the 1988 Agreement and the provision in the English agreement to the effect that an arbitrator, chosen from a panel of Queen's Council appointed by the Secretary of State, hears an appeal when a complainant is dissatisfied with the amount of compensation offered. He also attached significance to

72. *Farrell v Whitty, the Minister for the Environment, Ireland, the Attorney General and the MIBI*, [2008] IEHC 124, (31 January 2008, unreported) HC, Birmingham J, at pp 31–33.

73. *Farrell v Whitty, the Minister for the Environment, Ireland, the Attorney General and the MIBI*, [2008] IEHC 124, (31 January 2008, unreported) HC, Birmingham J, at p 33.

74. *Farrell v Whitty, the Minister for the Environment, Ireland, the Attorney General and the MIBI*, [2008] IEHC 124, (31 January 2008, unreported) HC, Birmingham J, at pp 33–34.

75. *Farrell v Whitty, the Minister for the Environment, Ireland, the Attorney General and the MIBI*, [2008] IEHC 124, (31 January 2008, unreported) HC, Birmingham J, at p 34.

the fact that amendments to the memorandum and articles of association of the MIBI required the consent of the Minister for Employment and Enterprise.

[12.45] Furthermore, Birmingham J also considered that, under s 78 of the 1961 Act,[76] only a member of the MIBI can issue an approved policy of insurance and 'even more unusually', the fact that, before a body can become an exempted person and be freed of the obligations of compulsory insurance, that body must provide an undertaking to deal with third party claims in respect of its vehicles on terms similar to those agreed between the Minister and the MIBI.[77]

[12.46] Birmingham J said that all of the foregoing factors led him to the view that the MIBI, in substance if not in form, operated as a quasi-state claims agency giving effect to an important aspect of public social policy and therefore was to be regarded as an emanation of the State.[78]

[12.47] In addition, Birmingham J stated that, while it was his view that it was not appropriate to apply rigorously the *Foster* tripartite test to establish the status of the MIBI, he would have reached the same conclusion even if he had applied that test.[79] He had no hesitation in concluding that the MIBI performed a public service. The position in relation to state control and special powers was less clear-cut but Birmingham J was of the view that aspects, such as the operation of a veto on the alteration of the MIBI's memorandum and articles, as well as the Minister's entitlement to give a binding direction in the event of a disagreement between a claimant and the MIBI, were indicative of a significant level of state control. He considered that this was 'hardly surprising' given that it was the State that ultimately controlled the scope of the MIBI's obligations, insofar as the State determined the extent of the requirements of compulsory insurance.[80]

[12.48] On the foregoing basis, Birmingham J concluded that the MIBI was to be regarded as an emanation of the State and that the Plaintiff was entitled to recover from it pursuant to the 1988 Agreement.[81]

H. ENGLISH CASE LAW ON MIB AS AN EMANATION OF THE STATE

[12.49] In England the issue of whether or not the English MIB is an emanation of the State was considered, albeit *obiter*, in *White v White*.[82] As noted above, the trial judge

---

76. As substituted by the European Communities (Compulsory Insurance) (Amendment) Regulations 1992 (SI 347/1992), art 9 (the Second 1992 Regulations).

77. *Farrell v Whitty, the Minister for the Environment, Ireland, the Attorney General and the MIBI*, [2008] IEHC 124, (31 January 2008, unreported) HC, Birmingham J, at pp 34–35.

78. *Farrell v Whitty, the Minister for the Environment, Ireland, the Attorney General and the MIBI*, [2008] IEHC 124, (31 January 2008, unreported) HC, Birmingham J, at p 35.

79. *Farrell v Whitty, the Minister for the Environment, Ireland, the Attorney General and the MIBI*, [2008] IEHC 124, (31 January 2008, unreported) HC, Birmingham J, at p 35.

80. *Farrell v Whitty, the Minister for the Environment, Ireland, the Attorney General and the MIBI*, [2008] IEHC 124, (31 January 2008, unreported) HC, Birmingham J, at p 36.

81. *Farrell v Whitty, the Minister for the Environment, Ireland, the Attorney General and the MIBI*, [2008] IEHC 124, (31 January 2008, unreported) HC, Birmingham J, at p 36.

82. *White v White* [1999] 1 CMLR 1251 (Court of Appeal).

found that, while the plaintiff's compensation claim was excluded by the MIB agreement on the basis that he 'ought to have known' that he was travelling in an uninsured car, such an exclusion was not permitted by the Second Directive which only allowed Member States to exclude compensation for persons who 'knew' about the absence of insurance. The trial judge considered that the right afforded to the plaintiff by the Second Directive was directly enforceable against the MIB as an emanation of the State and that it was bound to satisfy the plaintiff's claim. On appeal to the English Court of Appeal,[83] Schiemann LJ considered that it was well established that rights afforded by a directive may have direct effect and that this route was available against the State, and bodies sufficiently closely identified with the State, to make it proper for the court to prevent them from relying on the State's failure to implement the directive.[84] With respect to the issue of whether or not the MIB was an emanation of the State, Schiemann LJ[85] considered it unnecessary to express a concluded opinion.[86] He did, however, comment as follows:

'For my part, I accept that there is substantial uncertainty surrounding the concept of 'emanation of the State'. That uncertainty springs in part from the uncertainty of the legal concept and in part from the difficulty of applying that concept to a particular factual situation. The latter is a task which the national courts have to fulfil although they may be helped by a reference. I would not regard it as *acte clair* that the MIB was not an emanation of the State, although that is my current opinion.'[87]

[12.50] More recently, however, in *McCall v Poulton, MIB, Helphire (UK) Ltd and Angel Assistants Ltd*,[88] the County Court ordered that a preliminary ruling should be sought from the ECJ on, *inter alia*, the issue of whether or not the MIB is an emanation of the State. The question arose in the context of whether or not the plaintiff could claim directly against the MIB under the Second Directive.[89]

---

83. *White v White* [1999] 1 CMLR 1251 (Court of Appeal).
84. *White v White* [1999] 1 CMLR 1251 (Court of Appeal) at p 1261.
85. With whom Swinton Thomas and Hobhouse LJJ agreed, at p 1269.
86. The fact that he had previously decided that the Second Directive did not have direct effect against Member States (and therefore any emanation of the State) rendered it unnecessary to decide whether or not the MIB was an emanation of the State.
87. At p 1264.
88. *McCall v Poulton, MIB, Helphire (UK) Ltd and Angel Assistants Ltd* [2009] 1 CMLR 45, [2008] EWCA Civ 1313, [2009] CP Rep 15, [2009] PIQR P8, [2009] RTR 11.
89. The plaintiff was the victim of a motor accident caused by the first defendant's negligent driving. The plaintiff's car, a taxi, was damaged. He needed a replacement and so hired one on credit from the third defendant. He was also provided with an insurance policy issued by the fourth defendant. This policy provided the plaintiff with post-accident cover for (a) the legal costs of the plaintiff's resulting claim and (b) the third defendant's charges in the event that they were not recovered from the first named defendant within the credit period. Thereafter, it transpired that the first defendant was uninsured and he did not pay the plaintiff any compensation. The plaintiff made a claim on the policy issued to him by the fourth defendant and it paid the hire charges, thereby discharging the plaintiff's debt to the third defendant. The MIB declined to pay compensation for the hire charges in reliance on either or both of two exclusions in the English Uninsured Drivers Agreement (1999) (the 1999 Agreement), (contd .../)

I. INDIRECT EFFECT

[12.51] The concept of indirect effect was developed by the ECJ to increase the enforceability of unimplemented directives. The concept requires national courts to interpret national law in light of the relevant directive. The concept was described in *Von Colson and Kamann v Land Nordrhein-Westfalen*[90] as follows:

> '... The Member States' obligation arising from a directive to achieve the result envisaged by the directive and their duty under Article 5 of the Treaty[91] to take all appropriate measures, whether general or particular, to ensure the fulfilment of that obligation, is binding on all the authorities of Member States including, for matters within their jurisdiction, the courts.'[92]

[12.52] This principle was applied by the Circuit Court in *Dublin Bus v MIBI*[93] in which Judge McMahon held that cl 7(2) of the 1988 Agreement went beyond the terms of art 1(4) of the Second Directive. Judge McMahon proceeded to interpret cl 7(2) in a manner that was consistent with the Second Directive, having regard to the fact that:

> 'it has been clearly indicated by the [ECJ] that when there is a duty to transpose on a Member State, that duty and the concomitant duty to correct national responses which do not properly respond to the Community Directive falls on all organs of the State, including the judiciary, and not only on the legislature.[94] ... The courts must, therefore, assist where possible in this regard, by providing appropriate responses and remedies, always conscious, however, that they do not usurp the functions exclusively reserved for the legislature and the executive.'[95]

---

89. (contd) namely (1) cl 6(1)(c), which excludes the MIB's liability to meet claims made: '[b]y, or for the benefit of a person ("the beneficiary") other than the person suffering death, injury or damage which is made ... pursuant to a right of subrogation or contractual or other right belonging to the beneficiary'; and (2) cl 17(1) providing 'Where a claimant has received compensation from ... (b) an insurer under an insurance agreement or arrangement, or (c) any other source ... MIB may deduct ... an amount equal to that compensation'. In the County Court, the third and fourth defendants contended that, as a matter of Community law, interpreting the Second Directive, art 1(4), the MIB could not rely on either exclusion. The parties were in dispute as to whether the principle of interpretation identified in *Marleasing SA v La Comercial Internacional de Alimentación SA* (Case C–106/89) [1990] ECR I–4135, [1992] 1 CMLR 305 should be applied to the 1999 Agreement and as to whether the MIB was an emanation of the State such that the plaintiff might claim directly against the MIB under the Second Directive. The reference has not yet been heard by the ECJ.

90. *Von Colson and Kamann v Land Nordrhein-Westfalen* (Case 14/83) [1984] ECR 1891, [1986] 2 CMLR 430.

91. Now art 10 of the EC Treaty.

92. *Von Colson and Kamann v Land Nordrhein-Westfalen* (Case 14/83) [1984] ECR 1891, [1986] 2 CMLR 430 at para 26. See also *Marleasing SA v La Comercial Internacional de Alimentacion SA* (Case C–106/89) [1990] ECR I–4135, (1992) 1 CMLR 305.

93. *Dublin Bus v MIBI* (29 October 1999, unreported) CC.

94. Citing *Von Colson and Kamann v Land Nordrhein-Westfalen* (Case 14/83) [1984] ECR 1891, [1986] 2 CMLR 430.

95. *Dublin Bus v MIBI* (29 October 1999, unreported) CC at p 5.

J. DAMAGES AGAINST A MEMBER STATE FOR ITS FAILURE TO IMPLEMENT A DIRECTIVE

[12.53] Aside from pleading direct effect of a directive as against a Member State or an emanation of the State, a person may claim damages from a guilty Member State for its failure to implement a directive. This alternative course of action is of enormous value in circumstances where the directive does not satisfy the requirements of direct effect and was established in *Francovich and Others v Italy*.[96] Following its finding that the directive at issue did not have direct effect, the ECJ held that individuals aggrieved by non-implementation of the directive were entitled to claim damages from Italy for its non-implementation.

K. CONDITIONS PRECEDENT TO CLAIMING DAMAGES FOR NON-IMPLEMENTATION OF DIRECTIVE

[12.54] Three conditions must be satisfied before an individual will succeed in a claim for damages against a Member State for its non-implementation of a directive. First, the result prescribed by the directive must have been intended to confer rights on individuals. Second, the breach must be sufficiently serious. Third, there must be a direct causal link between the breach of the obligation resting on the State and the loss or damage sustained by the injured party.[97]

[12.55] This issue was raised in the context of the motor insurance directives before the ECJ in *Evans v Secretary of State for the Environment, Transport and the Regions and the MIB*.[98] By way of background, Evans claimed that he was entitled to be paid interest on compensation awarded to him by the MIB on the basis that the English Agreement provided for the payment of an amount assessed according to what the applicant would have been entitled to recover if he had successfully brought proceedings against the untraced person in court.[99]

[12.56] The claim for interest was refused by the High Court and Evans appealed. The Court of Appeal dealt with the appeal simultaneously with the appeal in *White v White*[100]

---

96. *Francovich and Others v Italy* (Joined Cases C–6/90 and C–9/90) [1991] ECR I–5357, [1993] 2 CMLR 66.

97. See *Francovich and Others v Italy* (Joined Cases C–6/90 and C–9/90) [1991] ECR I–5357, [1993] 2 CMLR 66 (at para 40); *Brasserie de Pecheur* and *Factortame* (Joined Cases C–46/93 and C–48/93) [1996] ECR I–1029 (at para 54 *et seq.*); and *Haim* (Case C–424/97) [2000] ECR I–5 123 (at para 36 *et seq*).

98. *Evans v Secretary of State for the Environment, Transport and the Regions and the MIB* (Case C–63/01) [2005] All ER (EC) 763, [2003] ECR I–14447, [2004] RTR 32, [2004] 1 CMLR 47, [2004] Lloyd's Rep IR 391, ECJ (5th Chamber).

99. Evans' application for compensation had previously been determined by the MIB and, on appeal to arbitration, the amount was reduced and he was ordered to pay the costs of the arbitration. He was granted leave to appeal to the High Court against the arbitrator's refusal to award him interest.

100. *White v White* [1999] 1 CMLR 1251. The Court of Appeal dealt with this appeal at the same time as the similar case of *Mighell v Reading* [1999] 1 CMLR 1251 (Court of Appeal). The Court of Appeal upheld the trial judge's finding that *Mighell* actually knew about the absence of insurance and dismissed the appeal.

referred to above. The Court of Appeal held that Evans was not entitled to interest and the House of Lords refused his application for leave to appeal.

[12.57] One month later, Evans commenced proceedings against the Secretary of State for the Environment, as the person responsible for the implementation of the First and Second Directives in the United Kingdom, and the MIB. He submitted, *inter alia,* that the United Kingdom failed to implement the Second Directive in that its agreement with the MIB failed to provide for the payment of interest on an award of damages. The High Court stayed the proceedings and referred various questions of law to the ECJ for a preliminary ruling. The ECJ delivered its decision on 4 December 2003.[101] It is important to emphasise that Evans did not claim that the directives had direct effect or that the MIB was an emanation of the State.

[12.58] The ECJ noted that the First and Second Directives did not expressly oblige the Member States to require the body responsible for paying compensation to pay interest. The ECJ held that art 1(4) of the Second Directive must be interpreted as meaning that an award of compensation must take account of the effluxion of time until actual payment of the sums awarded in order to guarantee 'adequate compensation' and that it was incumbent on the Member States to lay down the rules to be applied for that purpose.[102]

[12.59] Evans further submitted that the payment of costs incurred in relation to an application for compensation also constituted an essential component of the right to compensation.[103] The ECJ applied the same principles and held that, in the absence of Community legislation on the question of costs, it was for the Member States to lay down procedural rules in conformity with the principles of equivalence and effectiveness[104] and it was incumbent upon the national courts to verify that the procedures adopted complied with these principles. In this regard, it considered that it was for the national courts to:

> 'assess whether, in view of the less advantageous position in which victims find themselves *vis-à-vis* the MIB and the conditions under which such victims are able to submit their comments on matters that may be used against them, it appears reasonable, or indeed necessary, for them to be given legal assistance.'[105]

---

101. *Evans v Secretary of State for the Environment, Transport and the Regions and the MIB* (Case C–63/01) [2005] All ER (EC) 763, [2003] ECR I–14447, [2004] RTR 32, [2004] 1 CMLR 47, [2004] Lloyd's Rep IR 391, ECJ (5th Chamber).

102. *Evans v Secretary of State for the Environment, Transport and the Regions and the MIB* (Case C–63/01) [2005] All ER (EC) 763, [2003] ECR I–14447, [2004] RTR 32, [2004] 1 CMLR 47, [2004] Lloyd's Rep IR 391, ECJ (5th Chamber) at para 71.

103. *Evans v Secretary of State for the Environment, Transport and the Regions and the MIB* (Case C–63/01) [2005] All ER (EC) 763, [2003] ECR I–14447, [2004] RTR 32, [2004] 1 CMLR 47, [2004] Lloyd's Rep IR 391, ECJ (5th Chamber) at para 72.

104. *Evans v Secretary of State for the Environment, Transport and the Regions and the MIB* (Case C–63/01) [2005] All ER (EC) 763, [2003] ECR I–14447, [2004] RTR 32, [2004] 1 CMLR 47, [2004] Lloyd's Rep IR 391, ECJ (5th Chamber) at para 73.

105. *Evans v Secretary of State for the Environment, Transport and the Regions and the MIB* (Case C–63/01) [2005] All ER (EC) 763, [2003] ECR I–14447, [2004] RTR 32, [2004] 1 CMLR 47, [2004] Lloyd's Rep IR 391, ECJ (5th Chamber) at para 77.

[12.60] On this basis, the ECJ held that art 1(4) of the Second Directive was to be interpreted as meaning that compensation awarded by the authorised body was not required to include reimbursement of the costs incurred by a victim in connection with the processing of a compensation application, except to the extent to which such reimbursement was necessary to safeguard the rights derived from the Second Directive in conformity with the principles of equivalence and effectiveness. Thus, it was for the national court to consider whether that was the case under the procedural arrangements adopted in the Member State concerned.[106]

[12.61] The court reiterated the pronouncements made in *Francovich and Others v Italy*[107] regarding the circumstances in which a Member State may be required to make reparation to an individual for its breach of Community law. The court held that, if an examination of the compensation system by the national court was to disclose a defect in the transposition of the Second Directive, and if the defect had adversely affected the claimant, it was incumbent upon the national court to determine whether the breach of the obligation of transposition was sufficiently serious to warrant a claim for damages for failure to properly implement it.[108]

[12.62] The Court noted that all the factors which characterise the situation must be taken into account, including, in particular, the clarity and precision of the rule infringed, whether the infringement or the damage caused was intentional or involuntary, whether any error of law was excusable or inexcusable and the fact that the position taken by a Community institution may have contributed towards the adoption or maintenance of national measurescontrary to Community law.[109]

---

106. *Evans v Secretary of State for the Environment, Transport and the Regions and the MIB* (Case C–63/01) [2005] All ER (EC) 763, [2003] ECR I–14447, [2004] RTR 32, [2004] 1 CMLR 47, [2004] Lloyd's Rep IR 391, ECJ (5th Chamber) at para 78.

107. *Francovich and Others v Italy* (Joined Cases C–6/90 and C–9/90) [1991] ECR I–5357, [1993] 2 CMLR 66.

108. *Evans v Secretary of State for the Environment, Transport and the Regions and the MIB* (Case C–63/01) [2005] All ER (EC) 763, [2003] ECR I–14447, [2004] RTR 32, [2004] 1 CMLR 47, [2004] Lloyd's Rep IR 391, ECJ (5th Chamber) at paras 82–84.

109. *Evans v Secretary of State for the Environment, Transport and the Regions and the MIB* (Case C–63/01) [2005] All ER (EC) 763, [2003] ECR I–14447, [2004] RTR 32, [2004] 1 CMLR 47, [2004] Lloyd's Rep IR 391, ECJ (5th Chamber) at paras 86–87. *Byrne v MIB* [2009] QB 66 is an example of a case in which the plaintiff succeeded in an action for damages for the UK's failure to properly implement the Second Directive. As a child in 1993, the plaintiff was injured by an untraced driver. A claim for compensation on his behalf was rejected by the MIB on the basis that it was made outside the three-year time period prescribed by the MIB (Compensation of Victims of Untraced Drivers) Agreement 1972 (the 1972 Agreement). While still a child, the plaintiff brought an action for damages against the MIB on the ground that its rejection of the claim was in breach of the 1972 Agreement as properly interpreted in accordance with the Second Directive. In the alternative, the plaintiff claimed damages against the Secretary of State for Transport, on the ground that he was liable for the failure to properly implement the Second Directive. At first instance, a declaration was made that the 1972 Agreement did not provide the plaintiff with the protection that art 1(4) of the Second Directive required and that the plaintiff was entitled to damages against the Secretary of State. (contd .../)

L. THE CIRCUIT COURT DECISION IN *DUBLIN BUS V MIBI*

[12.63] In *Dublin Bus v MIBI*,[110] Judge McMahon held that cl 7(2) of the 1988 Agreement did not properly transpose the requirements of the Second Directive into Irish law. Judge McMahon cited *Francovich and Others v Italy*[111] and stated:

'It is equally clear that an individual in the State who suffers damage as a result of the State's failure to implement properly or at all the [Second Directive] can sue the State for these damages.'[112]

[12.64] Judge McMahon further noted that this right of action existed regardless of whether or not the directive had direct effect.[113] Having considered the general Community principles applicable to a situation where the issue of a Member State's liability for failure to obey its Community obligations comes before a Member State,[114] Judge McMahon held:

'I have already held that as the body authorised and appointed by the Minister for the Environment to manage the scheme on a day-to-day basis under the [1988] Agreement, the [MIBI] is the Minister's agent and partner in this scheme. The State's yoke of responsibility for transforming community responsibility in this regard lies equally on the shoulders of the Bureau as well as on the shoulders of the Minister. Indeed, in so far as the Bureau knew of the State's failure in this transforming process for several years and failed to remedy the matter it cannot

---

109. (contd) Upholding the declarations the Court of Appeal held that the three-year limitation period in the 1972 Agreement was less favourable that that which applied to proceedings for personal injury in tort against a traced driver and in respect of which the plaintiff could have sued at any time prior to his 21st birthday and the UK had failed to implement the Second Directive correctly (applying *Evans v Secretary of State for the Environment, Transport and the Regions and the MIB* (Case C–63/01) [2005] All ER (EC) 763, [2003] ECR I–14447, [2004] RTR 32, [2004] 1 CMLR 47, [2004] Lloyd's Rep IR 391, ECJ (5th Chamber)). Applying the *Francovich* principles, the Court was satisfied that the breach was 'sufficiently serious' to give rise to a remedy in damages. Significance was attached to the fact that the judgment of the ECJ in *Evans* was an authoritative statement of the legal context in which the 1972 Agreement had to be considered and was 'at the very least a warning of the need to revisit this issue' and 'had that been done, it would have signalled at the very least a serious risk of the agreement being found non-compliant in this respect' and it should have been clear that failure to remedy the defect would cause serious prejudice to a significant group of potential claimants' (at p 113). See *Carswell v Secretary of State for Transport and MIB* [2010] EWHC 3230 (QB) as an example of a case in which the plaintiff failed in her action for a declaration that, by reason of the provisions concerning costs in the 2003 Agreement between the Secretary of State and the MIB providing for Compensation for Victims of Untraced Drivers, the UK had failed to properly implement Second Directive, art 1(4) (now Sixth Directive, art 10).

110. *Dublin Bus v MIBI* (29 October 1999, unreported) CC.

111. *Francovich and Others v Italy* (Joined Cases C–6/90 and C–9/90) [1991] ECR I–5357, [1993] 2 CMLR 66.

112. *Dublin Bus v MIBI* (29 October 1999, unreported) CC at p 9.

113. *Dublin Bus v MIBI* (29 October 1999, unreported) CC at p 9, and citing *Tate v Minister for Social Welfare, Ireland and the Attorney General* [1995] 1 IR 418, [1995] 1 ILRM 507 (in which case the ECJ had already held that the directive at issue had direct effect) and *Francovich and Others v Italy* (Joined Cases C–6/90 and C–9/90) [1991] ECR I–5357, [1993] 2 CMLR 66 (which concerned a directive that did not have direct effect).

114. *Dublin Bus v MIBI* (29 October 1999, unreported) CC at pp 12–14.

avoid responsibility. In spite of public assurances that the Bureau has not been relying on Clause 7(2) since 1996, but was in fact abiding, in practice, by the provisions of the Directive, the present proceedings give a lie to this assurance. It is clearly flaunting the Directive in an unacceptable way. In the event, as already stated earlier in this judgment, in any event, it is not sufficient for the Member States to say [that] they are not enforcing the law which is clearly an improper transposition of Community Law. Member States must do more. They must take positive action to eliminate any doubt in the matter. Clearly this was not done here and for this the [MIBI] must take responsibility, with the Minister. It is quite clear that had the Directive been properly transposed into Irish law, Clause 7(2) would not be in the form it is in now, and the [respondent] would only be facing a restrictive provision which conforms with the terms of the Directive. In that event it would be clearly entitled to recover its property loss from the [MIBI]. In these circumstances, the failure to transpose the Directive into Irish law and the continued failure by the relevant Irish authorities to rectify the situation once the improper implementation was recognised caused the [respondent's] loss. In failing to rectify the situation, and in failing to implement properly the Directive at the outset, there has been a breach of Article 10, EC Treaty [formerly Article 5, EC Treaty], and it is proper for this Court to grant to the [respondent] an appropriate remedy.'[115]

---

115. *Dublin Bus v MIBI* (29 October 1999, unreported) CC at pp 14–15. Judge McMahon affirmed the District Court orders and awarded the respondent interest on the District Court award and costs to include the costs of the appeal.

Chapter 13

FOREIGN VEHICLES IN IRELAND AND IRISH VEHICLES AND RESIDENTS ABROAD

A. INTRODUCTION

[13.01] When one considers the international movement of persons and motor vehicles, numerous categories of claims arising from road traffic accidents may be identified. In this chapter, it is proposed to consider four categories of such claims, namely:

1. an Irish resident who is caused damage and / or injury (injured) in Ireland by a person driving a motor vehicle from another country (foreign vehicle);[1]

2. an Irish resident who is injured abroad by a foreign vehicle;[2]

3. a non-Irish resident who is injured in Ireland by a vehicle;[3]

4. a non-Irish resident who is injured abroad by a vehicle that is normally based in Ireland.[4]

[13.02] As will be seen below, there are various agreements affecting motorists and insurance that operate between the various members of the EU, EEA[5] and other countries. In general terms, however, the manner in which a person who is injured (injured party), in any of the above categories, will depend on a number of factors, such as:

1. whether or not the vehicle that caused the injury is insured;

2. the country in which the vehicle that caused the injury is normally based and insured (if it is insured);

3. the country in which the accident occurred, and whether or not that country is an EEA State, another country that is a party to certain international agreements or a country that is not a party to any such agreements; and

4. whether or not the injured party is a resident of an EEA State and whether the accident occurred in or outside his EEA State of residence.

Before discussing the four categories identified above, it is appropriate to outline the background and evolution of the international agreements that are currently in operation.

---

1. See paras **13.56–13.63** below and **Table 13.2** at p 225.
2. See paras **13.64–13.80** below and **Table 13.3** at p 233.
3. See paras **13.81–13.87** below and **Table 13.4** at p 237.
4. See paras **13.88–13.98** below and **Table 13.5** at p 242.
5. An 'EEA State' means a State that is a contracting party to the Agreement on the European Economic Area signed at Oporto on 2 May 1992, and the protocol adjusting the Agreement signed at Brussels on 17 March 1993 (reg 2(1)), and as amended by the 2004 and 2007 EEA Enlargement Agreements. In essence, the EEA States are the EU Member States and Iceland, Norway and Liechtenstein.

B. THE GREEN CARD SYSTEM

1. The Council of Bureaux

[13.03] Following a recommendation made by a working group of the United Nations,[6] representatives of various Member States met in 1949 to consider the establishment of an international system of motor insurance. Each Member State agreed to establish a national insurers' bureau.[7] The Member States also agreed to establish the Council of Bureaux, of which each national insurers' bureau would be a member. An Inter-Bureaux Agreement was adopted in 1951. Against this background, the green card system was established in June 1952.[8]

2. Commencement of the green card system

[13.04] The Council of Bureaux sought to introduce a means by which a person who takes his vehicle abroad (foreign vehicle) could:

1.   meet the compulsory insurance requirements of the country being visited (participating country[9]); and
2.   ensure that a person injured by a foreign vehicle would not be disadvantaged by the fact that his injury was caused by a foreign vehicle.

[13.05] The Council of Bureaux commenced the green card system on 1 January 1953.[10] A green card is a uniform and readily identifiable certificate of motor insurance. The green card system is an arrangement whereby the production of a green card in respect of a foreign vehicle abroad in a participating country is accepted as evidence that there is, in respect of the foreign vehicle, at least the minimum compulsory third party liability motor insurance required in the country being visited.

[13.06] In 1996, a new Uniform Agreement was adopted by the Council of Bureaux to govern the green card system (the 1996 Uniform Agreement).[11] The Council of Bureaux

---

6.   The recommendation was Recommendation No 5, adopted on 25 January 1949 by the Working Party on Road Transport of the Inland Transport Committee of the European Economic Commission of the United Nations. The recommendation invited Member States to ask motor vehicle insurers in the respective Member States to enter into agreements to establish a uniform system that would enable motorists to be satisfactorily insured upon entry into Member States in which third party liability motor insurance was compulsory. Recommendation No 5, in its current form, was superseded by Annex 1 of the Consolidated Resolution on the Facilitation of Road Transport (R.E.4) adopted by the Inland Transport Committee at the sixty-sixth session held on 17–19 February 2004. It is still referred to as Recommendation No 5.

7.   A national insurers' bureau is comprised of and financed by the domestic insurers that are authorised to transact compulsory motor vehicle insurance in the national market of a Member State.

8.   This was established by the adoption of Resolution No 42 by the Economic Commission for Europe of the United Nations.

9.   Also referred to herein as 'green card country'.

10. At this time, there were eight participating countries: Austria, Belgium, France, Federal Republic of Germany, Great Britain, Netherlands, Sweden and Switzerland.

11. The Uniform Agreement was adopted by the Council of Bureaux at the General Assembly in Casablanca on 30 and 31 May 1996, and applied to claims arising from accidents occurring on or after 1 July 1997.

replaced the 1996 Uniform Agreement with Section II of the Internal Regulations on 1 July 2003.[12] This was subsequently revised by Section II of the Internal Regulations which applies since 1 July 2008 (the Internal Regulations).[13]

[13.07] As of 1 August 2012, 46 countries were participating in the green card system.[14] As will be seen below, however, the requirement for the issuing and production of green cards was diminished by the First Directive, as amended, and decisions of the European Commission directing each Member State to refrain from making insurance checks on vehicles that are normally based in another Member State and certain other countries.[15] To a great extent, the green card system has also been overtaken by the operation of subsequent international agreements, including Section III of the Internal Regulations. The Internal Regulations and the current position regarding the obligation to obtain a green card, in terms of Irish vehicles abroad and foreign vehicles visiting Ireland, is discussed below.[16] It will be seen that the issue and production of green cards is now only necessary in respect of foreign vehicles moving to and from 13[17] of the 46 participating countries.[18]

3. National Insurers' Bureaux

[13.08] With respect to those countries for which the production of a green card is required, a national insurers' bureau[19] ('bureau') has two functions. It is required to:

1. print green cards (or authorise its member insurers to do so) and authorise a member insurer to issue a green card to a person insured by it in advance of that insured travelling abroad with his vehicle to a participating country in which

---

12. The 2002 Internal Regulations were adopted by the General Assembly of the Council of Bureaux on 30 May 2001.

13. The Internal Regulations were revised by the General Assembly of the Council of Bureaux on 29 May 2008 and are discussed below at paras **13.21–13.29** and are reproduced in **Appendix 6**. References herein to 'Internal Regulations' are to the Regulations as revised in 2008.

14. The 46 countries are: Albania, Andorra, Austria, Belarus, Belgium, Bosnia and Herzegovina, Bulgaria, Croatia, Cyprus, Czech Republic, Denmark (and the Faroe Islands), Estonia, Finland, Former Yugoslav Republic of Macedonia, France (and Monaco), Germany, Greece, Hungary, Iceland, Ireland, Islamic Republic of Iran, Israel, Italy (and the Republic of San Marino and the Vatican State), Latvia, Lithuania, Luxembourg, Malta, Moldova, Montenegro, Morocco, Netherlands, Norway, Poland, Portugal, Romania, Russia, Serbia, Slovakia, Slovenia, Spain, Sweden, Switzerland (and Liechtenstein), Tunisia, Turkey, Ukraine, and the United Kingdom. See **Table 13.1.** at p 201. Iraq was suspended from membership in 1992.

15. See paras **13.16–13.20**.

16. See paras **13.21–13.29**.

17. The 13 countries are: Albania, Belarus, Bosnia and Herzegovina, Former Yugoslav Republic of Macedonia, Islamic Republic of Iran, Israel, Morocco, Moldova, Montenegro, Russia, Tunisia, Turkey and Ukraine. See **Table 13.1** at p 201.

18. See fn **14** for a list of the 46 countries. See **Table 13.1** at p 201.

19. This is the term used in the Internal Regulations. While green cards are only required in respect of vehicles travelling to and from the 13 countries that are parties to only Section II of the Internal Regulations (see the list at fn **17**), all 46 countries that are parties to the Internal Regulations (see the list at fn **14**) have the obligations set out above at para **13.08**. (contd .../)

the production of a green card is required. In general terms, a green card may only be issued by the bureau (or member insurer) in the country in which the vehicle is registered.[20] If a foreign vehicle, in respect of which there is a green card, causes an accident in a participating country, the insurer that issued the green card is liable to reimburse the bureau of the country of accident[21] if the latter pays out compensation in settlement of a claim or on foot of award.[22] If the insurer fails in its reimbursement obligations, the bureau of which the insurer is a member must pay.[23]

2.   investigate the circumstances of an accident in its territory involving a vehicle from another participating country in respect of which a green card issued. In this situation, it must give notice of any such accident to the insurer who issued the green card. If the insurer that issued the green card has an approved correspondent[24] in the country of accident, the bureau of the country of accident must forward any claim to that approved correspondent and the latter must handle the claim. If there is no approved correspondent, the bureau of the country of accident must advise the insurer that issued the green card that it has received a claim and will handle it. Thereafter, the bureau of the country of accident may accept service of proceedings arising out of the claim and/or settle the claim.[25] Thereafter, the bureau of the country of accident may claim reimbursement from the insurer.

---

19.   (contd) For example, as will be seen below, Ireland is a party to Section III of the Internal Regulations, which means that an Irish vehicle visiting any of the other 32 countries that are also parties to Section III of the Internal Regulations (see the list at fn **70**) does not require a green card (and vice-versa). However, an Irish vehicle travelling to any of the 13 countries that are only parties to Section II of the Internal Regulations (see the list at fn **17**) requires a green card (and vice-versa) and Ireland must investigate an accident caused by a foreign vehicle (that has a green card) from any one of those 13 countries.

20.   Internal Regulations, art 7(2). However, a member insurer may be authorised by its bureau to issue green cards to its insured in another country in which no bureau exists, provided that the member insurer is established and the vehicle is registered in that other country (art 7(3)).

21.   Internal Regulations, art 5.

22.   Internal Regulations, art 9, provides that each bureau guarantees that any green card presented in a participating country is deemed to have been issued under its authority even if transpires that it is false, unauthorised or illegally altered. Such a guarantee will not apply, however, if the vehicle is not registered in the country that purportedly issued the green card, unless the provisions of art 7(3) apply (see fn **20**).

It is important to note that, where a foreign vehicle visiting a participating country (that should have but does not have a green card) causes an accident, Section II of the Internal Regulations does not apply because of the absence of the green card.

23.   Internal Regulations, art 6(1). A bureau acting in this capacity used to be referred to as a 'paying bureau'. However, this term was removed by the 2002 Internal Regulations.

24.   Internal Regulations, art 4, prescribes the means by which an insurer based in a participating country may have a correspondent (or agent) approved to act on its behalf in another participating country. The approval process is conducted by the bureau of the country in which the correspondent is established.

25.   A bureau acting in this capacity used to be referred to as a 'handling bureau'. However, this term was removed by the 2002 Internal Regulations.

4. The operation of the green card system in Ireland

[13.09] In 1953, the Irish Visiting Motorists' Bureau Ltd.[26] (IVMB) entered into an agreement with the Minister for Local Government whereby the IVMB became the bureau responsible for operating the green card system in Ireland (the 1953 Agreement).[27] Under the 1953 Agreement, if a foreign vehicle (in respect of which there was a green card) caused an accident in Ireland, the IVMB dealt with any claim by a third party in respect of that foreign vehicle. Now, however, the MIBI performs the functions that were formerly discharged by the IVMB.[28]

[13.10] Under the 1953 Agreement, where an Irish vehicle (in respect of which there was a green card[29] issued by the IVMB[30]) caused an accident abroad in a participating country, the IVMB was deemed to be the vehicle insurer that issued the certificate of insurance and to be competent to act as insurer.[31] This meant that the IVMB was liable to pay damages to the injured party in the country of accident (as 'paying bureau'), although, in general terms and assuming that the vehicle was insured, any money that was paid out would have emanated from the insurer that issued the green card. Likewise, if a foreign vehicle (in respect of which there was a green card) caused an accident in Ireland, the IVMB would discharge any third party claim arising out of the accident as

---

26. The Irish Visiting Motorists' Bureau Limited was incorporated under the Companies Acts 1908–1924, and entered into the 1953 Agreement as an agent of the insurance companies that were authorised to transact compulsory motor vehicle insurance in Ireland.

27. The 1953 Agreement was entered into on 7 January 1953 and became operative the following day. The 1953 Agreement, art 4 rendered the agreement determinable by either party on one year's notice. The 1953 Agreement was preceded by the conclusion of another agreement between the IVMB and Irish insurance companies on 2 January 1953.

28. Road Traffic Act 1961, s 72A (the 1961 Act), as inserted by the European Communities (Road Traffic) (Compulsory Insurance) Regulations 1975 (SI 178/1975), art 7, and amended by the EC (Road Traffic) (Compulsory Insurance) (Amendment) Regulations 1992 (SI 347/1992), art 8, and which Regulations were implemented to give effect to certain provisions of the Third Directive. Article 8 of the 1992 Regulations altered the body to be notified from the IVMB to the MIBI.

29. The form of International Motor Insurance Card (ie the format of the green card itself) was originally contained in the Road Traffic (Third Party Risks) (Visiting Motorists) Regulations 1952 (SI 383/1952), Sch. It was replaced by the Road Traffic (Third Party Risks) (Visiting Motorists) Regulations 1958 (SI 82/1958), Sch and then by the Mechanically Propelled Vehicles (International Circulation) Order 1961 (SI 269/1961), Sch 2. The current form of international motor insurance card is contained in the Mechanically Propelled Vehicles (International Circulation) Order 1992 (SI 384/1992), Sch 2 (amended in an insignificant way by the Mechanically Propelled Vehicles (International Circulation) (Amendment) Orders 1998 and 2010 (SI 111/1998 and SI 489/2010 respectively).

30. Essentially, the IVMB was required to issue green cards to its member insurance companies and a member insurance company could distribute them to persons insured by it.

31. Road Traffic (Third Party Risks) (Visiting Motorists) Regulations 1952 (SI 383/1952), art 4. These Regulations were repealed and replaced by the Mechanically Propelled Vehicles (International Circulation) Order 1961 (SI 269/1961). The Mechanically Propelled Vehicles (International Circulation) Order 1992 (SI 384/1992), repealed and replaced the 1961 Regulations. The vehicle insurer was the one who issued a certificate of insurance under the Road Traffic Act 1933, s 68.

though it was the foreign vehicle's insurer (as 'handling bureau'). Again, this meant that the IVMB was liable to pay damages to a person injured by a foreign vehicle in Ireland, although any money paid could be recouped from the bureau of the country that issued the green card, or more particularly and assuming that there was in fact insurance, the insurer that issued the green card. The IVMB has been disbanded. Since 1 January 1993, the MIBI is deemed insurer of a vehicle in respect of which a green card is issued and it discharges the duties that were formerly performed by the IVMB.[32]

[13.11] The current position is governed by the Mechanically Propelled Vehicles (International Circulation) Order 1992 (the 1992 Order).[33] Article 8 provides, *inter alia*:

'(1) In this article

"Certificate" means a certificate of insurance issued in accordance with section 66 of the Road Traffic Act, 1961 by a vehicle insurer certifying that an approved policy of insurance has been issued.

(2) For the purposes of Part VI of the [1961 Act] ... and any regulation made [thereunder], the following provisions shall apply regarding an international motor insurance card[34] in respect of the use of the vehicle referred to in the said card:

(a) the said card shall be deemed to be evidence that a certificate issued to the insured named thereon for the period shown thereon as the period of validity in Ireland;

(b) the [MIBI] shall be deemed to be the vehicle insurer which issued the evidence that a certificate was issued, and to be competent to act as a vehicle insurer;

(c) ...'

[13.12] Section 66(1) of the Road Traffic Act 1961 (the 1961 Act) provides:

'Where a vehicle insurer issues an approved policy of insurance he shall give to the person to whom it is issued the prescribed number of certificates (each of which is referred to in this Act as a certificate of insurance) and stating the prescribed particulars thereof.'

[13.13] Section 58(1) of the 1961 Act[35] defines 'vehicle insurer' as, *inter alia,* an undertaking that carries on vehicle insurance business in the State. It is subject to s 78 of the 1961 Act which prohibits a person from carrying on such business unless it is a member of the MIBI.

---

32. The Mechanically Propelled Vehicles (International Circulation) Order 1992 (SI 384/1992), art 4(1) which became operative on 1 January 1993. This also governs the issue of green cards (art 8) (see below at para **13.11**).

33. Mechanically Propelled Vehicles (International Circulation) Order 1992 (SI 384/1992).

34. Art 4(1) of the 1992 Order defines 'international motor insurance card' as meaning 'a duly completed international motor insurance card issued by a bureau or by the [MIBI] in, or substantially in, the form set out in the Second Schedule to this Order'.

35. As amended by the EC (Road Traffic) (Compulsory Insurance) (Amendment) Regulations 1992 (SI 347/1992).

[13.14] The effect of art 8 of the 1992 Order was explained by Finnegan J in the Supreme Court in *Director of Public Prosecutions v Leipina and Suhanovs*[36] as follows:

'A Green Card is not a policy of insurance. More importantly it is not an approved policy of insurance for the purposes of [section 56 of the 1961 Act][37] ...

[W]here the [1992 Order] has application the Green Card is deemed to be a certificate of insurance for the purposes of section 66 of the [1961 Act]. It is not a certificate of insurance. However the effect of the provision in [art 8 of the 1992] Order is that a person injured by the motor vehicle in respect of which the certificate exists, whether the vehicle is insured or not, the vehicle is deemed to be insured and the [MIBI] will satisfy any claim and in turn recoup the amount from the foreign insurer who issued the Green Card or the Bureau of the country in which the vehicle is registered if the vehicle is in fact uninsured.'[38]

[13.15] Having reviewed the Irish and European law on the issue, Finnegan J stated:

'For present purposes it is sufficient to state that the Green Card is not a policy of insurance. It is a device whereby a motor vehicle is deemed to be insured whether insured or not. The Green Card operates in favour of a vehicle registered in one State visiting another State. A Green Card does not operate in respect of a vehicle within the State of registration of the vehicle: in the State of registration of a vehicle the domestic law relating to compulsory insurance applies ...

The [1992 Order] is concerned with the recognition of the Green Card as evidence in the case of temporarily imported motor vehicles from outside the EU or designated territories. For the purposes of Part VI of the [1961 Act] Article 8 of the [1992] Order provides that the Green Card shall be deemed to be evidence that a certificate issued to the insured named thereon for the period shown thereon as the period of validity in Ireland'.[39]

---

36.   *Director of Public Prosecutions v Leipina and Suhanovs* [2011] IESC 3, (2 February 2011, unreported) SC (*per* Finnegan J).

37.   *Director of Public Prosecutions v Leipina and Suhanovs* [2011] IESC 3, at p 5.

38.   *Director of Public Prosecutions v Leipina and Suhanovs* [2011] IESC 3, at p 7.

39.   At pp 13–14. This prosecution arose out of the accused (the driver) driving a vehicle (owned by the second appellant) that bore an Irish registration plate. The driver had a green card for the vehicle. The green card, together with the policy on which it was based, was issued by a Latvian insurance company that was not a member of the MIBI. Latvia had joined the EU by the date of the alleged offence. In a case stated, the Circuit Court judge asked (a) whether the vehicle in question was covered for use in Ireland under the green card system; and (b) whether, on a charge for an offence contrary to s 56(1) and (3) of the 1961 Act, a policy of insurance attested to by way of a green card for a vehicle bearing an Irish registration plate may be a defence to such charge? The Supreme Court held, *inter alia*, that the various directives and the 1992 Order applied to vehicles registered in one country travelling within another and that, where the regulations apply, a green card is deemed evidence of insurance, whether or not the vehicle is actually insured. In this regard, the vehicle is deemed insured for the purposes of compensating a victim of an accident in which the vehicle is involved that occurs outside the country of the vehicle's registration but '[a] green card issued in respect of a vehicle registered in Ireland is of no effect or relevance in Ireland' (at p 14) and '[t]he deeming provision has no relevance whatsoever to the domestic law of the State requiring compulsory insurance of vehicles registered within the State' (at p 15). (contd .../)

C. EFFECT OF FIRST AND SECOND DIRECTIVES ON GREEN CARD SYSTEM

1. Compulsory minimum insurance and abolition of green card checks

[13.16] The First Directive directed each Member State, *inter alia*, to take measures to ensure that civil liability in respect of the use of vehicles normally based in its territory was covered by insurance.[40] The Member States were also directed to ensure that this insurance also covered loss or injury caused in any Member State and accorded with the law of the other Member States in this regard.[41] The Second Directive directed the Member States, *inter alia*, to introduce *minimum* compulsory third party liability motor vehicle insurance to be applied in all Member States.[42]

[13.17] Section 56(2A) of the Road Traffic Act 1961 (the 1961 Act), implemented the compulsory insurance provisions of the First and Second Directives.[43] It provides that the cover provided by an approved policy of insurance extends to damage to persons or property incurred by the negligent use of a vehicle by its user in any of the designated territories, and to the extent of the compulsory insurance requirements of the relevant

---

39.   (contd) This is because s 56(1) requires an approved policy of insurance (as defined by the 1961 Act, s 62) issued by a vehicle insurer (defined by the 1961 Act, s 58) and such a vehicle insurer must be a member of the MIBI (the 1961 Act, s 78). Furthermore, a policy of insurance, in accordance with the national laws on compulsory insurance in any of the designated territories where vehicles are based, is an approved policy (s 56(2A) of the 1961 Act). The territory in which a vehicle is 'normally based' (the 1961 Act, s 56(8)) is ascertained by reference to the territory of the State of which the vehicle bears a registration plate. The car was normally based in Ireland (being registered in Ireland) and so the Latvian green card (while deemed for the purposes of compensating victims to be an approved policy) was not an approved policy of insurance.

40.   The concept of normally based is discussed at para **13.20**.

41.   First Directive, art 3. Prior to this, various Member States had entered into bilateral agreements that accepted vehicle registration plates as evidence of insurance cover.

42.   Sixth Directive, arts 9 and 10. As of 1 August 2012, the current minimum amounts prescribed by the Sixth Directive, art 9(1) (as amended by the European Commission's Notice regarding the adaptation in line with inflation of certain amounts laid down in the Motor Insurance Directive 2009/103/EC (2010/C 332/01)) are: in the case of personal injury, €1,120,000 per victim or €5,600,000 per claim whatever the number of victims; in the case of property damage, €1,120,000 per claim. The 1961 Act, s 56(1), however, requires unlimited insurance for personal injury and, with respect to property damage, the minimum insurance is €1,120,000 per claim, whatever the number of victims.

43.   The original s 56(2A) was inserted by the EC (Road Traffic) (Compulsory Insurance) Regulations 1975 (SI 178/1975), art 3(a) which were introduced to implement the provisions of the First Directive dealing with the abolition of insurance checks on vehicles moving between Member States of the EEC and certain other countries which had made arrangements with the EEC. Section 56(2A) in its current form was substituted by the EC (Road Traffic) (Compulsory Insurance) (Amendment) Regulations 1992 (SI 347/1992), art 4(1), which were introduced to implement the provisions of the First Directive, as amended by the Second and Third Directives and by Council Directive 90/618/EC of 8 November 1990 which amended Directives 73/239 and 88/357 concerning the co-ordination of laws, regulations and administrative provisions relating to direct insurance other than life assurance (the 1990 Directive). The 1990 Directive obliges insurers authorised in other Member States, and who transact compulsory third party motor insurance business in Ireland, to be members of the MIBI (art 9) (see 1961 Act, s 78).

territory or under Irish law, whichever is greater. Section 62(1)(cc) of the 1961 Act correspondingly increased the liability of an insurer in the designated territories.[44] The designated territories are the territories of the Member States[45] (other than the State) and Croatia,[46] Iceland, Norway and Switzerland (including Liechtenstein).[47]

[13.18] Since 1 May 1962, section 56(1)(a) of the 1961 Act has required unlimited third party insurance against personal injury.[48] Since 21 December 2011, section 56(2)(a) requires third party insurance of €1,120,000 for property damage, regardless of the number of victims.[49]

2. Abolition of border motor insurance checks

[13.19] The First Directive directed Member States to refrain from making anything other than random insurance checks in respect of vehicles normally based in the

---

44.　Section 62(1)(cc) in its current form was substituted by the EC (Motor Insurance) Regulations 2008 (SI 248/2008), reg 3(a)(iii) (the 2008 Regulations). Prior to that, it was substituted by the EC (Road Traffic) (Compulsory Insurance) (Amendment) Regulations 1992 (SI 347/1992), art 4(2). The original s 62(1)(cc) was inserted by the EC (Road Traffic) (Compulsory Insurance) Regulations 1975 (SI 178/1975), art 4.

45.　There are currently 27 EU Member States: Austria, Belgium, Bulgaria, Cyprus, Czech Republic, Denmark, Estonia, Finland, France, Germany, Greece, Hungary, Ireland, Italy, Latvia, Lithuania, Luxembourg, Malta, Netherlands, Poland, Portugal, Romania, Slovakia, Slovenia, Spain, Sweden and the United Kingdom. See **Table 13.1** at p 201.

46.　Croatia will become an EU Member State on 1 July 2013.

47.　Road Traffic Act 1961, s 56(9), as substituted by the 2008 Regulations, reg 2.

　　Previously, the designated territories were prescribed by the 1961 Act, s 56(7), which was inserted by the EC (Road Traffic) (Compulsory Insurance) Regulations 1975 (SI 178/1975), art 3(b), and pursuant to which the associated countries were Austria, Finland, Norway, Sweden, Switzerland, Hungary, Czechoslovakia and the German Democratic Republic. Section 56(7) of the 1961 Act was then substituted by the EC (Road Traffic) (Compulsory Insurance) (Amendment) Regulations 1995 (SI 353/1995), reg 3(2), and pursuant to which the associated countries were Iceland, Norway (both of which are EEA States), Czech Republic, Hungary, Slovakia (all of whom have since joined the EU) and Switzerland (including Lichtenstein) (Lichtenstein is in the EEA). The 1995 Regulations became effective on 1 January 1996. The effect of the EC (Road Traffic) (Compulsory Insurance) (Amendment) Regulations 2001 (SI 463/2001), which operated from 12 October 2001 until the 2008 Regulations, was to extend the associated countries to incorporate Slovenia and Cyprus (both of which are now EU Member States) and Croatia.

48.　The Road Traffic Act, 1961 (Commencement) Order 1962 (SI 11/1962). Under the Sixth Directive, art 9, however, the minimum insurance requirement for personal injury was, initially, €1,000,000 per victim or €5,000,000 whatever the number of victims.

49.　Road Traffic Act 1961, s 56(2)(a), as amended by the 2008 Regulations, reg 2(b) (which applied from 4 July 2008) required minimum insurance against property damage of €1,000,000 per claim, whatever the number of victims. On 9 December 2010, and following a review provided for in the Sixth Directive, the European Commission published a Notice regarding the adaptation in line with inflation of certain amounts laid down in the Sixth Directive (2010/C 332/01) whereby the minimum insurance in respect of property damage was increased from €1,000,000 to €1,120,000 per claim, whatever the number of victims. Thereafter, on 21 December 2011, the 1961 Act, s 56(2)(a) was amended to reflect the foregoing increase by the European Union (Motor Insurance) (Limitation of Insurance in relation to property) Regulations 2011 (SI 702/2011).

territory of another Member State.[50] This was akin to raising a presumption of insurance in respect of vehicles from Member States. It was predicated, however, on the national insurers' bureaux of the Member States concluding an agreement whereby each bureau would guarantee the settlement, in accordance with the provisions of its own national law on compulsory insurance, of claims in respect of accidents occurring in its territory caused by vehicles normally based in the territory of another Member State, regardless of whether or not such vehicles were insured.[51] This led the way to waiving the requirement for issuing and producing green cards as evidence of insurance in certain circumstances. From 1 August 2003, Members States were directed by the Commission to refrain from making insurance checks on vehicles that were normally based in either another Member State or a number of other countries (many of which have since joined the EU). [52] The decision was extended over the years to incorporate other countries, most of which have since joined the EU. As of 1 August 2012, the countries outside the EEA to which the decision applies are Andorra, Croatia, Serbia, and Switzerland.[53]

3. Ascertaining a vehicle's territory by registration plate

[13.20] Section 56(8) of the 1961 Act was inserted to implement the First Directive.[54] It has been amended over time,[55] most recently by the European Communities (Motor Insurance) Regulations 2008 (the 2008 Regulations)[56] and now provides:

---

50.   First Directive, art 2(1). Prior to the First Directive, various Member States had entered into bilateral agreements that accepted vehicle registration plates as evidence of insurance cover.

51.   First Directive, art 2(2).

52.   2003/564/EC Commission Decision of 28 July 2003, on the application of Council Directive 72/166/EEC relating to checks on insurance against civil liability in respect of the use of motor vehicles (Text with EEA relevance) (notified under document number C(2003) 2626) (OJ L 192, 31 July 2003, p 23).

53.   These countries are, in any event, signatories to Section III of the Internal Regulations. The most recent Commission Decision prohibits checks on Serbian vehicles from 1 January 2012. This follows from the fact that, on 26 May 2011, the Internal Regulations were extended to the national insurers' bureau of Serbia (see 2011/754/EC Commission Implementing Decision of 22 November 2011, on the application of Directive 2009/103/EC of the European Parliament and of the Council with regard to on the application of Directive 2009/103/EC of the European Parliament and of the Council with regard to checks on insurance against civil liability in respect of the use of motor vehicles (notified under document number C(2011) 8289) (OJ L 310, 25 November 2011, pp 17–18)).

54.   Road Traffic Act 1961, s 56(8), was inserted by the EC (Road Traffic) (Compulsory Insurance) Regulations 1975 (SI 178/1975), art 3(b). It defined the 'territory in which a vehicle is normally based' by reference to, *inter alia*, 'the territory of the State in which it is registered'.

55.   A registration plate is the most convenient means of determining the Member State in which a vehicle is normally based. For this reason, the Second Directive, art 4 amended the definition of 'territory in which the vehicle is normally based' in the First Directive, art 1(4), such that 'the territory of the State of which the vehicle bears a registration' replaced the words 'the territory of the State in which the vehicle is registered'. The Road Traffic Act 1961, s 56(8), was amended accordingly (by the EC (Road Traffic) (Compulsory Insurance) Amendment Regulations 1987 (SI 322/1987), reg 4(2)). The Fifth Directive, art 1(1), amended the definition of 'territory in which the vehicle is normally based' in the First Directive, art 1(4).

56.   European Communities (Motor Insurance) Regulations 2008 (SI 248/2008).

'In [Part VI of the 1961 Act] a reference to the territory in which a vehicle is normally based is a reference to:

(a)   the territory of the state of which the vehicle bears a registration plate, irrespective of whether the plate is permanent or temporary,

(b)   in a case where no registration plate is required for a type of vehicle, but the vehicle bears an insurance plate or a distinguishing sign analogous to the registration plate, the territory of the state in which the plate or sign is issued, or

(c)   in a case where a registration or insurance plate or distinguishing sign is not required for a vehicle, the territory of the state in which the person who has custody of the vehicle is resident.'[57]

Thus, the registration plate is the means by which a vehicle's territory is ascertained.[58]

D. INTERNAL REGULATIONS[59]

[13.21] The partial elimination of the green card system commenced with various Member States entering into bilateral agreements that accepted vehicle registration plates as evidence of insurance cover. The various bilateral agreements were supplemented by a Supplementary Inter-Bureaux Agreement between several countries in 1972.[60] Subsequent agreements, based on the same principles, enabled the bureaux of other countries to become members and the agreements were collected into a single document called the Multilateral Guarantee Agreement (MGA) that was entered into in 1991. By 30 June 2002, the MGA was operating as between 24 of the then 44 countries participating in the green card system.[61] Although the green card system remained (and continues) in place, the MGA removed the need for motorists travelling between those 24 participating countries to obtain green cards in advance of travel.

[13.22] Thereafter, on 30 May 2002, a new Multilateral Agreement was entered between the National Insurers' Bureaux of the Member States of the European Economic Area and Other Associate States and it became operative on 1 July 2003 (the 2002

---

57.   The Road Traffic Act 1961, s 56(8), as amended by the 2008 Regulations, reg 2, and which repeats, almost verbatim, the text of the Sixth Directive, art 1(4).

58.   The Internal Regulations, Section III (discussed at paras **13.21–13.29**) is entitled "Rules Governing Contractual Relations Between Bureaux Based On Deemed Insurance Cover (Optional Provisions)" and art 11 defines 'normally based' in the same terms as the 1961 Act, s 56(8). It further provides that if a vehicle (that is required to bear a registration plate) bears no plate or bears one that is no longer legally issued to it, is involved in an accident, the territory in which the accident occurred shall, for the settlement of any resulting claim, be deemed to be the territory where the vehicle is normally based (art 11(2)).

59.   The Internal Regulations are reproduced in **Appendix 6**.

60.   The Supplementary Inter-Bureaux Agreement between several countries signed on 16 October 1972, became operative in 1973.

61.   Austria, Belgium, Croatia, Cyprus, Czech Republic, Denmark (and Faroe Islands), Finland, France (and Monaco), Germany, Greece, Hungary, Iceland, Ireland, Italy (and the Republic of San Marino and the Vatican State), Luxembourg, Netherlands, Norway, Portugal, Slovakia, Slovenia, Spain, Sweden, Switzerland (and Liechtenstein) and the United Kingdom.

Multilateral Agreement).[62] This replaced the MGA (*and* the 1996 Uniform Agreement through which the green card system was previously operated[63]).

[13.23] At the same time as the 2002 Multilateral Agreement was concluded, the Council of Bureaux incorporated all provisions governing the relations between bureaux into a single document, entitled the Internal Regulations.[64]

[13.24] The 2002 Multilateral Agreement was extended in 2008,[65] at which time the Internal Regulations were revised. The Internal Regulations referred to hereunder are the revised regulations which came into force on 1 July 2008.[66]

[13.25] Section II of the Internal Regulations is entitled 'Specific Rules Governing Contractual Relations between Bureaux Based on the Green Card' and states the rules that govern the operation of the green card system in those countries in which a green card must be produced. Forty-six countries have subscribed to Section II.[67] However, as will be seen below, the issue and production of green cards is now only necessary in respect of a vehicle that is travelling from any one of the 13 participating countries that have not signed up to Section III of the Internal Regulations[68] to another of the 46 countries, or vice-versa.

[13.26] Section III of the Internal Regulations is entitled 'Specific Rules Governing Contractual Relations Between Bureaux Based on Deemed Insurance Cover (Optional Provisions)'. Section III governs the position where a green card is not a prerequisite for travel in the relevant countries and where liability is determined by reference to the country in which the vehicle is normally based.[69] As of 1 August 2012, there are 33 signatories to Section III of the Internal Regulations (Section III countries).[70]

---

62. The 2002 Internal Regulations applied to all claims occurring after and claims not finally settled by 1 July 2003. While the national bureaux of the Member States of the EEA and the associated countries signed the multilateral aspect of the new agreement at that time, the individual bureaux proceeded to sign the bilateral aspect of the Internal Regulations in the succeeding months.

63. See above at paras **13.05–06**.

64. The 2002 Internal Regulations were adopted by the General Assembly of the Council of Bureaux on 30 May 2002.

65. The Agreement between the national insurers' bureaux of the Member States of the EEA and other Associate States 2008. In 2008, the signatories were the EEA States (see fn **5** above) and Andorra, Croatia and Switzerland. This was extended to Serbia on 26 May 2011.

66. As revised by the General Assembly in Lisbon on 29 May 2008 and comprising Appendix I to the revised 2008 Agreement.

67. See fn **14** for a list of the 46 countries.

68. See fn **17** for a list of the 13 countries.

69. The Internal Regulations, Section III, is entitled 'Specific Rules Governing Contractual Relations Between Bureaux Based On Deemed Insurance Cover (Optional Provisions)', defines 'normally based' (in art 11) in the same terms as the 1961 Act, s 56(8). It further provides that if a vehicle (that is required to bear a registration plate) bears no plate, or bears one that is no longer legally issued to it, is involved in an accident, the territory in which the accident occurred shall, for the settlement of any resulting claim, be deemed to be the territory where the vehicle is normally based (art 11(2)).

70. The 33 countries are: Andorra, Austria, Belgium, Bulgaria, Croatia, Cyprus, Czech Republic, Denmark (and the Faroe Islands), (contd .../)

[13.27] Where a vehicle that is normally based in one of the Section III countries[71] causes an accident in another Section III country, the bureau of the country in which the vehicle is normally based is liable to reimburse the bureau of the country of accident in respect of all monies paid out by the latter as compensation for injury caused. This is so regardless of whether or not the vehicle is actually insured.[72] Claims are investigated and handled in a similar fashion to those under Section II of the Internal Regulations[73] and in Ireland the bureau is the MIBI.

[13.28] Article 11 of the Internal Regulations defines the concept of the territory in which a vehicle is 'normally based' in the same terms as s 56(8) of the 1961 Act.[74]

[13.29] For this reason, a bureau in a Section III country has two functions:

1. In general terms, if a vehicle, that is normally based in a Section III country, visits and causes an accident in another Section III country, the insurer of the vehicle that caused the accident is liable to reimburse the bureau of the country of accident if the latter pays out compensation in settlement of a claim or on foot of an award. If, however, the insurer fails in its reimbursement obligations, the bureau of which the insurer is a member must reimburse the bureau of the country of accident.[75]

2. The bureau of the country of accident must investigate the circumstances of an accident in its territory involving a vehicle from another Section III country. Precisely what happens thereafter will depend upon whether or not the vehicle that caused the accident is insured or not:

    (a) the bureau of the country of accident must give notice of the accident to the insurer that issued the insurance policy, if the insurer is identified. If an identified insurer has an approved correspondent[76] in the country of

---

70. (contd) Estonia, Finland, France (and Monaco), Germany, Greece, Hungary, Iceland, Ireland, Italy (and the Republic of San Marino and the Vatican State), Latvia, Lithuania, Luxembourg, Malta, Netherlands, Norway, Poland, Portugal, Romania, Serbia, Slovakia, Slovenia, Spain, Sweden, Switzerland (and Liechtenstein) and the United Kingdom. See **Table 13.1.** at p 201. Iraq was suspended from membership in 1992.

   A country that is a signatory to Section III is also a signatory to Section II so that the latter governs the position of position of motorists travelling between it and a country that is only a signatory to Section II.

71. The 'normally based' concept is defined by the Internal Regulations, art 11.

72. The Internal Regulations, art 10.

73. The investigation and handling of claims under Section II (Green Cards) are considered at para **13.08**. It must be noted, however, that the Internal Regulations, Section III, do not apply where a green card has been issued in the circumstances provided for in art 7(3). See fn **20** above.

74. See para **13.20** above. Article 11 should this be sectionfurther provides that a vehicle (required to bear a registration plate) that bears no plate, or bears one that is no longer legally issued to it, shall, for the settlement of any resulting claim, be deemed to be normally based in the territory in which the accident occurred.

75. Internal Regulations, art 6(1). A bureau acting in this capacity used to be referred to as a 'paying bureau'. However, this term was removed by the 2002 Internal Regulations.

76. Internal Regulations, art 4 prescribes the means by which an insurer based in a participating country may have a correspondent (or agent) approved to act on its behalf in another participating country. The approval process is conducted by the bureau of the country in which the correspondent is established.

accident, the bureau of the country of accident must forward any claim to that correspondent who must handle it. If there is no approved correspondent, the bureau of the country of accident must advise the insurer that it has received a claim and will handle it. Thereafter, the bureau of the country of accident may accept service of proceedings arising out of the claim and/or settle the claim.[77] The bureau of the country of accident may claim reimbursement from the insurer.

(b)   where there is no identified insurer or no insurance actually exists, the bureau of the country of accident must give notice of the accident to the bureau of the country in which the vehicle that caused the accident is normally based (the bureau concerned). Thereafter, the bureau concerned will determine whether or not the relevant vehicle bore a valid registration plate. The bureau of the country of accident must advise the bureau concerned that it has received a claim and will handle it. Thereafter, the bureau of the country of accident may accept service of proceedings arising out of the claim and/or settle it and it may ultimately claim reimbursement from the bureau concerned. If, however, the vehicle does not bear a registration plate or bears one that does not correspond or no longer corresponds to the vehicle, then the bureau of the country of accident cannot claim reimbursement.

---

77.   A bureau acting in this capacity used to be referred to as a 'handling bureau'. However, this term was removed by the 2002 Internal Regulations.

Table 13.1 Position of various countries as of 1 August 2012

EEA States		Parties to Internal Regulations (Sections II and III) Green Card not required between these 33 countries	Parties to Internal Regulations (Section II only) Green Card required for: 1. vehicles travelling between these 13 countries; and 2. vehicles travelling from any one of these 13 countries to any one of the 33 countries that are parties to Section III and vice-versa.
EU States	**EFTA States**		
			Albania
		Andorra	
Austria		Austria	
			Belarus
Belgium		Belgium	
			Bosnia and Herzegovina
Bulgaria		Bulgaria	
		Croatia	
Cyprus		Cyprus	
Czech Republic		Czech Republic	
Denmark		Denmark (and Faroe Islands)	
Estonia		Estonia	
Finland		Finland	
			Former Yugoslav Republic of Macedonia
France		France (and Monaco)	
Germany		Germany	
Greece		Greece	
Hungary		Hungary	
	Iceland	Iceland	
Ireland		Ireland	
			Islamic Republic of Iran
			Israel
Italy		Italy (and the Republic of San Marino and the Vatican State)	
Latvia		Latvia	
Lithuania		Lithuania	
Luxembourg		Luxembourg	

EEA States		Parties to Internal Regulations (Sections II and III) Green Card not required between these 33 countries	Parties to Internal Regulations (Section II only) Green Card required for: 1. vehicles travelling between these 13 countries; and 2. vehicles travelling from any one of these 13 countries to any one of the 33 countries that are parties to Section III and vice-versa.
EU States	**EFTA States**		
Malta		Malta	
			Moldova
			Montenegro
			Morocco
Netherlands		Netherlands	
	Norway	Norway	
Poland		Poland	
Portugal		Portugal	
Romania		Romania	
			Russia
		Serbia	
Slovakia		Slovakia	
Slovenia		Slovenia	
Spain		Spain	
Sweden		Sweden	
	Liechtenstein	Switzerland (and Liechtenstein)	
			Tunisia
			Turkey
			Ukraine
United Kingdom		United Kingdom	

E. THE FOURTH AND FIFTH DIRECTIVES

1. Objectives of the Fourth Directive

[13.30] Unlike the earlier directives, the Fourth Directive was concerned with accidents that occur *outside* an injured party's EEA State of residence.[78] The national implementing legislation was the European Communities (Fourth Motor Insurance Directive) Regulations 2003 (the 2003 Regulations).[79] The corresponding provisions of the Sixth Directive are discussed below.

[13.31] In general terms, the Fourth Directive sought to simplify and accelerate the means by which compensation could be recovered by an injured party who resides in an EEA State and is caused loss or injury (injured) in an accident that:

(a)   occurs in an EEA State (other than his EEA State of residence) or a *non* EEA State that is a party to the green card system;[80] and

(b)   is caused by the use of a vehicle that is insured and normally based in an EEA State (other than the injured party's EEA State of residence).

[13.32] These 'special provisions' did not apply to an injured party if the vehicle that caused the injury was either insured or normally based in the injured party's EEA State of residence.[81] Injured parties covered by the Fourth Directive were given a direct right of action against the insurance undertaking that covered the responsible person against civil liability. It also made provision for claiming compensation where a resident of an EEA State was injured in another EEA State by a vehicle from a third country.

2. Objectives of the Fifth Directive

[13.33] In very general terms, the Fifth Directive[82] required each EEA State to establish a compensation procedure whereby the victim of any accident, caused by a vehicle that is normally based in *any* EEA State, may claim compensation in his EEA State of residence[83] and this is regardless of whether or not the vehicle that caused the injury was insured. In addition, where there was insurance, such injured parties were given a direct right of action against the insurance undertaking that covered the responsible person against civil liability.

---

78.   The Fourth Directive was added to Annex IX EEA Agreement by Decision No 4/2001 (OJ No L 66, 8.3.2001, p 46 and EEA Supplement No 12, 8.3.2001, p 4) and entered into force on 1 September 2001.

79.   European Communities (Fourth Motor Insurance Directive) Regulations 2003 (SI 651/2003) and are reproduced in **Appendix 4.1**. The Regulations became operative on 27 November 2003 and were amended by the European Communities (Motor Insurance) Regulations 2008 (SI 248/2008) and are reproduced in **Appendix 4.2**.

80.   This second category is stated to be without prejudice to the legislation of third countries on civil liability and private international law (see Sixth Directive, art 20).

81.   Sixth Directive, art 20(2).

82.   The Fifth Directive was added to Annex IX EEA Agreement by Decision No 86/2006 (OJ No L 289, 19.10.2006, p 21 and EEA Supplement No 52, 19.10.2006, p 17), and entered into force 1 March 2008.

83.   The Sixth Directive, art 19.

F. THE SIXTH DIRECTIVE

1. EEA residents injured in EEA

[13.34] The provisions of the Sixth Directive[84] affecting an EEA resident who is injured in an EEA State may be summarised as follows:

1. *Direct right of action against insurer*: a resident of an EEA State who is injured in *any* EEA State by a vehicle that is normally based in *any* EEA State enjoys a direct right of action against the insurance undertaking covering the responsible party against civil liability (the insurer).[85] Where an injured party brings proceedings against the insurer, the proceedings may be brought in the EEA State in which the injured party is domiciled, provided that the insurer is domiciled in an EEA State.[86]

2. The issues that arise, in terms of conflicts of law, are beyond the scope of this work and in respect of which the reader is directed elsewhere.[87] However,

---

84. The Sixth Directive was added to Annex IX EEA Agreement by Decision No 117/2011 (OJ No L 341, 22.12.2011, p 81 and EEA Supplement No 70, 22.12.2011, p 17), and entered into force on 1 November 2011. The Sixth Directive is reproduced in **Appendix 3**.

85. Sixth Directive, art 18.

86. See Council Regulation (EC) No 44/2001 of 22 December 2000, on jurisdiction and the recognition and enforcement in civil and commercial matters (OJ L 12, 16.1.2001, p 1), art 11(2) and art 9(1)(b), and the Sixth Directive, recital 32. See further *FBTO Schadeverzekeringen v Odenbreit* (Case C–463/06) [2008] 2 All ER (Comm) 733, [2007] ECR I–11321 (ECJ), in which the ECJ confirmed that a person domiciled in Germany, who was injured in the Netherlands by a vehicle that was insured and normally based in the Netherlands, was entitled to sue the insurer (which was established in the Netherlands) in Germany.

Council Regulation (EC) No 44/2001 provides, for the purpose of the Council Regulation, 'a company or other legal person or association of natural and legal persons is domiciled at the place where it has its: (a) statutory seat, or (b) central administration, or (c) principal place of business' (art 60(1)). With respect to Ireland and the UK 'statutory seat' is defined to mean 'the registered office or, where there is no such office anywhere, the place of incorporation or, where there is no such place anywhere, the place under the law of which the formation took place' (art 60(2)). Furthermore, it provides that 'an insurer who is not domiciled in a Member State but has a branch, agency or other establishment in one of the Member States shall, in disputes arising out of the operations of the branch, agency or establishment, be deemed to be domiciled in that Member State' (art 9(2)).

Initially, Denmark opted out of Council Regulation (EC) No 44/2001. However, its terms were effectively extended to Denmark (see Council Decision of 27 April 2006 concerning the conclusion of the Agreement between the European Community and the Kingdom of Denmark on jurisdiction and the recognition and enforcement of judgments in civil and commercial matters (2006/325/EC)). This entered into force on 1 July 2007. With respect to the Norway, Iceland and Switzerland, the Lugano Convention of 16 September 1988 was replaced by the Convention on jurisdiction and the recognition and enforcement of judgments in civil and commercial matters, which was initialled at Brussels on 28 March 2007, and the signing thereof was approved by the Council Decision of 15 October 2007 on the signing, on behalf of the Community on jurisdiction and the recognition and enforcement of judgments in civil and commercial matters (2007/712/EC) OJ L 339 21.12.07. It mirrors the provisions contained in Council Regulation (EC) No 44/2001.

87. See for example Dicey, Morris and Collins, *The Conflict of Laws* (14th edn, Sweet & Maxwell, 2006).

Regulation (EC) No 864/2007 of the European Parliament and of the Council of 11 July 2007 on the law applicable to non-contractual obligations (Rome II)[88] should be observed. It provides, as a general rule and subject to exception, that the law applicable to a non-contractual obligation arising out of a tort/delict shall be the law of the country in which the damage occurs.[89] Thus, in *Kelly v Groupama*,[90] in which an Irish resident sued the insurer of a French vehicle for injuries suffered by him in France, the Irish High Court proceeded on the basis that damages should be awarded in accordance with French law.[91,92] In England, however, in a case concerning an accident that pre-dated the applicability of Rome II, and in which an English resident sued the insurer of a French vehicle in England for injuries suffered by him in France, the English Court of Appeal held that damages were to be assessed by reference to English law as the *lex fori*.[93]

3. *Direct claim for compensation to insurer*: a resident of an EEA State who is injured in *any* EEA State by a vehicle that is normally based in *any* EEA State may apply directly to the insurer for compensation, regardless of where the insurer is established in the EEA. If liability is not contested and damages have been quantified, a reasoned offer of compensation must be made to an injured party within three months of the presentation of his claim to the insurer.[94] If liability is denied or not clearly determined, or damages have not been fully quantified, a reasoned reply to the compensation claim must be made to an injured party within this three-month period.[95]

---

88. Which came into force on 11 January 2009 and only applies to events giving rise to damage after its entry into force (art 31).

89. This is stated to be irrespective of the country in which the event giving rise to the damage occurred and irrespective of the country or countries in which the indirect consequences of that event occur (art 4(1)). Article 4(2) provides, however, that where the person claimed to be liable and the person who sustained the damage are habitually resident in the same country at the time that the damage occurs, the law of that country shall apply. Further, where it is clear 'from all the circumstances of the case' that the tort/delict is manifestly more closely connected with a country other than that indicated in art 4(1) or 4(2), the law of that other country shall apply (art 4(3)).

90. *Kelly v Groupama* [2012] IEHC 177, (20 April 2012, unreported) HC, O'Neill J.

91. In so doing, O'Neill J observed that it was common case, by reference to Rome II, that the substantive law applicable to the assessment of damages was French law, as the law of the place where the damage occurred (at p 3).

92. The complexities are illustrated by *Jacobs v MIB* [2010] EWCA Civ 1208, [2011] 1 WLR 2609. In that case, a UK resident sued the MIB in respect of injuries caused to him in Spain by an uninsured vehicle that was ordinarily based in Spain. The English Court of Appeal held that Rome II did not apply to the assessment of compensation payable by the MIB under the UK regulations that implemented the Fourth Directive (the relevant provisions of which are now contained in the Sixth Directive). The MIB was obliged to pay compensation in accordance with English law.

93. *Maher v Groupama Grand Est* [2009] EWCA Civ 1191, [2010] 1 WLR 1564.

94. Sixth Directive, art 22. Where this is not done, art 22 directs Member States to adopt provisions requiring the payment of interest on any compensation ultimately offered or awarded by a court.

95. Sixth Directive, art 22. Furthermore, art 22 obliges the Member States to 'create a duty, backed by appropriate effective and systematic financial or equivalent administrative penalties' to comply with this three-month time period.

4. *Claiming compensation from claims representative*: a resident of an EEA State who is injured in an EEA State (other than that of his residence) may apply for compensation to the insurer's claims representative in the EEA State of his residence. Quite sensibly, however, the right does not apply if the vehicle that caused the injury is either normally based or insured in the injured party's EEA State of residence.[96] An insurer must appoint a claims representative in each EEA State, other than the EEA State in which it received its official authorisation.[97] A claims representative is responsible for collecting all necessary information in connection with the settlement of claims and for negotiating settlements.[98] A claims representative shall have sufficient powers to represent the insurer and meet claims in full. It must also be capable of examining cases in the official language of the injured party's EEA State of residence.[99]

5. If liability is not contested and damages have been quantified, a reasoned offer of compensation must be made to an injured party within three months of the presentation of his claim to a claims representative.[100] If liability is denied or not clearly determined, or damages have not been fully quantified, a reasoned reply to a compensation claim must be made within this three-month period.[101]

6. *Information Centres*: provision is made for the establishment of an information centre in each EEA State with responsibility for the co-ordination, compilation and dissemination of information on a register maintained by it. The register must include particulars of the registration numbers of motor vehicles normally based in its territory, their insurance policies, and each insurer's claims representatives.[102]

7. The information centre must provide certain information from the register to an injured party, namely the particulars of insurance and motor vehicle ownership relevant to the injured party's claim and the particulars of the insurer's claims representative in the injured party's EEA State of residence.[103]

8. *Compensation bodies*: a resident of an EEA State who is injured in an EEA State (other than that of his residence) may apply for compensation in his EEA

---

96. Sixth Directive, art 20(2) and art 1(6).
97. Sixth Directive, art 21(1).
98. Sixth Directive, art 21(4), which also provides that the requirement of appointing a claims representative shall not affect the right of an injured party (or his insurance undertaking) from instituting proceedings directly against the person who caused the accident (or his insurance undertaking).
99. Sixth Directive, art 21(5).
100. Sixth Directive, art 22. Where this is not done, art 22 directs Member States to adopt provisions requiring the payment of interest on any compensation ultimately offered or awarded by a court.
101. Sixth Directive, art 22. Article 22 further obliges the Member States to 'create a duty, backed by appropriate effective and systematic financial or equivalent administrative penalties' to comply with this three-month time period.
102. Sixth Directive, art 23(1).
103. Sixth Directive, art 23(3)–(4).

State of residence in certain circumstances. To this end, a compensation body, with responsibility for paying compensation to injured parties must be established in each EEA State.[104] The injured party may present a claim to the compensation body in his EEA State of residence if:

(a) no reasoned reply is received from the insurer or claims representative in the injured party's EEA State of residence within three months of the claim for compensation; or

(b) the insurer has failed to appoint a claims representative in the injured party's EEA State of residence. If, however, the injured party has presented a claim directly to the insurer, the injured party cannot present a claim to the compensation body unless he has not received a reasoned reply from that insurer within three months.[105]

9. The compensation body in the injured party's EEA State of residence must take action within two months of a compensation claim being presented to it. However, it must terminate its action if the insurer or its claims representative subsequently makes a reasoned reply.[106]

10. The compensation body in the injured party's EEA State of residence must inform a number of persons about the claim and the fact that it will respond to the claim within two months of its presentation, namely, the insurer or claims representative, the compensation body of the EEA State in which the insurer that issued the policy is established, and the responsible party (if known).[107]

11. Where the compensation body in the injured party's EEA State of residence compensates the injured party, that compensation body is entitled to claim reimbursement from the compensation body in the EEA State in which the

---

104. Sixth Directive, art 24(1). The Sixth Directive, art 20(2) provides that art 24 only applies to an accident caused by a vehicle that is normally based and insured in an EEA State other than that of the injured party's residence. The Fourth Directive, art 6 (the predecessor to the Sixth Directive, art 24) provided that it would take effect after an agreement was concluded between the compensation bodies established or approved by the Member States relating to their functions and obligations and the procedures for reimbursement and from the date fixed by the Commission upon its having ascertained that such an agreement had been concluded. The relevant agreement is the 'Agreement Between Compensation bodies and Guarantee Funds' and was entered into on 29 April 2002. Thereafter, on 27 December 2002, the Commission adopted its Decision 2003/20/EC, which was addressed to the Member States and which ascertained the agreement concluded between the compensation bodies. The Decision specified that art 6 should be applicable from 20 January 2003 and that Member States were to inform the Commission about their implementing measures. The Agreement was extended with the enlargement of the EU.

105. Sixth Directive, art 24(1). Likewise, if the injured party has taken action directly against the responsible party's insurance undertaking, he cannot present a claim to the compensation body.

106. Sixth Directive, art 24(1).

107. Sixth Directive, art 24(1).

insurer that issued the policy is established. Thereafter, the latter body shall be subrogated to the injured party in his rights against the responsible person or his insurer with respect to the compensation that has been paid.[108]

12. Obviously, the above assumes the existence of insurance and, quite sensibly, an injured party cannot avail of the provisions pertaining to compensation bodies if the vehicle that caused his injury is insured in the injured party's EEA State of residence.[109] Likewise, the compensation body provisions do not apply if the vehicle that caused the accident is normally based in the injured party's EEA State of residence.[110]

13. *Penalties*: it directs EEA States to fix effective, proportional and dissuasive penalties for breach of the domestic legislation implementing the Sixth Directive and to take steps to secure their application.[111]

14. *Unidentified or uninsured vehicle*: a resident of an EEA State who is injured in an EEA State (other than that of his residence) may make a claim to the compensation body in his EEA State of residence if it is either impossible to identify the vehicle that caused the accident or, within two months following the accident, it is impossible to identify the relevant insurer (for example if there is no insurance).[112] If the compensation body in the

---

108. Sixth Directive, art 24(2). Art 24(3) provides that art 24(2) will take effect after an agreement has been entered into between the compensation bodies established or approved by the Member States relating to their functions and obligations and the procedures for reimbursement and from the date fixed by the Commission upon its having determined that such an agreement has been concluded. Previously, the Fourth Directive, art 10(3) (which introduced these provisions) directed each Member State to establish or approve the compensation body before 20 January 2003. Following the conclusion of an agreement between the various compensation bodies on 29 April 2002 in Brussels, and notified to the Commission by letter of 19 July 2002, Commission Decision 2003/20/EC of 27 December 2002 (OJ L 008, 14 January 2003, p 355) declared the provisions of the Fourth Directive that corresponded to arts 24 and 25 of the Sixth Directive effective from 20 January 2003. This explains why the provisions of the Fourth Directive, art 10(4) are not reproduced.

109. Sixth Directive, art 20(2) and art 1(6).

110. Sixth Directive, art 20(2). The position in respect of an unidentified or uninsured vehicle is dealt with below at paras 14–15.

111. Sixth Directive, art 27.

112. Sixth Directive, art 25(1). The Sixth Directive, art 19, provides that the compensation procedure provided for in art 22 shall apply for the settlement of 'all claims arising from any accident caused by a vehicle covered by insurance as referred to in article 3'. It also provides that, in cases of claims that may be settled by the system of national insurers' bureaux guaranteeing the settlement of claims occurring in their respective territories, Member States shall establish the same compensation procedure that is provided for in the Sixth Directive, art 22. This means, *inter alia*, that, where a resident of an EEA State is injured in another EEA State, then, provided he is not resident in the EEA State in which the vehicle that injures him is normally based, the compensation body in the injured party's EEA State of residence must deal with his claim if the injured party so requires. Hence, art 19 provides that, for the purpose of applying the art 22 compensation procedure, any reference to an insurance undertaking shall be understood as a reference to a national insurers' bureau.

injured party's EEA State of residence pays compensation,[113] it may recoup this cost as follows:[114]

(a)   where the insurer cannot be found, against the guarantee fund[115] of the EEA State where the vehicle is normally based;[116]

(b)   where it concerns an unidentified vehicle, against the guarantee fund in the EEA State in which the accident occurred;[117] and

(c)   in the case of a third country vehicle, against the guarantee fund in the EEA State in which the accident took place.[118]

15.   Furthermore, this provision is stated to apply to accidents caused by third country vehicles that are covered by arts 7–8. In essence, this refers to a vehicle that is actually from a non-EEA country (non-EEA vehicle) but which is physically present in the EEA.[119] In this regard, apart from non-EEA vehicles emanating from Andorra, Croatia, Switzerland or Serbia,[120] every EEA State is obliged to ensure that any non-EEA vehicle entering its territory has either a green card (if it is from one of the 13 countries that are parties to Section II of the Internal Regulations) *or* appropriate frontier insurance.

2. EEA residents injured in non-EEA green card countries

[13.35] *Vehicle insured and normally based in EEA injures EEA resident in non-EEA green card country*: the Sixth Directive also makes provision for an EEA resident who is injured in a third country (ie a non EEA State) that is a party to the green card system by a vehicle that is insured and normally based in an EEA State.[121] In this situation, the injured party may apply for compensation from the insurer or, provided that the vehicle that caused the injury is neither normally based nor insured in the injured party's EEA State of residence,[122] from the insurer's claims representative in the EEA State of his residence. If a reasoned reply is not received from the insurer or claims representative within three months (or the insurer has failed to appoint a claims representative in the injured party's EEA State of residence), the injured party may apply to the compensation

---

113.   According to the Sixth Directive, art 25, the compensation body must compensate the injured party in either situation in accordance with the Sixth Directive, art 10, and which, *inter alia*, obliges each Member State to set up a body with the responsibility of providing compensation in respect of injury caused by an unidentified or uninsured vehicle in that Member State.

114.   This is subject to the conditions prescribed by the Sixth Directive, art 24(2).

115.   This term refers to the obligation imposed on Member States in the Sixth Directive, art 10(1) (formerly Second Directive, art 1(4)) to establish a body that would compensate victims of uninsured and unidentified drivers.

116.   Sixth Directive, art 25(1)(a).

117.   Sixth Directive, art 25(1)(b).

118.   Sixth Directive, art 25(1)(c).

119.   Sixth Directive, art 25(2).

120.   Which countries are parties to Internal Regulations, Section III.

121.   Sixth Directive, art 20(1).

122.   Sixth Directive, art 20(2) and art 1(6).

body in his EEA State of residence. If that compensation body pays out,[123] it may recoup any monies it pays out from the compensation body in the EEA State in which the insurer that issued the policy is established.[124]

G. EC (FOURTH MOTOR INSURANCE DIRECTIVE) REGULATIONS 2003

1. Purpose of the 2003 Regulations

[13.36] The purpose of the 2003 Regulations[125, 126] as originally enacted was to implement those provisions of the Fourth Directive that are now contained in the Sixth Directive.[127] To this end, the 2003 Regulations *generally applied* (subject to exclusions) to an injured party who is either:

(a) normally resident in an EEA State[128] and injured in an accident in an EEA State other than the EEA State in which the injured party is normally resident;[129] or

(b) normally resident in an EEA State and injured in a specified territory (ie Croatia and Switzerland).[130]

In either situation, the vehicle that caused the loss or injury (the injury) must have been insured and normally based in an EEA State at the time of the accident.

[13.37] The Fourth Directive provided, *inter alia*, that an EEA resident who is injured in a third country (ie a non-EEA State) that is a party to the green card system, by a vehicle that insured and normally based in an EEA State, could, in certain circumstances, apply for compensation from the insurer (or its claims representative) in his EEA State of residence and if the claim was not satisfactorily dealt with, the injured party could apply

---

123. The compensation must be provided in accordance with Sixth Directive, arts 9 and 10, which direct, *inter alia*, each Member State to set up a body with the task of providing compensation to persons injured by an unidentified vehicle or a vehicle in respect of which the insurance obligations prescribed by the directive have not been satisfied (art 10(1)).

124. Sixth Directive, art 24(2). Thereafter, the latter body shall be subrogated to the injured party in his rights against the responsible person or his insurance undertaking with respect to the compensation that has been paid.

125. EC (Fourth Motor Insurance Directive) Regulations 2003 (SI 651/2003), operative from 27 November 2003 (the 2003 Regulations).

126. As amended by the 2008 Regulations, reg 5.

127. And discussed above at paras **13.34–13.35**.

128. An 'EEA State' means a state that is a contracting party to the Agreement on the European Economic Area signed at Oporto on 2 May 1992, and the protocol adjusting the Agreement signed at Brussels on 17 March 1993 (reg 2(1)), and as amended by the 2004 and 2007 EEA Enlargement Agreements. In essence, the EEA States are the EU Member States and Iceland, Norway and Liechtenstein.

129. Reg 3(1).

130. Reg 3(2). The 2003 Regulations, reg 2(1), defines 'specified territories' as 'designated territories'. 'Designated territories' is defined as having the meaning assigned by the EC (Road Traffic) (Compulsory Insurance) (Amendment) Regulations 2001 (SI 463/2001) which comprises the Member States of the EU, together with Iceland, Norway, Switzerland (including Liechtenstein), and Croatia.

to the compensation body in his EEA State of residence.[131] Other than providing for the specified territories of Croatia and Switzerland, however, the 2003 Regulations make no provision for an injured party in this situation making a compensation claim to the insurer (or its claims representative) or indeed to the MIBI. The position has not been altered by the amendments made by the European Communities (Motor Insurance) Regulations 2008 (the 2008 Regulations).[132]

2. Provisions of the 2003 Regulations

[13.38] The main provisions of the 2003 Regulations, as amended by the 2008 Regulations, are set out below.

1. *Direct right of action against insurer*: Regulation 3(1) of the 2003 Regulations states that, subject to reg 3(2)–(3), the Regulations apply to an injured party:[133]

    (a)   who is normally resident in an EEA State;

    (b)   who is entitled to compensation resulting from an accident in an EEA State other than the EEA State in which he is normally resident; and

    (c)   the accident was caused by a vehicle that, at the time of the accident, was insured and normally based in an EEA State.

2. Regulation 3(2) of the 2003 Regulations states that the Regulations shall also apply to an injured party:

    (a)   who is normally resident in an EEA State;

    (b)   who is entitled to compensation resulting from an accident in a 'specified territory' (ie Croatia and Switzerland); and

    (c)   the accident was caused by the use of a vehicle that, at the time of the accident, was insured and normally based in an EEA State.[134]

3. Regulation 3(5) of the 2003 Regulations states that, an injured party shall be entitled to issue proceedings against an insurance undertaking[135] that is authorised to transact compulsory motor insurance business in the State (insurer) in respect of an accident caused by a vehicle insured by it.[136]

4. The 2008 Regulations inserted a new reg 3(7) into the 2003 Regulations. This provides, *inter alia*, that reg 3(5) applies 'to all injured parties normally resident in an EEA State'.[137] A literal interpretation of the foregoing suggests that a

---

131. Fourth Directive, art 1(1) (now Sixth Directive, art 20(1)). See above at para **13.35**.
132. European Communities (Motor Insurance) Regulations 2008 (SI 248/2008).
133. Reg 2(1) defines 'injured party' as 'any person entitled to compensation in respect of any loss or injury caused by vehicles'.
134. This is stated to be without prejudice to the legislation of third countries on civil liability and private international law.
135. 'Insurance undertaking' is defined as an undertaking that has received its official authorisation in accordance with art 6 or art 23(2) of 73/239/EEC, OJ L 228, 24 July 1973, p 3.
136. This is without prejudice to the injured party's right to issue proceedings against the insured person. Furthermore, the insurance undertaking is deemed to be directly liable to the injured party to the extent that it is liable to the insured person.
137. The 2003 Regulations, reg 3(7), as inserted by the 2008 Regulations, reg 5(a).

person who resides in any EEA State may sue, in Ireland, an insurer in respect of an accident caused by a vehicle insured by that insurer regardless of where the accident occurred. It is highly unlikely that the creation of such a broad sweeping third category was intended. However, if the new reg 3(7) is to be construed (in conjunction with reg 3(1)–(2)) as providing that any injured party who is normally resident in an EEA State may directly claim in Ireland against an insurer for an accident occurring in any EEA State or in a specified territory (ie Croatia and Switzerland), that was caused by one of its insured vehicles (that was at the time of the accident insured and normally based in an EEA State), then the new provision appears to properly implement the corresponding provision of the Sixth Directive, although the Sixth Directive does not require that such a right of action be afforded to an injured party who is injured in an accident in a specified territory.[138]

5. *Claiming compensation from claims representatives or insurers*: the following provisions of reg 4 of the 2003 Regulations only apply to an accident caused by the use of a vehicle which, at the time of the accident, was insured through an establishment[139] in an EEA State and normally based in an EEA State (other than the injured party's EEA State of normal residence).[140] While reg 4 fails to expressly specify the countries of accident to which it applies, the only reasonable construction that can be afforded to it is that it applies to accidents in an EEA State (where the injured party normally resides in another EEA State) or in a specified territory (and where the injured party is normally resident in an EEA State):[141]

   (a) every insurer authorised to transact compulsory motor insurance business in Ireland must appoint a claims representative in each of the other EEA States;[142]

   (b) each claims representative must be granted sufficient representational authority and powers to enable it to settle claims.[143] The claims representative is responsible for handling and settling claims against the insurer,[144] collecting all necessary information in connection with the consideration and settlement of claims, negotiating settlements,

---

138. Sixth Directive, art 18.
139. 'Establishment' is defined as 'the head office, agency or branch of an insurance undertaking as defined by article 2(c) of [the First Directive]'.
140. The 2003 Regulations, reg 3(3) and reg 3(7) (as inserted by the 2008 Regulations, reg 5(1)).
141. See 2003 Regulations, reg 3(3). While reg 3(3) does not specify the countries of accident, reg 3(1) is stated to be subject to reg 3(3) (and reg 3(2)) which supports this construction.
142. Reg 4(1). Each insurance undertaking is required to notify the information centre (ie the MIBI) of all the contact details for its claims representative in each EEA State (reg 4(4)). The requirement to appoint a claims representative in each other EEA State pursuant to reg 4(1) does not limit the entitlement of an injured party as provided for in reg 3(5) (reg 3(6)).
143. Regulation 4(2). The provisions of reg 4 only apply in respect of an accident caused by the use of a vehicle which at the time of the accident was insured and normally based in an EEA State other than the state of residence of the injured party (reg 3(3)).
144. The 2008 Regulations, reg 4(6).

examining claims and communicating with a claimant in respect of a claim in the official language of the EEA State of the claimant's normal residence.[145] The interpretation suggested herein complies with the objectives of the Sixth Directive.[146]

6. The following provisions of reg 4 of the 2003 Regulations apply to an accident caused by the use of a vehicle which, at the time of the accident, was insured through an establishment in an EEA State and was normally based in an EEA State (other than the EEA State in which the injured party is normally resident)[147] and are also stated to apply to 'all injured parties normally resident in an EEA State':[148]

    (a) an insurer or claims representative must make a reasoned offer of compensation within three months of the presentation of a claim in which liability is not contested and the damages have been quantified;[149]

    (b) if liability is denied or has not been clearly determined or damages have not been fully quantified, a reasoned reply to the claim must be issued by the insurer or claims representative within the three month period.[150]

7. An insurer or claims representative who fails to comply with the above obligations in terms of issuing replies or offers within the stated timeframe may be subjected to prosecution and interest penalties.[151] The same applies to the MIBI.[152]

8. *Information Centre*: the MIBI is deemed to be the information centre for the purposes of the Sixth Directive.[153] It must, *inter alia*, co-ordinate the compilation and dissemination of information concerning the insurance policies in force for vehicles normally based in Ireland to the extent that requests of this

---

145. The 2008 Regulations, reg 4(7).
146. See the Sixth Directive, art 21.
147. The 2003 Regulations, reg 3(3). By reason of an amendment made by the 2008 Regulations (reg 5(a) inserting reg 3(7) into the 2003 Regulations), it is arguable that it also applies 'to all injured parties normally resident in an EEA State' (without reference to the country of accident), although the most reasonable construction of this provision is discussed at para **13.38** above.
148. The 2003 Regulations, reg 3(7), as inserted by the 2008 Regulations, reg 5(a).
149. The 2008 Regulations, reg 4(8)(a).
150. The 2008 Regulations, reg 4(8)(b). Reg 4(9) provides that an insurance undertaking of claims representative that fails to comply with reg 4(8) shall be guilty of an offence within the meaning of the EC (Non-Life Insurance) Framework Regulations 1994 (SI 359/1994), reg 59, as amended and liable on summary conviction. The 2008 Regulations, reg 4(10) also provides for the payment of interest where the insurance undertaking or claims representative breaches reg 4(8).
151. The 2008 Regulations, reg 4(9) provides that an insurer or claims representative that fails to comply with reg 4(8) shall be guilty of an offence within the meaning of the EC (Non-Life Insurance) Framework Regulations 1994 (SI 359/1994), reg 59, as amended and liable on summary conviction. Regulation 4(10) also provides for the payment of interest where the insurance undertaking or claims representative breaches reg 4(8).
152. The 2003 Regulations, reg 4(12), as inserted by the 2008 Regulations, reg 5(b).
153. The 2003 Regulations, reg 5(1).

nature are submitted to it.[154] The MIBI must provide an injured party with particulars of the relevant insurance policy[155] and of ownership of the motor vehicle.[156]

9.   *Compensation body*: The MIBI is nominated as the compensation body required by the Sixth Directive.[157] An injured party[158] who is normally resident in Ireland and who claims compensation for an accident occurring in an EEA State (other than Ireland) or in a specified territory (ie Croatia and Switzerland), arising out of the use of a vehicle that is normally based and insured through an insurer in an EEA State (other than Ireland), may present a compensation claim to the MIBI if:

(a)   the injured party has presented a compensation claim to the insurer or its claims representative and no reasoned reply is provided to him within three months thereof;[159] or

(b)   the insurer 'has failed to appoint a claims representative in Ireland, unless such [insurer] has not provided a reasoned reply within three months of a claim for compensation in accordance with reg 4(8)(b)'.[160]

It appears that the second category was intended to cover a situation in which an injured party availed of his right to claim compensation directly against the

---

154. The 2003 Regulations, reg 5(2). While reg 5(3) (as amended by the 2008 Regulations, reg 5(c)) specifies the information that is necessary for compliance with reg 5(2), it is arguable that the obligations imposed on the MIBI do not go as far as the Sixth Directive, art 23(1), which requires that the Information Centre is responsible for keeping 'a register' containing information pertaining to insurance policies in force.

155. The 2003 Regulations, reg 5(5)(b). If the vehicle is owned by an exempted person or is a State vehicle, particulars of the relevant person or Minister must be furnished.

156. The 2003 Regulations, reg 5(5)(a). Again, by reason of the insertion of the 2003 Regulations, reg 3(7), by the 2008 Regulations, reg 5(a), it seems that the 2003 Regulations, reg 5, applies 'to all injured parties normally resident in an EEA State', without reference to the country of accident.

157. The 2003 Regulations, reg 6(1).

158. As defined by the 2003 Regulations, reg 3(1)–3(2).

159. The 2003 Regulations, reg 6(2)(c). Notably, this refers to the obligation on an insurance undertaking or claims representative to issue 'a reasoned reply' under reg 4(8)(a). Regulation 4(8)(a) is, however, concerned with the making of 'a reasoned offer of compensation', despite the fact that it appears that this provision was intended to implement the Sixth Directive, art 24(1)(a), which is concerned with the claims representative's failure to issued a reasoned reply.

160. The 2003 Regulations, reg 6(2)(d). This does not make sense and it appears that an error has been made. The Sixth Directive, art 24(1)(b), allows such an injured party to claim against the compensation body in his own Member State 'if the insurance undertaking has failed to appoint a claims representative in the Member State of residence of the injured party in accordance with article 20(1); in such a case, injured parties may not present a claim to the compensation body if they have presented a claim for compensation directly to the insurance undertaking of the vehicle the use of which caused the accident and if they have received a reasoned reply within three months of presenting the claim'. Hence, the inclusion of the word 'not' in reg 6(2)(d) appears erroneous, as does the failure to make correct provision for a claims representative (if one has been appointed) issuing a reasoned reply within three months as is provided for in reg 4(8)(b).

insurer. However, if the injured party has taken legal action directly against the insurer, no claim may be presented to the MIBI.[161]

10. On receipt of a compensation claim, the MIBI must inform a number of persons of its receipt and advise them that it will respond to it within two months. It must inform the person allegedly responsible for the accident (if known), the relevant insurer or its claims representative and the compensation body in the EEA State in which the accident is alleged to have occurred.[162] The MIBI must cease to act if the insurer or its claims representative subsequently makes a reasoned reply.[163]

11. Where the MIBI compensates an injured party, it can claim reimbursement from the compensation body in the EEA State where the relevant insurer is established.[164] Thereafter, the compensation body in the relevant EEA State shall be subrogated to the injured party in his rights against the responsible person or the relevant insurer with respect to the compensation that has been paid.[165]

12. *Unidentified or uninsured vehicles*: Regulation 7[166] provides that an injured party may also obtain compensation from the MIBI in circumstances where it is impossible to identify:

(a)   a vehicle involved in an accident which gives rise to a claim to which the Regulations apply,[167] or

(b)   an insurer that has issued the policy for the relevant vehicle within two months of the accident.[168]

13. According to the Sixth Directive,[169] the MIBI must compensate the injured party in either situation in accordance with what is now art 10 of the Sixth Directive and which, *inter alia*, obliges each EEA State to set up a body with the responsibility of providing compensation in respect of injury caused by an unidentified or uninsured vehicle in that EEA State. Regulation 7(2) provides that, in the event of a claim to the compensation body, it shall compensate the injured party in accordance with art 10 'as if it was the body authorised [under art 10] and the accident occurred in the State'. Curiously, reg 7(2) suggests that the MIBI must only pay compensation on this basis in respect of an unidentified vehicle.[170] Notwithstanding this, it does mean, at least as regards an Irish

---

161. The 2003 Regulations, reg 6(3).
162. The 2003 Regulations, reg 6(4).
163. The 2003 Regulations, reg 6(5).
164. The 2003 Regulations, reg 6(9).
165. The 2003 Regulations, reg 6(11).
166. The 2003 Regulations, reg 7, also applies in respect of an accident caused by a vehicle that at the time of the accident was normally based in one of the specified territories (reg 3(3)).
167. The 2003 Regulations, reg 7(1)(a).
168. The 2003 Regulations, reg 7(1)(b).
169. Sixth Directive, art 25.
170. If reg 7(2) is only concerned with the payment of compensation in respect of an unidentified vehicle, the Regulations omit to state the manner in which compensation is to be calculated where an insurance undertaking is unidentifiable, notwithstanding the fact that the Sixth Directive, art 25, (contd .../)

resident that is injured in another EEA State by an unidentified vehicle, he may (if needs be) issue proceedings against the MIBI in the State pursuant to the 2009 MIBI Agreement for compensation for his injuries. In order to achieve the intention of the Sixth Directive, it is likely that the relevant provisions will be judicially interpreted to include the payment of compensation in respect of persons who are injured by uninsured vehicles.

14. Thereafter, reg 7(3) provides that, in the event of paying out monies in accordance with reg 7(2),[171] the MIBI can recover same as follows:[172]

   (a) where the insurer cannot be identified,[173] against the guarantee fund[174] in the EEA State in which the vehicle that caused the accident was normally based;

   (b) where it concerns an unidentified vehicle, against the guarantee fund in the EEA State in which the accident occurred; and

   (c) in the event of a third country vehicle,[175] against the guarantee fund of the EEA State in which the accident took place.[176]

15. Regulation 3(4) provides that, notwithstanding reg 3(1)–(2), reg 7 shall also apply in respect of an accident caused by a vehicle that at the time of the accident was normally based in one of the specified territories. In circumstances where reg 7 permits an Irish resident to claim compensation from the MIBI in circumstances where it is not possible to identify a vehicle involved in an accident which gives rise to a claim under the Regulations or where, within two months of the accident, it is not possible to identify an

---

170. (contd) provides that the MIBI must compensate the injured party in accordance with the provisions of arts 9 and 10.

171. It would appear from reg 7(3)(a) that it was intended that the MIBI would recover compensation from the guarantee fund of the EEA State in which the vehicle that caused the accident was normally based and insured. Reg 7(2), however, appears to confine the ability of the MIBI to recover from other guarantee funds in circumstances in which it compensates for injuries suffered by an Irish resident in an EEA State by an unidentified vehicle. This appears to be an error caused by the fact that reg 7(2) refers to 'subparagraph (a)' when the more appropriate reference would have been to 'paragraph (1)'. The MIBI can, however, recover this money pursuant to the Internal Regulations.

172. Reg 7(3) states that the compensation body's right to reclaim the monies that it pays out is subject to the conditions set out in reg 7(7) which does not exist.

173. Reg 7(3)(a).

174. Provided for in the Sixth Directive, art 10(1) (in Ireland the MIBI).

175. The 2003 Regulations, reg 2(2) defines 'third country' as one other than an EEA State or the specified territories.

176. The Regulations do not envisage the MIBI recovering from any guarantee fund in the specified territories (ie Croatia and Switzerland). This is probably because the MIBI's recovery rights in this regard (as national insurers' bureau) is provided for in the Internal Regulations. It is curious that having made provision for accidents in the 'specified territories' of Croatia and Switzerland, that this was not extended to include Andorra and Serbia in circumstances where the 2002 Multilateral Agreement was extended to Andorra in 2005 and its successor, the 2008 Multilateral Agreement, was extended to Serbia in 2011 (see fn **65** above) with the result that (as with Croatia and Switzerland) EEA States are not obliged to ensure the existence of a green card or frontier insurance for vehicles that are normally based there.

insurance undertaking that has issued a policy for the vehicle in question, it is difficult to decipher precisely what was intended by reg 3(4). A literal reading suggests that an Irish resident, who is injured in an EEA State or specified territory by a vehicle that is normally based in a specified territory, may claim compensation from the MIBI where it is not possible to identify an insurance undertaking that issued the policy or it is uninsured. It does not suggest, however, that the Irish resident may claim compensation from the MIBI if in fact the insurance undertaking has been identified.

H. DEEMED INSURER

1. Introduction

[13.39] The MIBI is deemed to be the insurer of a foreign vehicle holding a green card in Ireland.[177] When an Irish vehicle holding a green card causes an accident in another green card country, the bureau of the country of accident may handle any claim arising out of the use of the Irish vehicle (unless the insurer has a correspondent in Ireland). The MIBI can recover any monies it pays out from the insurer or bureau of the country that issued the green card as appropriate.[178]

[13.40] With respect to a vehicle travelling abroad to a green card country in which liability is determined by reference to the country in which it normally based (and for the most part determined by registration plate), Section III of the Internal Regulations apply. It is entitled 'Specific Rules Governing Contractual Relations Between Bureaux Based on Deemed Insurance Cover (Optional Provisions)', although the words 'deemed insurer' do not otherwise appear therein.[179] It provides that the bureau of the country of accident may handle any claim arising out of the use of the foreign vehicle (unless its insurer has an approved correspondent in the country of accident) and, if there is no insurance, the bureau of the country of accident will deal with the claim. Any monies paid out by the bureau of the country of accident may be recouped from the insurer or bureau of the country in which the foreign vehicle is normally based, as appropriate.[180]

2. Section 76 of the Road Traffic Act 1961

[13.41] Section 76(1)(d) of the 1961 Act provides, *inter alia*, that where a person claims to be entitled to recover from the owner or user of a vehicle for a sum, against the liability for which the owner or user was insured by 'an approved policy of insurance', the claimant may serve a notice in writing of the claim by registered post, and having done so, the claimant may apply to court for leave to institute and prosecute the proceedings against the insurer. The court, if satisfied that the owner or user is not in the State, or cannot be found or served with the process of the court, or that it is just and

---

177. The Mechanically Propelled Vehicles (International Circulation) Order 1992 (SI 384/ 1992), art 8(2)(b). See para **13.11**.
178. Section II of the Internal Regulations. See para **13.08**.
179. Article 15 is, however, entitled 'Unilateral application of guarantee based on deemed insurance cover' (Section III).
180. See paras **13.26–13.29**.

equitable that the application should be granted, may grant leave to the claimant to institute and prosecute the proceedings against the insurer and to recover from it the sum which the claimant would be entitled to recover from the owner or user and the payment of which the insurer has insured.

[13.42] Section 76(1)(b)–(c) of the 1961 Act provides, *inter alia*, that where a person claims to be entitled to recover from the owner or user of a vehicle, or has, in court proceedings (of which the vehicle insurer had prior notification), recovered judgment against the owner or user for a sum, against the liability for which the owner or user was insured by 'an approved policy of insurance', the claimant may serve a notice in writing of the claim or judgment by registered post. Having done so, where the claimant recovers judgment, the insurer shall pay the claimant the amount of the judgment as the insurer has insured and the payment shall be a valid payment under the policy. If the amount of the judgment is not recovered from the owner, user or insurer, the claimant may apply to the court that gave the judgment for leave to execute the judgment against the insurer.

3. *Director of Public Prosecutions v Donnelly*

[13.43] In effect, s 56(1) prohibits a person from using a vehicle in a public place unless either a vehicle insurer (or an exempted person) 'would be liable for injury caused by the negligent use of the vehicle' by him or 'there is in force ... an approved policy of insurance whereby the user (or some other person who would be liable for injury caused by the negligent use of the vehicle ... by the user), is insured'. In this regard, section 68 of the 1961 Act allows a vehicle insurer to issue a certificate of exemption in respect of a vehicle owned by it. This certifies ownership and states the particulars in respect of its liability for injury caused by the negligent use of the vehicle.

[13.44] Section 56(1) of the 1961 Act was recently interpreted by the Supreme Court in *Director of Public Prosecutions v Donnelly*[181] in a consultative case stated from the Circuit Court arising out of a prosecution for the offence of driving without insurance under s 56(3) of the 1961 Act. In that case, the appellant drove his father's vehicle, with the father's consent, but the appellant was not insured on the father's policy. In defending the charge, the appellant contended that, if he had caused injury to a third party, the father's insurer (as vehicle insurer) would have been 'liable' to the third party. The DPP, on the other hand, contended that s 56(1) had to be construed in light of s 68 and, on this basis, s 56(1) was only concerned with a situation where the vehicle insurer would be liable directly in tort for the injury caused by the negligent driving of a vehicle owned by it.

[13.45] In the Supreme Court, the essential issue was reduced to whether the reference to 'vehicle insurer' in s 56(1) included the situation that had arisen, namely where an approved policy of insurance exists at the relevant time but did not cover the appellant's driving.[182] The Supreme Court was satisfied that the first reference to 'liable for injury'

---

181. *Director of Public Prosecutions v Donnelly* [2012] IESC 44, (23 July 2012, unreported) SC (*per* Fennelly J).
182. At para 11.

in s 56(1) was concerned with injury suffered by a third party as a result of the negligent driving of a vehicle owned by the vehicle insurer.[183] The Court stated that the plain meaning of 'liable' is that the vehicle insurer 'is liable as a matter of law to pay damages to an injured party for the consequences of its own acts, including acts of the drivers of vehicles which it owns for which it is vicariously liable. The insurer is legally liable in that way only when it owns the vehicle'.[184] On the other hand, where an insured person causes injury to a third party, the insured is liable to the third party. The liability of the insurer in this situation is to indemnify the insured and that '[i]t is not a liability owed directly to the injured party. That liability remains the liability of the insured.'[185]

4. *Director of Public Prosecutions v Leipina and Suhanovs*

[13.46] *Director of Public Prosecutions v Leipina and Suhanovs*[186] concerned a prosecution for the offence of driving without insurance. The driver had a green card for the vehicle which, together with the insurance policy on which it was based, was issued by a Latvian insurance company that was not a member of the MIBI.[187] However, the vehicle was registered in Ireland and therefore bore an Irish registration plate. While the Supreme Court was principally concerned with the question of whether or not the vehicle was covered for use in Ireland under the green card system, the Court commented (albeit *obiter*) that the registration plate of the country of registration (for Section III countries) 'is evidence of insurance and has the like effect to a Green Card: see *Jacobs v Motor Insurers' Bureau* [2010] EWHC 231'.[188] In *Jacobs v MIB*,[189] it was common ground between the parties that a UK resident, who was injured in Spain by a vehicle that was ordinarily based in Spain, and then being driver by an uninsured German national, was entitled to proceed against the MIB in its capacity as a compensation body under the UK regulations implementing what are now arts 24–25 of the Sixth Directive.[190] The Court of Appeal commented that, under the scheme provided for by the Sixth Directive, an injured party may recover from the compensation body in

---

183. At para 22.
184. At para 27.
185. At para 23. The foregoing statement was made in the context of liability, rather than the manner in which an indemnity might be enforced and should therefore not be considered to conflict with s 76 of the 1961 Act and/or the Sixth Directive, art 18.

   The second question asked of the Supreme Court in the case stated was whether or not, having regard to the Second Directive, art 2(1) (now the Sixth Directive, art 13(1)), liability could be avoided by an insurer on the basis that the insurance policy limited cover to the persons named therein. In light the Court's conclusion on the appropriate interpretation of s 56(1), however, it was not necessary for the court to answer this question.

186. *Director of Public Prosecutions v Leipina and Suhanovs* [2011] IESC 3, (2 February 2011, unreported) SC (*per* Finnegan J).
187. See further paras **13.14–13.15** above.
188. At pp 12–13. The decision in *Jacobs* was subsequently appealed to the Court of Appeal.
189. *Jacobs v MIB* [2010] EWCA Civ 1208, [2011] 1 WLR 2609.
190. The Motor Vehicles (Compulsory Insurance) (Information Centre and Compensation Body) Regulations 2003. The dispute in that case, however, concerned whether the MIB was required to assess the compensation payable in accordance with Spanish or English law and whether Parliament and Council Regulation (EC) No 864/2007 on the law applicable to non-contractual obligations applied to determine the applicable law. (contd .../)

his state of residence 'if the driver's insurer fails to respond promptly to his claim or the driver is uninsured or a relevant insurer cannot be identified'.[191]

5. The MIBI as deemed insurer?

[13.47] The foregoing raise an issue as to the precise legal status of the MIBI when it deals with a claim arising out of an accident in Ireland in which a foreign vehicle which has a green card is the only or one of a number of vehicles responsible. Likewise, it raises an issue as to the status of the MIBI when it deals with a claim that is brought against a vehicle that is normally based in another country that is a party to Section III of the Internal Regulations, whether as the only vehicle or one of the vehicles responsible for an accident in Ireland. At the outset, it should be noted that the fact that an accident in Ireland involves a foreign vehicle does not change Irish domestic law. Accordingly, the provisions of the 1961 Act still apply.[192]

[13.48] As noted, where injury is caused to an Irish resident by a foreign vehicle in Ireland with a green card (Section II vehicle), the MIBI 'shall be deemed to be the vehicle insurer which issued the evidence that a certificate was issued, and to be competent to act as a vehicle insurer'.[193] One might therefore consider that the Irish resident might therefore avail of s 76 of the 1961 Act. However, s 76 is predicated on the basis that there is 'an approved policy of insurance'. All the indicators from the Supreme Court decision in *DPP v Leipina and Suhanovs*[194] are that, while a green card is deemed evidence of insurance (whether or not the vehicle is actually insured) and the Section II vehicle is deemed insured for the purposes of compensating a victim of an accident that is caused by it, the deeming provision 'has no relevance whatsoever to the domestic law of the State'.[195] The Supreme Court considered an approved policy of insurance (as defined by s 62) must be issued by a vehicle insurer (defined by s 58) and such a vehicle insurer must be a member of the MIBI (s 78), and this would obviously not be the position with a foreign insurer. Furthermore, it is significant that art 8(3) of the 1992 Order expressly provides that s 58 shall not apply to the MIBI ie it is not a vehicle insurer. On this reasoning, it seems that the Irish resident injured party must proceed on the basis of art 8 of the 1992 Order.

[13.49] The foregoing also raises the question of what is the position where an Irish resident is injured in an accident that is caused by both a Section II vehicle (that is actually insured) and another vehicle which, for the purposes of this example, is an Irish insured vehicle. The issue is whether or not the MIBI may be treated as a concurrent

---

190. (contd) The Court of Appeal held that the compensation should be assessed in accordance with English law. See further paras **13.34**, point 2.

191. At p 2614.

192. The Internal Regulations allow claims to be handled by a bureau in conformity with legal and regulatory provisions applicable in the country of accident (art 3(4)).

193. Mechanically Propelled Vehicles (International Circulation) Order 1992, art 8. Although, in practical terms, where the Section II vehicle is in fact insured, the MIBI will only deal with the claim if the insurer that issued the green card does not have a correspondent in Ireland.

194. *DPP v Leipina and Suhanovs* [2011] IESC 3, (2 February 2011, unreported) SC (per Finnegan J).

195. *DPP v Leipina and Suhanovs* [2011] IESC 3, (2 February 2011, unreported) SC (per Finnegan J) at p 15.

wrongdoer such that, if liability for the accident was apportioned between the owner and / or driver of the insured Section II vehicle and the Irish insured, the injured party might proceed to recover the entire judgment from the MIBI (or vice-versa).[196] Again, in light of *DPP v Leipina and Suhanovs* and art 8(3) of the 1992 Order, it appears that the MIBI would not be considered to be a concurrent wrongdoer, although even if it was, it could obviously recover the full amount of the judgment from the insurer of the Section II vehicle.[197] In this regard, it is notable that there is no MIBI agreement regulating the manner in which an Irish resident is to proceed against it in terms of recovering damages for injury suffered by him at the hands of a insured Section II vehicle in Ireland, although this situation is unlikely to arise in circumstances where the insurer of the Section II vehicle is likely to have a correspondent in Ireland that will handle the claim.

[13.50] The significance of the foregoing is further highlighted by an example in which an Irish resident is injured in Ireland in an accident that is caused by both a Section II vehicle (that is not actually insured) and another vehicle which, for the purpose of this example, is an Irish insured vehicle. Again, the issue is whether or not the MIBI might be treated as a concurrent wrongdoer such that, if liability was apportioned between the owner and / or user of the Section II uninsured vehicle and the Irish insured, the injured party might proceed to recover the entire judgment from the MIBI. Again, in light of *DPP v Leipina and Suhanovs* and art 8(3) of the 1992 Order, it appears that the MIBI would not be considered to be a concurrent wrongdoer. This accords with the position that would follow if the Irish resident proceeded against the MIBI under the 2009 Agreement in respect of the actions of the owner and / or driver of the Section II uninsured vehicle (where the owner and / or driver are also co-defendants) and the Irish insured. In this case, the MIBI would not be a concurrent wrongdoer and, provided that some liability was apportioned to the Irish insured, the MIBI might avoid having to pay out anything on foot of any judgment that might be entered jointly and severally against the Irish insured and the owner and / or driver of the Section II vehicle on the basis that, assuming that the insurer of the Irish insured discharged the judgment, there would be no unsatisfied judgment that the MIBI might be required to discharge.

[13.51] For the above reasons, it is submitted that there is no valid legal reason why an uninsured Section II vehicle should be treated any differently to an uninsured Irish vehicle, although it is notable that if the claim is dealt with under the 2009 Agreement as opposed to art 8 of the 1992 Order, it is questionable as to whether or not the MIBI may be in a position to recoup any monies it pays out from the bureau of the green card country from which the Section II vehicle emanated.

[13.52] Where injury is caused by a foreign vehicle in Ireland that is normally based in a country that is a party to Section III of the Internal Regulations ('Section III vehicle'), the MIBI takes the view that it is 'deemed insurer' of the Section III vehicle and deals with such a claim on behalf of the bureau of the country in which the Section III vehicle is 'normally based' and on the basis that it will ultimately be reimbursed by that

---

196. Pursuant to the Civil Liability Act 1961, Pt III, and on the basis that notices of indemnity and contribution are exchanged.

197. Or from the bureau of the green card country from it was visiting.

bureau.[198] The significance, however, is that, if the MIBI is to be treated in law as the insurer of the Section III vehicle, a claimant may be in a position to recover from the MIBI as the insurer of the foreign vehicle.[199] Indeed, the MIBI itself takes the view that the 2009 Agreement has no part to play in such claims although, as a matter of practice, claimants invariably cite the 2009 Agreement when dealing with a Section III vehicle that is uninsured and this would appear to accord with good sense.[200] However, the MIBI's approach in terms of treating itself as 'deemed insurer' is questionable in light of the Supreme Court's comments in *DPP v Leipina and Suhanovs* and the fact that there is no 'approved policy of insurance' as defined by s 62 of the 1961 Act and which appears to be a prerequisite to the operation of s 76.

[13.53] The significance of the foregoing becomes apparent when one considers a situation where an Irish resident is injured in Ireland in an accident that is caused by both a Section III vehicle (that is actually insured) and another vehicle which, for the purpose of this example, is an Irish insured vehicle. The issue is whether or not the MIBI may be treated as a concurrent wrongdoer such that, if liability for the accident was apportioned between the insured Section III vehicle and the Irish insured, the injured party might proceed to recover the entire judgment from the MIBI. This suggests that, if the MIBI treats itself as 'deemed insurer', then it should consider serving a notice of indemnity on the Irish insured (and vice-versa). In this regard, it is notable that there is no MIBI Agreement regulating the manner in which an Irish resident is to proceed against it in terms of recovering damages for injury suffered by him at the hands of an insured Section III vehicle in Ireland, although this situation is unlikely to arise in circumstances where the insurer of the Section III vehicle is likely to have a correspondent in Ireland that will handle the claim and the Irish resident also has a direct right of action against the insurer.

[13.54] The significance of the foregoing is further illustrated by an example in which an Irish resident is injured in Ireland in an accident that is caused by both a Section III vehicle (that is not actually insured) and another vehicle which, for the purpose of this example, is an Irish insured vehicle. Again, the issue is whether or not the MIBI and the Irish insured might be treated as concurrent wrongdoers such that, if liability was

---

198. Although, in practical terms, where the Section III vehicle is in fact insured, the MIBI will only deal with the claim if the insurer of the Section III vehicle does not have a correspondent in Ireland.

199. Pursuant to Road Traffic Act 1961, s 76, subject to prior notification. The MIBI will ultimately be reimbursed by the insurer of the Section III vehicle or, in default, by the bureau of the country in which the vehicle is normally based.

200. The Internal Regulations provide that the MIBI is the only body that may deal with the claim in Ireland where the Section III vehicle is not in fact insured. See para **13.54** below in relation to uninsured Section III vehicles. Note, however, that the Internal Regulations are concerned with the manner in which a bureau pays out money to an injured party and then seeks reimbursement from the bureau of the country in which the Section II (or indeed Section III) vehicle is normally based. It is not concerned with the manner in which an injured party should proceed against the bureau of the country in which the injured party is seeking to recover. Likewise, in terms of a person claiming compensation from or issuing proceedings against the MIBI in respect of injury caused to him by an uninsured vehicle, the 2009 Agreement does not distinguish between injuries caused by a vehicle that is normally based inside or outside the State.

apportioned between the Section III uninsured vehicle and the Irish insured, the injured party might proceed to recover the entire judgment from the MIBI. On the basis that the MIBI treats itself as 'deemed insurer', it seems that it may be treated as a concurrent wrongdoer with the Irish insured. Contrast this with the position if the MIBI is sued under the 2009 Agreement in respect of the actions of the owner and / or driver of the Section III uninsured vehicle (where the owner and / or driver are also co-defendants) and the Irish insured. In this case, the MIBI would not be a concurrent wrongdoer and, provided that some liability was apportioned to the Irish insured, it could avoid having to pay out anything on foot of any judgment that might be entered jointly and severally against the Irish insured and the owner and / or driver of the Section III vehicle.

[13.55] For the above reasons, it is submitted that there is no valid legal reason why an uninsured Section III vehicle should be treated any differently to an uninsured vehicle that is normally based in Ireland, although it is notable that if the claim is dealt with under the 2009 Agreement as opposed to the deemed insurance provisions of the Internal Regulations, it is questionable as to whether or not the MIBI may be in a position to recoup any monies it pays out from the bureau of the country in which the Section III vehicle is normally based.

I. IRISH RESIDENT INJURED IN IRELAND BY A FOREIGN VEHICLE[201]

1. Injury caused by vehicle that is normally based in the EEA

[13.56] An Irish resident who is injured in an accident in Ireland that is caused by a vehicle that is normally based in an EEA State (other than Ireland), that is in fact insured, may apply to the MIBI for compensation. The MIBI appears to deal with the claim on the basis that it is 'deemed insurer' and will recover any monies that it pays out from the bureau of the country in which the Section III insured vehicle is normally based. The foregoing applies unless, assuming that there is insurance, the insurer has an approved correspondent in Ireland, in which case it must handle the claim. In this situation, the Irish resident also has a direct right of action against the insurer. This applies regardless of where the insurer is established in the EEA (provided it is in fact domiciled in the EEA) and the proceedings may be brought in Ireland.[202] There is, however, no domestic MIBI Agreement regulating the manner in which the Irish resident should proceed against the MIBI should he choose to do so, although the Internal Regulations provide that it may accept service of proceedings arising out of the claim.

[13.57] Thus, by way of example, if a person is injured in Donegal by a vehicle that is insured and normally based in Northern Ireland, he may have recourse to the MIBI unless the insurer has a correspondent in the State. Likewise, he has a direct right of

---

201. The most important points of this paragraph are summarised in **Table 13.2** at p 225.
202. See, for example, *Kelly v Groupama* [2012] IEHC 177, (20 April 2012, unreported), HC in which an Irish resident who suffered injuries in France sued the French motorist's insurers directly before the Irish courts.

action against the insurer and, provided that the insurer is domiciled in the EEA,[203] the injured party may sue the insurer in Ireland, provided that the injured party is domiciled here.[204]

[13.58] An Irish resident who is injured in an accident in Ireland that is caused by a vehicle that is normally based in an EEA State (other than Ireland), that is in fact uninsured, may apply to the MIBI for compensation. The MIBI appears to deal with such a claim on the basis that it is 'deemed insurer' and will recover any monies that it pays out from the bureau of the country in which the Section III uninsured vehicle is normally based. In this regard, it seems that the Irish resident may proceed against the MIBI under the relevant terms of the 2009 Agreement, in the same way that he would if he was injured by an uninsured Irish vehicle.

[13.59] Thus, by way of example, if a person is injured in Donegal by a vehicle that is normally based in Northern Ireland, but which is in fact uninsured, he may proceed against the MIBI and may join the uninsured as a co-defendant to the proceedings.

2. Injury caused by vehicle that is normally based in Andorra, Croatia, Switzerland or Serbia

[13.60] An Irish resident who is injured in an accident in Ireland that is caused by a vehicle that is normally based in Andorra, Croatia, Switzerland or Serbia[205] (a Section III vehicle), that is in fact insured, may apply to the MIBI for compensation. The foregoing applies unless the insurer has an approved correspondent in Ireland, in which case it must handle the claim. The MIBI appears to deal with such claims on the basis that it is 'deemed insurer' and will recover any monies that it pays out from the bureau of the country in which the Section III vehicle is normally based. There is, however, no domestic MIBI Agreement regulating the manner in which the Irish resident should pursue the MIBI in the event that court proceedings are necessary, although the Internal Regulations provide that it may accept service of proceedings arising out of the claim.

[13.61] If the Section III vehicle from one of these four countries is not in fact insured, then the MIBI deals with the claim on the same basis as it deals with one in respect of which the Section III vehicle is insured (ie as 'deemed insurer'). In this regard, it seems that the Irish resident may proceed against the MIBI under the relevant terms of the 2009 Agreement, in the same way as he would if he was injured by an uninsured Irish vehicle.

3. Injury caused by Section II vehicle

[13.62] An Irish resident that is injured in an accident in Ireland that is caused by a vehicle from one of the 13 countries that have subscribed only to Section II of the

---

203. See fn **86** above.
204. The Irish resident who is injured in Ireland may also wish to join the insured owner / driver of the vehicle as a co-defendant to his direct action against the insurer. This can be done on the basis of Council Regulation (EC) No 44/2001, art 5(3) which provides that, in matters relating to tort, a person domiciled in a Member State may be sued in the courts of the place where the harmful event occurred.
205. These countries are parties to Section III of the Internal Regulations but are not in the EEA.

Internal Regulations (a Section II vehicle) and in respect of which a green card exists, may apply to the MIBI for compensation. The foregoing applies unless, assuming that there is insurance, the insurer has an approved correspondent in Ireland, in which case it must handle the claim. If the compensation claim is not resolved, it seems that the Irish resident may proceed against the MIBI in reliance upon art 8 of the 1992 Regulations and the Internal Regulations provide that it may accept service of proceedings arising out of the claim.

[13.63] Where there is an Irish resident who is injured in an accident in Ireland that is caused by a Section II vehicle from one of the 13 countries, and in respect of which there is no green card, it seems that the appropriate course of action is to claim compensation from the MIBI in the same way as the Irish resident would if injured by an uninsured Irish vehicle and pursuant to the 2009 Agreement.

Table 13.2 Irish resident injured in Ireland by foreign vehicle[206]

Country of Accident	Origin of Vehicle		Claims Procedure	
	Section II only Green card country –	Section III country – vehicle normally based	Insured	Uninsured
Ireland		EEA State other than Ireland[207]	MIBI or Insurer's correspondent Alternatively, pursue person responsible and / or direct right of action against insurer. These proceedings may be brought in Ireland.[208]	MIBI
		Andorra, Croatia, Switzerland or Serbia	MIBI or insurer's correspondent	MIBI
	Any one of 13 countries[209]		MIBI or insurer's correspondent	MIBI

J. IRISH RESIDENT INJURED ABROAD BY FOREIGN VEHICLE[210]

[13.64] The position of an Irish resident who is injured abroad by a foreign vehicle may fall into four categories, namely an Irish resident who is injured abroad:

1.   in another EEA State or specified territory (ie Croatia and Switzerland);[211]

---

206.   This table must be considered in conjunction with the content of paras **13.56–13.63**.
207.   Being the EU Member States and Iceland, Norway and Liechtenstein.
208.   This is subject to what is stated at para **13.57**, including that the insurer is domiciled in a Member State as defined by Council Regulation No 44/2001 (see para **13.34**, point 1).
209.   Albania, Belarus, Bosnia and Herzegovina, Former Yugoslav Republic of Macedonia, Islamic Republic of Iran, Israel, Morocco, Moldova, Montenegro, Russia, Tunisia, Turkey and Ukraine.
210.   The most important points of this paragraph are summarised in **Table 13.3** at 233.
211.   See paras **13.65–13.76**.

2. in one of the 13 countries that are parties to the green card system (but outside the EEA and specified territories)[212] by a vehicle that is insured and normally based in an EEA State;[213]

3. in a country (outside the EEA) that is a party to the green card system by a vehicle that is normally based in that country or another country that is a party to the green card system;[214]

4. in a county that is a not a party to the green card system.[215]

1. Irish resident injured in another EEA State or a specified territory by foreign vehicle

[13.65] The position of an Irish resident who is injured by a foreign vehicle in *another* EEA State or specified territory depends on a number of factors, such as whether the foreign vehicle is:

(a) identified or not;

(b) insured and normally based in an EEA State;

(c) normally based in a specified territory; or

(d) a vehicle from outside the EEA and specified territories.

[13.66] *Identified or unidentified foreign vehicle*: if the foreign vehicle cannot be identified, the Irish resident who is injured in another EEA State or specified territory may make a claim to the MIBI,[216] which must compensate the injured party as if he were injured by an unidentified or uninsured vehicle in Ireland.[217] If the foreign vehicle is identified, the position will depend whether or not the vehicle falls within (b), (c) or (d) above.

[13.67] *Foreign vehicle insured and normally based in an EEA State*: an Irish resident who is injured in another EEA State or a specified territory by a vehicle that is insured and normally based in an EEA State other than Ireland (foreign vehicle),[218] may make a compensation claim directly to the insurer or its claims representative in Ireland.[219]

---

212. The 13 countries are: Albania, Belarus, Bosnia and Herzegovina, Former Yugoslav Republic of Macedonia, Islamic Republic of Iran, Israel, Morocco, Moldova, Montenegro, Russia, Tunisia, Turkey and Ukraine.

213. See paras **13.77–13.78**.

214. See para **13.79**.

215. See para **13.80**.

216. The 2003 Regulations, reg 7(1)(a). Alternatively, the Irish resident could make a claim against the bureau of the country of accident.

217. The 2003 Regulations, reg 7(2). See also points 14–15 at para **13.38**, regarding the MIBI's recovery rights in relation to any monies paid out by it in respect of an unidentified vehicle and which seems to depend upon whether the accident occurred in an EEA State or a specified territory.

218. The 2003 Regulations, reg 3(1) and (3).

219. The 2003 Regulations, reg 4. If the foreign vehicle was insured by an authorised insurance undertaking in Ireland, the Irish resident could issue proceedings directly against it in Ireland (reg 3(5)).

However, if there is no claims representative in Ireland or no reasoned offer of compensation or reasoned reply is forthcoming within three months of the claim, the Irish resident may claim compensation from the MIBI.[220] Furthermore, the Irish resident has a direct right of action against the insurer.

[13.68] Furthermore, where it is not possible to identify an insurance undertaking that has issued a policy for the foreign vehicle within two months of the accident, an Irish resident may be permitted to make a direct claim to the MIBI.[221] The same applies if it there is in fact no insurance.

[13.69] Thus, by way of example, if an Irish resident is injured in the United Kingdom by a vehicle that is insured and normally based there, the Irish resident may claim compensation from the insurer's claims representative in Ireland. If there is no such claims representative, or the claims representative does not comply with the time limits for making a reasoned offer or reply, the Irish resident may have recourse to the MIBI. As indicated, the Irish resident also has a direct right of action against the insurer and, assuming that the insurer is domiciled in the EEA,[222] the Irish resident may sue it in Ireland, if the Irish resident is also domiciled here.[223] As indicated above, if the vehicle in this scenario is uninsured, the Irish resident may also have recourse to the MIBI, regardless of his domicile.

[13.70] *Foreign vehicle normally based in a specified territory*: the position with respect to an Irish resident who is injured in another EEA State or specified territory by

---

220. The 2008 Regulations, reg 6(2). See also point 9 at para **13.38**. The right to claim compensation from the MIBI is without prejudice to the direct right of action afforded to the Irish resident against the liable insurer, although both courses cannot be pursued (2008 Regulations, reg 3(5) and reg 6(3)).

221. The 2008 Regulations, reg 7(1)(b). However, this is subject to the observations made at para **13.38** which identifies difficulties with the wording of the 2003 Regulations.

222. See para **13.34**, point 1, in respect of domicile.

223. The position is not as clear if the Irish resident wishes to join the insured driver as a co-defendant and it seems there may be little to be gained by doing so. Council Regulation (EC) No 44/2001 of 22 December 2000, on jurisdiction and the recognition and enforcement in civil and commercial matters (OJ L 12, 16.1.2001, p 1) provides that, in matters relating to tort, a person domiciled in a Member State may be sued in the courts of the place where the harmful event occurred (art 5(3)). Where there are multiple defendants, a person domiciled in a Member State may also be sued 'in the courts for the place where any one of them is domiciled, provided the claims are so closely connected that it is expedient to hear and determine them together to avoid the risk of irreconcilable judgments resulting from separate proceedings (art 6(1)). However, where, for example, a person who is domiciled in Ireland is injured abroad by a foreign vehicle and he exercises his direct right of action against the insurer (that is domiciled elsewhere in the EEA) and sues the insurer in Ireland (as opposed to in the insurer's EEA State of domicile), art 6(1) does not expressly provide a basis upon which to name the insured as a co-defendant. This would suggest that a plaintiff who wants to sue both the insurer and insured would have to sue in the EEA State in which one or other of them was domiciled. Council Regulation (EC) No 44/2001 also provides that '[i]n respect of liability insurance, the insurer may also, if the law of the court permits it, be joined in proceedings which the injured party has brought against the insured' (art 11(1)) and that 'if the law governing such direct actions provides that the policyholder or the insured may be joined as a party to the action, the same court shall have jurisdiction over them' (art 11(3)). (contd .../)

a vehicle that is normally based in one of the specified territories (ie Croatia or Switzerland) is different and somewhat unclear.

[13.71] With respect to a vehicle that is normally based in one of the specified territories causing injury to an Irish resident in either another EEA State or in a specified territory, it should be noted at the outset that, in general terms, a vehicle from outside the EEA must be provided with either a valid green card or a certificate of insurance before it enters an EEA State. However, this requirement does not extend to Croatia or Switzerland in circumstances where they are parties to Section III of the Internal Regulations[224] and the Commission has directed the EEA States to refrain from conducting checks on such vehicles.[225] It appears to be against this background that the 2003 Regulations provides that reg 7 shall apply to a vehicle that is normally based in a specified territory.[226] This suggests that where a vehicle, that is normally based in one of the specified territories, injures an Irish resident in either another EEA State or a specified territory, the Irish resident may apply to the MIBI for compensation. However, reg 7 applies only in respect of an unidentified vehicle or one in respect of which it is not possible to identify an insurance undertaking within two months of the accident. Thus, it would seem that the only circumstance under which an Irish resident, who is caused injury in another EEA State or a specified territory by a vehicle that is normally based in a specified territory, may claim compensation from the MIBI, is if it is not possible to identify the insurance undertaking within the two-month period or it is in fact uninsured.[227]

[13.72] For the foregoing reason, it seems that, if a vehicle that is normally based in Croatia or Switzerland (and insured by an identifiable insurer) causes injury to an Irish resident in another EEA State or a specified territory, the 2003 Regulations do not otherwise avail him and he must make a claim to the national insurers' bureau (bureau) of the country of accident or otherwise pursue the person responsible for the accident and / or his insurer. That said, the specified territories are both parties to Section III of

---

223. (contd) In Ireland, the direct right of action against an insurer is provided for in the EC (Fourth Motor Insurance Directive) Regulations 2003 (SI 651/2003), reg 3(5) which states '[a]n injured party shall be entitled, without prejudice to his right to issue proceedings against the insured person, to issue proceedings against an insurance undertaking that is authorised to transact compulsory motor insurance business in the State in respect of an accident caused by a vehicle insured by that undertaking and the insurance undertaking shall be directly liable to the injured party to the extent that it is liable to the insured person'. The Sixth Directive, art 18, directs the Member States to ensure that a person who is injured by a vehicle for which compulsory insurance is required 'enjoys a direct right of action against' the insurer. It therefore remains to be seen whether or not the foregoing is interpreted as permitting a plaintiff to name the driver of a foreign vehicle that is insured and normally based in the EEA (but outside Ireland) as a co-defendant to a direct action that is brought against that insured driver's insurer in Ireland.

224. See the Sixth Directive, arts 7–8.

225. This has applied since 1 August 2003 (2003/564/EC Commission Decision of 28 July 2003, on the application of Council Directive 72/166/EEC relating to checks on insurance against civil liability in respect of the use of motor vehicles (Text with EEA relevance) (notified under document number C(2003) 2626) (OJ L 192, 31 July 2003, p 23)).

226. Regulation 3(4), which makes no reference to insurance.

227. The 2008 Regulations, reg 7(1)(b). However, this is subject to the observations made at para **13.38**, which identifies difficulties with the wording of the 2003 Regulations.

the Internal Regulations and so insurers in either country may well have approved correspondents in Ireland and so, on a practical basis, it may be possible to make a claim in this way. Alternatively, it may be that the MIBI will agree to handle claims of this nature on behalf of Irish residents.

[13.73] *Foreign vehicle emanates from outside EEA and specified territories*: the 2003 Regulations make no provision in respect of any Irish resident who is injured in another EEA State or specified territory by a foreign vehicle that emanates from outside the EEA or specified territories. That said, such vehicles will either be from Andorra or Serbia, one of the 13 countries that are required to have green cards,[228] or another country.

[13.74] Andorra and Serbia are parties to Section III of the Internal Regulations and are countries in respect of which the European Commission has directed the EEA States to refrain from making insurance checks on such vehicles entering the EEA. However, the reality is that the 2003 Regulations do not make provision for a situation where a vehicle that is normally based in either country injures an Irish resident in another EEA State or specified territory. Thus, where there is insurance, it seems that an Irish resident in such a situation must make a claim to the bureau of the country of accident. Alternatively, the Irish resident might be in a position to pursue the person responsible for the accident and / or his insurer.[229] If there is no insurance, and provided that the accident occurred in the EEA, then it appears that the 2003 Regulations permit the Irish resident to make a claim to the MIBI.[230] If there is no insurance, and the accident occurred in a specified territory, it seems that the Irish resident must make a claim to the bureau of the country of accident.

[13.75] If the vehicle is from one of the 13 countries that are parties to Section II of the Internal Regulations, then, assuming that there is a valid green card, it appears that the Irish resident cannot look to the MIBI for compensation under the 2003 Regulations, but may claim compensation from the bureau of the country of accident.[231] Alternatively, the Irish resident might be in a position to pursue the person responsible for the accident and / or his insurer. If, however, there is no valid green card in respect of the vehicle such that it is uninsured, then despite the fact that it appears that the Sixth Directive intended that the Irish resident would be in a position to claim against the MIBI in respect of an

---

228. Being one of the 13 countries that are signatories to Part II of the Internal Regulations (Albania, Belarus, Bosnia and Herzegovina, Former Yugoslav Republic of Macedonia, Islamic Republic of Iran, Israel, Morocco, Moldova, Montenegro, Russia, Tunisia, Turkey and Ukraine).
229. If the insurer is in the EEA and the accident occurred in the EEA, the Irish resident may be in a position to pursue the insurer directly.
230. Alternatively, he may apply to the bureau of the country of accident.
231. Internal Regulations, art 3. It must investigate the accident and notify any correspondent of the relevant insurer if one has been approved. Such an approved correspondent can handle the claim (Internal Regulations, art 4). If there is no such correspondent, the MIBI must give notice to the insurer who issued the green card or insurance policy or, if appropriate, to the bureau concerned being the bureau of the country that issued the green card (art 3). The national bureau of the country of accident can recoup any monies it pays out from the foreign vehicle's insurer or the bureau of the country that issued the green card, as appropriate.

accident caused by it in the EEA,[232] no such provision appears to be made in the 2003 Regulations and hence the necessity for the Irish resident to look to the bureau of the country of accident.

[13.76] If the vehicle is from a country that is not a party to the Internal Regulations, and insurance has been taken out before the foreign vehicle entered the EEA State or specified territory (other than Ireland), then neither the 2003 Regulations nor the Internal Regulations assist the Irish resident in terms of claiming compensation in the State. He could, however, claim directly against the person responsible for the accident and rely on his insurance. If, however, the vehicle is not insured at all, then despite the fact that it appears that the Sixth Directive intended that the Irish resident would be in a position to claim against the MIBI in respect of an accident caused by such a vehicle in the EEA,[233] no such provision appears to be made in the 2003 Regulations and hence the necessity for the Irish resident to look to the bureau of the country of accident.

2. Irish resident injured in a country (outside EEA and specified territories) that is a party to the green card system by a vehicle insured and normally based in EEA

[13.77] An Irish resident who is injured in one of the 15 countries[234] that are parties to the green card system (but which are not included in the EEA and specified territories) by a vehicle that is insured and normally based in an EEA State, is not provided for in the 2003 Regulations. This suggests that such a person must claim compensation from the bureau of the country of accident.

[13.78] The Sixth Directive, however, expressly provides for a situation in which a resident of an EEA State seeks compensation for injury suffered in a country that is a party to the green card system (but which is not an EEA State) as a result of the use of a vehicle that is insured and normally based in an EEA State (other than the State of the injured party's residence).[235] It clearly envisages that an Irish resident who is injured in these circumstances may, where the insurer has not appointed a claims representative or if a reasoned reply is not given within three months, be compensated by the MIBI.[236] It also envisages that the MIBI would compensate in the event of no insurance and that it would recover any monies paid by it from the compensation body in the EEA State of the establishment of the insurance undertaking that issued the policy or, in the event of no insurance, from the bureau of the country of accident.[237] The 2003 Regulations make no provision for this situation, and so it seems that even if the vehicle was insured, the

---

232. Sixth Directive, art 25(2).
233. Sixth Directive, art 25(2).
234. Being the 13 countries that are parties to Section II of the Internal Regulations (Albania, Belarus, Bosnia and Herzegovina, Former Yugoslav Republic of Macedonia, Islamic Republic of Iran, Israel, Morocco, Moldova, Montenegro, Russia, Tunisia, Turkey and Ukraine) and Andorra and Serbia which are parties to Section III of the Internal Regulations.
235. Sixth Directive, art 20(1).
236. Sixth Directive, art 24(1).
237. Sixth Directive, art 24(2).

Irish resident may be forced to make a claim to the bureau of the country of accident (unless the insurer has an approved correspondent in that country) in either situation.[238]

3. Irish resident injured in a country (outside the EEA) that is a party to the green card system by a vehicle from the same or another green card country

[13.79] Seventeen countries outside the EEA are parties to the Internal Regulations (the 17 countries[239]). Of those 17 countries, 13 are parties to Section II of the Internal Regulations only (the 13 countries [240]) and the other four are parties to both Sections II and III of the Internal Regulations (the four countries [241]). Neither the 2003 Regulations nor the Sixth Directive make provision for an Irish resident who seeks compensation for an accident that occurs in any of the 17 countries and that is caused by a vehicle that is from that country of accident or one of the other 17 countries. In this situation, it seems that the following provisions apply:

(a) If the Irish resident is injured in one of the 13 countries by a vehicle that is from that country of accident, then, if the vehicle is insured, he may have recourse to whatever legal avenues are available for recovering from an insured motorist in that country of accident. If the vehicle is uninsured, the Irish resident may look to the bureau in the country of accident.

(b) If the Irish resident is injured in one of the 13 countries by a vehicle from another one of the 17 countries (ie where a green card is required), then the available options depend upon whether or not there was a green card in existence for the vehicle that caused the accident. If there was a green card, the Irish resident may claim compensation from the approved correspondent (or the insurer that issued the green card) in the country of accident and, if there is none, against the bureau in the country of accident. If there was no insurance, then he must claim against the bureau in the country of accident.

(c) If the Irish resident is injured in one of the four countries by a vehicle that is insured and normally based in that same country, then the Irish resident must claim from the insurer (or his approved correspondent) in the country of accident. If there is none, he may claim against the bureau in the country of accident. If there was no insurance, he must claim against the bureau in the country of accident.

---

238. Alternative remedies, such as claiming direct effect, indirect effect and/or pursuing the State for failing to properly implement a directive are considered in **Ch 12**.

239. Being the 13 countries that are parties to Section II of the Internal Regulations (Albania, Belarus, Bosnia and Herzegovina, Former Yugoslav Republic of Macedonia, Islamic Republic of Iran, Israel, Morocco, Moldova, Montenegro, Russia, Tunisia, Turkey and Ukraine) and Andorra, Croatia, Serbia and Switzerland which are parties to Section II and Section III of the Internal Regulations.

240. Being Albania, Belarus, Bosnia and Herzegovina, Former Yugoslav Republic of Macedonia, Islamic Republic of Iran, Israel, Morocco, Moldova, Montenegro, Russia, Tunisia, Turkey and Ukraine.

241. Being Andorra, Croatia, Serbia and Switzerland.

(d) If the Irish resident is injured in one of the four countries by a vehicle that is insured and normally based in another of the four countries, then the Irish resident must claim from the insurer's approved correspondent in the country of accident. If there is none, he may claim against the bureau in the country of accident. If there was no insurance, he must claim against the bureau in the country of accident.

(e) If the Irish resident is injured in one of the four countries by a vehicle that is from one of the 13 countries (ie where a green card is required), then the position will depend upon whether or not there was a green card. If there was a green card, then the Irish resident must claim against the approved correspondent (of the insurer that issued the green card) in the country of accident and, if there is none, against the bureau in the country of accident. If there was no insurance, then he must claim against the bureau in the country of accident.

4 Irish resident injured in a country that is not a party to the green card system

[13.80] Regardless of the origin of the responsible vehicle, an Irish resident who is injured in an accident in a country that is not a party to the green card system must pursue the person who caused the accident directly or perhaps through any insurance that may be in place in that country.

Table 13.3 Irish resident injured abroad by foreign vehicle[242]

Country of accident (not Ireland)	Country vehicle normally based	Country vehicle insured and normally based	Unidentified/ Insured/ Uninsured	Claims Procedure
An EEA State or Specified Territory			Unidentified	MIBI
				Alternatively, bureau of country of accident
An EEA State or Specified Territory		EEA State	Insured	Insurer regardless of where in the EEA the insurer is established
				Alternatively, claims representative in Ireland
				Alternatively, MIBI if no claims representative in Ireland or no reasoned offer of compensation or reasoned reply to claim within three months of the claim
				Alternatively, MIBI if not possible to identify insurance undertaking within two months of accident
				Alternatively, pursue person responsible and / or direct right of action against insurer. The proceedings may be brought in Ireland.[243]
An EEA State or Specified Territory	EEA State		Uninsured	MIBI
				Alternatively, bureau in country of accident
An EEA State or Specified Territory	Specified Territory		Insured	Bureau in country of accident[244]
				Alternatively, MIBI if impossible to identify an insurance undertaking within two months of accident[245]
An EEA State or Specified Territory	Specified Territory		Uninsured	MIBI
				Alternatively, bureau in country of accident
An EEA State or Specified Territory	Andorra / Serbia		Insured	Bureau in country of accident
				Alternatively, the person responsible and / or insurer[246]
EEA State	Andorra / Serbia		Uninsured	MIBI
				Alternatively, bureau in country of accident.
Specified Territory	Andorra / Serbia		Uninsured	Bureau in country of accident

Country of accident (not Ireland)	Country vehicle normally based	Country vehicle insured and normally based	Unidentified/ Insured/ Uninsured	Claims Procedure
An EEA State or Specified Territory	One of 13 countries[247] or other country		Insured	Bureau in country of accident
			Uninsured	
One of 15 countries that are parties to green card system but not in EEA and specified territories[248]		EEA State	Insured	Bureau in country of accident or approved correspondent of insurer in that country
				Alternatively person responsible and / or any insurer
			Uninsured	Bureau in country of accident
One of 17 countries that are parties to green card system but not in EEA[249]	One of 17 countries that are parties to green card system but not in EEA		Insured	Bureau in country of accident unless insurer has an approved correspondent in country of accident[250]
				Alternatively person responsible and / or any insurer
			Uninsured	Bureau in country of accident
Non-green card country	Any origin		Insured	Person responsible or relevant insurance
			Uninsured	Person responsible

---

242. This table must be considered in conjunction with the content of paras **13.64–13.80**.
243. This is subject to what is stated above at para **13.69** and fn **223**.
244. Although insurers of vehicles in the specified territories are likely to have approved correspondents in Ireland. Hence, it might be possible to advance such claims via such an approved correspondent. On a practical level, the MIBI may agree to handle such claims.
245. Alternatively, a claim could be made to the bureau in the country of the accident if the vehicle that caused the accident was normally based in a specified territory other the EEA State or specified territory in which the accident occurred.
246. If the insurer is in the EEA and the accident occurred there, it may be possible to pursue it directly.
247. Albania, Belarus, Bosnia and Herzegovina, Former Yugoslav Republic of Macedonia, Islamic Republic of Iran, Israel, Morocco, Moldova, Montenegro, Russia, Tunisia, Turkey and Ukraine.
248. Being the 13 countries that are parties to the Internal Regulations, Section II (Albania, Belarus, Bosnia and Herzegovina, Former Yugoslav Republic of Macedonia, Islamic Republic of Iran, Israel, Morocco, Moldova, Montenegro, Russia, Tunisia, Turkey and Ukraine) and Andorra and Serbia which are parties to Section III of the Internal Regulations.
249. Being the 13 countries that are parties to the Internal Regulations, Section II (Albania, Belarus, Bosnia and Herzegovina, Former Yugoslav Republic of Macedonia, Islamic Republic of Iran, Israel, Morocco, Moldova, Montenegro, Russia, Tunisia, Turkey and Ukraine) and Andorra, Croatia, Serbia and Switzerland which are parties the Internal Regulations, Sections II and Section III.
250. This is of course unless the accident was caused by a vehicle from the same one of the 17 countries. If the vehicle is from the same country as the country of accident, and is insured, then recourse must be taken to whatever legal avenues are available for recovering from an insured motorist in that country.

K. NON-IRISH RESIDENT INJURED IN IRELAND BY A VEHICLE[251]

[13.81] The position of a vehicle in Ireland causing injury to a person who is not an Irish resident depends upon whether or not the injured person is a resident of an EEA State.

1. Vehicle in Ireland injures resident of an EEA State (other than Ireland) in Ireland

[13.82] The position of a resident of an EEA State other than Ireland (EEA resident), who is injured by a vehicle in Ireland, further depends on a number of factors, including whether or not the vehicle was insured and normally based in Ireland or another EEA State, is uninsured, unidentified or normally based outside the EEA.

[13.83] *Vehicle insured and normally based in Ireland*: if the vehicle that caused the accident in Ireland is insured and normally based in Ireland, the EEA resident can claim compensation from the Irish insurer's claims representative in his EEA State of residence.[252] If there is no claims representative, or a reasoned offer or reply is not made within three months of the claim, the compensation body in the EEA State of residence may be required to deal with the claim.[253] It can then recover any monies paid out from the MIBI.[254] The foregoing is without prejudice to any claim that might be brought by the EEA resident (or his insurer) against the person responsible for the accident (or his insurer and in respect of which there is a direct right of action).[255] Alternatively, the EEA resident can also bring proceedings in Ireland in the normal way.

[13.84] *Vehicle insured and normally based in another EEA State*: if the vehicle that caused the accident in Ireland is insured and normally based in another EEA State, the EEA resident can claim compensation from the insurer's claims representative in his EEA State of residence.[256] If there is no claims representative, or a reasoned offer of compensation is not made within three months of the claim, the compensation body in the EEA State of residence may be required to deal with the claim.[257] It can then recover the money paid out from the compensation body in the EEA State in which the insurance undertaking which issued the policy is established.[258] These rights will only apply if the vehicle that caused the accident is insured and normally based in an EEA

---

251. The most important points of this paragraph are summarised in **Table 13.4** at p 237.
252. Sixth Directive, arts 20–22.
253. Sixth Directive, art 24. Assuming of course that the Member State has implemented the provisions of the Sixth Directive. In the absence of implementation, remedies such as claiming direct effect, indirect effect and/or pursuing the relevant Member State for failing to properly implement the Sixth Directive (see **Ch 12**) may also be considered.
254. Sixth Directive, art 24(2). The MIBI can thereafter recover against the person who caused the accident or the relevant insurance undertaking.
255. Sixth Directive, arts 18 and 21(4). If, however, the EEA resident has taken action directly against insurance undertaking, he cannot present a claim to the compensation body (Sixth Directive, art 24(1)).
256. Sixth Directive, arts 20–22.
257. Sixth Directive, art 24.
258. Sixth Directive, art 24(2).

State other than that of the EEA State of residence.[259] The foregoing is without prejudice to any claim that might be brought by the EEA resident (or his insurer) against the person responsible for the accident (or his insurer and in respect of which there is a direct right of action). Alternatively, the EEA resident can also bring proceedings in Ireland in the normal way.

[13.85] *Vehicle in Ireland is uninsured*: if the vehicle that caused the injury in Ireland is uninsured, the EEA resident may apply for compensation from the compensation body in his EEA State of residence. Thereafter, the compensation body in the EEA State of residence can recover the money it pays out from the MIBI on the basis that the accident occurred in Ireland.[260] Alternatively, the EEA resident can also bring proceedings in Ireland in the normal way.

[13.86] *Vehicle in Ireland is unidentified:* if the vehicle that caused the injury in Ireland is unidentified, the EEA resident may apply for compensation from the compensation body in his EEA State of residence. Thereafter, the compensation body in the EEA State of residence can recover the money it pays out from the MIBI on the basis that the accident occurred in Ireland.[261] Alternatively, the EEA resident can also bring proceedings in Ireland in the normal way.

2. Irish vehicle injures person in Ireland who does not reside in the EEA (non EEA resident)

[13.87] Where an Irish vehicle in Ireland injures a person who is resident outside the EEA, the injured party must claim directly against the insured or through his insurer.[262] If there is no insurance, or the vehicle that caused the accident is either unidentified or uninsured, then, regardless of the origin of the non-EEA resident, he may make a claim against the MIBI under the 2009 Agreement.

---

259.   Sixth Directive, art 20(2).

260.   Sixth Directive, art 25(1)(a).

261.   Sixth Directive, art 25(1)(b). Alternatively, the EEA resident could make a claim directly to the MIBI for injury caused to him by an unidentified vehicle in Ireland.

262.   If, however, the non-EEA resident is injured by a foreign vehicle visiting Ireland, the non-EEA resident may be in a position to claim compensation from the MIBI.

Table 13.4 Non-Irish resident injured in Ireland by a vehicle[263]

COUNTRY OF ACCIDENT IS IRELAND				
Country of residence of injured party	Country vehicle insured and normally based	Country vehicle normally based	Unidentified/ Insured/ Uninsured	Claims Procedure
EEA State other than Ireland	Ireland		Insured	Insurer or claims representative for insurer of Irish vehicle in injured party's EEA State of residence.
				Alternatively, compensation body of EEA State of residence if no claims representative or no reasoned offer or reply to claim within three months.
				Alternatively, pursue person responsible and / or direct right of action against insurer. The non-Irish resident may bring proceedings in Ireland or in the EEA State of which he is resident.[264]
		Ireland	Uninsured or unidentified	Compensation body in EEA State of residence.
				Alternatively, MIBI.
	EEA State other than Ireland (and other than injured party's EEA State of residence)		Insured	Insurer or claims representative for insurer of Irish vehicle in injured party's EEA State of residence.
				Alternatively, compensation body of EEA State of residence if no claims representative or no reasoned offer or reply to claim within three months.
				Alternatively, pursue person responsible and / or direct right of action against insurer. The non-Irish resident may bring proceedings in Ireland or in the EEA State of which he is resident.[265]
		EEA State other than Ireland (and other than injured party's EEA State of residence)	Uninsured	Compensation body in EEA State of residence.
				Alternatively, MIBI.
			Unidentified	Compensation body in EEA State of residence.
				Alternatively, MIBI

COUNTRY OF ACCIDENT IS IRELAND				
Country of residence of injured party	Country vehicle insured and normally based	Country vehicle normally based	Unidentified/ Insured/ Uninsured	Claims Procedure
Non-EEA State	Ireland		Insured	Person responsible or insurer.
		Ireland	Uninsured or unidentified	MIBI

L. NON-IRISH RESIDENT INJURED ABROAD BY A VEHICLE THAT IS NORMALLY BASED IN IRELAND[266]

[13.88] The claims procedure for a person who is injured by an Irish vehicle abroad depends upon whether the accident occurs inside or outside the EEA and, if within the EEA, whether the injury is caused in the injured party's EEA State of residence. The position further depends on whether or not there was insurance in respect of the use of the vehicle.

1. Vehicle insured and normally based in Ireland injures person in another EEA State

[13.89] The position of a non-Irish resident who is injured outside Ireland by a vehicle that is insured and normally based in Ireland depends upon whether or not the non-Irish resident is actually resident in the EEA State in which the accident occurs ('the EEA State of the accident').

[13.90] *Injured party is resident in EEA State of the accident*: if the injured party is resident in the EEA State of the accident in which he was injured by a vehicle that is insured and normally based in Ireland, the Sixth Directive does not apply. The Internal Regulations, however, make provision for such an injured party making a compensation claim directly to the bureau of the EEA State of the accident (also his residence in this example). It is obliged to investigate the circumstances of the accident and must give notice of any such accident to the insurer who issued the insurance policy. If the insurer of the Irish vehicle is identified and it has an approved correspondent in the EEA State of the accident, the bureau of the EEA State of the accident must forward any claim to the insurer's approved correspondent who must handle it. If there is no approved correspondent, the bureau of the EEA State of the accident must advise the insurer that it has received the claim and that it will handle it. Thereafter, the bureau of the EEA State of the accident may accept service of proceedings arising out of the claim and/or settle the claim. Thereafter, the bureau of the EEA State of the accident may claim

---

263. This table must be considered in conjunction with the content of paras **13.81–13.87**.
264. This is subject to what is stated above at para **13.69** and fn **223**.
265. This is subject to what is stated above at para **13.69** and fn **223**.
266. The most important points of this paragraph are summarised in **Table 13.5** at p 242.

reimbursement from the insurer.[267] The foregoing is without prejudice to any claim that might be brought by the EEA resident (or his insurer) against the person responsible for the accident (or his insurer and in respect of which there is a direct right of action).[268]

[13.91] *Injured party is resident in EEA State other than the EEA State of the accident*: if the injured party is resident in an EEA State other than that in which he was injured by a vehicle that is insured and normally based in Ireland, the Sixth Directive applies.[269] In this situation, the EEA resident may claim compensation from the insurer or its representative in the EEA State of his residence.[270] If there is no claims representative, or a reasoned offer or reply is not made within three months of the claim, the compensation body in the EEA State of residence may be required to deal with the claim.[271] It can then recover the compensation paid out from the MIBI.[272] The foregoing is without prejudice to any claim that might be brought by the EEA resident (or his insurer) against the person responsible for the accident (or his insurer and in respect of which there is a direct right of action).[273] In the alternative, there is nothing to prevent an application being made for compensation to the bureau of the EEA State of the accident.

2. Uninsured vehicle normally based in Ireland injures person in another EEA State

[13.92] The position of a non-Irish resident who is injured outside Ireland by a vehicle that is normally based in Ireland, but not insured, depends upon whether or not the non-Irish resident that is injured is actually resident in the EEA State of the accident.

[13.93] *Injured party is resident in EEA State of the accident*: if the injured party is resident in the EEA State of the accident in which he was injured by the uninsured vehicle that is normally based in Ireland, the Sixth Directive does not apply and he must apply to the bureau of the EEA State of the accident.

[13.94] *Injured party is resident in EEA State other than the EEA State of the accident*: If the injured party is not resident in the EEA State of the accident, he may claim compensation from the compensation body in his EEA State of residence. Thereafter,

---

267. Internal Regulations, art 5.
268. Sixth Directive, arts 18 and 21(4). If, however, the EEA resident has taken action directly against the insurance undertaking, he cannot present a claim to the compensation body (Sixth Directive, art 24(1)).
269. See Sixth Directive, arts 20–26.
270. Sixth Directive, arts 20–22.
271. Sixth Directive, art 24, assuming of course that the Member State has implemented the provisions of the Sixth Directive. In the absence of implementation, remedies such as claiming direct effect, indirect effect and/or pursuing the relevant Member State for failing to properly implement the Sixth Directive (see **Ch 12**) may also be considered.
272. Sixth Directive, art 24(2). The MIBI can thereafter recover against the person who caused the accident or his insurance undertaking.
273. Sixth Directive, arts 18 and 21(4). If, however, the EEA resident has taken action directly against the insurance undertaking, he cannot present a claim to the compensation body (Sixth Directive, art 24(1)).

the compensation body in the EEA State of residence can recover any monies it pays out from the MIBI.[274]

3. Vehicle insured and normally based in Ireland injures a resident of another EEA State in a country that is a party to the green card system but is not in the EEA

[13.95] The Sixth Directive provides that, if a vehicle that is insured and normally based in Ireland injures a resident of another EEA State while the vehicle is outside the EEA but in a country that is a party to the green card system, the EEA resident may claim compensation in the EEA State of residence. It provides that he may so claim from the insurer or its claims representative in the EEA State of residence.[275] If there is no claims representative, or if a reasoned offer of compensation or reasoned reply is not issued within three months, the compensation body in the EEA State of residence may be required to deal with the claim.[276] Provision is then made for the recovery of any monies paid out from the MIBI.[277] The foregoing is without prejudice to any claim that might be brought by the EEA resident (or his insurer) against the person responsible for the accident (or his insurer and in respect of which there is a direct right of action).[278] The Internal Regulations also envisage a compensation claim being made to the bureau of the country of accident.[279] Obviously, an injured party in this situation would have to consider the domestic legislation in his EEA State of residence to confirm that the Sixth Directive has been properly implemented there and allows him to apply to the compensation body there.[280]

4. Vehicle normally based in Ireland (but not insured) injures a resident of another EEA State in a country that is a party to the green card system but is not in the EEA

[13.96] As with the previous paragraph, the Sixth Directive envisages that, if a vehicle that is normally based in Ireland injures a resident of another EEA State while the vehicle is outside the EEA but in a country that is a party to the green card system, the

---

274. Sixth Directive, art 25(1)(a).
275. Sixth Directive, art 20(1).
276. Sixth Directive, art 24.
277. Sixth Directive, art 24(2). The MIBI can thereafter recover against the person who caused the accident or his insurance undertaking.
278. Sixth Directive, arts 18 and 21(4). If, however, the EEA resident has taken action directly against the insurance undertaking, he cannot present a claim to the compensation body (Sixth Directive, art 24(1)).
279. This can investigate and handle the claim unless the insurer has a correspondent approved to act on its behalf in the country of accident. If there is such a correspondent, it may take over and deal with the claim. Any monies that the correspondent pays out to the injured party are ultimately paid by the insurer (Internal Regulations, arts 3–5).
280. The 2003 Regulations, however, make no provision for the converse situation, namely one whereby an Irish resident claims from the MIBI in respect of his being injured in a green card country that is outside the EEA by a vehicle that is insured and normally based in an EEA State (other than Ireland) and in the absence of a claims representative or reasoned offer or reply being made.

EEA resident may claim compensation from the compensation body in the EEA State of residence.

5. Vehicle normally based in Ireland injures a person (other than an EEA resident) in a country that is party to the green card system but not in the EEA.

[13.97] If a vehicle that is normally based in Ireland injures a non-EEA resident in a country that is a green card country but not in the EEA, then any compensation claim will be dealt with by the bureau of the country of accident in accordance with Section III of the Internal Regulations (Andorra, Croatia, Switzerland or Serbia) or Section II of the Internal Regulations in respect of the 13 countries that are party to it.[281]

6. Vehicle normally based in Ireland injures a person in a country that is not a party to the green card system

[13.98] If a vehicle normally based in Ireland injures a person in a country that is not a party to the green card system, the injured party (whether or not a resident of the EEA) may have to claim against the responsible party directly or through any relevant insurance that was obtained in respect of the Irish vehicle in advance of entering the relevant country and generally in accordance with the law of the country of accident.

---

281. Albania, Belarus, Bosnia and Herzegovina, Former Yugoslav Republic of Macedonia, Islamic Republic of Iran, Israel, Morocco, Moldova, Montenegro, Russia, Tunisia, Turkey and Ukraine.

Table 13.5 Non-Irish resident injured abroad by a vehicle that is normally based in Ireland[282]

Country vehicle insured and normally based	Country vehicle normally based	Country of Accident (other than Ireland)	Country of victims's residence	Unidentified/ Insured/ Uninsured	Claims Procedure
Ireland		EEA State	EEA State of the accident	Insured	Bureau in injured party's EEA State of accident or insurer's correspondent.
Ireland		EEA State	EEA State other than that in which accident occurred	Insured	Insurer or claims representative for insurer of Irish vehicle in injured party's EEA State of residence.
					Alternatively, compensation body of EEA State of residence if no claims representative or no reasoned offer or reply to claim within three months.
					Alternatively, pursue person responsible and / or direct right of action against insurer.
	Ireland	EEA State	EEA State of the accident	Uninsured	Bureau in injured party's EEA State of residence.
	Ireland	EEA State	EEA State other than that in which accident occurred	Uninsured	Compensation body in EEA State of residence.
Ireland		Green card country that is outside the EEA	EEA State	Insured	Insurer or claims representative for insurer of Irish vehicle in injured party's EEA State of residence.
					Alternatively, compensation body of EEA State of residence if no claims representative or no reasoned offer or reply to claim within three months.
					Alternatively, direct right of action against the liable insurer.
	Ireland	Green card country that is outside the EEA	EEA State	Uninsured	Compensation body in EEA State of residence

Country vehicle insured and normally based	Country vehicle normally based	Country of Accident (other than Ireland)	Country of victims's residence	Unidentified/ Insured/ Uninsured	Claims Procedure
	Ireland	Green card country that is outside the EEA	Country outside EEA	Insured or Uninsured	Bureau of the country of accident.
Ireland		Any country outside green card system	Any country outside EEA and green card system	Insured or Uninsured	Person responsible or claim under any insurance that might apply.

---

282.   This table must be considered in conjunction with the content of paras **13.88–13.98**.

Appendix 1

AGREEMENT DATED 29 JANUARY 2009 BETWEEN THE MINISTER FOR TRANSPORT AND THE MOTOR INSURERS' BUREAU OF IRELAND ('THE 2009 AGREEMENT')

MOTOR INSURERS' BUREAU
OF IRELAND

COMPENSATION OF UNINSURED
ROAD ACCIDENT VICTIMS

Agreement dated 29th January 2009 between the Minister for Transport and the Motor Insurers' Bureau of Ireland (MIBI)

AGREEMENT

Text of an Agreement dated the 29th day of January 2009 between the Minister for Transport and the Motor Insurers' Bureau of Ireland, extending, with effect from dates specified in the Agreement, the scope of the Bureau's liability, with certain exceptions, for compensation for victims of road accidents involving uninsured or stolen vehicles and unidentified or untraced drivers to the full range of compulsory insurance in respect of injury to person and damage to property under the Road Traffic Act, 1961.

MEMORANDUM OF AGREEMENT made the 29th day of January 2009 between the MINISTER FOR TRANSPORT (hereinafter referred to as "the Minister") of the one part and MOTOR INSURERS' BUREAU OF IRELAND (hereinafter referred to as MIBI) whose registered office is at 39 Molesworth St. in the city of Dublin of the other part SUPPLEMENTAL to an Agreement (hereinafter called "the Principal Agreement") made the 10th day of March, 1955 between the Minister for Local Government of the one part and Those Insurers Granting Compulsory Motor Vehicle Insurance in Ireland by or on behalf of whom the said Agreement was signed (thereinafter and hereinafter referred to as "the Insurers") of the other part,

WHEREAS in pursuance of the undertaking given by the Insurers in paragraph 1 of the Principal Agreement a Company stands incorporated under the Companies Act, 1963 with the name of Motor Insurers' Bureau of Ireland (being a party to this Agreement and hereinafter referred to as "MIBI"):

AND WHEREAS a memorandum of Agreement (hereinafter referred to as "the Agreement of 1955") was made between the Minister and MIBI on the 30th day of November, 1955:

AND WHEREAS the Agreement of 1955 was amended by an Addendum thereto made between the Minister and MIBI on the 12th day of March 1962:

245

AND WHEREAS a memorandum of Agreement (hereinafter referred to as "the Agreement of 1964") was made between the Minister and MIBI on the 30th day of December, 1964:

AND WHEREAS the Agreement of 1955 was determined by the Agreement of 1964:

AND WHEREAS the Agreement of 1964 was determined by the Agreement of 1988:

AND WHEREAS the Agreement of 1988 was determined by the Agreement of 2004:

NOW THEREFORE IT IS HEREBY AGREED between the parties hereto as follows:

1. Determination of Agreement of 2004

1.1   The Agreement of 2004 is hereby determined but without prejudice to the continued operation of the said Agreement in respect of accidents occurring before the 30th day of January 2009.

1.2   This Agreement encompasses the Sixth Motor Insurance Directive which codifies the Five existing EU Motor Insurance Directives.

2. Enforcement of Agreement

A person claiming compensation by virtue of this Agreement (hereinafter referred to as "the claimant") must seek to enforce the provisions of this Agreement by:-

2.1   making a claim directly to MIBI for compensation which may be settled with or without admission of liability, or

2.2   making an application to the Injuries Board citing MIBI as a respondent under the terms of the PIAB Act 2003 which, pursuant to s.12(1), provides that unless and until such an application is made, no proceedings in court may be brought in respect of the claim,

2.3   citing MIBI as co-defendants in any proceedings against the owner and or/ user of the vehicle giving rise to the claim except where the owner and user of the vehicle remain unidentified or untraced, or

2.4   citing MIBI as sole defendant where the claimant is seeking a court order for the performance of the Agreement by MIBI provided the claimant has first applied for compensation to MIBI under the clause 2.1 and has either been refused compensation by MIBI or has been offered compensation by MIBI which the claimant considers to be inadequate and/or applied to the Injuries Board as at 2.2 and having received a release from the Injuries Board to proceed with legal action.

3. Conditions precedent to MIBI's liability

The following shall be conditions precedent to MIBI's liability:

3.1   The claimant or the claimant's legal representative shall have given prior notice, by registered post or electronic mail as specified in the website (www.mibi.ie), of intention to seek compensation within the time limits prescribed in the Statutes of Limitation.

3.2   The claimant shall upon demand furnish MIBI with all material information (including all medical reports) reasonably required in relation to the processing of the compensation claim including information relating to the relevant accident, personal injuries or death, medical treatment, funeral expenses, damage to property, and legal, professional or other costs reasonably incurred by or on behalf of the claimant.

3.3   In the event of a claim arising from an accident caused or contributed to by an untraced motorist since MIBI is unable to obtain details of the accident from the driver, the claimant shall also make himself available for interview by the authorized agents of MIBI. The claimant shall have the right to have his solicitor present at such interview. The claimant must answer all reasonable questions relating to the circumstances of the accident. All answers by the claimant shall be used solely for the purpose of progressing the claimant's claim against MIBI and for no other purpose and may not be used by any party other than MIBI or its servants or agents. All such answers may be used in the course of any subsequent court hearing which may arise to determine MIBI's liability to the claimant and may not be used in any circumstances in any criminal proceedings. The claimant shall make himself available for interview within 30 days of completing an application to the Injuries Board so as to enable the Injuries Board and the MIBI to reach a decision on the claim within 90 days.

3.4   The claimant shall co-operate fully with An Garda Síochána or any other authorised person in their investigations of the circumstances giving rise to the claim.

3.5   The claimant shall furnish MIBI with copies of all relevant documentation in relation to the accident and any subsequent legal proceedings relating thereto, including copies of all correspondence, statements and pleadings.

3.6   The claimant shall endeavour to establish if an approved policy of insurance covering the use of any vehicle involved in the accident exists by demanding or arranging for the claimant's legal representative to demand insurance particulars (including policy number if available) of the user or owner of the vehicle in accordance with the provisions of Section 73 of the Road Traffic Act, 1961. Provided the claimant or his legal advisers have made this demand in writing and he has been unsuccessful in so establishing after two months from the date of the accident, notification to MIBI may then take place. If within that two month period the claimant can present to MIBI written confirmation from a member of An Garda Síochána or the owner and/or user of the vehicle giving rise to the claim, then notification may take place immediately.

3.7   The claimant shall furnish MIBI with details of any claim of which the claimant is aware made in respect of the damage to property arising from the accident under any policy of insurance or otherwise and any report made of which the claimant is aware or notification given to any person in respect of that damage or the use of the vehicle giving rise thereto, as MIBI may reasonably require.

3.8 Notice of proceedings or application to the Injuries Board shall be given by the claimant by registered post before commencement of such proceedings or application:-

    3.8.1 to the insurer in any case in which there was in force at the time the accident occurred an approved policy of insurance purporting to cover the use of the vehicle and the existence of which is known to the claimant before the commencement of proceedings or application;

    3.8.2 to MIBI in any other case.

    3.8.3 to the owner and/or user of the vehicle giving rise to the claim except where the owner and user of the vehicle remains unidentified.

3.9 The claimant shall give not less than twenty eight days notice to MIBI before issuing a motion for judgement against any person which may give rise to an obligation on MIBI.

3.10.1 In the event of a dispute relating to compliance with these clauses the claimant can refer same to be decided by an arbitrator agreed by the parties or, in default of agreement, appointed by the President for the time being of the Law Society of Ireland or in the event of his being unwilling or unable to do so by the next senior officer of the Society who is willing and able to make the appointment provided always that these provisions shall apply also to the appointment (whether by agreement or otherwise) of any replacement arbitrator where the original arbitrator (or any replacement) has been removed by Order of the High Court, or refuses to act, or is incapable of acting or dies. Subject to the provisions of (ii) below, the Arbitration Acts 1954–1998 (or any subsequent legislation amending or replacing same and having like effect) shall apply to such arbitrations.

3.10.2 Any party to a determination under clause 3.10.1 may appeal such determination to the Minister whose decision shall be final.

3.10.3 This clause will be reviewed in the light of the Supreme Court judgement in the Case of Elaine Farrell v Whitty, The Minister for the Environment, Ireland and The Attorney General and The Motor Insurers' Bureau of Ireland; Record Number 1997 NO. 10802 P when received.

3.11 All judgements shall be assigned to MIBI or its nominee.

3.12 The Claimant shall give credit to MIBI for any amounts paid to him or due to be paid to him from any source in respect of any liability for injury to person or property arising out of the event which occasioned the claim against MIBI.

3.13 Any accident giving rise to a claim made to the MIBI shall be reported by the claimant to An Garda Síochána within two days of the event or as soon as the claimant reasonably could.

3.14   A claim shall not be deemed to be notified to the MIBI unless all the following information is supplied or good cause is shown as to why it is not available:

3.14.1   name, date of birth, PPS number and address of claimant.

3.14.2   registration of vehicle alleged to be uninsured and where available the type and make of such vehicle.

3.14.3   name of Garda Station to which the accident has been reported.

3.14.4   reason why the claimant considers the vehicle to be uninsured.

3.14.5   what steps have been taken to establish insurance position.

3.14.6   name and address of owner and/or driver of the uninsured vehicle.

3.14.7   date and time of accident.

3.14.8   place of accident.

3.14.9   brief description of accident.

3.14.10   if any other vehicle(s) involved, its registration number, and where available the type and make of such vehicle.

3.14.11   name and address of owner and/or driver, and insurance details.

4. Satisfaction of Judgements by MIBI

4.1.1   Subject to the provisions of clause 4.4, if Judgement/Injuries Board Order to Pay in respect of any liability for injury to person or death or damage to property which is required to be covered by an approved policy of insurance under Section 56 of the Act is obtained against any person or persons in any court established under the Courts (Establishment and Constitution) Act, 1961 (No.38 of 1961) or the Injuries Board established by the PIAB Act, 2003 whether or not such person or persons be in fact covered by an approved policy of insurance and any such judgement is not satisfied in full within 28 days from the date upon which the person or persons in whose favour such judgement is given become entitled to enforce it then MIBI will so far as such judgement relates to injury to person or damage to property and subject to the provisions of this Agreement pay or cause to be paid to the person or persons in whose favour such judgement was given any sum payable or remaining payable thereunder in respect of the aforesaid liability including taxed costs (or such proportion thereof as is attributable to the relevant liability) or satisfy or cause to be satisfied such judgement whatever may be the cause of the failure of the judgement debtor.

4.1.2   Subject to the provisions of clause 4.4, the MIBI shall satisfy, as soon as reasonably possible, any judgement in favour of a person who has issued proceedings pursuant to clause 2.3.

4.2   The claimant shall not be entitled to recover legal costs or expenses for the provision of information to MIBI as may be required by virtue of this Agreement except where MIBI have interviewed the claimant pursuant to Clause 3.3 of this Agreement in which case MIBI will be liable to pay the reasonable costs of such interview.

4.3   The claimant shall not be entitled to legal costs or expenses in excess of what would be payable:

     4.3.1   if the owner or user of the vehicle were covered by an approved policy of insurance.

     4.3.2   by virtue of the fact that MIBI is or may be a defendant or codefendant to any legal proceedings relating to his claim.

4.4   Where a claimant has received or is entitled to receive benefit or compensation from any source, including any insurance policy in respect of damage to property, MIBI shall deduct from the sum payable or remaining payable under clause 4.1 an amount equal to the amount of that benefit or compensation in addition to the deduction of any amounts by virtue of clauses 7.2 and 7.3.

4.5   The MIBI as the Compensation Body shall take action within two months of the date when the injured party presents a claim for compensation to it but shall terminate its action if the insurance undertaking, or its claims representative, subsequently makes a reasoned reply to the claim.

4.6   Where MIBI and the claimant agree an amount in respect of compensation, MIBI shall pay such amount to the claimant within 28 days of such agreement being reached.

5. Exclusion of Certain User and Passenger Claims

5.1   Where at the time of the accident the vehicle had been stolen or taken by violence, the liability of MIBI shall not extend to any judgement or claim in respect of injury, death or damage to property sustained while the person injured or killed or the owner of the property damaged voluntarily entered the vehicle which caused the damage or injury and MIBI can prove that they knew it was stolen or taken by violence.

5.2   Where at the time of the accident the person injured or killed or who sustained damage to property voluntarily entered the vehicle which caused the damage or injury and MIBI can prove that they knew that there was not in force an approved policy of insurance in respect of the use of the vehicle, the liability of MIBI shall not extend to any judgement or claim either in respect of injury or death of such person while the person injured or killed was by his consent in or on such vehicle or in respect of damage to property while the owner of the property was by his consent in or on the vehicle.

6. Unidentified or Untraced Vehicle, Owner or User

The liability of MIBI shall, subject to the exclusions of Clause 5 above, extend to the payment of compensation for the personal injury or death of any person caused by the negligent use of a vehicle in a public place, where the owner or user of the vehicle remains unidentified or untraced.

7. Damage to Property

7.1   The liability of MIBI for damage to property shall not extend to damage caused by an unidentified vehicle unless compensation for substantial personal injuries involving an inpatient hospital stay for five days or more has also been paid in respect of the event causing the damage subject to an excess of €500.

7.2   The liability of MIBI for damage to property shall not exceed the minimum property damage cover required by Section 56(2)(a) of the Road Traffic Act, 1961 applying at the time of the event giving rise to the claim.

7.3   The liability of MIBI shall not extend to the first €220 of damage to property suffered by any one property owner due to the negligent use of a vehicle stolen or obtained by violence or threats of violence or used or taken possession of without the consent of the owner of the vehicle or other lawful authority.

7.4   In cases where the claimant and MIBI agree to accept an Injuries Board award, and if that award includes an allowance for property damage, the acceptance of that award by both parties is subject always to the provisions of Clause 4.4 and this Clause of the Agreement.

8. Period of Agreement

This Agreement shall be determinable by the Minister at any time or by MIBI on two years' notice, without prejudice to the continued operation of the Agreement in respect of accidents occurring before the date of termination.

9. Recoveries

Nothing in this Agreement shall prevent any vehicle insurer from providing by conditions in its contracts of insurance or by collateral agreements that all sums paid by it on behalf of MIBI or by MIBI by virtue of the Principal Agreement or of this Agreement in or towards the discharge of the liability of its policyholders shall be recoverable by it or by MIBI from the policyholder or from any other person.

10. Offers in Satisfaction

When notice of proceedings has been given under Clause 3 it shall be competent for MIBI not later than ten days before trial to offer to the claimant in full satisfaction of the obligation of MIBI such sum as it considers sufficient in respect of damages together with the equivalent of the taxed costs to date and if in that action the claimant is awarded in respect of damages a sum (exclusive of any amounts for which MIBI would not be liable under this Agreement) which is not more than the sum offered under this Clause (exclusive of the sum for such taxed costs) then in satisfaction of this Agreement MIBI shall not be required to pay more than the total of such damages awarded less any amounts for which it would not be liable under this Agreement and the sum offered in respect of costs and shall be entitled to set off any costs incurred by them after the date of the offer. MIBI reserves the right to vary the amount offered in satisfaction.

11. State Vehicles and Exempted Persons

11.1   MIBI's acceptance of liability in respect of vehicles the use of which is required to be covered by an approved policy of insurance shall extend to vehicles owned by or in possession of the State or of an "exempted person" as defined in Section 60 of the Act only so long as there is in force an approved policy of insurance purporting to cover the use of the vehicle.

11.2   For the purpose of this Clause a vehicle which has been unlawfully removed from the possession of the State or from an "exempted person" shall be taken to continue in that possession whilst it is so removed.

12. Information Centre and Central Body

The MIBI shall act as both the Information Centre and the Central Body in accordance with the requirements of EU Motor Insurance Directives 2000/26/EC and 2005/14/EC.

13. Domestic Agreement

The Agreement entered into between MIBI and the insurers of even date with the Agreement of 1955 and referred to in the Agreement of 1955 as "the Domestic Agreement" or any subsequent or amended agreement made in renewal or replacement of the said Domestic Agreement or incorporated into the Memorandum and Articles of Association shall not discharge MIBI from its liabilities or obligations under this Agreement.

14. Operation

This Agreement shall come into operation on the XXst day of January 2009 in respect of claims arising out of the use of a vehicle in a public place on or after that date.

15. Definitions

In this Agreement, "the Act" means the Road Traffic Act, 1961 (No.24 of 1961).

"Injury to person" does not include any injury by way of loss of services of the person injured.

The "Injuries Board" means the Personal Injuries Assessment Board set up under the Personal Injuries Assessment Board Act, 2003.

IN WITNESS whereof the parties hereto have hereunto set their hands and affixed their seals on the day and year first herein written.

GIVEN under the Official Seal of the Minister for Transport in the presence of:

L.S.

_____

Noel Dempsey

Minister for Transport

_____

Andrew Cullen

_____

Mary Lally

Civil Servants, Department of Transport

Present when the Common Seal of the Motor Insurers' Bureau of Ireland was affixed hereto:

L.S.

_____

John Sheehy

Chairperson, MIBI

_____

John Casey

Chief Executive, MIBI

_____

Dáithí Ó Maolchoille

Company Secretary, MIBI

Appendix 2

AGREEMENT DATED 31 MARCH 2004 BETWEEN THE MINISTER FOR TRANSPORT AND THE MOTOR INSURERS' BUREAU OF IRELAND ('THE 2004 AGREEMENT')

MIBI AGREEMENT 2004

Text of an Agreement dated the 31st day of March 2004 between the Minister for Transport and the Motor Insurers' Bureau of Ireland, extending, with effect from dates specified in the Agreement, the scope of the Bureau's liability, with certain exceptions, for compensation for victims of road accidents involving uninsured or stolen vehicles and unidentified or untraced drivers to the full range of compulsory insurance in respect of injury to person and damage to property under the Road Traffic Act, 1961.

MEMORANDUM OF AGREEMENT made the 31st day of March 2004 between the MINISTER FOR TRANSPORT (hereinafter referred to as "the Minister") of the one part and MOTOR INSURERS' BUREAU OF IRELAND (hereinafter referred to as MIBI) whose registered office is at 39 Molesworth St. in the city of Dublin of the other part SUPPLEMENTAL to an Agreement (hereinafter called "the Principal Agreement") made the 10th day of March, 1955 between the Minister for Local Government of the one part and Those Insurers Granting Compulsory Motor Vehicle Insurance in Ireland by or on behalf of whom the said Agreement was signed (thereinafter and hereinafter referred to as "the Insurers") of the other part,

WHEREAS in pursuance of the undertaking given by the Insurers in paragraph 1 of the Principal Agreement a Company stands incorporated under the Companies Act, 1963 with the name of Motor Insurers' Bureau of Ireland (being a party to this Agreement and hereinafter referred to as "MIBI"):

AND WHEREAS a memorandum of Agreement (hereinafter referred to as "the Agreement of 1955") was made between the Minister and MIBI on the 30th day of November, 1955:

AND WHEREAS the Agreement of 1955 was amended by an Addendum thereto made between the Minister and MIBI on the 12th day of March 1962:

AND WHEREAS a memorandum of Agreement (hereinafter referred to as "the Agreement of 1964") was made between the Minister and MIBI on the 30th day of December, 1964:

AND WHEREAS the Agreement of 1955 was determined by the Agreement of 1964:

AND WHEREAS the Agreement of 1964 was determined by the Agreement of 1988:

255

NOW THEREFORE IT IS HEREBY AGREED between the parties hereto as follows:

1. Determination of Agreement of 1988

The Agreement of 1988 is hereby determined but without prejudice to the continued operation of the said Agreement in respect of accidents occurring before the 1st day of May 2004.

2. Enforcement of Agreement

A person claiming compensation by virtue of this Agreement (hereinafter referred to as "the claimant") must seek to enforce the provisions of this Agreement by:-

2.1 making a claim to MIBI for compensation which may be settled with or without admission of liability, or

2.2 citing MIBI as co-defendants in any proceedings against the owner and/or user of the vehicle giving rise to the claim except where the owner and user of the vehicle remain unidentified or untraced, or

2.3 citing MIBI as sole defendant where the claimant is seeking a court order for the performance of the Agreement by MIBI provided the claimant has first applied for compensation to MIBI under the clause 2.1 and has either been refused compensation by MIBI or has been offered compensation by MIBI which the claimant considers to be inadequate.

3. Conditions precedent to MIBI's liability

The following shall be conditions precedent to MIBI's liability:

3.1 The claimant or the claimant's legal representative shall have given prior notice, by registered post or electronic mail as specified in the website (www.mibi.ie) of intention to seek compensation.

   (a) in respect of personal injuries or death within the time limits prescribed in the Statutes of Limitation.

   (b) in respect of damage to property not later than one year from the date of the accident giving rise to the damage to property.

3.2 The claimant shall upon demand furnish MIBI with all material information (including all medical reports) reasonably required in relation to the processing of the compensation claim including information relating to the relevant accident, personal injuries or death, medical treatment, funeral expenses, damage to property, and legal, professional or other costs reasonably incurred by or on behalf of the claimant.

3.3 In the event of a claim arising from an accident caused or contributed to by an untraced motorist since MIBI is unable to obtain details of the accident from the driver, the claimant shall also make himself available for interview by the authorized agents of MIBI. The claimant shall have the right to have his solicitor present at such interview. The claimant must answer all reasonable questions relating to the circumstances of the accident. All answers by the claimant shall be used solely for the purpose of progressing the claimant's claim against MIBI and for no other purpose and may not be used by any party other than MIBI or its servants or agents. All such answers may be used in the course of any subsequent court hearing which may arise to determine MIBI's liability to the claimant and may not be used in any circumstances in any criminal proceedings.

3.4 The claimant shall co-operate fully with An Garda Siochana or any other authorized person in their investigations of the circumstances giving rise to the claim.

3.5 The claimant shall furnish MIBI with copies of all relevant documentation in relation to the accident and any subsequent legal proceedings relating thereto, including copies of all correspondence, statements and pleadings.

3.6 The claimant shall endeavour to establish if an approved policy of insurance covering the use of any vehicle involved in the accident exists by demanding or arranging for the claimant's legal representative to demand insurance particulars (including policy number if available) of the user or owner of the vehicle in accordance with the provisions of Section 73 of the Act. Provided the claimant or his legal advisers have made this demand in writing and he has been unsuccessful in so establishing after three months from the date of the accident, notification to MIBI may then take place. If within that three month period the claimant can present to MIBI written confirmation from a member of An Garda Siochana or the owner and/or user of the vehicle giving rise to the claim, then notification may take place immediately.

3.7 The claimant shall furnish MIBI with details of any claim of which the claimant is aware made in respect of the damage to property arising from the accident under any policy of insurance or otherwise and any report made of which the claimant is aware or notification given to any person in respect of that damage or the use of the vehicle giving rise thereto, as MIBI may reasonably require.

3.8 Notice of proceedings shall be given by the claimant by registered post before commencement of such proceedings:-

(a) to the insurer in any case in which there was in force at the time the accident occurred an approved policy of insurance purporting to cover the use of the vehicle and the existence of which is known to the claimant before the commencement of proceedings;

(b) to MIBI in any other case.

3.9 The claimant shall give not less than twenty eight days notice to MIBI before obtaining Judgement against any person which may give rise to an obligation on MIBI.

3.10 If so required by MIBI and subject to full indemnity from MIBI as to reasonable costs, the Claimant shall take all reasonable steps against any person against whom the Claimant may have a remedy in respect of or arising out of the injury or death or damage to property provided that any dispute as to the reasonableness of a requirement by MIBI that any particular step should be taken to obtain judgement against any such person shall be referred to the Minister whose decision shall be final.

3.11   All judgements shall be assigned to MIBI or its nominee.

3.12   The Claimant shall give credit to MIBI for any amounts paid to him or due to be paid to him from any source in respect of any liability for injury to person or property arising out of the event which occasioned the claim against MIBI.

3.13   Any accident giving rise to a claim made to the MIBI shall be reported by the claimant to An Garda Siochana within two days of the event or as soon as the claimant reasonably could.

3.14   A claim shall not be deemed to be notified to the MIBI unless all the following information is supplied or good cause is shown as to why it is not available:

(a)   name, PPS number and address of claimant.

(b)   registration of vehicle alleged to be uninsured and where available the type and make of such vehicle.

(c)   name of Garda Station to which the accident has been reported.

(d)   reason why the claimant considers the vehicle to be uninsured.

(e)   what steps have been taken to establish insurance position.

(f)   name and address of owner and/or driver of the uninsured vehicle.

(g)   date and time of accident.

(h)   place of accident.

(i)   brief description of accident.

(j)   if any other vehicles involved, its registration number, and where available the type and make of such vehicle.

(k)   name and address of owner and/or driver, and insurance details.

4. Satisfaction of Judgements by MIBI

4.1   Subject to the provisions of clause 4.4, if Judgement in respect of any liability for injury to person or death or damage to property which is required to be covered by an approved policy of insurance under Section 56 of the Act is obtained against any person or persons in any court established under the Courts (Establishment and Constitution) Act, 1961 (No.38 of 1961) whether or not such person or persons be in fact covered by an approved policy of insurance and any such judgement is not satisfied in full within 28 days from the date upon which the person or persons in whose favour such judgement is given become entitled to enforce it then MIBI will so far as such judgement relates to injury to person or damage to property and subject to the provisions of this Agreement pay or cause to be paid to the person or persons in whose favour such judgement was given any sum payable or remaining payable thereunder in respect of the aforesaid liability including taxed costs (or such proportion thereof as is attributable to the relevant liability) or satisfy or cause to be satisfied such judgement whatever may be the cause of the failure of the judgement debtor.

4.2   The claimant shall not be entitled to recover legal costs or expenses for the provision of information to MIBI as may be required by virtue of this Agreement except where MIBI have interviewed the claimant pursuant to Clause 3.3 of this Agreement in which case MIBI will be liable to pay the reasonable costs of such interview.

4.3   The claimant shall not be entitled to legal costs or expenses in excess of what would be payable.

(a)   if the owner or user of the vehicle were covered by an approved policy of insurance.

(b)   by virtue of the fact that MIBI is or may be a defendant or co-defendant to any legal proceedings relating to his claim.

4.4   Where a claimant has received or is entitled to receive benefit or compensation from any source, including any insurance policy in respect of damage to property, MIBI may deduct from the sum payable or remaining payable under clause 4.1 an amount equal to the amount of that benefit or compensation in addition to the deduction of any amounts by virtue of clauses 7.2 and 7.3.

4.5   Where a claimant applies to the MIBI for compensation and no judgement has been obtained or is obtainable, MIBI shall, as soon as is reasonably practicable, give a decision on the application and shall give reasons for the decision.

4.6   Where MIBI and the claimant agree an amount in respect of compensation, MIBI shall pay such amount to the claimant within 28 days of such agreement being reached.

5. Exclusion of Certain User and Passenger Claims

5.1   Where at the time of an accident, the vehicle had been stolen or obtained by violence or threats of violence or used or taken possession of without the consent of the owner of the vehicle or other lawful authority, the liability of MIBI shall not extend to any judgement or claim in respect of injury, death or damage to property sustained while the person injured or killed or the owner of the property damaged was the person or one of the persons who stole or obtained by violence or threats of violence the vehicle or who was in or on such vehicle in collusion with such person or persons, or knew it was stolen, taken by violence or threats of violence or without the consent of the owner.

5.2   Where at the time of the accident the person injured or killed or who sustained damage to property knew, or ought reasonably to have known, that there was not in force an approved policy of insurance in respect of the use of the vehicle, the liability of MIBI shall not extend to any judgement or claim either in respect of injury or death of such person while the person injured or killed was by his consent in or on such vehicle or in respect of damage to property while the owner of the property was by his consent in or on the vehicle or the property was in or on the vehicle with the consent of the owner of the property.

5.3   Where a vehicle, the use of which is not covered by an approved policy of insurance, collides with another vehicle and the use of that other vehicle is also not covered by an approved policy of insurance, the liability of MIBI shall not extend to any judgement or claim in respect of injury, death or damage to the property of the user of either vehicle.

6. Unidentified or Untraced Vehicle, Owner or User

The liability of MIBI shall, subject to the exclusions of Clause 5 above, extend to the payment of compensation for the personal injury or death of any person caused by the negligent use of a vehicle in a public place, where the owner or user of the vehicle remains unidentified or untraced.

7. Damage to Property

7.1   The liability of MIBI for damage to property shall not extend to damage caused by an unidentified vehicle.

7.2   The liability of MIBI for damage to property shall not exceed the minimum property damage cover required by Section 56(2)(a) of the Act applying at the time of the event giving rise to the claim.

7.3   The liability of MIBI shall not extend to:

(a)   the first €220 of damage to property suffered by any one property owner due to the negligent use of a vehicle stolen or obtained by violence or threats of violence or used or taken possession of without the consent of the owner of the vehicle or other lawful authority;

(b)   subject to the provisions of the foregoing paragraph, the first €440 of damage to property suffered by any one property owner due to the negligent use of a vehicle, the use of which is not covered by an approved policy of insurance.

8. Period of Agreement

This Agreement shall be determinable by the Minister at any time or by MIBI on two years' notice, without prejudice to the continued operation of the Agreement in respect of accidents occurring before the date of termination.

9. Recoveries

Nothing in this Agreement shall prevent any vehicle insurer from providing by conditions in its contracts of insurance or by collateral agreements that all sums paid by it on behalf of MIBI or by MIBI by virtue of the Principal Agreement or of this Agreement in or towards the discharge of the liability of its policyholders shall be recoverable by it or by MIBI from the policyholder or from any other person.

10. Offers in Satisfaction

When notice of proceedings has been given under Clause 3 it shall be competent for MIBI not later than ten days before trial to offer to the claimant in full satisfaction of the obligation of MIBI such sum as it considers sufficient in respect of damages together with the equivalent of the taxed costs to date and if in that action the claimant is awarded in respect of damages a sum (exclusive of any amounts for which MIBI would not be liable under this Agreement) which is not more than the sum offered under this Clause (exclusive of the sum for such taxed costs) then in satisfaction of this Agreement MIBI shall not be required to pay more than the total of such damages awarded less any amounts for which it would not be liable under this Agreement and the sum offered in respect of costs and shall be entitled to set off any costs incurred by them after the date of the offer. MIBI reserves the right to vary the amount offered in satisfaction.

11. State Vehicles and Exempted Persons

11.1 MIBI's acceptance of liability in respect of vehicles the use of which is required to be covered by an approved policy of insurance shall extend to vehicles owned by or in possession of the State or of an "exempted person" as defined in Section 60 of the Act only so long as there is in force an approved policy of insurance purporting to cover the use of the vehicle.

11.2 For the purpose of this Clause a vehicle which has been unlawfully removed from the possession of the State or from an "exempted person" shall be taken to continue in that possession whilst it is so removed.

12. Domestic Agreement

The Agreement entered into between MIBI and the insurers of even date with the Agreement of 1955 and referred to in the Agreement of 1955 as "the Domestic Agreement" or any subsequent or amended agreement made in renewal or replacement of the said Domestic Agreement shall not discharge MIBI from its liabilities or obligations under this Agreement.

13. Fund of Last Resort

Subject to the generality of the foregoing, the Guarantee Fund is a Fund of Last Resort.

14. Operation

This Agreement shall come into operation on the 1st day of May 2004 in respect of claims arising out of the use of a vehicle in a public place on or after that date.

15. Definitions

In this Agreement, "the Act" means the Road Traffic Act, 1961 (No.24 of 1961): "Injury to person" does not include any injury by way of loss of services of the person injured.

IN WITNESS whereof the parties hereto have hereunto set their hands and affixed their seals on the day and year first herein written.

GIVEN under the Official Seal of the Minister for Transport in the presence of:

John Murphy

Des Coppins

Civil Servants,

Custom House, Dublin

Seámus Brennan

Minister for Transport

Present when the Common Seal of the Motor Insurers' Bureau of Ireland was affixed hereto:-

Philip Bradley

Chairperson, MIBI

John Casey

Chief Executive, MIBI

Robert Thompson

Company Secretary, MIBI

Appendix 3

DIRECTIVE 2009/103/EC OF THE EUROPEAN PARLIAMENT AND OF THE COUNCIL OF 16 SEPTEMBER 2009 ('THE SIXTH DIRECTIVE')

OJ L 263,7.10.2009, p 11

DIRECTIVE 2009/103/EC

of the European Parliament and of the Council

of 16 September 2009

relating to insurance against civil liability in respect of the use of motor vehicles, and the enforcement of the obligation to insure against such liability

(codified version)

(Text with EEA relevance)

THE EUROPEAN PARLIAMENT AND THE COUNCIL OF THE EUROPEAN UNION,

Having regard to the Treaty establishing the European Community, and in particular Article 95(1) thereof,

Having regard to the proposal from the Commission,

Having regard to the opinion of the European Economic and Social Committee[1],

Acting in accordance with the procedure laid down in Article 251 of the Treaty[2],

Whereas:

(1) Council Directive 72/166/EEC of 24 April 1972 on the approximation of the laws of Member States relating to insurance against civil liability in respect of the use of motor vehicles, and to the enforcement of the obligation to insure against such liability[3], Second Council Directive 84/5/EEC of 30 December 1983 on the approximation of the laws of the Member States relating to insurance against civil liability in respect of the use of motor vehicles[4], Third Council Directive 90/232/EEC of 14 May 1990 on the approximation of the laws of the Member States relating to insurance against civil liability in respect of the use of motor vehicles[5] and Directive 2000/26/EC of the European Parliament and of the Council of 16 May 2000 on the approximation of the laws of the Member States relating to insurance against civil liability in respect of the

---

1. OJ C 224, 30.8.2008, p 39.
2. Opinion of the European Parliament of 21 October 2008 (not yet published in the Official Journal) and Council Decision of 13 July 2009.
3. OJ L 103, 2.5.1972, p 1.
4. OJ L 8, 11.1.1984, p 17.
5. OJ L 129, 19.5.1990, p 33.

use of motor vehicles (Fourth motor insurance Directive)[6] have been substantially amended several times[7]. In the interests of clarity and rationality those four Directives should be codified, as well as Directive 2005/14/EC of the European Parliament and of the Council of 11 May 2005 amending Council Directives 72/166/EEC, 84/5/EEC, 88/357/EEC and 90/232/EEC and Directive 2000/26/EC of the European Parliament and of the Council relating to insurance against civil liability in respect of the use of motor vehicles[8].

(2) Insurance against civil liability in respect of the use of motor vehicles (motor insurance) is of special importance for European citizens, whether they are policyholders or victims of an accident. It is also a major concern for insurance undertakings as it constitutes an important part of non-life insurance business in the Community. Motor insurance also has an impact on the free movement of persons and vehicles. It should therefore be a key objective of Community action in the field of financial services to reinforce and consolidate the internal market in motor insurance.

(3) Each Member State must take all appropriate measures to ensure that civil liability in respect of the use of vehicles normally based in its territory is covered by insurance. The extent of the liability covered and the terms and conditions of the insurance cover are to be determined on the basis of those measures.

(4) In order to exclude any possible misinterpretation of this Directive and to make it easier to obtain insurance cover for vehicles bearing temporary plates, the definition of the territory in which the vehicle is normally based should refer to the territory of the State of which the vehicle bears a registration plate, irrespective of whether such a plate is permanent or temporary.

(5) While respecting the general criterion of the registration plate to determine the territory in which the vehicle is normally based, a special rule should be laid down for accidents caused by vehicles without a registration plate or bearing a registration plate which does not correspond or no longer corresponds to the vehicle. In this case and for the sole purpose of settling the claim, the territory in which the vehicle is normally based should be deemed to be the territory in which the accident took place.

(6) A prohibition of systematic checks on motor insurance should apply to vehicles normally based in the territory of another Member State as well as to vehicles normally based in the territory of a third country but entering from the territory of another Member State. Only non-systematic checks which are not discriminatory and are carried out as part of a control not aimed exclusively at insurance verification may be permitted.

(7) The abolition of checks on green cards for vehicles normally based in a Member State which enter the territory of another Member State can be effected by means of an agreement between the national insurers' bureaux, whereby each national bureau would guarantee compensation in accordance with the provisions of national law in respect of any loss or injury giving entitlement to compensation caused in its territory by one of those vehicles, whether or not insured.

---

6. OJ L 181, 20.7.2000, p 65.
7. See Annex I, Part A.
8. OJ L 149, 11.6.2005, p 14.

(8) Such a guarantee agreement presupposes that all Community motor vehicles travelling in Community territory are covered by insurance. The national law of each Member State should, therefore, provide for the compulsory insurance of vehicles against civil liability, such insurance to be valid throughout Community territory.

(9) The system provided for in this Directive could be extended to vehicles normally based in the territory of any third country in respect of which the national bureaux of the Member States have concluded a similar agreement.

(10) Each Member State should be able to act in derogation from the general obligation to take out compulsory insurance in respect of vehicles belonging to certain natural or legal persons, public or private. For accidents caused by such vehicles, the Member State so derogating should designate an authority or body to compensate for the damage to victims of accidents caused in another Member State. Steps should be taken to ensure that due compensation is paid not only to the victims of accidents caused by these vehicles abroad but also the victims of accidents occurring in the Member State in which the vehicle is normally based, whether or not they are resident in its territory. Furthermore, Member States should ensure that the list of persons exempt from compulsory insurance and the authorities or bodies responsible for compensation of victims of accidents caused by such vehicles is communicated to the Commission for publication.

(11) Each Member State should be able to act in derogation from the general obligation to take out compulsory insurance in respect of certain types of vehicles or certain vehicles having a special plate. In that case, the other Member States are allowed to require, at the entry into their territory, a valid green card or a frontier insurance contract, in order to ensure the provision of compensation to victims of any accident which may be caused by those vehicles in their territories. However, since the elimination of border controls within the Community means that it is not possible to ensure that vehicles crossing frontiers are covered by insurance, compensation for victims of accidents caused abroad cannot be guaranteed. Steps should also be taken to ensure that due compensation is awarded to the victims of accidents caused by those vehicles not only abroad but also in the Member State in which the vehicle is normally based. For this purpose, Member States should treat the victims of accidents caused by those vehicles in the same way as victims of accidents caused by uninsured vehicles. Indeed, compensation to victims of accidents caused by uninsured vehicles should be paid by the compensation body of the Member State in which the accident took place. Where payments are made to victims of accidents caused by vehicles subject to the derogation, the compensation body should have a claim against the body of the Member State in which the vehicle is normally based. After a certain period to allow for the implementation and application of this possibility of derogation, and taking into account the lessons drawn therefrom, the Commission should, when appropriate, submit proposals for its replacement or repeal.

(12) Member States' obligations to guarantee insurance cover at least in respect of certain minimum amounts constitute an important element in ensuring the protection of victims. The minimum amount of cover for personal injury should be calculated so as to compensate fully and fairly all victims who have suffered very serious injuries, while taking into account the low frequency of accidents involving several victims and the

small number of accidents in which several victims suffer very serious injuries in the course of one and the same event. A minimum amount of cover per victim or per claim should be provided for. With a view to facilitating the introduction of these minimum amounts, a transitional period should be established. However, a period shorter than the transitional period should be provided for, in which Member States should increase these amounts to at least half the levels provided for.

(13) In order to ensure that the minimum amount of cover is not eroded over time, a periodic review clause should be provided using as a benchmark the European Index of Consumer Prices (EICP) published by Eurostat, as provided for in Council Regulation (EC) No 2494/95 of 23 October 1995 concerning harmonised indices of consumer prices[1]. Procedural rules governing such a review should also be laid down.

(14) It is necessary to make provision for a body to guarantee that the victim will not remain without compensation where the vehicle which caused the accident is uninsured or unidentified. It is important to provide that the victim of such an accident should be able to apply directly to that body as a first point of contact. However, Member States should be given the possibility of applying certain limited exclusions as regards the payment of compensation by that body and of providing that compensation for damage to property caused by an unidentified vehicle may be limited or excluded in view of the danger of fraud.

(15) It is in the interest of victims that the effects of certain exclusion clauses be limited to the relationship between the insurer and the person responsible for the accident. However, in the case of vehicles stolen or obtained by violence, Member States may specify that compensation will be payable by the abovementioned body.

(16) In order to alleviate the financial burden on that body, Member States may make provision for the application of certain excesses where the body provides compensation for damage to property caused by uninsured vehicles or, as the case may be, vehicles stolen or obtained by violence.

(17) The option of limiting or excluding legitimate compensation for victims on the basis that the vehicle is unidentified should not apply where the body has paid compensation for significant personal injuries to any victim of the accident in which damage to property was caused. Member States may provide for an excess, up to the limit prescribed in this Directive, to be borne by the victim of the damage to property. The conditions in which personal injuries are to be considered significant should be determined by the national legislation or administrative provisions of the Member State where the accident takes place. In establishing those conditions, the Member State may take into account, inter alia, whether the injury has required hospital care.

(18) In the case of an accident caused by an uninsured vehicle, the body which compensates victims of accidents caused by uninsured or unidentified vehicles is better placed than the victim to bring an action against the party liable. Therefore, it should be provided that that body cannot require that victim, if he is to be compensated, to establish that the party liable is unable or refuses to pay.

---

1.   OJ L 257, 27.10.1995, p 1

(19) In the event of a dispute between the body referred to above and a civil liability insurer as to which of them should compensate the victim of an accident, Member States, to avoid any delay in the payment of compensation to the victim, should ensure that one of those parties is designated as being responsible in the first instance for paying compensation pending resolution of the dispute.

(20) Motor vehicle accident victims should be guaranteed comparable treatment irrespective of where in the Community accidents occur.

(21) The members of the family of the policyholder, driver or any other person liable should be afforded protection comparable to that of other third parties, in any event in respect of their personal injuries.

(22) Personal injuries and damage to property suffered by pedestrians, cyclists and other non-motorised road users, who are usually the weakest party in an accident, should be covered by the compulsory insurance of the vehicle involved in the accident where they are entitled to compensation under national civil law. This provision does not prejudge the issue of civil liability, or the level of awards of damages in respect of a given accident, under national legislation.

(23) The inclusion within the insurance cover of any passenger in the vehicle is a major achievement of the existing legislation. This objective would be placed in jeopardy if national legislation or any contractual clause contained in an insurance policy excluded passengers from insurance cover because they knew or should have known that the driver of the vehicle was under the influence of alcohol or of any other intoxicating agent at the time of the accident. The passenger is not usually in a position to assess properly the level of intoxication of the driver. The objective of discouraging persons from driving while under the influence of intoxicating agents is not achieved by reducing the insurance cover for passengers who are victims of motor vehicle accidents. Cover of such passengers under the vehicle's compulsory motor insurance does not prejudge any liability they might incur pursuant to the applicable national legislation, nor the level of any award of damages in a specific accident.

(24) All compulsory motor insurance policies should cover the entire territory of the Community.

(25) Some insurance undertakings insert into insurance policies clauses to the effect that the contract will be cancelled if the vehicle remains outside the Member State of registration for longer than a specified period. This practice is in conflict with the principle set out in this Directive, according to which compulsory motor insurance should cover, on the basis of a single premium, the entire territory of the Community. It should therefore be specified that the insurance cover is to remain valid during the whole term of the contract, irrespective of whether the vehicle remains in another Member State for a particular period, without prejudice to the obligations under Member States' national legislation with respect to the registration of vehicles.

(26) In the interests of the party insured, every insurance policy should guarantee for a single premium, in each Member State, the cover required by its law or the cover required by the law of the Member State where the vehicle is normally based, when that cover is higher.

(27) Steps should be taken to make it easier to obtain insurance cover for vehicles imported from one Member State into another, even though the vehicle is not yet registered in the Member State of destination. A temporary derogation from the general rule determining the Member State where the risk is situated should be made available. For a period of 30 days from the date when the vehicle is delivered, made available or dispatched to the purchaser, the Member State of destination should be considered to be the Member State where the risk is situated.

(28) Any person wishing to take out a new motor insurance contract with another insurer should be in a position to justify his accident and claims record under the old contract. The policyholder should have the right to request at any time a statement concerning the claims, or the absence of claims, involving the vehicle or vehicles covered by the insurance contract at least during the preceding five years of the contractual relationship. The insurance undertaking, or any body which may have been appointed by a Member State to provide compulsory insurance or to supply such statements, should provide this statement to the policyholder within 15 days of the request.

(29) In order to ensure due protection for victims of motor vehicle accidents, Member States should not permit insurance undertakings to rely on excesses against an injured party.

(30) The right to invoke the insurance contract and to claim against the insurance undertaking directly is of great importance for the protection of victims of motor vehicle accidents. In order to facilitate an efficient and speedy settlement of claims and to avoid as far as possible costly legal proceedings, a right of direct action against the insurance undertaking covering the person responsible against civil liability should be provided for victims of any motor vehicle accident.

(31) In order to obtain an adequate level of protection for victims of motor vehicle accidents, a 'reasoned offer' procedure should be extended to any kind of motor vehicle accident. This same procedure should also apply *mutatis mutandis* where the accident is settled by the system of national insurers' bureaux.

(32) Under Article 11(2) read in conjunction with Article 9(1)(b) of Council Regulation (EC) No 44/2001 of 22 December 2000 on jurisdiction and the recognition and enforcement of judgments in civil and commercial matters[1], injured parties may bring legal proceedings against the civil liability insurance provider in the Member State in which they are domiciled.

(33) The green card bureau system ensures the ready settlement of claims in the injured party's country of residence even where the other party comes from a different European country.

(34) Parties injured as a result of a motor vehicle accident falling within the scope of this Directive and occurring in a State other than that of their residence should be entitled to claim in their Member State of residence against a claims representative appointed there by the insurance undertaking of the responsible party. This solution would enable

---

1.   OJ L 12, 16.1.2001, p 1.

damage suffered by injured parties outside their Member State of residence to be dealt with under procedures which are familiar to them.

(35) This system of having claims representatives in the injured party's Member State of residence affects neither the substantive law to be applied in each individual case nor the matter of jurisdiction.

(36) The existence of a direct right of action for the injured party against the insurance undertaking is a logical supplement to the appointment of such representatives and moreover improves the legal position of parties injured as a result of motor vehicle accidents occurring outside their Member State of residence.

(37) It should be provided that the Member State where the insurance undertaking is authorised should require that undertaking to appoint claims representatives resident or established in the other Member States to collect all necessary information in relation to claims resulting from such accidents and to take appropriate action to settle the claims on behalf and for the account of the insurance undertaking, including the payment of compensation. Claims representatives should have sufficient powers to represent the insurance undertaking in relation to persons suffering damage from such accidents, and also to represent the insurance undertaking before national authorities including, where necessary, before the courts, in so far as this is compatible with the rules of private international law on the conferral of jurisdiction.

(38) The activities of the claims representative are not sufficient in order to confer jurisdiction on the courts in the injured party's Member State of residence if the rules of private international law on the conferral of jurisdiction do not so provide.

(39) The appointment of representatives responsible for settling claims should be one of the conditions for access to and carrying on the activity of insurance listed in class 10 of point A of the Annex to First Council Directive 73/239/EEC of 24 July 1973 on the coordination of laws, regulations and administrative provisions relating to the taking-up and pursuit of the business of direct insurance other than life assurance[1], except for carriers' liability. That condition should therefore be covered by the single official authorisation issued by the authorities of the Member State where the insurance undertaking establishes its head office, as specified in Title II of Council Directive 92/49/EEC of 18 June 1992 on the coordination of laws, regulations and administrative provisions relating to direct insurance other than life assurance and amending Directives 73/239/EEC and 88/357/EEC (third non-life insurance Directive)[2]. That condition should also apply to insurance undertakings having their head office outside the Community which have secured an authorisation granting them access to the activity of insurance in a Member State of the Community.

(40) In addition to ensuring that the insurance undertaking has a representative in the State where the injured party resides, it is appropriate to guarantee the specific right of the injured party to have the claim settled promptly. It is therefore necessary to include in national law appropriate effective and systematic financial or equivalent administrative penalties — such as injunctions combined with administrative fines,

---

1.   OJ L 228, 16.8.1973, p 3.
2.   OJ L 228, 11.8.1992, p 1.

reporting to supervisory authorities on a regular basis, on-the-spot checks, publications in the national official journal and in the press, suspension of the activities of the company (prohibition on the conclusion of new contracts for a certain period), designation of a special representative of the supervisory authorities responsible for verifying that the business is run in line with insurance laws, withdrawal of the authorisation for this business line, sanctions to be imposed on directors and management staff — in the event that the insurance undertaking or its representative fails to fulfil its obligation to make an offer of compensation within a reasonable period of time. This should not prejudice the application of any other measure, especially under the law applicable to supervisory matters, which may be considered appropriate. However, it is a condition that liability and the damage and injury sustained should not be in dispute, so that the insurance undertaking is able to make a reasoned offer within the prescribed period of time. The reasoned offer of compensation should be in writing and should contain the grounds on the basis of which liability and damages have been assessed.

(41) In addition to those sanctions, it is appropriate to provide that interest should be payable on the amount of compensation offered by the insurance undertaking or awarded by the court to the injured party when the offer has not been made within the prescribed time limit. If Member States have existing national rules which cover the requirement for late-payment interest, this provision could be implemented by a reference to those rules.

(42) Injured parties suffering loss or injury as a result of motor vehicle accidents sometimes have difficulty in establishing the name of the insurance undertaking providing insurance against civil liability in respect of the use of motor vehicles involved in an accident.

(43) In the interests of such injured parties, Member States should set up information centres to ensure that such information concerning any accident involving a motor vehicle is made available promptly. Those information centres should also make available to injured parties information concerning claims representatives. It is necessary that such centres should cooperate with each other and respond rapidly to requests for information about claims representatives made by centres in other Member States. It seems appropriate that such centres should collect information about the actual termination date of the insurance cover but not about the expiry of the original validity of the policy if the duration of the contract is extended owing to non-cancellation.

(44) Specific provision should be made with respect to vehicles (for example, government or military vehicles) which fall within the exemptions from the obligation to be insured against civil liability.

(45) The injured party may have a legitimate interest in being informed about the identity of the owner or usual driver or the registered keeper of the vehicle, for example if he can obtain compensation only from those persons because the vehicle is not duly insured or the damage exceeds the sum insured, in which event this information should also be provided.

(46) Certain information provided, such as the name and address of the owner or usual driver of the vehicle and the number of the insurance policy or the registration number

of the vehicle, constitutes personal data within the meaning of Directive 95/46/EC of the European Parliament and of the Council of 24 October 1995 on the protection of individuals with regard to the processing of personal data and on the free movement of such data[3]. The processing of such data which is required for the purposes of this Directive should therefore comply with the national measures taken pursuant to Directive 95/46/EC. The name and address of the usual driver should be communicated only if national legislation provides for such communication.

(47) In order to ensure that the injured party will not remain without the compensation to which he is entitled, it is necessary to make provision for a compensation body to which the injured party may apply where the insurance undertaking has failed to appoint a representative or is manifestly dilatory in settling a claim or where the insurance undertaking cannot be identified. The intervention of the compensation body should be limited to rare individual cases where the insurance undertaking has failed to comply with its duties in spite of the deterrent effect of the potential imposition of penalties.

(48) The role played by the compensation body is that of settling the claim in respect of any loss or injury suffered by the injured party only in cases which are capable of objective determination and therefore the compensation body should limit its activity to verifying that an offer of compensation has been made in accordance with the time limits and procedures laid down, without any assessment of the merits.

(49) Legal persons who are subrogated by law to the injured party in his claims against the person responsible for the accident or the latter's insurance undertaking (such as, for example, other insurance undertakings or social security bodies) should not be entitled to present the corresponding claim to the compensation body.

(50) The compensation body should have a right of subrogation in so far as it has compensated the injured party. In order to facilitate enforcement of the compensation body's claim against the insurance undertaking where the latter has failed to appoint a claims representative or is manifestly dilatory in settling a claim, the body providing compensation in the injured party's State should also enjoy an automatic right of reimbursement with subrogation to the rights of the injured party on the part of the corresponding body in the State where the insurance undertaking is established. This body is the best placed to institute proceedings for recourse against the insurance undertaking.

(51) Even though Member States may provide that the claim against the compensation body is to be subsidiary, the injured person should not be obliged to present his claim to the person responsible for the accident before presenting it to the compensation body. In such a case the injured party should be in at least the same position as in the case of a claim against the guarantee fund.

(52) This system can be made to function by means of an agreement between the compensation bodies established or approved by the Member States, defining their functions and obligations and the procedures for reimbursement.

---

3.   OJ L 281, 23.11.1995, p 31.

(53) Where it is impossible to identify the insurer of a vehicle, it should be provided that the ultimate debtor in respect of the damages to be paid to the injured party is the guarantee fund provided for this purpose situated in the Member State where the uninsured vehicle, the use of which has caused the accident, is normally based. Where it is impossible to identify the vehicle, it should be provided that the ultimate debtor is the guarantee fund provided for this purpose situated in the Member State in which the accident occurred.

(54) This Directive should be without prejudice to the obligations of the Member States relating to the time limits for transposition into national law and application of the Directives set out in Annex I, Part B,

HAVE ADOPTED THIS DIRECTIVE:

CHAPTER 1
GENERAL PROVISIONS

Article 1
Definitions

For the purposes of this Directive:

1. 'vehicle' means any motor vehicle intended for travel on land and propelled by mechanical power, but not running on rails, and any trailer, whether or not coupled;

2. 'injured party' means any person entitled to compensation in respect of any loss or injury caused by vehicles;

3. 'national insurers' bureau' means a professional organisation which is constituted in accordance with Recommendation No 5 adopted on 25 January 1949 by the Road Transport Sub-committee of the Inland Transport Committee of the United Nations Economic Commission for Europe and which groups together insurance undertakings which, in a State, are authorised to conduct the business of motor vehicle insurance against civil liability;

4. 'Territory in which the vehicle is normally based' means:

(a) the territory of the State of which the vehicle bears a registration plate, irrespective of whether the plate is permanent or temporary; or

(b) in cases where no registration is required for a type of vehicle but the vehicle bears an insurance plate, or a distinguishing sign analogous to the registration plate, the territory of the State in which the insurance plate or the sign is issued; or

(c) in cases where neither a registration plate nor an insurance plate nor a distinguishing sign is required for certain types of vehicle, the territory of the State in which the person who has custody of the vehicle is permanently resident; or

(d) in cases where the vehicle does not bear any registration plate or bears a registration plate which does not correspond or no longer corresponds to the vehicle and has been involved in an accident, the territory of the State in which the accident took place, for the purpose of settling the claim as provided for in the first indent of Article 2(a) or in Article 10;

5. 'green card' means an international certificate of insurance issued on behalf of a national bureau in accordance with Recommendation No 5 adopted on 25 January 1949 by the Road Transport Sub-committee of the Inland Transport Committee of the United Nations Economic Commission for Europe;

6. 'insurance undertaking' means an undertaking which has received its official authorisation in accordance with Article 6 or Article 23(2) of Directive 73/239/EEC;

7. 'establishment' means the head office, agency or branch of an insurance undertaking as defined in Article 2(c) of Second Council Directive 88/357/EEC of 22 June 1988 on the coordination of laws, regulations and administrative provisions relating to direct insurance other than life assurance and laying down provisions to facilitate the effective exercise of freedom to provide services[1].

Article 2
Scope

The provisions of Articles 4, 6, 7 and 8 shall apply to vehicles normally based on the territory of one of the Member States:

  (a) after an agreement has been concluded between the national insurers' bureaux under the terms of which each national bureau guarantees the settlement, in accordance with the provisions of national law on compulsory insurance, of claims in respect of accidents occurring in its territory, caused by vehicles normally based in the territory of another Member State, whether or not such vehicles are insured;

  (b) from the date fixed by the Commission, upon its having ascertained in close cooperation with the Member States that such an agreement has been concluded;

  (c) for the duration of that agreement.

Article 3
Compulsory insurance of vehicles

Each Member State shall, subject to Article 5, take all appropriate measures to ensure that civil liability in respect of the use of vehicles normally based in its territory is covered by insurance.

The extent of the liability covered and the terms and conditions of the cover shall be determined on the basis of the measures referred to in the first paragraph.

Each Member State shall take all appropriate measures to ensure that the contract of insurance also covers:

  (a) according to the law in force in other Member States, any loss or injury which is caused in the territory of those States;

---

1.   OJ L 172, 4.7.1988, p. 1.

(b) any loss or injury suffered by nationals of Member States during a direct journey between two territories in which the Treaty is in force, if there is no national insurers' bureau responsible for the territory which is being crossed; in such a case, the loss or injury shall be covered in accordance with the national laws on compulsory insurance in force in the Member State in whose territory the vehicle is normally based.

The insurance referred to in the first paragraph shall cover compulsorily both damage to property and personal injuries.

Article 4
Checks on insurance

Member States shall refrain from making checks on insurance against civil liability in respect of vehicles normally based in the territory of another Member State and in respect of vehicles normally based in the territory of a third country entering their territory from the territory of another Member State. However, they may carry out non-systematic checks on insurance provided that those checks are not discriminatory and are carried out as part of a control which is not aimed exclusively at insurance verification.

Article 5
Derogation from the obligation in respect of compulsory insurance of vehicles

1. A Member State may derogate from Article 3 in respect of certain natural or legal persons, public or private; a list of such persons shall be drawn up by the State concerned and communicated to the other Member States and to the Commission.

A Member State so derogating shall take the appropriate measures to ensure that compensation is paid in respect of any loss or injury caused in its territory and in the territory of other Member States by vehicles belonging to such persons.

It shall in particular designate an authority or body in the country where the loss or injury occurs responsible for compensating injured parties in accordance with the laws of that State in cases where Article 2(a) is not applicable.

It shall communicate to the Commission the list of persons exempt from compulsory insurance and the authorities or bodies responsible for compensation.

The Commission shall publish that list.

2. A Member State may derogate from Article 3 in respect of certain types of vehicle or certain vehicles having a special plate; the list of such types or of such vehicles shall be drawn up by the State concerned and communicated to the other Member States and to the Commission.

Any Member State so derogating shall ensure that vehicles referred to in the first subparagraph are treated in the same way as vehicles for which the insurance obligation provided for in Article 3 has not been satisfied.

The guarantee fund of the Member State in which the accident has taken place shall then have a claim against the guarantee fund in the Member State where the vehicle is normally based.

From 11 June 2010 Member States shall report to the Commission on the implementation and practical application of this paragraph.

The Commission, after examining those reports, shall, if appropriate, submit proposals for the replacement or repeal of this derogation.

Article 6
National insurers' bureaux

Each Member State shall ensure that, where an accident is caused in its territory by a vehicle normally based in the territory of another Member State, the national insurers' bureau shall, without prejudice to the obligation referred to in Article 2(a), obtain information:

(a) as to the territory in which the vehicle is normally based, and as to its registration mark, if any;

(b) in so far as is possible, as to the details of the insurance of the vehicle, as they normally appear on the green card, which are in the possession of the person having custody of the vehicle, to the extent that those details are required by the Member State in whose territory the vehicle is normally based.

Each Member State shall also ensure that the bureau communicates the information referred to in points (a) and (b) to the national insurers' bureau of the State in whose territory the vehicle referred to in the first paragraph is normally based.

CHAPTER 2
PROVISIONS CONCERNING VEHICLES NORMALLY BASED IN THE TERRITORY OF THIRD COUNTRIES

Article 7
National measures concerning vehicles normally based on the territory of third countries

Each Member State shall take all appropriate measures to ensure that vehicles normally based in the territory of a third country which enter the territory in which the Treaty is in force shall not be used in its territory unless any loss or injury caused by those vehicles is covered, in accordance with the requirements of the laws of the various Member States on compulsory insurance against civil liability in respect of the use of vehicles, throughout the territory in which the Treaty is in force.

Article 8
Documentation concerning vehicles normally based in the territory of third countries

1. Every vehicle normally based in the territory of a third country must, before entering the territory in which the Treaty is in force, be provided either with a valid green card or

with a certificate of frontier insurance establishing that the vehicle is insured in accordance with Article 7.

However, vehicles normally based in a third country shall be treated as vehicles normally based in the Community if the national bureaux of all the Member States severally guarantee, each in accordance with the provisions of its own national law on compulsory insurance, settlement of claims in respect of accidents occurring in their territory caused by such vehicles.

2. Having ascertained, in close cooperation with the Member States, that the obligations referred to in the second subparagraph of paragraph 1 have been assumed, the Commission shall fix the date from which and the types of vehicles for which Member States shall no longer require production of the documents referred to in the first subparagraph of paragraph 1.

CHAPTER 3
MINIMUM AMOUNTS COVERED BY COMPULSORY INSURANCE

Article 9
Minimum amounts

1. Without prejudice to any higher guarantees which Member States may prescribe, each Member State shall require the insurance referred to in Article 3 to be compulsory at least in respect of the following amounts:

(a) in the case of personal injury, a minimum amount of cover of EUR 1000000 per victim or EUR 5000000 per claim, whatever the number of victims;

(b) in the case of damage to property, EUR 1000000 per claim, whatever the number of victims.

If necessary, Member States may establish a transitional period extending until 11 June 2012 at the latest within which to adapt their minimum amounts of cover to the amounts provided for in the first subparagraph.

Member States establishing such a transitional period shall inform the Commission thereof and indicate the duration of the transitional period.

However, until 11 December 2009 at the latest, Member States shall increase guarantees to at least a half of the levels provided for in the first subparagraph.

2. Every five years after 11 June 2005 or the end of any transitional period as referred to in the second subparagraph of paragraph 1, the amounts referred to in that paragraph shall be reviewed in line with the European Index of Consumer Prices (EICP) established pursuant to Regulation (EC) No 2494/95.

The amounts shall be adjusted automatically. Such amounts shall be increased by the percentage change indicated by the EICP for the relevant period, that is to say, the five years immediately preceding the review referred to in the first subparagraph, and rounded up to a multiple of EUR 10000.

The Commission shall communicate the adjusted amounts to the European Parliament and to the Council and shall ensure their publication in the *Official Journal of the European Union*.

CHAPTER 4
COMPENSATION FOR DAMAGE CAUSED BY AN UNIDENTIFIED VEHICLE OR A VEHICLE FOR WHICH THE INSURANCE OBLIGATION PROVIDED FOR IN ARTICLE 3 HAS NOT BEEN SATISFIED

Article 10
Body responsible for compensation

1. Each Member State shall set up or authorise a body with the task of providing compensation, at least up to the limits of the insurance obligation for damage to property or personal injuries caused by an unidentified vehicle or a vehicle for which the insurance obligation provided for in Article 3 has not been satisfied.

The first subparagraph shall be without prejudice to the right of the Member States to regard compensation by the body as subsidiary or non-subsidiary and the right to make provision for the settlement of claims between the body and the person or persons responsible for the accident and other insurers or social security bodies required to compensate the victim in respect of the same accident. However, Member States may not allow the body to make the payment of compensation conditional on the victim establishing in any way that the person liable is unable or refuses to pay.

2. The victim may in any event apply directly to the body which, on the basis of information provided at its request by the victim, shall be obliged to give him a reasoned reply regarding the payment of any compensation.

Member States may, however, exclude the payment of compensation by that body in respect of persons who voluntarily entered the vehicle which caused the damage or injury when the body can prove that they knew it was uninsured.

3. Member States may limit or exclude the payment of compensation by the body in the event of damage to property by an unidentified vehicle.

However, where the body has paid compensation for significant personal injuries to any victim of the same accident in which damage to property was caused by an unidentified vehicle, Member States may not exclude the payment of compensation for damage to property on the basis that the vehicle is unidentified. Nevertheless, Member States may provide for an excess of not more than EUR 500 to be borne by the victim of such damage to property.

The conditions in which personal injuries are to be regarded as significant shall be determined in accordance with the legislation or administrative provisions of the Member State in which the accident takes place. In this regard, Member States may take into account, inter alia, whether the injury required hospital care.

4. Each Member State shall apply its laws, regulations and administrative provisions to the payment of compensation by the body, without prejudice to any other practice which is more favourable to the victim.

Article 11
Disputes

In the event of a dispute between the body referred to in Article 10(1) and the civil liability insurer as to which must compensate the victim, the Member States shall take the appropriate measures so that one of those parties is designated to be responsible in the first instance for paying compensation to the victim without delay.

If it is ultimately decided that the other party should have paid all or part of the compensation, that other party shall reimburse accordingly the party which has paid.

CHAPTER 5
SPECIAL CATEGORIES OF VICTIM, EXCLUSION CLAUSES, SINGLE PREMIUM, VEHICLES DISPATCHED FROM ONE MEMBER STATE TO ANOTHER

Article 12
Special categories of victim

1. Without prejudice to the second subparagraph of Article 13(1), the insurance referred to in Article 3 shall cover liability for personal injuries to all passengers, other than the driver, arising out of the use of a vehicle.

2. The members of the family of the policyholder, driver or any other person who is liable under civil law in the event of an accident, and whose liability is covered by the insurance referred to in Article 3, shall not be excluded from insurance in respect of their personal injuries by virtue of that relationship.

3. The insurance referred to in Article 3 shall cover personal injuries and damage to property suffered by pedestrians, cyclists and other non-motorised users of the roads who, as a consequence of an accident in which a motor vehicle is involved, are entitled to compensation in accordance with national civil law.

This Article shall be without prejudice either to civil liability or to the quantum of damages.

Article 13
Exclusion clauses

1. Each Member State shall take all appropriate measures to ensure that any statutory provision or any contractual clause contained in an insurance policy issued in accordance with Article 3 shall be deemed to be void in respect of claims by third parties who have been victims of an accident where that statutory provision or contractual clause excludes from insurance the use or driving of vehicles by:

   (a) persons who do not have express or implied authorisation to do so;

(b) persons who do not hold a licence permitting them to drive the vehicle concerned;

(c) persons who are in breach of the statutory technical requirements concerning the condition and safety of the vehicle concerned.

However, the provision or clause referred to in point (a) of the first subparagraph may be invoked against persons who voluntarily entered the vehicle which caused the damage or injury, when the insurer can prove that they knew the vehicle was stolen.

Member States shall have the option — in the case of accidents occurring on their territory — of not applying the provision in the first subparagraph if and in so far as the victim may obtain compensation for the damage suffered from a social security body.

2. In the case of vehicles stolen or obtained by violence, Member States may provide that the body specified in Article 10(1) is to pay compensation instead of the insurer under the conditions set out in paragraph 1 of this Article. Where the vehicle is normally based in another Member State, that body can make no claim against any body in that Member State.

Member States which, in the case of vehicles stolen or obtained by violence, provide that the body referred to in Article 10(1) is to pay compensation may fix in respect of damage to property an excess of not more than EUR 250 to be borne by the victim.

3. Member States shall take the necessary measures to ensure that any statutory provision or any contractual clause contained in an insurance policy which excludes a passenger from such cover on the basis that he knew or should have known that the driver of the vehicle was under the influence of alcohol or of any other intoxicating agent at the time of an accident, shall be deemed to be void in respect of the claims of such passenger.

Article 14
Single premium

Member States shall take the necessary steps to ensure that all compulsory policies of insurance against civil liability arising out of the use of vehicles:

(a) cover, on the basis of a single premium and during the whole term of the contract, the entire territory of the Community, including for any period in which the vehicle remains in other Member States during the term of the contract; and

(b) guarantee, on the basis of that single premium, in each Member State, the cover required by its law or the cover required by the law of the Member State where the vehicle is normally based when that cover is higher.

Article 15
Vehicles dispatched from one Member State to another

1. By way of derogation from the second indent of Article 2(d) of Directive 88/357/EEC, where a vehicle is dispatched from one Member State to another, the Member State where the risk is situated shall be considered to be the Member State of destination, immediately upon acceptance of delivery by the purchaser, for a period of

30 days, even though the vehicle has not formally been registered in the Member State of destination.

2. In the event that the vehicle is involved in an accident during the period mentioned in paragraph 1 of this Article while being uninsured, the body referred to in Article 10(1) in the Member State of destination shall be liable for the compensation provided for in Article 9.

CHAPTER 6
STATEMENT, EXCESS, DIRECT ACTION

Article 16
Statement relating to the third party liability claims

Member States shall ensure that the policyholder has the right to request at any time a statement relating to the third party liability claims involving the vehicle or vehicles covered by the insurance contract at least during the preceding five years of the contractual relationship, or to the absence of such claims.

The insurance undertaking, or a body which may have been appointed by a Member State to provide compulsory insurance or to supply such statements, shall provide that statement to the policyholder within 15 days of the request.

Article 17
Excess

Insurance undertakings shall not require any party injured as a result of an accident to bear any excess as far as the insurance referred to in Article 3 is concerned.

Article 18
Direct right of action

Member States shall ensure that any party injured as a result of an accident caused by a vehicle covered by insurance as referred to in Article 3 enjoys a direct right of action against the insurance undertaking covering the person responsible against civil liability.

CHAPTER 7
SETTLEMENT OF CLAIMS ARISING FROM ANY ACCIDENT CAUSED BY A VEHICLE COVERED BY INSURANCE AS REFERRED TO IN ARTICLE 3

Article 19
Procedure for the settlement of claims

Member States shall establish the procedure referred to in Article 22 for the settlement of claims arising from any accident caused by a vehicle covered by insurance as referred to in Article 3.

In the case of claims which may be settled by the system of national insurers' bureaux provided for in Article 2 Member States shall establish the same procedure as in Article 22.

For the purpose of applying this procedure, any reference to an insurance undertaking shall be understood as a reference to national insurers' bureaux.

Article 20
Special provisions concerning compensation for injured parties following an accident in a Member State other than that of their residence

1. The object of Articles 20 to 26 is to lay down special provisions applicable to injured parties entitled to compensation in respect of any loss or injury resulting from accidents occurring in a Member State other than the Member State of residence of the injured party which are caused by the use of vehicles insured and normally based in a Member State.

Without prejudice to the legislation of third countries on civil liability and private international law, these provisions shall also apply to injured parties resident in a Member State and entitled to compensation in respect of any loss or injury resulting from accidents occurring in third countries whose national insurer's bureaux have joined the green card system whenever such accidents are caused by the use of vehicles insured and normally based in a Member State.

2. Articles 21 and 24 shall apply only in the case of accidents caused by the use of a vehicle:

    (a)   insured through an establishment in a Member State other than the State of residence of the injured party; and

    (b)   normally based in a Member State other than the State of residence of the injured party.

Article 21
Claims representatives

1. Each Member State shall take all measures necessary to ensure that all insurance undertakings covering the risks classified in class 10 of point A of the Annex to Directive 73/239/EEC, other than carrier's liability, appoint a claims representative in each Member State other than that in which they have received their official authorisation.

The claims representative shall be responsible for handling and settling claims arising from an accident in the cases referred to in Article 20(1).

The claims representative shall be resident or established in the Member State where he is appointed.

2. The choice of its claims representative shall be at the discretion of the insurance undertaking.

The Member States may not restrict this freedom of choice.

3. The claims representative may act for one or more insurance undertakings.

4. The claims representative shall, in relation to such claims, collect all information necessary in connection with the settlement of the claims and shall take the measures necessary to negotiate a settlement of claims.

The requirement of appointing a claims representative shall not preclude the right of the injured party or his insurance undertaking to institute proceedings directly against the person who caused the accident or his insurance undertaking.

5. Claims representatives shall possess sufficient powers to represent the insurance undertaking in relation to injured parties in the cases referred to in Article 20(1) and to meet their claims in full.

They must be capable of examining cases in the official language(s) of the Member State of residence of the injured party.

6. The appointment of a claims representative shall not in itself constitute the opening of a branch within the meaning of Article 1(b) of Directive 92/49/EEC and the claims representative shall not be regarded as an establishment within the meaning of Article 2(c) of Directive 88/357/EEC or an establishment within the meaning of Regulation (EC) No 44/2001.

Article 22
Compensation procedure

The Member States shall create a duty, backed by appropriate, effective and systematic financial or equivalent administrative penalties, whereby, within three months of the date when the injured party presented his claim for compensation either directly to the insurance undertaking of the person who caused the accident or to its claims representative,

(a) the insurance undertaking of the person who caused the accident or its claims representative is required to make a reasoned offer of compensation in cases where liability is not contested and the damages have been quantified; or

(b) the insurance undertaking to whom the claim for compensation has been addressed or its claims representative is required to provide a reasoned reply to the points made in the claim in cases where liability is denied or has not been clearly determined or the damages have not been fully quantified.

Member States shall adopt provisions to ensure that, where the offer is not made within the three-month time limit, interest shall be payable on the amount of compensation offered by the insurance undertaking or awarded by the court to the injured party.

Article 23
Information centres

1. In order to enable the injured party to seek compensation, each Member State shall establish or approve an information centre responsible:

(a) for keeping a register containing the following information:

   (i) the registration numbers of motor vehicles normally based in the territory of the State in question;

(ii)   the numbers of the insurance policies covering the use of those vehicles for the risks classified in class 10 of point A of the Annex to Directive 73/239/EEC, other than carrier's liability and, where the period of validity of the policy has expired, the date of termination of the insurance cover;

(iii)   insurance undertakings covering the use of vehicles for the risks classified in class 10 of point A of the Annex to Directive 73/239/EEC, other than carrier's liability, and claims representatives appointed by such insurance undertakings in accordance with Article 21 of this Directive whose names are to be notified to the information centre in accordance with paragraph 2 of this Article;

(iv)   the list of vehicles which, in each Member State, benefit from the derogation from the requirement for civil liability insurance cover in accordance with Article 5(1) and (2);

(v)   as regards the vehicles provided for in point (iv):

    –   the name of the authority or body designated in accordance with the third subparagraph of Article 5(1) as responsible for compensating injured parties in the cases where the procedure provided for in Article 2(2)(a) is not applicable, if the vehicle benefits from the derogation provided for in the first subparagraph of Article 5(1),

    –   the name of the body covering the vehicle in the Member State where it is normally based if the vehicle benefits from the derogation provided for in Article 5(2);

(b)   or for coordinating the compilation and dissemination of that information; and

(c)   for assisting entitled persons to be apprised of the information mentioned in points (a)(i) to (v).

The information under points (a)(i), (ii) and (iii) must be preserved for a period of seven years after the termination of the registration of the vehicle or the termination of the insurance contract.

2. Insurance undertakings referred to in point (a)(iii) of paragraph 1 shall notify to the information centres of all Member States the name and address of the claims representative appointed by them in accordance with Article 21 in each of the Member States.

3. Member States shall ensure that the injured party is entitled for a period of seven years after the accident to obtain without delay from the information centre of the Member State where he resides, the Member State where the vehicle is normally based or the Member State where the accident occurred the following information:

(a)   the name and address of the insurance undertaking;

(b)   the number of the insurance policy; and

(c)   the name and address of the insurance undertaking's claims representative in the State of residence of the injured party.

Information centres shall cooperate with each other.

4. The information centre shall provide the injured party with the name and address of the owner or usual driver or registered keeper of the vehicle if the injured party has a legitimate interest in obtaining this information. For the purposes of this provision, the information centre shall address itself in particular:

    (a) to the insurance undertaking; or

    (b) to the vehicle registration agency.

If the vehicle benefits from the derogation provided for in the first subparagraph of Article 5(1) the information centre shall inform the injured party of the name of the authority or body designated in accordance with the third subparagraph of Article 5(1) as responsible for compensating injured parties in cases where the procedure provided for in Article 2(a) is not applicable.

If the vehicle benefits from the derogation provided for in Article 5(2) the information centre shall inform the injured party of the name of the body covering the vehicle in the country where it is normally based.

5. Member States shall ensure that, without prejudice to their obligations under paragraphs 1 and 4, the information centres provide the information specified in these paragraphs to any party involved in any traffic accident caused by a vehicle covered by insurance as referred to in Article 3.

6. The processing of personal data resulting from paragraphs 1 to 5 must be carried out in accordance with national measures taken pursuant to Directive 95/46/EC.

Article 24
Compensation bodies

1. Each Member State shall establish or approve a compensation body responsible for providing compensation to injured parties in the cases referred to in Article 20(1).

Such injured parties may present a claim to the compensation body in their Member State of residence:

    (a) if, within three months of the date when the injured party presented his claim for compensation to the insurance undertaking of the vehicle the use of which caused the accident or to its claims representative, the insurance undertaking or its claims representative has not provided a reasoned reply to the points made in the claim; or

    (b) if the insurance undertaking has failed to appoint a claims representative in the Member State of residence of the injured party in accordance with Article 20(1); in such a case, injured parties may not present a claim to the compensation body if they have presented a claim for compensation directly to the insurance undertaking of the vehicle the use of which caused the accident and if they have received a reasoned reply within three months of presenting the claim.

Injured parties may not however present a claim to the compensation body if they have taken legal action directly against the insurance undertaking.

The compensation body shall take action within two months of the date when the injured party presents a claim for compensation to it but shall terminate its action if the insurance undertaking, or its claims representative, subsequently makes a reasoned reply to the claim.

The compensation body shall immediately inform:

(a) the insurance undertaking of the vehicle the use of which caused the accident or the claims representative;

(b) the compensation body in the Member State in which the insurance undertaking which issued the policy is established;

(c) if known, the person who caused the accident;

that it has received a claim from the injured party and that it will respond to that claim within two months of the presentation of that claim.

This provision shall be without prejudice to the right of the Member States to regard compensation by that body as subsidiary or non-subsidiary and the right to make provision for the settlement of claims between that body and the person or persons who caused the accident and other insurance undertakings or social security bodies required to compensate the injured party in respect of the same accident. However, Member States may not allow the body to make the payment of compensation subject to any conditions other than those laid down in this Directive, in particular the injured party's establishing in any way that the person liable is unable or refuses to pay.

2. The compensation body which has compensated the injured party in his Member State of residence shall be entitled to claim reimbursement of the sum paid by way of compensation from the compensation body in the Member State in which the insurance undertaking which issued the policy is established.

The latter body shall be subrogated to the injured party in his rights against the person who caused the accident or his insurance undertaking in so far as the compensation body in the Member State of residence of the injured party has provided compensation for the loss or injury suffered.

Each Member State shall be obliged to acknowledge this subrogation as provided for by any other Member State.

3. This Article shall take effect:

(a) after an agreement has been concluded between the compensation bodies established or approved by the Member States relating to their functions and obligations and the procedures for reimbursement;

(b) from the date fixed by the Commission upon its having ascertained in close cooperation with the Member States that such an agreement has been concluded.

Article 25
Compensation

1. If it is impossible to identify the vehicle or if, within two months of the date of the accident, it is impossible to identify the insurance undertaking, the injured party may apply for compensation from the compensation body in the Member State where he resides. The compensation shall be provided in accordance with the provisions of

Articles 9 and 10. The compensation body shall then have a claim, on the conditions laid down in Article 24(2):

    (a) where the insurance undertaking cannot be identified: against the guarantee fund in the Member State where the vehicle is normally based;

    (b) in the case of an unidentified vehicle: against the guarantee fund in the Member State in which the accident took place;

    (c) in the case of a third-country vehicle: against the guarantee fund in the Member State in which the accident took place.

2. This Article shall apply to accidents caused by third-country vehicles covered by Articles 7 and 8.

Article 26
Central body

Member States shall take all appropriate measures to facilitate the timely provision to the victims, their insurers or their legal representatives of the basic data necessary for the settlement of claims.

Those basic data shall, where appropriate, be made available in electronic form in a central repository in each Member State, and be accessible by parties involved in the case at their express request.

Article 27
Penalties

Member States shall fix penalties for breaches of the national provisions which they adopt in implementation of this Directive and shall take the steps necessary to secure the application thereof. The penalties shall be effective, proportional and dissuasive. The Member States shall notify to the Commission as soon as possible any amendments concerning provisions adopted pursuant to this Article.

CHAPTER 8
FINAL PROVISIONS

Article 28
National provisions

1. Member States may, in accordance with the Treaty, maintain or bring into force provisions which are more favourable to injured parties than the provisions needed to comply with this Directive.

2. Member States shall communicate to the Commission the text of the main provisions of domestic law which they adopt in the field governed by this Directive.

Article 29
Repeal

Directives 72/166/EEC, 84/5/EEC, 90/232/EEC, 2000/26/EC and 2005/14/EC, as amended by the Directives listed in Annex I, Part A, are hereby repealed, without prejudice to the obligations of the Member States relating to the time limits for transposition into national law and application of the Directives set out in Annex I, Part B.

References to the repealed Directives shall be construed as references to this Directive and shall be read in accordance with the correlation table in Annex II.

Article 30
Entry into force

This Directive shall enter into force on the 20th day following its publication in the *Official Journal of the European Union*.

Article 31
Addressees

This Directive is addressed to the Member States.

Done at Strasbourg, 16 September 2009.

For the European Parliament

The President

J. Buzek

For the Council

The President

C. Malmström

ANNEX I
PART A

Repealed Directive with list of its successive amendments
(referred to in Article 29)

Council Directive 72/166/EEC (OJ L 103, 2.5.1972, p 1)

Council Directive 72/430/EEC (OJ L 291, 28.12.1972, p 162)

Council Directive 84/5/EEC (OJ L 8, 11.1.1984, p 17)   Only Article 4

Directive 2005/14/EC of the European Parliament and   Only Article 1
Council (OJ L 149, 11.6.2005, p 14)

Council Directive 84/5/EEC (OJ L 8, 11.1.1984, p 17)

Annex I, point IX.F of the 1985 Act of Accession (OJ L
302, 15.11.1985, p 218)

Council Directive 90/232/EEC (OJ L 129, 19.5.1990,   Only Article 4
p 33)

Directive 2005/14/EC of the European Parliament and   Only Article 2
Council (OJ L 149, 11.6.2005, p 14)

Council Directive 90/232/EEC (OJ L 129, 19.5.1990, p 33)

Directive 2005/14/EC of the European Parliament and   Only Article 4
Council (OJ L 149, 11.6.2005, p 14)

Directive 2000/26/EC of the European Parliament and
Council (OJ L 181, 20.7.2000, p 65)

Directive 2005/14/EC of the European Parliament and   Only Article 5
Council (OJ L 149, 11.6.2005, p 14)

Directive 2005/14/EC of the European Parliament and
Council (OJ L 149, 11.6.2005, p 14)

PART B
List of time limits for transposition into national law and application
(referred to in Article 29)

Directive	Time limit for transposition	Date of application
72/166/EEC	31 December 1973	—
72/430/EEC	—	1 January 1973
84/5/EEC	31 December 1987	31 December 1988
90/232/EEC	31 December 1992	—
2000/26/EC	19 July 2002	19 January 2003
2005/14/EC	11 June 2007	—

ANNEX II
CORRELATION TABLE

Directive 72/166/EEC	Directive 84/5/EEC	Directive 90/232/EEC	Directive 2000/26/EC	This Directive
Article 1, points (1) to (3)				Article 1, points (1) to (3)
Article 1, point (4), first indent				Article 1, point (4)(a)
Article 1, point (4), second indent				Article 1, point (4)(b)
Article 1, point (4), third indent				Article 1, point (4)(c)
Article 1, point (4), fourth indent				Article 1, point (4)(d)
Article 1, point (5)				Article 1, point (5)
Article 2(1)				Article 4
Article 2(2), introductory wording				Article 2, introductory wording
Article 2(2), first indent				Article 2, point (a)
Article 2(2), second indent				Article 2, point (b)
Article 2(2), third indent				Article 2, point (c)
Article 3(1), first sentence				Article 3, first paragraph
Article 3(1), second sentence				Article 3, second paragraph
Article 3(2), introductory wording				Article 3, third paragraph, introductory wording
Article 3(2), first indent				Article 3, third paragraph, point (a)
Article 3(2), second indent				Article 3, third paragraph, point (b)

Directive 72/166/EEC	Directive 84/5/EEC	Directive 90/232/EEC	Directive 2000/26/EC	This Directive
Article 4, introductory wording				Article 5(1), first subparagraph
Article 4, point (a), first subparagraph				Article 5(1), first subparagraph
Article 4, point (a), second subparagraph, first sentence				Article 5(1), second subparagraph
Article 4, point (a), second subparagraph, second sentence				Article 5(1), third subparagraph
Article 4, point (a), second subparagraph, third sentence				Article 5(1), fourth subparagraph
Article 4, point (a), second subparagraph, fourth sentence				Article 5(1), fifth subparagraph
Article 4, point (b), first subparagraph				Article 5(2), first subparagraph
Article 4, point (b), second subparagraph, first sentence				Article 5(2), second subparagraph
Article 4, point (b), second subparagraph, second sentence				Article 5(2), third subparagraph
Article 4, point (b), third subparagraph, first sentence				Article 5(2), fourth subparagraph
Article 4, point (b), third subparagraph, second sentence				Article 5(2), fifth subparagraph
Article 5, introductory wording				Article 6, first subparagraph, introductory wording

Appendix 3: Directive 2009/103/EC (The Sixth Directive)

Directive 72/166/EEC	Directive 84/5/EEC	Directive 90/232/EEC	Directive 2000/26/EC	This Directive
Article 5, first indent				Article 6, first paragraph, point (a)
Article 5, second indent				Article 6, first paragraph, point (b)
Article 5, final wording				Article 6, second paragraph
Article 6				Article 7
Article 7(1)				Article 8(1), first subparagraph
Article 7(2)				Article 8(1), second subparagraph
Article 7(3)				Article 8(2)
Article 8				—
	Article 1(1)			Article 3, fourth paragraph
	Article 1(2)			Article 9(1)
	Article 1(3)			Article 9(2)
	Article 1(4)			Article 10(1)
	Article 1(5)			Article 10(2)
	Article 1(6)			Article 10(3)
	Article 1(7)			Article 10(4)
	Article 2(1), first subparagraph, introductory wording			Article 13(1), first subparagraph, introductory wording
	Article 2(1), first indent			Article 13(1), first subparagraph, point (a)
	Article 2(1), second indent			Article 13(1), first subparagraph, point (b)

Directive 72/166/EEC	Directive 84/5/EEC	Directive 90/232/EEC	Directive 2000/26/EC	This Directive
	Article 2(1), third indent			Article 13(1), first subparagraph, point (c)
	Article 2(1), first subparagraph, final wording			Article 13(1), first subparagraph, introductory wording
	Article 2(1), second and third subparagraphs			Article 13(1), second and third subparagraphs
	Article 2(2)			Article 13(2)
	Article 3			Article 12(2)
	Article 4			—
	Article 5			—
	Article 6			—
		Article 1, first paragraph		Article 12(1)
		Article 1, second paragraph		Article 13(3)
		Article 1, third paragraph		—
		Article 1a, first sentence		Article 12(3), first subparagraph
		Article 1a, second sentence		Article 12(3), second subparagraph
		Article 2, introductory wording		Article 14, introductory wording
		Article 2, first indent		Article 14, point (a)
		Article 2, second indent		Article 14, point (b)
		Article 3		—
		Article 4		Article 11
		Article 4a		Article 15
		Article 4b, first sentence		Article 16, first paragraph

Directive 72/166/EEC	Directive 84/5/EEC	Directive 90/232/EEC	Directive 2000/26/EC	This Directive
		Article 4b, second sentence		Article 16, second paragraph
		Article 4c		Article 17
		Article 4d	Article 3	Article 18
		Article 4e, first paragraph		Article 19, first paragraph
		Article 4e, second paragraph, first sentence		Article 19, second paragraph
		Article 4e, second paragraph, second sentence		Article 19, third paragraph
		Article 5(1)		Article 23(5)
		Article 5(2)		—
		Article 6		—
			Article 1(1)	Article 20(1)
			Article 1(2)	Article 20(2)
			Article 1(3)	Article 25(2)
			Article 2, introductory wording	—
			Article 2, point (a)	Article 1, point (6)
			Article 2, point (b)	Article 1, point (7)
			Article 2, points (c), (d) and (e)	—
			Article 4(1), first sentence	Article 21(1), first subparagraph
			Article 4(1), second sentence	Article 21(1), second subparagraph
			Article 4(1), third sentence	Article 21(1), third subparagraph
			Article 4(2), first sentence	Article 21(2), first subparagraph

Directive 72/166/EEC	Directive 84/5/EEC	Directive 90/232/EEC	Directive 2000/26/EC	This Directive
			Article 4(2), second sentence	Article 21(2), second subparagraph
			Article 4(3)	Article 21(3)
			Article 4(4), first sentence	Article 21(4), first subparagraph
			Article 4(4), second sentence	Article 21(4), second subparagraph
			Article 4(5), first sentence	Article 21(5), first subparagraph
			Article 4(5), second sentence	Article 21(5), second subparagraph
			Article 4(6)	Article 22
			Article 4(7)	—
			Article 4(8)	Article 21(6)
			Article 5(1), first subparagraph, introductory wording	Article 23(1), first subparagraph, introductory wording
			Article 5(1), first subparagraph, point (a), introductory wording	Article 23(1), first subparagraph, point (a), introductory wording
			Article 5(1), first subparagraph, point (a)(1)	Article 23(1), first subparagraph, point (a)(i)
			Article 5(1), first subparagraph, point (a)(2)	Article 23(1), first subparagraph, point (a)(ii)
			Article 5(1), first subparagraph, point (a)(3)	Article 23(1), first subparagraph, point (a)(iii)

Directive 72/ 166/EEC	Directive 84/5/ EEC	Directive 90/ 232/EEC	Directive 2000/ 26/EC	This Directive
			Article 5(1), first subparagraph, point (a)(4)	Article 23(1), first subparagraph, point (a)(iv)
			Article 5(1), first subparagraph, point (a)(5), introductory wording	Article 23(1), first subparagraph, point (a)(v), introductory wording
			Article 5(1), first subparagraph, point (a)(5)(i)	Article 23(1), first subparagraph, point (a)(v), first indent
			Article 5(1), first subparagraph, point (a)(5)(ii)	Article 23(1), first subparagraph, point (a)(v), second indent
			Article 5(1), second subparagraph	Article 23(1), second subparagraph
			Article 5(2), (3) and (4)	Article 23(2), (3) and (4)
			Article 5(5)	Article 23(6)
			Article 6(1)	Article 24(1)
			Article 6(2), first subparagraph	Article 24(2), first subparagraph
			Article 6(2), second subparagraph, first sentence	Article 24(2), second subparagraph
			Article 6(2), second subparagraph, second sentence	Article 24(2), third subparagraph
			Article 6(3), first subparagraph	Article 24(3)
			Article 6(3), second subparagraph	—

Directive 72/166/EEC	Directive 84/5/EEC	Directive 90/232/EEC	Directive 2000/26/EC	This Directive
			Article 6a	Article 26
			Article 7, introductory wording	Article 25(1), introductory wording
			Article 7, point (a)	Article 25(1), point (a)
			Article 7, point (b)	Article 25(1), point (b)
			Article 7, point (c)	Article 25(1), point (c)
			Article 8	—
			Article 9	—
			Article 10(1) to (3)	—
			Article 10(4)	Article 28(1)
			Article 10(5)	Article 28(2)
				Article 29
			Article 11	Article 30
			Article 12	Article 27
Article 9	Article 7	Article 7	Article 13	Article 31
				Annex I
				Annex II

Appendix 4.1

EUROPEAN COMMUNITIES (FOURTH MOTOR INSURANCE DIRECTIVE) REGULATIONS 2003 (SI 651/2003)

European Communities (Fourth Motor Insurance Directive) Regulations 2003 (SI 651/2003) ('the 2003 Regulations') incorporating the amendments made thereto by the European Communities (Motor Insurance) Regulations 2008 (SI 248/2008) (fns 6–9 inserted by Authors)

EUROPEAN COMMUNITIES (FOURTH MOTOR INSURANCE DIRECTIVE) REGULATIONS 2003
SI 651 OF 2003

I, Seamus Brennan, Minister for Transport, in exercise of the powers conferred on me by section 3 of the European Communities Act 1972 (No. 27 of 1972) and for the purposes of giving effect to Directive No. 2000/26/EC of the European Parliament and of the Council of 16 May 2000[1] concerning the approximation of the laws of the Member States relating to insurance against civil-liability in respect of the use of motor vehicles and amending Council Directive 73/239/EEC and 88/357/EEC (Fourth Motor Insurance Directive), hereby make the following regulations:-

Citation

1. These Regulations may be cited as the European Communities (Fourth Motor Insurance Directive) Regulations 2003.

Interpretation

2. (1) In these Regulations—

"accident" means an accident to which these Regulations apply;

"Directive" means Directive 2000/26/EC of the European Parliament and of the Council of 16 May 2000;

"Directive 72/166/EEC[2]" means Council Directive 72/166/EEC on the approximation of the laws of the Member States relating to insurance against civil liability in respect of the use of motor vehicles, and to the enforcement of the obligation to insure against such liability;

"Directive 84/5/EEC[3]" means Council Directive 84/5/EEC on the approximation of the laws of the Member States relating to insurance against civil liability in respect of the use of motor vehicles;

---

1.   OJ No. L181/65 of 20.7.2000.
2.   OJ No. L103, 2.5.1972, p. 6.
3.   OJ No. L8 30.12.1983, p. 17.

"designated territories" has the meaning assigned by the European Communities (Road Traffic) (Compulsory Insurance) (Amendment) Regulations 2001 (S.I. No. 463 of 2001);

"EEA State" means a State which is a contracting party to the Agreement on the European Economic Area signed at Oporto on 2nd May 1992[4] and the protocol adjusting the Agreement signed at Brussels on 17th March 1993;

"enactment" means a statute or an instrument made under a power conferred by statute;

"establishment" means the head office, agency or branch of an insurance undertaking as defined in Article 2(c) of Directive 72/166/EEC;

"exempted person" has the meaning assigned to it by section 60 of the Road Traffic Act, 1961 (No. 24 of 1961) (as amended);

"insurance undertaking" means an undertaking which has received its official authorisation in accordance with article 6 or article 23(2) of 73/239/EEC[5];

"insured vehicle" means a vehicle for which a policy of insurance issued by an insurance undertaking is in force and other cognate words shall be construed accordingly;

"injured party" means any person entitled to compensation in respect of any loss or injury caused by vehicles;

"Member State" means a Member State of the European Communities;

"EEA State of residence" means the EEA State of normal residence of an injured party;

"Minister" means Minister for Transport;

"normally resident in EEA State" means a person whose place of normal residence is in that State;

"normal residence" has the meaning assigned to it by regulation 3 of the Vehicle Registration Tax (Permanent Reliefs Regulations 1993 (S.I. No. 59 of 1993) and other cognate words shall be construed accordingly;

"specified territories" means "designated territories" other than an EEA State;

"State vehicles" has the meaning assigned to it by section 4(2) of the Road Traffic Act, 1961;

"Third Country" means a country other than an EEA State or specified territories;

"vehicle" has the meaning assigned to it by article 1(1) of Directive 72/166/EEC;

"the EEA State in which the vehicle is normally based" means the territory of the EEA State in which the vehicle is normally based as defined in Article 1(4) of Directive 72/166/EEC.

---

4.   Directive 2000/26/EC was added to annex 1X of the European Economic Area Agreement by decision No. 4/2001 of the European Economic Area Joint Committee which came into force on 1 September 2001 (OJ No L66, 8.3.2001, p 46).

5.   OJ L.228, 24.7.1973, p 3.

(2) In these Regulations, unless otherwise indicated—

(a) a reference to a Regulation is to a Regulation of these Regulations, and

(b) a reference to a paragraph or subparagraph is a reference to paragraph or subparagraph of the provision in which the reference occurs.

(c) Except for a word or phrase defined in paragraph (1), or where otherwise indicated, a word or phrase to which a meaning has been assigned by a Directive referred to in these Regulations has that meaning.

(3) In these Regulations a reference to an enactment shall be construed as a reference to the enactment as amended by any subsequent enactment, including these Regulations.

Parties to whom these Regulations apply

3. (1) Subject to paragraphs (2) and (3), these Regulations shall apply to an injured party, who is normally resident in an EEA State, and who is entitled to compensation in respect of any loss or injury resulting from an accident in an EEA State other than an EEA State where the party is normally resident and which was caused by a vehicle that at the time of the accident was insured and normally based in an EEA State.

(2) Without prejudice to the legislation of Third countries on civil liability and private international law, these regulations shall apply in respect of an injured party who is normally resident in an EEA State and who is entitled to compensation as a result of an accident in a specified territory where such accident was caused by the use of a vehicle that at the time of the accident was insured and normally based in an EEA State.

(3) Regulations 4 and 6 shall only apply in respect of an accident caused by the use of a vehicle which at the time of the accident was insured through an establishment in an EEA State and normally based in an EEA State other than the state of residence of the injured party:

(4) Notwithstanding paragraphs (1) and (2), Regulation 7 shall also apply in respect of an accident caused by a vehicle that at the time of the accident was normally based in one of the specified territories.

Direct right of action

(5) An injured party shall be entitled, without prejudice to his right to issue proceedings against the insured person, to issue proceedings against an insurance undertaking that is authorised to transact compulsory motor insurance business in the State in respect of an accident caused by a vehicle insured by that undertaking and the insurance undertaking shall be directly liable to the injured party to the extent that it is liable to the insured person.

(6) The requirement to appoint a claims representative in accordance with Regulation 4(1) does not limit in any way the entitlement of an injured party as provided for in paragraph (5).

[(7) Paragraphs (5) and (6) of this Regulation, paragraphs (8) to (10) of Regulation 4 and Regulation 5 apply to all injured parties normally resident in an EEA State.][6]

Claims Representative

4. (1) Each insurance undertaking that is authorised to transact compulsory motor insurance business in the State shall appoint a claims representative in each other EEA State, which claims representative shall be selected at the discretion of the appointing insurance undertaking.

(2) Each claims representative shall be granted sufficient representational authority and powers by the insurance undertaking that appointed it as will enable the said claims representative to settle claims in full.

(3) A common claims representative may be appointed to represent more than one insurance undertaking.

(4) Each insurance undertaking shall notify to the Information Centre, the name, address, telephone number, fax number and electronic mail address of the claims representative that it has appointed in each EEA State.

(5) The claims representatives shall be resident or established in the respective EEA State for which they have been appointed.

(6) A claims representative shall handle and settle claims by injured parties to whom Regulation 3 applies that are made against the insurance undertaking which he or she represents.

(7) The duties of a claims representative shall include—

  (a) the collection of all the information necessary to the full consideration and settlement of a claim,

  (b) the taking of all measures necessary to negotiate a settlement of a claim.

  (c) where so required by a claimant, the examination of a claim and the carrying on of all communications with the claimant in relation thereto, in the official language of the EEA State in which the claimant normally resides.

(8) Not more than 3 months after the date on which an injured party presents a claim for compensation either directly to an insurance undertaking or to a claims representative, the said insurance undertaking or claims representative shall either—

  (a) make a reasoned offer of compensation in any case where liability is not contested and the damages have been quantified, or

  (b) provide a reasoned reply to the points made in the claim in any case where liability is denied, or has not been clearly determined, or the damages have not been fully quantified.

(9) An insurance undertaking or claims representative which fails to comply with paragraph 8 shall be guilty of an offence within the meaning of Regulation 59 of the

---

6. Inserted by authors: Regulation 3(7) was inserted by Regulation 5(a) of the European Communities (Motor Insurance) Regulations 2008 (SI 248/2008).

European Communities (Non-Life Insurance) Framework Regulations 1994, (S.I. No 359 of 1994) (as amended) and shall on summary conviction be liable to the fine specified therein.

(10) Where the insurance undertaking or claims representative is in breach of paragraph 8, the interest at the rate per annum specified for the time being in section 26 of the Debtors (Ireland) Act, 1840, as varied from time to time pursuant to section 20 of the Courts Act 1981 (No. 11 of 1981) (as amended), is payable by the said insurance undertaking, on any sum awarded to an injured party from the day on which the said breach occurred.

[(11) The appointment of a claims representative does not in itself constitute a head office, agency or branch of an insurance undertaking or does not constitute an establishment in any EEA State.][7]

[(12) Paragraphs (8) to (10) apply to the Motor Insurers' Bureau of Ireland as they apply to insurance undertakings and claims representatives.][8]

Information Centre

5. (1) The Motor Insurers' Bureau of Ireland is hereby approved as the Information Centre in accordance with Regulation 5 of the Directive.

(2) The Information Centre shall co-ordinate the compilation and dissemination of information concerning the insurance policies in force in respect of vehicles normally based in the State to the extent to which requests have been submitted to it.

(3) The information necessary for compliance with paragraph (2) shall include—

   (a)   the registration numbers of all vehicles that are normally based in the State,

   (b)   the policy reference numbers of each policy of insurance covering insured vehicles that are normally based in Ireland for all liability, other than carrier's liability arising out of the use of vehicles on land or the date of termination of the insurance cover, where the period of validity of an insurance policy has expired,

   [...][9]

   (d)   The name, address, telephone number, fax number and electronic mail address of each relevant insurance undertaking and of the claims representative appointed in accordance with Regulation 4.

   (e)   The name, address, telephone number, fax number and electronic mail address of an exempted person or person designated by the exempted person to act on its behalf in relation to the matters provided for in these Regulations,

---

7.   Inserted by authors: the original regulation 4(11) was substituted by Regulation 5(b) of the European Communities (Motor Insurance) Regulations 2008 (SI 248/2008).

8.   Inserted by authors: Regulation 4(12) was inserted by Regulation 5(b) of the European Communities (Motor Insurance) Regulations 2008 (SI 248/2008).

9.   Inserted by authors: Regulation 5(3)(c) was deleted by Regulation 5(c) of the European Communities (Motor Insurance) Regulations 2008 (SI 248/2008).

(f)   The name, address, telephone number, fax number and electronic mail address of the person designated by the relevant Minister to act on his behalf in relation to State vehicles provided for in these Regulations,

(4) (a)   An insurance undertaking that is authorised to transact compulsory motor insurance business in the State, an exempted person or person designated by him and person designated by the Minister in relation to State vehicles, shall maintain and provide any information that the Information Centre is obliged to compile and disseminate in accordance with paragraphs (2) and (3), upon request by the Information Centre.

(b)   Subject to subparagraph (c), a request from the Information Centre pursuant to subparagraph (a) shall be complied with by whom it was addressed or in the event that addressee does not possess the required information, a response to that effect, such that the required information or response is in the possession of the Information Centre within 7 working days or as soon as practicable thereafter following the making of such request.

(c)   The information referred to at subparagraph (a) and (b) shall be maintained for a period of 7 years;

   (i)   after the termination of the period of cover of the insurance policy in the case of an insurance undertaking, and

   (ii)   after the ownership or control of the vehicle ceases in the case of an exempted person,

   (iii)   after the vehicle ceases to be a State vehicle in the case of a person designated by the relevant Minister.

(5) (a)   On request, the Information Centre shall provide to an injured party, or a party authorised to act on his or her behalf, if the injured party has a legitimate interest in obtaining this information, involving one or more vehicles, with the name and address of the registered owner or keeper of the vehicle or vehicles in question,

(b)   For the purposes of subparagraph (a) the Information Centre shall provide:

   (i)   the name and address of the insurance undertaking that provided insurance policies in respect of each vehicle involved in the accident, or

   (ii)   the name and address of the exempted person that is the owner of any such vehicle, or

   (iii)   the name and address of the relevant Minister in relation to the State vehicle, if applicable.

(6) A request made under this regulation shall be made in writing or by electronic mail, shall contain sufficient information to identify the vehicle in respect of which the information is being sought and shall be received no later than 7 years after the date of the accident.

(7) The Information Centre shall co-operate with the information centres in each other EEA State in relation to the provision of information in accordance with these Regulations.

Compensation Body

6 (1)   The Motor Insurers' Bureau of Ireland is hereby approved as the Compensation Body for the State for the purposes of the Directive.

(2) Subject to paragraph (3) an injured party to which these Regulations apply and normally resident in the State may present a claim for compensation to the Compensation Body where:

    (a) that person claims to be entitled to compensation in respect of an accident occurring either in an EEA State other than the State or in the specified territories,

    (b) the loss or injury to which the claim relates has been caused by or arises out of the use of a vehicle which is normally based in an EEA state other than the State, and insured through an insurance undertaking established in an EEA State other than the State, and

    (c) the injured party had presented a prior claim for compensation to the said insurance undertaking or its claims representative and the said insurance undertaking or claims representative had not provided a reasoned reply within 3 months of such presentation, in accordance with Regulation 4(8)(a), or

    (d) the said insurance undertaking has failed to appoint a claims representative in the State, unless such insurance undertaking has not provided a reasoned reply within 3 months of the presentation of a claim for compensation in accordance with Regulation 4(8)(b).

(3) Paragraph (2) shall not apply in any case where an injured party has taken legal action directly against the insurance undertaking concerned in respect of the vehicle which caused the accident.

(4) On receipt of a claim pursuant to paragraph (2), the Compensation Body shall immediately inform—

    (a) the insurance undertaking in respect of the vehicle the use of which is alleged to have caused the accident or the claims representative,

    (b) the Compensation Body in the EEA State where the insurance undertaking which issued the insurance policy is established,

    (c) the person alleged to have caused the accident, if the name of that person is known,

of the making of such claim and will respond to the said claim within a period of 2 months of presentation thereof.

(5) The Compensation Body shall cease forthwith to act in respect of a claim if the insurance undertaking or its claims representative, subsequently makes a reasoned reply to the claim.

(6) The Compensation Body shall determine the validity of a claim and make compensation payments in respect of a claim, it deems valid, as if it were the insurance

undertaking liable to the injured party for the loss and damage in respect of the accident which is the subject of the claim.

(7) Subject to paragraph (6), the provisions of this Regulation shall be without prejudice to—

    (a) the right of the State to regard a payment of compensation by the Compensation Body as subsidiary or non-subsidiary to any legal proceedings which may be issued by the injured party, and

    (b) the right to make provision for the settlement of claims between the Compensation Body and the person or persons who caused the accident and other insurance undertakings, Government Department or Health Board that may be required to make payments to the injured person in respect of the same accident.

(8) The Compensation Body may not make the payment of compensation subject to the injured party being required to establish in any way that the person liable for compensation is unable to or is unwilling to, pay the said compensation, or any conditions other than those specified in these Regulations.

(9) Where the Compensation Body has paid compensation to a person normally resident in the State, it shall be entitled to claim reimbursement of the amount of compensation so paid from the compensation body in the EEA State in which the insurance undertaking which issued the policy in respect of the vehicle that gave rise to the liability, is established.

(10) Where a compensation body in another EEA State has paid compensation to a person normally resident in that EEA State in respect of an accident involving a vehicle the policy for which was issued by an insurance undertaking established in the State, the compensation body shall be liable to indemnify the foreign compensation body.

(11) Whenever any compensation body receives a claim pursuant to paragraphs (7) or (8), it shall be subrogated to the injured party's rights against the person liable for the payment of compensation or his insurance undertaking.

7. (1) Where

    (a) it is not possible to identify a vehicle involved in an accident which gives rise to a claim to which these Regulations are applicable, or,

    (b) where, within 2 months of the date of such accident, it is not possible to identify an insurance undertaking that has issued a policy for the vehicle in question,

an injured party that is normally resident in the State may make a claim for compensation to the Compensation Body.

(2) In the event of a claim on the Compensation Body on foot of subparagraph (a) the Compensation Body shall compensate the injured party in accordance with the provisions of article 1 of Directive 84/5/EEC as if it were the body authorised under paragraph 4 of that article and the accident had occurred in the State.

(3) In the event of the payment of compensation by the compensation body under paragraph (2) the compensation body shall then have a claim under the conditions set out in paragraph (7)

(a) where the insurance undertaking cannot be identified, against the guarantee fund provided for in Regulation 1(4) of Directive 84/5/EEC in the EEA State in which the vehicle which caused the accident was normally based;

(b) in the case of an unidentified vehicle, against the guarantee fund in the EEA State in which the accident took place;

(c) in the event of a third country vehicle, against the guarantee fund of the EEA State in which the accident took place.

8. (1) Subject to paragraph (2), the Information Centre and the Compensation Body shall be responsible for the regulation of the systems and procedures that are required for the discharge of their functions under these Regulations.

(2) In the event of a failure by the Information Centre or the Compensation Body to discharge its functions under these Regulations, the Minister may direct that the said functions be discharged within a specified period.

(3) The European Communities (Non-Life Insurance) Framework Regulations 1994 (S.I. No. 359 of 1994) (as amended) shall, with the following modifications and any other necessary modifications, to those Regulations, apply to these Regulations, and references in those Regulations or the provisions of those regulations shall, unless the context otherwise requires, be construed as including references to these Regulations or the provisions of these Regulations—

(a) by the insertion in Regulation 2 of the following definition:

"'Claims representative' means a person appointed as a claims representative by an insurance undertaking pursuant to Regulation 4(1) of the European Communities (Fourth Motor Insurance Directive) Regulations 2003 (S.I. No. 651 of 2003) and shall be construed as a 'person concerned' within the meaning of Regulation 59"

(b) by the insertion in Regulation 7(2) of the following paragraph:

"(f) It shall communicate the name and address of the claims representative appointed or to be appointed in each EEA State other than the EEA State in which the authorisation is sought if the risks to be covered are classified in class 10 of point A of Annex 1, other than carrier's liability."

(c) by the insertion in Regulation 49 of the following paragraph

"(h) It shall communicate the name and address of the claims representative appointed or to be appointed in each EEA State other than the EEA State in which the authorisation is sought if the risks to be covered are classified in class 10 of point A of Annex 1, other than carrier's liability."

GIVEN under my Official Seal

27th November 2003.

Séamus Brennan

Minister for Transport

Explanatory Note

(This note is not part of the Instrument and does not purport to be a legal interpretation)

These regulations give legal effect to the provisions of Directive 2000/26/EEC of the European Parliament and of the Council of 16 May 2000 on the approximation of the laws of the Member States relating to insurance against civil liability in respect of the use of motor vehicles and amending Council Directives 73/239/EEC and 88/357/EEC (Fourth Motor Insurance Directive)

The Directive makes special provisions for the processing of certain claims for compensation for injury or damage arising as a result of accidents occurring in a Member State of the European Communities other than the Member State of residence of the injured party.

These regulations also provide for

- a direct right of action against insurers authorised to transact motor insurance business in the Republic of Ireland in the case of relevant accidents

- the appointment of claims representatives by such insurers in each of the other Member States with sufficient powers and authority to handle and settle relevant claims in the language of the state to which they have been appointed; the appointment of such claims representatives will be a threshold condition for insurers who wish to transact motor insurance business in Republic of Ireland

- the approval of the Motor Insurers' Bureau of Ireland (MIBI) as the Information Centre in Republic of Ireland for the purpose of providing information on insurers and insurance policies in force in respect of relevant accidents

- the approval of MIBI as the Compensation Body for relevant accidents in the case of failure of an insurer authorised to transact motor insurance business in Republic of Ireland to appoint a claims representative, settle a claim within three months of its receipt or to make a reasoned response within three months. Compensation for uninsured and unidentified accidents to which the regulations apply will also be dealt with in the first instance by the MIBI as compensation body.

These regulations also apply to those States which are parties to the European Economic Area Agreement though not Member States of the European Community, currently Iceland, Norway and Liechtenstein.

Appendix 4.2

EUROPEAN COMMUNITIES (MOTOR INSURANCE) REGULATIONS 2008 (SI 248/2008) ('THE 2008 REGULATIONS')

EUROPEAN COMMUNITIES (MOTOR INSURANCE) REGULATIONS 2008

SI 248/2008

I, NOEL DEMPSEY, Minister for Transport, in exercise of the powers conferred on me by section 3 of the European Communities Act 1972 (No. 27 of 1972) and for the purposes of giving effect to Directive No. 2005/14/EC of the European Parliament and of the Council of 11 May 2005,[1] hereby make the following regulations:

Citation

1. These Regulations may be cited as the European Communities (Motor Insurance) Regulations 2008.

Compulsory Motor Insurance

2. Section 56 of the Road Traffic Act 1961 is amended—

    (a)   in paragraph (a) of subsection (1), by deleting "(exclusive of the excepted persons)",

    (b)   in subsection (2) (inserted by Regulation 3(1) of the European Communities (Road Traffic) (Compulsory Insurance) (Amendment) Regulations 1995 (S.I. No. 353 of 1995)) by substituting for paragraph (a) the following:

        "(a)   it may, in so far as it relates to injury to property, be limited to the sum of €1,000,000 per claim, whatever the number of victims,", and

        (c)   by substituting for subsection (7) (inserted by Regulation 3 of European Communities (Road Traffic) (Compulsory Insurance) (Amendment) Regulations 2001 (S.I. No. 463 of 2001)) subsection (8) (inserted by Regulation 4(2) of the European Communities (Road Traffic) (Compulsory Insurance) (Amendment) Regulations 1987 (S.I. No. 322 of 1987)) and subsections (9) and (10) (inserted by the European

---

1.   OJ No. L149, 11.6.2005.

Notice of the making of this Statutory Instrument was published in "Iris Oifigiúil" of 8th July, 2008.

Communities (Road Traffic) (Compulsory Insurance) (Amendment) Regulations 1992 (S.I. No. 347 of 1992)) the following:

"(8) In this Part a reference to the territory in which a vehicle is normally based is a reference to—

(a)   the territory of the state of which the vehicle bears a registration plate, irrespective of whether the plate is permanent or temporary,

(b)   in a case where no registration plate is required for a type of vehicle, but the vehicle bears an insurance plate or a distinguishing sign analogous to the registration plate, the territory of the state in which the plate or sign is issued, or

(c)   in a case where a registration or insurance plate or distinguishing sign is not required for a vehicle, the territory of the state in which the person who has custody of the vehicle is resident.

(9) In this Part—

'designated territories' means the territories of the Member States (other than the State) and Croatia, Iceland, Norway and Switzerland;

'mechanically propelled vehicle' includes a semi-trailer or trailer when used in a public place.".

3. Section 62 of the Road Traffic Act 1961 is amended—

(a)   in subsection (1) by—

(i)   in paragraph (*b*) by deleting "(exclusive of the excepted person)",

(ii)   in paragraph (*c*) by deleting "and" after "insurance",

(iii)   by substituting for paragraph (ii) (inserted by Regulation 4(2) of the European Communities (Road Traffic) (Compulsory Insurance) (Amendment) Regulations 1992 (S.I. No. 347 of 1992)) the following:

"(cc) The liability of the insurer extends, in addition to the negligent use of the mechanically propelled vehicle in the State, to the negligent use of the vehicle in the designated territories according to the law relating to compulsory insurance against civil liability in respect of the use of mechanically propelled vehicles in force in those territories or to the extent required by this Part, whichever is the greater;",

(iv)   in paragraph (*d*) by substituting "insured; and" for "insured.", and

(v)   by inserting after paragraph (*d*) the following:

"(e)   the liability of the insurer extends to any loss or injury suffered by the victim, due to the negligent use of a mechanically propelled vehicle, during a direct journey between two Member States, if there is no national insurers' bureau responsible for the territory which is being crossed in accordance with the law relating to compulsory insurance against civil liability in respect of the use of mechanically propelled vehicles in that territory.",

(b) by substituting for subsection (1A) (inserted by Regulation 5 of the European Communities (Road Traffic) (Compulsory Insurance) Regulations 1975 (S.I. No.178 of 1975)) the following:

"(1A) For the purpose of this Part a policy of insurance issued in accordance with the laws on compulsory insurance in force in any of the designated territories, other than the State, in respect of a mechanically propelled vehicle normally based in that territory is an approved policy of insurance."

(c) by inserting after subsection (3) the following:

"(4) In this section 'national insurers' bureau' means a professional organisation which is constituted in accordance with Recommendation No. 5 adopted on 25 January 1949 by the Road Transport Sub-committee of the Inland Transport Committee of the United Nations Economic Commission for Europe and which groups together insurance undertakings which, in a state, are authorised to conduct the business of motor vehicle insurance against civil liability.".

4. Regulation 5(2) of the Road Traffic (Compulsory Insurance) Regulations 1962 (S.I. No. 14 of 1962) is amended by deleting "or an excepted person".

Functions of Motor Insurers' Bureau of Ireland

5. European Communities (Fourth Motor Insurance Directive) Regulations 2003 (S.I. No. 651 of 2003) are amended—

(a) in Regulation 3, by inserting after paragraph (6) the following:

"(7) Paragraphs (5) and (6) of this Regulation, paragraphs (8) to (10) of Regulation 4 and Regulation 5 apply to all injured parties normally resident in an EEA State",

(b) in Regulation 4, by substituting for paragraph (11) the following:

"(11) The appointment of a claims representative does not in itself constitute a head office, agency or branch of an insurance undertaking or does not constitute an establishment in any EEA State.

(12) Paragraphs (8) to (10) apply to the Motor Insurers' Bureau of Ireland as they apply to insurance undertakings and claims representatives.", and

(c) In Regulation 5(3), by deleting subparagraph (c).

GIVEN under my Official Seal,

4 July 2008

NOEL DEMPSEY,

Minister for Transport

EXPLANATORY NOTE

These Regulations give legal effect to the provisions of Directive 2005/14/EC of the 11th May 2005 amending Council Directives 72/166/EEC, 84/5/EEC, 88/357/EEC and 90/232/EEC and Directive 2000/26/EC of the European Parliament and of the Council relating to insurance against civil liability in respect of the use of motor vehicles.

The Regulations provide for:

- the definition of the territory in which the vehicle is normally based as being the state of which the vehicle bears a registration plate, another plate or the state of residence of the custodian of the vehicle

- the liability of the insurer to cover, in accordance with local law, the negligent use of a vehicle in transit between two EU States where the territory being crossed has no national insurers' bureau

- the limit per claim for property damage being € 1,000,000.00 regardless of the number of victims

- the approval of the Motor Insurers' Bureau of Ireland (MIBI) as the Guarantee Fund for compensation in accidents where compulsory motor insurance is not in place and the requirement that the MIBI handle claims for compensation in the same manner as an insurance undertaking including the making of an offer of compensation within three months of a valid claim or providing a reasoned reply in the same period

- policy of motor insurance issued under the laws of any of the designated territories as being an approved policy of insurance

- the reference to Green Card details is deleted in the information to be supplied by the Information Centre.

These Regulations also specify that:

- all persons, other than the driver, travelling in a mechanically propelled vehicle are passengers for the purposes of third party compulsory motor insurance

- the definition of mechanically propelled vehicle is extended to include semi- trailer or trailer when used in a public place.

Appendix 5

'INSURER CONCERNED' AND OTHER DEFINITIONS IN ARTICLE 1 OF THE MIBI'S ARTICLES OF ASSOCIATION TOGETHER WITH ARTICLES 71–76 THEREOF

INTERPRETATION

1.1 The marginal notes hereto do not affect the construction hereof and in these Articles unless there is something in the subject or context inconsistent therewith.

1.2 In these Articles (except where the context otherwise requires) the following words shall have the following meanings:

Words	Meanings
'THE ACT'	The Companies' Acts 1963–2009 (as amended from time to time).
'THE BUREAU'	Motor Insurers' Bureau of Ireland, having its registered office at 39 Molesworth Street, Dublin 2.
'THE BOARD'	The Board of Directors for the time being of the Bureau.
...	
'THE DOMESTIC REGULATIONS'	The regulations between the Bureau and its Members more particularly referred to in these Articles.
...	
'MEMBER'	A member of the Bureau which transacts motor vehicle insurance in the State and Lloyd's Underwriters including a member who ceases to be a member for the purposes of Article 10 and Article 63.3
...	

For the purposes of Articles 71, 72, 73, 74, 75 and 76 please see Article 1.2 which contains the relevant definitions applicable to this Article.

'Execution date'	means the date upon which the Original Judgment Creditor became entitled to enforce a Road Traffic Act Judgment against the Judgment Debtor;

'Insurer concerned'　　　shall, subject to this Article, mean the Member who at the time of the accident which gave rise to a Road Traffic Act Liability was providing Motor Insurance in respect of the vehicle from the use and / or ownership of which the liability of the Judgment Debtor arose.

'Judgment Debtor'　　　means a person against whom a Court Order on foot of Road Traffic Acts 1961–2006 as amended or PIAB Payment Order has been obtained.

'Motor Insurance'　　　means the existence of any document or promise by or on behalf of any Member, whether legally or otherwise effecting or purporting to effect insurance cover against a Road Traffic Act Liability where such motor insurance is current at the time that such a liability was incurred whether or not such motor insurance was provided in Writing, *via* verbal representations, *via* electronic communications or other electronic record or otherwise.

'Original　Judgment　means the person in whose favour a Road Traffic
Creditor'　　　Act Judgment was given and who is entitled to enforce it and has complied or is able and willing to comply with the conditions precedent to the Bureau's liability as set out in any of the agreements entered into from time to time by the Bureau for the purposes of satisfying Road Traffic Act Judgments.

'PIAB'　　　means Personal Injuries Assessment Board established under the Personal Injuries Assessment Board Act, 2003.

'Relevant Foreign　　　shall mean:-
Country'

- a country having compensation body or guarantee fund as required under Article 6 of Directive 2000/26/EC with which the Bureau has concluded an agreement pursuant to Article 6(3) of such Directive; or

- any country having a national insurers' bureau (as defined in Article 1(3) of Directive 72/166/EEC, a **'Green Card Bureau'**), with which the Bureau has concluded an agreement under the Green Card system;

312

'Road Traffic Act Judgment'	means a judgment obtained in a court of competent jurisdiction in respect of a Road Traffic Act Liability or a payment order issued by PIAB in respect of a Road Traffic Act Liability;
'Road Traffic Act Liability'	means such liability (whether arising out of negligence, breach of statutory duty or otherwise) arising out of driving, management, ownership, use or control of a motor vehicle in a public place or otherwise under the Road Traffic Acts 1961–2006 as amended or under the equivalent legislation in a Relevant Foreign Country:-

(a) as is required to be covered by a policy of insurance or security under the Road Traffic Acts 1961–2006 as amended or under the equivalent legislation in a Relevant Foreign Country or

(b) as would fall within (a) above were it not for s 4 of RTA 1961 (as amended) or the equivalent provisions of any enactment within the State or of a Relevant Foreign Country and is in fact covered by a policy of insurance;

'Satisfy the Original Judgment Creditor'	means to pay or cause to be paid to the original judgment creditor such sum as is due and outstanding under a Road Traffic Act Judgment (including assessed costs or such proportion of the assessed costs as is attributable to the Road Traffic Act Liability) on terms that the judgment is assigned by the Original Judgment Creditor to the Bureau.

1.3   References to the singular number only shall include the plural number and *vice versa*; references to one gender only shall include all genders; and references to persons shall include corporations.

1.4   Headings are inserted for convenience only and shall not affect the construction of these Articles.

1.5   Words importing persons include corporations and firms. Unless the contrary intention appears, words or expressions contained in these Articles shall bear the same meaning as in the Act or in any modification thereof in force at the date at which these regulations became binding on the Bureau.

1.6   Reference herein to any enactment shall mean such enactment as the same may be amended and may be from time to time and for the time being in force.

71   **THE DOMESTIC REGULATIONS – INSURER CONCERNED**

71.1   **Interpretation of Articles 71, 72, 73, 74, 75 and 76**

For the purposes of Articles 71, 72, 73, 74, 75 and 76 please see Article 1.2 which contains the relevant definitions applicable to this Article.

71.2   Where something must be done under this Article within a specified period of days after a date or an event, the period shall begin on the day following that date or event and the days shall be taken to be calendar days.

Qualifications to the Application of Insurer Concerned Provisions

71.3   Without prejudice to the generality of the definition of Insurer Concerned, a Member is the Insurer Concerned notwithstanding that:

71.3.1 the Motor Insurance has been obtained by fraud, misrepresentation, non-disclosure of material facts, or mistake, whether or not such fraud, misrepresentation, non-disclosure of material facts or mistake renders the insurance void *ab initio* except in circumstances when, before the date on which the Road Traffic Act Liability was incurred there had been a prosecution and conviction which would entitle the Insurer Concerned to refuse payment pursuant to section 76(1)(e) of the Road Traffic Acts, 1961–2006 as amended; or

71.3.2 some term, description, limitation, exception or condition (whether express or implied) of the insurance or of the proposal form on which it is based expressly or by implication excludes the Insurer Concerned's liability whether generally or in the particular circumstances in which the Judgment Debtor's liability was incurred; or

71.3.3 the Judgment Debtor was in unauthorised possession of the vehicle arising out of the use of which the liability of the Judgment Debtor was incurred.

71.3.4 the use of the vehicle is other than that permitted under the policy.

71.4   A Member only ceases to the be the Insurer Concerned when the Motor Insurance has been cancelled in any of the circumstances set out below or in the case or Article 71.4.5 and Article 71.4.5 is void *ab initio*:-

71.4.1 the certificate of insurance has been returned for cancellation to the insurer, the effective date of the cancellation being the later of the date on which the certificate of insurance has been received by the insurer or the date from which the insured has requested that the insurance be cancelled;

71.4.2 the insured has made specific request in Writing to the insurer, the effective date of the cancellation being the later of the date on which the said request has been received by the insurer or the date from which the insured has requested that the insurance be cancelled;

71.4.3 the certificate of insurance has been returned for cancellation to the intermediary who is acting as agent or broker in relation to the insurance policy in question, the effective date of cancellation being the later of the date o which the certificate of insurance has been received by such intermediary or the date from which the insured has requested that the insurance be cancelled;

71.4.4   the insurer or any agent or broker as specified in Article 71.4.3 has written by letter to the insured and posted it *via* registered post (or such other method of communication as is unanimously resolved by the Board and communicated to the Members in Writing) to the insured cancelling the insurance and demanding return of the certificate of insurance, the effective date of the cancellation being the later of the date on which the said letter is registered by the postal authorities or the effective date of cancellation as stated in the letter.

71.4.5   when, before the date on which the Road Traffic Act Liability was incurred there had been a prosecution and conviction which would entitle the Insurer Concerned to refuse payment pursuant to section 76(1)(e) of the Road Traffic Acts 1961–2006 as amended and a letter declaring the Motor Insurance void is sent to the insured by the Member *via* registered post (or *via* such other method of communication unanimously resolved by the Board and communicated to the Members in writing) and the letter is registered by the postal authorities before the date on which the Road Traffic Liability was incurred.

71.4.6   when the Motor Insurance is void "*ab initio*" and a letter declaring the Motor Insurance void is sent to the insured by the Member *via* registered post (or *via* such other method of communication unanimously resolved by the Board and communicated to the Members in writing) and the letter is registered by the postal authorities before the date on which the Road Traffic Liability was incurred.

71.4.7   when the insurance has ceased to operate by reason of a transfer of interest in the vehicle involved in the accident, which the insurance purports to cover the onus of proof is on the Insured to prove the change of ownership.

INSURANCE OF UNSPECIFIED VEHICLES

71.5   For the purpose of these Articles an Insurer Concerned in respect of any Motor Insurance covering unspecified vehicles (i.e. vehicles which are insured in common with other vehicles are not the subject of a policy of insurance affecting individually identified vehicles insured as stand alone vehicles) shall in relation to such vehicles, and irrespective of the basis of the policy, be the Insurer Concerned and shall cease to be the Insurer Concerned in respect of:-

71.5.1.   vehicles not the property of the insured which have been taken into the custody or control of the insured, if, and only if the vehicle in respect of which the claim arises was released from his custody or control to the owner of any such vehicle;

71.5.2 any vehicle which is specifically excluded from the insurance provided by the policy by reference to its registration number or by other vehicle identification; or

71.5.3 any vehicle which is specifically insured in the name of the insured with another insurer.

71.6 Where an Insurer Concerned under such an unspecified motor vehicle insurance and an Insurer Concerned under another insurance in respect of the same particular vehicle are both involved in circumstances in which neither insurer is liable under its policy the claim shall be handled by agreement between the relevant Insurers Concerned each being liable for one half of the damages and costs in default of agreement.

71.7 If there is more than one Insurer Concerned in respect of a particular vehicle then the handling of any claims will be by agreement between the relevant Insurers Concerned (and, in default of agreement, as determined by the Board) and the administrative costs of handling and settling the claims shall be shared equally between all relevant Insurers Concerned.

INSURER CONCERNED – BURDEN AND ONUS OF PROOF

72. Where a Member contends that it is not the Insurer Concerned, for whatever reason the onus and burden of proving such contention shall rest upon such Member.

PERSONS VISITING RELEVANT FOREIGN COUNTRIES

73. Where persons visiting Relevant Foreign Countries are insured against a Road Traffic Act Liability under policies issued abroad (other than policies issued in a Relevant Foreign Country) by branch office, agent or subsidiary or associated company or a Member, such Member shall be the Insurer Concerned in the event of such visitor becoming a Judgment Debtor.

OBLIGATION TO SATISFY JUDGMENTS

74.1 If a Road Traffic Act Judgment is obtained the Insurer Concerned will satisfy the original judgment creditor if, and to the extent that, the judgment has not within twenty eight days of the Execution Date has been satisfied by the Judgment Debtor.

74.2 The making of any payment by an Insurer Concerned under this Article shall not entitle that Member to any reimbursement in respect thereof from the Bureau.

74.3 Where judgment is obtained in respect of a liability which by reason only of section 60 of the Road Traffic Act 1961 (or any similar section as applied by virtue of any enactment or any corresponding provisions of a Relevant Foreign Country) is not required to be covered by insurance it shall is such liability is covered for the purposes of this Article be deemed to be a judgment obtained in respect of a Road Traffic Act Liability and a vehicle which has been unlawfully removed from the possession of the Government or of an "exempted person" (as defined under the Road Traffic Acts 1961–

2006 as amended) shall be deemed to continue in that possession while it is so removed.

74.4　Subject to complying in all respects with this Article 74, nothing contained in this Article shall affect or be deemed to affect any right of a Member to indemnity or contribution from another Member whether such right arises at common law, by statute, from a claims sharing or other agreement, by subrogation or by assignment of the original judgment creditor's judgment and all such rights shall be determined according to the facts and circumstances of each particular case without reference to this Article.

SATISFACTION OF CLAIMS BY THE BUREAU

75.1　If it appears to the Bureau to be expedient, the Bureau may itself, at its discretion, settle or compromise any claim in respect of a Road Traffic Act Liability or satisfy any Road Traffic Act Judgment or refund any amount paid by any bureau or other person in any Relevant Foreign Country on foot of any settlement of or compromising of any claim in respect of a Road Traffic Liability or on foot of any satisfaction or any Road Traffic Act Judgment and in any such case the Bureau shall be entitled to recover the sum paid by it from the Insurer Concerned and/or the insurer and the Insurer Concerned and/or the insurer shall refund or pay any amounts paid by the Bureau to the Bureau within fourteen days of being requested to do so by the Bureau in writing.

75.2　If a judgment is obtained against any Judgment Debtor and remains unsatisfied and no Member is liable to satisfy same under this Article the Bureau will after the expiry of twenty eight days from the Execution Date satisfy this claim itself.

INSURER CONCERNED LITIGATION

76　In respect of any claim in which a Member is an Insurer Concerned pursuant to these Articles relating to:-

76.1　Any matter relating to the interpretation of these Memorandum and Articles of Association or any other statutory, national or international agreement, which the Bureau is a party to;

76.2　Any matter relating to the interpretation of EU legislation concerning the provision of insurance against civil liability in respect of the use of motor vehicles;

76.3　Any litigation or dispute in whole or in part relating to constitutional or other precedent issues which are of concern to the Bureau given its principal objects;

76.4　Any other litigation or dispute in whole or in part where the Bureau's role, obligations and rights are directly affected;

in addition to their obligations and responsibilities to the Bureau pursuant to these Articles, the relevant Insurer Concerned shall immediately notify the Secretary of the Bureau in Writing of such litigation or dispute and at which point the Bureau shall, in addition to any other rights which it may have pursuant to these Articles, have the right to adopt and conduct such litigation or dispute in the stead of the Insurer Concerned as it sees fit and shall have the right to recover all reasonable costs, damages and/or other expenses from the Insurer Concerned, the insured or any third party as the case may be. In circumstances where the Bureau adopts and conducts such litigation or dispute pursuant to this Article in the stead of the Insurer Concerned such Insurer Concerned may make an application to the Board to have the Bureau bear some or all of the costs of the litigation or dispute on the basis that the litigation or dispute properly concerns all the members and accordingly should be properly borne by the Bureau. Upon such application from a Member the Board may in its absolute discretion decide that the Bureau will bear some or all of the costs of such precedent litigation or dispute.

Appendix 6

INTERNAL REGULATIONS AS REVISED BY THE GENERAL ASSEMBLY OF THE COUNCIL OF BUREAUX ON 29 MAY 2008

INTERNAL REGULATIONS

Preamble

(1) Whereas in 1949 the Working Party on Road Transport of the Inland Transport Committee of the Economic Commission for Europe of the United Nations sent to the Governments of Member States a recommendation[1] inviting them to ask insurers covering third party liability risks in respect of the use of vehicles to conclude agreements for the establishment of uniform and practical provisions to enable motorists to be satisfactorily insured when entering countries where insurance against such risks is compulsory.

(2) Whereas this recommendation concluded that the introduction of a uniform insurance document would be the best way to achieve that end and set out the basic principles of agreements to be concluded between insurers in the different countries.

(3) Whereas the Inter-Bureaux Agreement, the text of which was adopted in November 1951 by representatives of the insurers in States which, at the time, had responded favourably to the recommendation, formed the basis of the relationship between these insurers.

(4) Whereas:

(a) the purpose of the system, commonly known as the Green Card System, was to facilitate the international circulation of motor vehicles by enabling insurance of third party liability risks in respect of their use to fulfil the criteria imposed by the visited country and, in the case of accidents, to guarantee compensation of injured parties in accordance with the national law and regulations of that country;

(b) the international motor insurance card (Green Card), which is officially recognised by the government authorities of the States adopting the United Nations Recommendation, is proof in each visited country of compulsory civil liability insurance in respect of the use of the motor vehicle described therein;

---

1. Recommendation No 5 adopted on January 1949, superseded by Annex 1 of the Revised Consolidated Resolution on the Facilitation of Road Transport (R.E.4) adopted by the Working Party on Road Transport of the Inland Transport Committee of the Economic Commission for Europe of the United Nations, the text of which is provided as Appendix I.

Internal Regulations adopted by the General Assembly in Crete on 30 May 2002 and revised in Lisbon on 29 May 2008

COUNCIL OF BUREAUX   CONSEIL DES BUREAUX

(c)   in each participating State a national bureau has been created and officially approved in order to provide a dual guarantee to:

–   its government that the foreign insurer will abide by the law applicable in that country and compensate injured parties within its limits,

–   the bureau of the visited country of the commitment of the member insurer covering third party liability in respect of the use of the vehicle involved in the accident;

(d)   as a consequence of this non-profit-making dual mandate, each bureau is required to have its own independent financial structure based on the joint commitment of insurers authorised to transact compulsory civil liability insurance in respect of the use of motor vehicles operating in its national market which enables it to meet obligations arising out of agreements between it and other bureaux.

(5) Whereas:

(a)   some States, in order to further facilitate international road traffic, have abolished Green Card inspection at their frontiers by virtue of agreements signed between their respective Bureaux, mainly based on vehicle registration;

(b)   by its Directive of 24 April 1972[2] the Council of the European Union proposed to the Bureaux of Member States the conclusion of such an agreement; then known as the Supplementary Inter-Bureaux Agreement, which was signed on 16 October 1972;

(c)   subsequent agreements, based on the same principles, enabled the bureaux of other countries to become members; and these agreements were then collected into a single document signed on 15 March 1991 and called the Multilateral Guarantee Agreement.

(6) Whereas it is now desirable to incorporate all provisions governing the relations between bureaux into a single document, the Council of Bureaux, at its General Assembly held in Rethymno (Crete) on 30 May 2002 adopted these Internal Regulations.

(7) Whereas the General Assembly of Lisbon (Portugal) ratified, on 29 May 2008, the updates which were made to the current Internal Regulations related principally to the application of the 5th Motor Insurance Directive (Directive 2005/14/EC of 11 May 2005).

---

2.   Directive of the Council of 24 April 1972 (72/166/EEC) on the approximation of the laws of Member States relating to insurance against civil liability in respect of the use of motor vehicles and to the enforcement of the obligation to insure against such liability, the text of which is provided as Appendix II.

Internal Regulations adopted by the General Assembly in Crete on 30 May 2002 and revised in Lisbon on 29 May 2008

COUNCIL OF BUREAUX   CONSEIL DES BUREAUX

SECTION I GENERAL RULES (MANDATORY PROVISIONS)

Article 1 Purpose

The purpose of these Internal Regulations is to govern the reciprocal relations between National Insurers' Bureaux thereby enforcing the provisions of Recommendation No 5 adopted on 25 January 1949 by the Working Party on Road Transport of the Inland Transport Committee of the European Economic Commission of the United Nations, superseded by Annex 1 of the Revised Consolidated Resolution on the Facilitation of Road Transport (R.E.4) adopted by the Inland Transport Committee at the sixty-sixth session which was held from 17 to 19 of February 2004 in its current version (hereinafter called recommendation No 5).

Article 2 Definitions

For the purpose of these Internal Regulations the following words and expressions shall have the meanings herein assigned to them and no other:

1. "national insurers' bureau" (hereinafter called bureau): means the professional organisation which is a Member of the Council of Bureaux and constituted in the country of its establishment pursuant to Recommendation No 5;

2. "insurer": means any undertaking authorised to conduct the business of compulsory third party liability insurance in respect of the use of motor vehicles;

3. "member": means any insurer who is a member of a bureau;

4. "correspondent": means any insurer or other person appointed by one or more insurers with the approval of the Bureau of the country in which the person is established with a view to handling and settling claims arising from accidents involving vehicles for which the insurer or insurers in question have issued an insurance policy and occurring in that country;

5. "vehicle": means any motor vehicle intended for travel on land and propelled by mechanical power but not running on rails as well as any trailer whether or not coupled but only where the motor vehicle or trailer is made subject to compulsory insurance in the country in which it is being used;

6. "accident": means any event causing loss or injury which may, pursuant to the law of the country where it occurs, fall within the scope of compulsory third party liability insurance in respect of the use of a vehicle;

7. "injured party": means any person entitled to claim compensation in respect of any loss or injury caused by a vehicle;

8. "claim": means any one or more claims for compensation presented by an injured party and arising out of the same accident;

9. "policy of insurance": means a contract of compulsory insurance issued by a member covering civil liability in respect of the use of a vehicle;

Internal Regulations adopted by the General Assembly in Crete on 30 May 2002 and revised in Lisbon on 29 May 2008

10. "insured": means any person whose third party liability is covered by a policy of insurance;

11. "Green Card": means the international certificate of motor insurance conforming to any of the models approved by the Council of Bureaux;

12. "Council of Bureaux": means the body to which all Bureaux must belong and which is responsible for the administration and the operation of the international motor civil liability insurance system (known as the Green Card System).

Article 3 Handling of claims

1. When a bureau is informed of an accident occurring in the territory of the country for which it is competent, involving a vehicle from another country it shall, without waiting for a formal claim, proceed to investigate the circumstances of the accident. It shall as soon as possible give notice of any such accident to the insurer who issued the Green Card or policy of insurance or, if appropriate, to the bureau concerned. Any omission to do so shall however not be held against it.

If, in the course of this investigation, the bureau notes that the insurer of the vehicle involved in the accident is identified and that a correspondent of this insurer has been approved in conformity with the provisions in Article 4, it shall forward this information promptly to the correspondent for further action.

2. On receipt of a claim arising out of an accident under the circumstances described above, if a correspondent of the insurer has been approved, the bureau shall forward the claim promptly to the correspondent so that it may be handled and settled in conformity with the provisions of Article 4. If there is no approved correspondent, it shall give immediate notice to the insurer who issued the Green Card or policy of insurance or, if appropriate, to the bureau concerned that it has received a claim and will handle it, or arrange for it to be handled, by an agent whose identity it shall also notify.

3. The bureau is authorised to settle any claim amicably or to accept service of any extra-judicial or judicial process likely to involve the payment of compensation.

4. All claims shall be handled by the bureau with complete autonomy in conformity with legal and regulatory provisions applicable in the country of accident relating to liability, compensation of injured parties and compulsory insurance in the best interests of the insurer who issued the Green Card or policy of insurance or, if appropriate, the bureau concerned.

The bureau shall be exclusively competent for all matters concerning the interpretation of the law applicable in the country of accident (even when it refers to the legal provisions applying in another country) and the settlement of the claim. Subject to this latter provision, the bureau shall, on express demand, inform the insurer, or the bureau concerned, before taking a final decision.

5. When the settlement envisaged is in excess of the conditions or limits applicable under the compulsory motor civil liability insurance law in force in the country of accident whilst covered under the policy of insurance, it shall consult the insurer in

COUNCIL OF BUREAUX   CONSEIL DES BUREAUX

relation to that part of the claim which exceeds those conditions or limits. The consent of such insurer is not required if the applicable law imposes on the bureau the obligation to take account of the contractual guarantees in excess of such limits and conditions provided in the law relating to insurance against civil liability in respect of the use of motor vehicles in the country of accident.

6. A bureau may not of its own volition or without the written consent of the insurer or Bureau concerned, entrust the claim to any agent who is financially interested in it by virtue of any contractual obligation. If it does so, without such consent, its right to reimbursement shall be limited to one half of the sum otherwise recoverable.

Article 4 Correspondents

1. Subject to any agreement to the contrary binding it to other bureaux and/or to any national legal or regulatory provisions, each bureau shall set out the conditions under which it grants, refuses or withdraws its approval to correspondents established in the country for which it is competent.

However, this approval shall be granted automatically when requested in the name of a member of another Bureau for any establishment of this member in the country of the Bureau receiving the request provided that such establishment is authorised to transact insurance against civil liability in respect of the use of motor vehicles.

2. Bureaux in the Member States of the European Economic Area undertake when receiving such a request, to approve as correspondents in their country claims representatives already appointed by insurers of the other Member States pursuant to Directive 2000/26/EC. This approval cannot be withdrawn as long as the correspondent concerned retains its capacity as a claims representative under the said Directive unless it is in serious breach of its obligations under this Article.

3. Only a bureau shall have the authority, on the request of one of its members, to send to another bureau a request for approval of a correspondent established in the country of that bureau. This request shall be sent by fax or e-mail and supported by proof that the proposed correspondent accepts the requested approval.

The bureau concerned shall grant or refuse its approval within three months from the date of receipt of the request and shall notify its decision and its effective date to the bureau that made the request as well as to the correspondent concerned. In the event of no response being received, approval shall be deemed to have been granted and to have taken effect on the expiry of that period.

4. The correspondent shall handle all claims in conformity with any legal or regulatory provisions applicable in the country of accident relating to liability, compensation of injured parties and compulsory motor insurance, in the name of the bureau that has approved it and on behalf of the insurer that requested its approval, arising out of accidents occurring in that country involving vehicles insured by the insurer that requested its approval.

When any settlement envisaged exceeds the conditions or limits applicable under the compulsory motor civil liability insurance law applicable in the country of accident, whilst covered under the policy of insurance, the correspondent must comply with the provisions set out in Article 3(5).

5. The bureau that has granted its approval to a correspondent recognises it as exclusively competent to handle and settle claims in the name of the bureau and on behalf of the insurer that requested its approval. The bureau shall inform injured parties of this competence and forward to the correspondent any notifications relating to such claims. However it may, at any time and without any obligation to justify its decision, take over the handling and settlement of a claim from a correspondent.

6. If, for whatever reason, the bureau that granted the approval is required to compensate any injured party in place of the correspondent, it shall be reimbursed directly by the bureau through which the request for approval was sent, in accordance with the conditions set out in Article 5.

7. Subject to the provisions of Article 4(4), the correspondent is free to agree with the insurer that requested its approval the conditions for reimbursement of sums paid to injured parties and the method for calculating its handling fees which agreement, however, shall not be enforceable against any bureau.

If a correspondent is unable to obtain reimbursement of advance payments it has made in accordance with the conditions set out in Article 4.4 on behalf of the insurer that requested its approval, it shall be reimbursed by the bureau that approved it. The latter bureau shall subsequently be reimbursed by the bureau of which the insurer in question is a member in accordance with the conditions set out in Article 5.

8. When a bureau is informed that one of its members has decided to dismiss a correspondent, it shall immediately so inform the bureau that granted the approval. This latter bureau shall be at liberty to determine the date on which its approval will cease to have effect.

When a bureau that granted approval to a correspondent decides to withdraw it or is informed that the correspondent wishes to have its approval withdrawn, it shall immediately so inform the bureau that forwarded the request for the approval of the correspondent. It shall also inform the bureau of the date of the correspondent's effective withdrawal or the date on which its approval will cease to have effect.

Article 5 Conditions of reimbursement

1. When a bureau or the agent it has appointed for the purpose has settled all claims arising out of the same accident it shall send, within a maximum period of one year from the date of the last payment made in favour of an injured party, by fax or e-mail to the member of the bureau which issued the Green Card or policy of insurance or, if appropriate, to the bureau concerned a demand for reimbursement specifying:

1.1. the sums paid as compensation to injured parties under either an amicable settlement or a court order;

1.2. the sums disbursed for external services in the handling and settlement of each claim and all costs specifically incurred for the purposes of a legal action which would

COUNCIL OF BUREAUX   CONSEIL DES BUREAUX

have been disbursed in similar circumstances by an insurer established in the country of the accident;

1.3. a handling fee to cover all other charges calculated under the rules approved by the Council of Bureaux.

When claims arising out of the same accident are defended and settled without any compensation being paid, such sums as provided in subparagraph (1)(2) above and the minimum fee fixed by the Council of Bureaux in conformity with subparagraph (1)(3) above may be claimed.

2. The demand for reimbursement shall specify that the amounts due are payable in the country and in the national currency of the beneficiary, free of costs, within a period of two months from the date of demand and that, on expiry of that period, late interest at 12 % per annum on the amount due from the date of the demand until the date of receipt of the remittance by the bank of the beneficiary shall apply automatically.

The demand for reimbursement may also specify that amounts expressed in the national currency are payable in euro, at the official rate of exchange current in the country of the claiming bureau at the date of the demand.

3. Under no circumstances shall demands for reimbursement include payments for fines, bail bonds or other financial penalties imposed upon an insured which are not covered by insurance against civil liability in respect of the use of motor vehicles in the country of accident.

4. Supporting documents, including the objective proof that compensation due to injured parties has been paid, shall be sent promptly on demand but without delay to the reimbursement.

5. Reimbursement of all sums cited in subparagraphs (1)(1) and (1)(2) above may be claimed in accordance with the conditions set out in this Article notwithstanding that the bureau may not have settled all claims arising out of the same accident. The handling fee provided for under subparagraph (1)(3) above may also be claimed if the principal sum which is the subject of the reimbursement is in excess of the amount fixed by the Council of Bureaux.

6. If, after satisfaction of a reimbursement demand, a claim is reopened or a further claim arising out of the same accident is made, the balance of the handling fee, if any, shall be calculated in accordance with the provisions in force at the time when the demand for reimbursement in respect of the re-opened or further claim is presented.

7. Where no claim for compensation has resulted from an accident, no handling fee may be claimed.

Article 6 Obligation of guarantee

1. Each bureau shall guarantee the reimbursement by its members of any amount demanded in accordance with the provisions of Article 5 by the bureau of the country of accident or by the agent that it has appointed for the purpose.

Internal Regulations adopted by the General Assembly in Crete on 30 May 2002 and revised in Lisbon on 29 May 2008

If a member fails to make the payment demanded within the period of two months specified in Article 5, the bureau to which this member belongs shall itself make the reimbursement in accordance with the conditions described hereunder, following receipt of a guarantee call made by the bureau of the country of accident or by the agent that it has appointed for the purpose.

The bureau standing as guarantor shall make the payment within a period of one month. On expiry of that period, late interest at 12 % per annum on the amount due, calculated from the date of the guarantee call to the date of receipt of the remittance by the beneficiary's bank, shall apply automatically.

The guarantee call shall be made by fax or e-mail within a period of 12 months after the date of despatch of the demand for reimbursement under Article 5. On expiry of that period and without prejudice to any late interest for which it may be liable, the liability of the Bureau standing as guarantor shall be limited to the amount claimed from its member plus 12 months interest calculated at 12 % per annum.

No guarantee call shall be admissible if made more than two years after the despatch of the demand for reimbursement

2. Each bureau guarantees that its members shall instruct the correspondents whose approval they have requested to settle claims in conformity with the provisions of the first paragraph of Article 4(4) above and forward to those correspondents or to the bureau of the country of accident all documents concerning all claims entrusted to them.

SECTION II SPECIFIC RULES GOVERNING CONTRACTUAL RELATIONS BETWEEN BUREAUX BASED ON THE GREEN CARD (OPTIONAL PROVISIONS)

The provisions of this section apply where contractual relations between bureaux are based on the Green Card.

Article 7 Issue and delivery of green cards

1. Each bureau shall be responsible for printing its Green Cards or shall authorise its members to print them.

2. Each bureau shall authorise its members to issue Green Cards to their insureds solely for vehicles registered in any country for which it is competent.

3. Any member may be authorised by its bureau to issue green cards to its insureds in any country where no bureau exists provided that the member is established in that country. This option is limited to vehicles registered in the country in question.

4. All Green Cards are deemed to be valid for at least 15 days from their date of inception. In the event that a Green Card is issued for a lesser period, the bureau having authorised the issuing of the Green Card shall guarantee cover to the bureaux in the countries for which the card is valid for a period of 15 days from the date of inception of its validity.

Internal Regulations adopted by the General Assembly in Crete on 30 May 2002 and revised in Lisbon on 29 May 2008

5. Where an agreement signed between two bureaux is cancelled under Article 16(3)(5), all Green Cards delivered in their name for use in their respective territories shall be null and void as soon as the cancellation becomes effective.

6. Where an agreement is cancelled or suspended by the application of Article 16(3)(6), the residual period of validity of the Green Cards delivered in the name of the bureaux concerned for use in their respective territories shall be determined by the Council of Bureaux.

Article 8 Confirmation of the validity of a Green Card

Any request for confirmation of the validity of an identified Green Card sent by fax or e-mail to a bureau by the bureau of the country of accident or by any agent appointed for the purpose shall be given a definitive answer within three months of the request. In the event of no such response then on expiry of that period, the Green Card shall be deemed to be valid.

Article 9 False, unauthorised or illegally altered Green Cards

Any Green Card presented in a country for which it is valid, purporting to be issued under the authority of a bureau shall be guaranteed by that bureau, even if it is false, unauthorised or illegally altered.

However, the bureau's guarantee shall not apply where a Green Card relates to a vehicle which is not legally registered in that bureau's country, with the exception of the circumstances specified in Article 7(3).

SECTION III SPECIFIC RULES GOVERNING CONTRACTUAL RELATIONS BETWEEN BUREAUX BASED ON DEEMED INSURANCE COVER (OPTIONAL PROVISIONS)

The provisions of this section apply when the relations between bureaux are based on deemed insurance cover, with certain exceptions.

Article 10 Obligations of the bureaux

The bureaux to which the provisions of this section apply shall guarantee, on a full reciprocity basis, the reimbursement of all amounts payable under these Regulations arising out of any accident involving a vehicle normally based in the territory of the State for which each of these bureaux is competent, whether the vehicle is insured or not.

Article 11 The normally based concept

1. The territory of the State in which the vehicle is normally based is determined on the basis of any of the following criteria:

1.1. the territory of the Member State of which the vehicle bears a registration plate, whether this be permanent or temporary;

Internal Regulations adopted by the General Assembly in Crete on 30 May 2002 and revised in Lisbon on 29 May 2008

1.2. where no registration is required for the type of vehicle but the vehicle bears an insurance plate, or a distinguishing sign analogous to a registration plate, the territory of the State in which the insurance plate or the sign is issued;

1.3. where neither registration plate nor insurance plate nor distinguishing sign is required for certain types of vehicles, the territory of the State in which the person who has custody of the vehicle is permanently resident.

2. If a vehicle required to bear a registration plate bears no plate or bears a registration plate which does not correspond or no longer corresponds to the vehicle has been involved in an accident, the territory in which the accident occurred shall, for the settlement for any resulting claim, be deemed to be the territory where the vehicle is normally based.

Article 12 Exemptions

The provisions of this section do not apply to:

1. vehicles registered in countries other than the countries of the bureaux subject to the provisions of this section and for which a Green Card has been delivered by a member of any of these bureaux. In the event of an accident involving a vehicle for which a Green Card has been issued the bureaux concerned shall act according to the rules set out in Section II;

2. vehicles belonging to certain persons, if the State in which they are registered has designated in the other States an authority or body responsible for compensating injured parties in accordance with the conditions prevailing in the country of accident;

3. certain types of vehicles or certain vehicles bearing a special plate of which the list is determined by each Member State and communicated to other Member States and to the Commission.

The list of vehicles referred to under 2 and 3 as well as the list of authorities or bodies appointed in the other States shall be drawn up by each State and communicated to the Council of Bureaux by the bureau of that State.

Article 13 Confirmation of the territory in which a vehicle is normally based

Any request for confirmation of the territory in which a vehicle is normally based sent by fax or e-mail to a bureau by the bureau of the country of the accident or by any agent appointed for the purpose shall be given a definitive answer within three months of the request. In the event of no such response being received then on the expiry of that period there shall be deemed to be confirmation that the vehicle is normally based in that bureau's territory.

Article 14 Duration of the guarantee

Bureaux may limit the duration of the guarantee due in accordance with Article 10 for all vehicles, on the basis of reciprocal agreements signed with other bureaux and communicated to the Council of Bureaux.

Internal Regulations adopted by the General Assembly in Crete on 30 May 2002 and revised in Lisbon on 29 May 2008

COUNCIL OF BUREAUX   CONSEIL DES BUREAUX

Article 15 Unilateral application of guarantee based on a deemed insurance cover

Save legal provisions to the contrary, bureaux may agree on any unilateral application of this section within the context of their bilateral relations.

SECTION IV RULES GOVERNING AGREEMENTS CONCLUDED BETWEEN NATIONAL INSURERS' BUREAUX (MANDATORY PROVISIONS)

Article 16 Bilateral agreements - conditions

1. Bureaux may conclude bilateral agreements between themselves whereby they undertake within the context of their reciprocal relations to abide by the mandatory provisions of these Internal Regulations, as well as the optional provisions specified herein.

2. Such agreements shall be signed in triplicate by the contracting bureaux, each of whom shall retain a copy. The third copy shall be sent to the Council of Bureaux which shall, after consultation with the concerned parties, inform them of the date commencement of their agreement.

3. Such agreements shall include clauses providing:

3.1. identification of the contracting bureaux, mentioning their status as members of the Council of Bureaux and the territories for which they are competent;

3.2. their undertaking to abide by the mandatory provisions of these Internal Regulations;
3.3. their undertaking to abide by such optional provisions as mutually chosen and agreed;

3.4. reciprocal authorities granted by these bureaux, in their own name and on behalf of their members, to settle claims amicably or to accept service of any extra-judicial or judicial process likely to lead to the payment of compensation resulting from any accident within the scope and purpose of these Internal Regulations;

3.5. unlimited duration of the agreement, subject to the right of each contracting bureau to terminate it on 12 months notice simultaneously notified to the other party and to the Council of bureaux.

3.6. automatic cancellation or suspension of the agreement if either contracting bureau ceases to be a Member of the Council of Bureaux or has its membership suspended.

4. A model of this agreement is appended (Annex III).

Article 17 Exception

1. By derogation to Article 16, the bureaux of Member States of the European Economic Area shall, in conformity with Article 2 of Directive 72/166/EEC of 24 April 1972 signify their reciprocal acceptance of these Internal Regulations by a multilateral agreement the commencement date of which is determined by the Commission of the European Union in collaboration with the Council of Bureaux.

Internal Regulations adopted by the General Assembly in Crete on 30 May 2002 and revised in Lisbon on 29 May 2008

COUNCIL OF BUREAUX   CONSEIL DES BUREAUX

2. The bureaux in non-member States of the European Economic Area may commit to this multilateral agreement by respecting the conditions fixed by the competent committee as acknowledged in the Constitution of the Council of Bureaux.

SECTION V PROCEDURE FOR AMENDING THE INTERNAL REGULATIONS (MANDATORY PROVISIONS)

Article 18 Procedure

1. Any amendment to these Regulations shall fall within the exclusive competence of the General Assembly of the Council of Bureaux.

2. By derogation to the above:

(a) any amendment to the provisions set out in Section III shall fall within the exclusive competence of the committee as acknowledged in the Constitution of the Council of bureaux. Those provisions are binding on bureaux which, although not members of this committee, have elected to apply Section III in their contractual relations with other bureaux; and

(b) any amendment to Article 4.2 shall fall within the exclusive competence of the bureaux of the European Economic Area.

SECTION VI Resolution of disputes between Bureaux (MANDATORY PROVISIONS)

Article 19 Resolution of disputes between Bureaux

Any dispute arising out of these Internal Regulations or related to them shall be resolved by mediation or by arbitration.

The rules of the mediation and the arbitration are dealt with in a separate regulation approved by the General Assembly of the Council of Bureaux

SECTION VII ENTRY INTO FORCE (MANDATORY PROVISION) Article 20 Entry into force

1. The provisions of the current Internal Regulations will come into force on the 1st of July 2008. On this date, it will supersede the version of the Internal Regulations adopted in Rethymno on the 30th of May 2002.

2. By way of derogation from Article 20.1, Article 11, Article 12.3 and Article 14 come into force retrospectively for accidents occurring from the 11th of June 2007 onwards.

ANNEXES

Annex I: Recommendation No 5

Annex II: Directive of 24 April 1972 (72/166/EEC)

Annex III: Model agreement between Bureaux.(See on the following page)

Internal Regulations adopted by the General Assembly in Crete on 30 May 2002 and revised in Lisbon on 29 May 2008

Appendix 7.1

CLAIM NOTIFICATION FORM USED BY THE MIBI

MIBI Ref

CLAIM NOTIFICATION FORM

Please note that only receipt by MIBI of a <u>fully completed & signed</u> claim notification form will constitute formal notification of a claim which should be returned to MIBI, Insurance House, 39 Molesworth Street, Dublin 2. Please use <u>BLOCK CAPITAL</u> letters only when completing this form.

Privacy Notice: The information you provide to us as part of your claim application will be processed by us to confirm your identity, process your application and to record and cross reference particulars of your claim in insurance industry databases, including Insurance Link, for fraud prevention purposes. Any queries in relation to this should be referred to the Claims Manager at MIBI. In certain cases, this may involve the sharing of your information with other insurance providers and private investigators. Guidelines for sharing of information in this regard are contained in a Code of Practice on Data Protection for the Insurance Sector which has been approved by the Data Protection Commissioner. For full details see the Data Protection Notice on our website www.mibi.ie.

SECTION A – CLAIMANT DETAILS		
1. Title: Mr/Mrs/Ms/etc.	**2. Male/Female**	**3. Date of Birth:**
4. Name:		**5. Email address:** **6. Telephone No:**
7. Address:		**8. PPS/Company Number:** **9. Occupation:** **10. Registered for VAT:** **Yes/NO**

331

11.What is the claimant's involvement in accident:

Driver, Passenger, Pedestrian, Vehicle Owner, Property Owner, Cyclist, Other (please specify):

SECTION B – CLAIMING FOR:

12. Vehicle Damage: Give details of vehicle damage sustained:

If any of the following documents are available you **must** supply them with this form: (a) estimate for repairs (b) engineers report (c) photographs of damaged vehicle.

Note: An excess is applicable to MIBI Vehicle Damage Claims in certain specific circumstances.

13. Property (non vehicle) Damage: Give details of property damage sustained.

Please advise if the damage was covered under a household, or any other, policy (Yes/No):

If any of the following documents are available you **must** supply them with this form: (a) estimate for repairs (b) engineers report (c) photographs of damaged property.

Note: An excess is applicable to MIBI Property (non vehicle) Damage Claims in certain specific circumstances.

14. Personal Injury: Give brief details of the injuries sustained:

Please supply the name and address of medical attendants. If a medical report is available you **must** supply it with this form.

15. Uninsured Losses: (E.g. Policy Excess) Give specific details:

Please furnish all documents supporting your uninsured losses claim.

SECTION C – CLAIMANT'S VEHICLE DETAILS:		
16. Registration Number:	17. Make & Model of Vehicle:	18. Country of Registration:
19. Vehicle Owner:	20. Vehicle Driver (at time of accident):	
21. Vehicle Insurer: (not broker)	22. Policy Number:	23. Cover Type: (please specify) Comprehensive Third Party Fire & Theft Third Party Only Policy Expiry Date:
SECTION D – ACCIDENT DETAILS		
24. Date of accident:	25. Time of accident:	26. Describe Road Conditions:
27. County where accident occurred:	28. Town where accident occurred:	29. Exact location of accident

30. Give brief circumstances of accident:

SECTION E – INVESTIGATING GARDA DETAILS:		
31. Date on which it was reported to Gardai?	32. Garda Station:	33. Name of Investigating Garda:

34. If accident was not reported to Gardai please explain why:

35. Name & contact details for any witnesses (including email address and telephone no.): (Furnish copies of all available statements from any witnesses).

Section F – OFFENDING VEHICLE DETAILS:		
36. Registration Number:	37.Make & Model of Vehicle:	38. Country of Registration:
39. Vehicle Owner:		40. Vehicle Driver (at time of accident):
41. Vehicle Owner Address & Telephone No.:		42. Vehicle Driver Address & Telephone No.:
43. Vehicle Insurer:	44. Policy Number:	45. Expiry Date:

---

46. What steps have been taken to establish if vehicle was insured:

47. Why does the claimant believe the vehicle to be uninsured:

48. If Foreign Registered Vehicle give Green Card No. & include photocopy if available:

Green Card No.

---

49. Any other vehicles involved in accident: Yes/No (If yes please supply details:)

I confirm all the above information to be true and accurate and I have read, and consent to, the Privacy Notice on this form.

Signature & Date: _____

For information on Terms & Conditions which apply in making a claim for compensation from MIBI please refer to the relevant MIBI Agreement available from www.mibi.ie   26.09.2011

Appendix 7.2

MANDATE FORM USED BY THE MIBI

CURRENT MANDATE FORM

(a) I consent to the Motor Insurers' Bureau of Ireland taking over and conducting, in my name, the defence of any claim or action for personal injury and/or damage to property made against me arising out of an accident which occurred on the   day of   20   .

(b) I further consent to the Motor Insurers' Bureau of Ireland making such admissions on my behalf, as appear to it to be necessary in the conduct of the case and I undertake to give them all possible assistance and information in the handling of the claim and the conduct of the proceedings.

(c) In the event of my having a claim for contribution against any person or party, I authorise the Motor Insurers' Bureau of Ireland to prosecute such claim in my name for its benefit.

(d) I agree to pay the Motor Insurers' Bureau of Ireland all sums paid by it, in respect of any settlements effected by it or on foot of any award of judgment made arising from the said accident. I am aware that the Motor Insurers' Bureau of Ireland may take legal proceedings against me in order to recover any sums that it may pay out in this regard.

(e) I understand the nature of the liability incurred and it has been made clear to me that I should seek independent legal advice, before signing this Mandate Form.

(f) I understand that the Motor Insurers' Bureau of Ireland will where necessary, instruct solicitors to act on my behalf and I consent to the Motor Insurers' Bureau of Ireland doing so.

DATED:

SIGNED:

WITNESSED:

Appendix 7.3

ASSIGNMENT FORM USED BY THE MIBI

CURRENT ASSIGNMENT

THE COURT[1]

BETWEEN:

A.B.

Plaintiff

and

THE MOTOR INSURERS' BUREAU OF IRELAND AND X.Y.Z.

Defendant

I, THE UNDERSIGNED OF

ACKNOWLEDGE RECEIPT from the Motor Insurers' Bureau of Ireland in full and final satisfaction of my claim against

arising out of an accident on the   day of   20   .

at   in (the City of)

AND IN CONSIDERATION OF THE SAID PAYMENT HEREBY SUBROGATE my rights against the said [name of Defendant/Co-Defendant] to the Motor Insurers' Bureau of Ireland AND AGREE to take all reasonable steps required of me by the Motor Insurers' Bureau of Ireland to assist them in pursuing recovery of the said sum of €   from the said [Defendant/Co-Defendant].

SIGNED: DATE:

WITNESSED BY:

---

1.   This form of assignment is adapted for use in circumstances where the MIBI takes an assignment of an Order to pay made by the Injuries Board.

Appendix 8.1

PRECEDENT INDORSEMENT OF CLAIM IN ACTION AGAINST AN UNINSURED MOTORIST AND THE MIBI AS CO-DEFENDANTS

PRECEDENT PERSONAL INJURY SUMMONS
INDORSEMENT OF CLAIM

THE HIGH COURT

BETWEEN

ROBERT JOHNSON

Plaintiff

AND

THURSTON MOORE AND THE MOTOR INSURERS' BUREAU OF IRELAND

Defendants

The plaintiff claim is for the reliefs set out herein for personal injuries suffered by the plaintiff as follows:

(a) Description of parties:

1. The plaintiff was born on the 8th day of May, 1911 resides at [   ]. The plaintiff is a musician and his PPS number is: [ ].

2. The first defendant is a youth worker who resides at [   ] and was at all material times the owner and\or driver of a motor vehicle registered letters and numbers [ ].

3. The second defendant is a company limited by guarantee with its registered offices at 39 Molesworth Street, Dublin and is sued pursuant to the provisions of the agreement made between the second defendant and the Minister for Transport dated 29th day of January, 2009.

(b) The wrong alleged against the defendants:

1. On or about the 13th day of September, 2012 the plaintiff was driving his motor vehicle on the public highway at O'Connell Street, Dublin when a motor vehicle owned and driven by the first defendant collided with the rear of the vehicle in which the plaintiff was travelling as a result of which the plaintiff suffered personal injury, loss and damage.

2. The aforesaid accident and the personal injury, loss and damage suffered by the plaintiff was caused and\or was contributed to as a result of the negligence and breach of duty (including breach of statutory duty) of the first defendant, his servants and\or agents in or about the driving,

341

management and upkeep of his vehicle. The first defendant was not insured to drive the aforesaid motor vehicle.

(c) Particulars of negligence of the defendant constituting the wrong:

    a.   Driving into the rear of the plaintiff's vehicle;

    b.   Failing to have any or any proper look out;

    c.   Driving too fast in the particular circumstances.

(d) Particulars of the injuries to the plaintiff occasioned by the wrong of the defendant:

    1.   The plaintiff was taken to the Mater Hospital in Dublin where he was diagnosed with a broken right leg. The plaintiff suffered a fracture of C6\7 of the cervical area. Further particulars will be furnished in due course.

(e) Reliefs claimed:

The plaintiff claims the following reliefs:

    a.   Damages against the first defendant for personal injury, loss and damage and\or expense caused and\or occasioned as a result of the negligence and breach of duty (including breach of statutory duty) of the first defendant, his servants and\or agents;

    b.   A declaration that the second defendant is obliged to satisfy in full any judgment or part of a judgment remaining unsatisfied within twenty eight days after the date upon which judgment is entered against the first defendant pursuant to the agreement entered into between the Minister for Transport and the second named defendant dated the 29th day of January, 2009;

    c.   An order directing the second defendant to satisfy in full any judgment or part of a judgment remaining unsatisfied within twenty eight days after the date upon which such judgment is entered against the first defendant;

    d.   Further and other relief;

    e.   Interest;

    f.   Costs.

(f) Schedule:

Particulars of items of special damage:

    (a)   Medical expenses;

    (b)   Hospital expenses;

(g) Particulars required by order 4 Rule 3A:

    (a)   Proceedings have been authorised pursuant to section 14 of the Personal Injuries Assessment Board Act 2003;

    (b)   The said authorisation was issued on the [ ] day of [ ] [20], authorisation number [ ].

Signed: _____

THOMAS VERLAINE BL.

This summons was issued by the plaintiff

OR

This summons was issued by [] plaintiff whose registered place of business is [], solicitor for the [ ].

The plaintiff's personal details are as follows:

[ ]

1. The address at which the plaintiff ordinarily resides is: [ ] (state address accurately). The plaintiff's address for services, if different from the plaintiff's address mentioned above, should also be stated here: [ ].

2. Plaintiff's occupation:

3. Plaintiff's date of birth :   Day: Month: Year:

4. Plaintiff's Personal Public Service Number: . (If the plaintiff has not been issued with a Personal Public Service Number, this must be stated).

Appendix 8.2

PRECEDENT INDORSEMENT OF CLAIM IN ACTION AGAINST THE MIBI IN RESPECT OF A VEHICLE WHOSE OWNER AND USER ARE UNIDENTIFIED AND UNTRACED

PRECEDENT PERSONAL INJURY SUMMONS INDORSEMENT OF CLAIM

THE HIGH COURT

BETWEEN

ROBERT JOHNSON

Plaintiff

AND

THE MOTOR INSURERS' BUREAU OF IRELAND

Defendant

The plaintiff claims for the reliefs set out herein for personal injuries suffered by the plaintiff as follows:

(a) Description of parties:

1. The plaintiff was born on the 8th day of May, 1911 resides at [   ]. The plaintiff is a musician and his PPS number is: [   ].

2. The defendant is a company limited by guarantee with its registered offices at 39 Molesworth Street, Dublin and is sued pursuant to the provisions of the agreement made between the second defendant and the Minister for Transport dated 29th day of January, 2009.

(b) The wrong alleged against the defendant:

1. On or about the 13th day of September, 2012 the plaintiff was driving his motor vehicle on the public highway at O'Connell Street, Dublin when a motor vehicle, the owner and user of which remains unidentified or untraced collided with the rear of the plaintiff's motor vehicle.

2. The aforesaid accident occurred wholly as a result of the negligence and breach of duty (including breach of statutory duty) of the untraced motorist in the driving, care, management and control of the aforesaid motor vehicle. The defendant is obliged to compensate the plaintiff pursuant to the provisions of the agreement entered into between it and the Minister for Transport dated the 29th January, 2009.

(c) Particulars of negligence of the defendant constituting the wrong:

a. Driving into the rear of the plaintiff's vehicle;

b. Failing to have any or any proper look out;

c. Driving too fast in the particular circumstances.

(d) Particulars of the injuries to the plaintiff occasioned by the wrong of the defendant:

1. The plaintiff was taken to the Mater Hospital in Dublin where he was diagnosed with a broken right leg. The plaintiff suffered a fracture of C6\7 of the cervical area. Further particulars will be furnished in due course.

(e) Reliefs claimed:

The plaintiff claims the following reliefs:

a. A declaration that the defendant is obliged to compensate the plaintiff pursuant to the agreement entered into between it and the Minister for Transport dated the 29th day of January 2009;

b. An order for the performance of the aforesaid agreement;

c. Compensation for personal injury, loss, damage and\or expense caused and\or occasioned as a result of the negligence and breach of duty (including breach of statutory duty) in and about the use of a motor vehicle on or about the 13th September, 2012, the owner and user of which remains unidentified or untraced and an order directing the defendant to pay the plaintiff such compensation as may be assessed by this honourable court;

d. Further and other relief;

e. Interest;

f. Costs.

(f) Schedule:

Particulars of items of special damage:

(a) Medical expenses;

(b) Hospital expenses;

(g) Particulars required by order 4 Rule 3A:

(a) Proceedings have been authorised pursuant to section 14 of the Personal Injuries Assessment Board Act 2003;

(b) The said authorisation was issued on the [ ] day of [ ] [20], authorisation number [ ].

Signed: _____

THOMAS VERLAINE BL.

This summons was issued by the plaintiff

OR

346

This summons was issued by [] plaintiff whose registered place of business is
[   ], solicitor for the [   ].

The plaintiff's personal details are as follows:

[   ]

1. The address at which the plaintiff ordinarily resides is: [   ] (state address
    accurately). The plaintiff's address for services, if different from the plaintiff's
    address mentioned above, should also be stated here: [   ].

2. Plaintiff's occupation:

3. Plaintiff's date of birth :   Day: Month: Year:

4. Plaintiff's Personal Public Service Number: . (If the plaintiff has not
    been issued with a Personal Public Service Number, this must be stated).

INDEX